Very best wishes

Goodbye to the Working Class

Goodbye to the Working Class

Published by The Conrad Press Limited in the United Kingdom 2021

Tel: +44(0)1227 472 874

www.theconradpress.com

info@theconradpress.com

ISBN 978-1-914913-02-0

Typesetting and Cover Design by:
Charlotte Mouncey, www.bookstyle.co.uk

The Conrad Press logo was designed by Maria Priestley.

Printed and bound in Great Britain by Clays Ltd, Elcograf S.p.A.

Goodbye to the Working Class

Social change, incompetence and
sleaze push Labour to the brink

Reg Race

ACKNOWLEDGEMENTS
AND CREDITS

I have relied on many people to develop the ideas in this book, and their evidence and concerns have in large part supported the conclusions that I have drawn about the plight of Labour, one of many social democratic parties in the Western World that are in terminal decline or serious trouble.

In order to produce the evidence required, I asked many leading members of the Party for an interview. I wanted to test whether the positions that I thought were correct would survive discussion, and by and large they did. I gave a specific promise to all of them – sitting MPs, former Ministers, leading Party officials, key activists – that I would not quote their views or attribute them directly in this book. I hope I have kept my promise. It is sad that so many people who know what is going on are not empowered to speak their minds in a constructive fashion, and that tells you something about the culture of the modern Labour Party.

I have also eschewed the Labour practice of blaming individuals for the failures of the Labour Party. This is a fruitless activity because there are much bigger forces at work; but misjudgements over key issues have contributed mightily at times to the decline of credibility, and at times have created mayhem.

In writing this contribution, I have also relied heavily on my own personal files from political and organisational activities over the last 60 years. I tend not to throw things away, which is useful when writing a book of this kind. But this is not a diary: diaries are subject to short term distortions based on what is thought important at the time, whereas reflection after time can lend perspective.

Over the years I have gained valuable insights from many people who have influenced the trend of my thinking: my university tutor, Fred Whitemore, whose utter realism was always a sheet anchor to ground over-enthusiastic views; David Cowling, who lent substantial amounts of his valuable time to harvesting election statistics; and many others in the grassroots organisations who contributed valuable ideas.

I would also like to thank the very good people who helped in the production of this book, especially Natascha Engel, a former Deputy Speaker of the House of Commons, who advised on editing; Victoria Simon-Shore, who was helpful on legal points; James Essinger, my publisher; Erica Martin, who provided excellent access to the photographic libraries of the pre-digital world; Charlotte Mouncey, who edited and collated the pictures and charts and supervised typesetting; Emma Lockley, who produced the invaluable index; the staff in the House of Commons Library who helped unearth long forgotten parts of Parliamentary history, and confirmed the non-existence of others; and most importantly of all my wife Mandy Moore, who encouraged and supported me throughout the gestation of this book and was extraordinarily tolerant. Mandy and I have worked together on many political projects over 40 years and this book could not have been written without her insights as a feminist.

Of course, all errors, miscalculations and misunderstandings are my responsibility alone.

It is, of course, entirely possible that I am wrong about everything.

Dr Reg Race
Blackheath June 2021

Contents

PICTURE CREDITS

1. Princess Marina at Kent University (Special Collections and Archives University of Kent)
2. Women MPs lobby for toy safety 1966 (Evening Standard/Hulton Archive/ Getty Images
3. There will be trouble ahead, dirty jobs strike 1969 (Mirrorpix/Reach Licensing)
4. Don't work for Tower Hamlets (Arthur Jones/Getty Images)
5. The great ungluing starts here, Harold and Mary Wilson 1970 (Romano Cagnoni/Report IFL archive/ Reportdigital.co.uk)
6. Break the Tory Stranglehold on Canterbury (author's archive)
7. Labour's victorious pro Europe lobby (PA images/Alamy stock photos)
8. Denis Healey Labour Conference 1976 (Mirrorpix/Reach Licensing)
9. Jim Callaghan lobbied by fire crews Labour Conference 1977 (John Sturrock/reportdigital.co.uk)
10. The fight back against Labour spending cuts Alan Fisher with marchers 1976 (Keystone Press/Alamy stock photo)
11. Head of the March 1976 (John Minihan/Evening Standard/Getty Images)
12. Boogying against the cuts (NLA/report-digital.co.uk)
13. Tony Benn and Michael Foot (Martin Mayer/reportdigital.co.uk)
14. Bernard Donoughue 1977 (Mike Hollist/Daily Mail/Shutterstock)
15. Cuts Man: Joel Barnett MP 1976 (Topfoto)
16. Not so matey: Alan Fisher and Frank Chapple Labour Party conference 1979 (ANL/Shutterstock)
17. Peter Shore a former friend of Benn (News/Popperfoto/Getty Images)
18. RR speaking at the Labour Party Conference 1979 (John Sturrock/report-digital.co.uk)
19. Equalising abortion rights: RR and Jo Richardson MP launch their Bill 1981 (photographer unknown)
20. Launching the round the clock picket to get Mandela and fellow prisoners out of gaol (Stefano Cagnoni/reportdigtal. co.uk)
21. RR supporting CPSA in Brixton 1980 (Shutterstock)
22. Sameena, Rubeena and Seema Waseem fighting child abduction: (photographer unknown, pic courtesy of Tribune)
23. Porn does for sex what Russia does for Socialism, Sex Shop pickets 1981: (Bill Cross/ANL/Shutterstock)
24. Let's negotiate: RR on Falklands Peace March with Harriet Harman 1982 (NLA/reportdigital.co.uk)
25. Newt fancier Ken Livingstone at Camley Street Natural Park: (pic GLC)
26. End of the road for the Miners January 1985 (John Harris/reportdigital.co.uk)
27. Nurses on a Nightingale Ward Bradford Royal Infirmary 1985 (PA images/Alamy stock photo)
28. Mandy Moore with Jo Richardson MP and Joan Maynard MP Labour Women's Conference 1986 (John Harris/report-digital.co.uk)
29. Creative destruction: demolition of Arkwright Town 1995 (Robert Brook/ Science Photo Library)
30. The decisive defeat 1981: some of Benn's foot soldiers (author's personal archive)
31. Saving Labour national newspaper advertisement 2016 (author's personal archive)
32. Fred Whitemore meets St Nicholas as Lord Mayor of Canterbury 2001 (photographer unknown)
33. Inside dustjacket: Reg Race when an MP, (photographer unknown, author's personal archive)
34. Front cover: Durham Miners Gala c. 1948 (Pictorial Press Ltd/Alamy stock photo)
35. Back cover: Lancashire cotton mill c. 1920s (Topfoto)

FIGURE CREDITS

PREFACE

This book is about power, who has it, who has lost it, and how the main party of progressive ideas in Britain, the Labour Party, has lost its way because of multiple failings over decades. Some claim that this is just the result of demographics or individuals. It isn't.

I started writing this book knowing that there was a problem: how to explain the upending of power in Labour, so far removed from the stable, consensual landscape that RT McKenzie, writing in 1955, described in the afterglow of the Attlee Government. I decided that I would tell this important story based on my own experiences, linked to insights from the academic world, national data and polling evidence, so that the reader could see the extraordinary and completely unprecedented changes that have taken place.

Let us be clear: the defeat of the PLP[1] leadership candidates in 2015 and 2016, and the election of an insurgent outsider with a wholly differing policy platform, is the only time in Labour's history when the membership has in fact taken over. There is reason to believe that some of the conditions for this upending of 'normal service' are still present, and that a repeat cannot be ruled out.

It is also true that the Labour Party's members and its Parliamentary representatives have undergone a total sea change. From being a working class party hammering on the gates of Parliament to win change, with working class members and a substantial presence of manual workers in the PLP, it has now been transformed into the most middle class party in Britain. Manual worker representation in the PLP has almost ceased to exist, and the membership is now very largely from the public sector middle class. None of this has been deliberate, but extraordinarily foolish actions by leaders have enabled it.

In addition, the party's electoral base has been transformed. Social democratic parties in Western Europe have had a hard time because of the significant reduction in working class voters, their electoral base, in recent years.

1. Parliamentary Labour Party

What is not so clearly understood, certainly if we are to go by discussions at Labour branch meetings and conferences, is the size of the change: the working class, utterly dominant at 75% of the population in 1911 and still over 60% in 1960,[2] has now been reduced to a declining rump, sized at perhaps 23%. Great industries have fallen: mining, entirely gone; manufacturing, significantly reduced; agricultural work, seriously cut; textile production, largely gone; and the world of coal, steel, steam and manufacturing that I grew up in in industrial Manchester and Salford has disappeared like sea mist on a warm autumn day.

In its place are swathes of shop workers. The retail sector is now the dominant and by far the largest occupational group in Britain. Napoleon's alleged phrase that we were 'a nation of shopkeepers' has become literally true 200 years later. Also dominant are the own-account workers, the 'white van man' beloved of the *Sun* newspaper, and criticised by some arrogant people in the Labour Party. Hugely important also are the growing ranks of the professional workers, greatly expanded in size and clout because of specialisation within the professions, and dominant in many places. The wider group of non-manual workers grew in size and overtook that of manual workers in the late 1970s, with the white collar labour force growing by 287% between 1911 and 1981.

It is also true that these great changes in the electorate are consequent on the underlying forces in the economy as technology drives forward, reducing the need for staff and thereby challenging the basis on which taxation is predicated. This further impacts on the provision of public services, and our ability to provide the essentials of life for those who cannot manage to provide expensive housing and other services for themselves.

This is not the only reason for Labour's decline. The Labour Party when in government also has a habit of facing the wrong way on economic issues when there is a crisis. The débacle of 1931 was caused by the inability of Labour ministers to understand that the Gold Standard was not an immutable and sacrosanct policy, even when none other than JM Keynes told them loudly that it wasn't. Labour in 1931 demonstrated an acceptance of the status quo, promptly reversed when the 1931 General Election was comfortably over and the more flexible political establishment was in charge again in a Conservative-dominated government, which ditched the Gold Standard in short order.

In the great crisis of 1975-6, when Labour ministers deliberately

---

2.   AH Halsey, *British Social Trends since 1900*, Macmillan 1988, page 9

performed a *volte face*, introduced monetarism and engineered a substantial attack on public services (some would say the most substantial attack ever mounted on them in Britain), the policy was based on an extraordinary misreading of the public accounts. The Labour leadership said they were in massive deficit when they were not, and they knew this, but they cut anyway, legitimising and paving the way for the Thatcher revolution. This was a different class of poor decision-making: a scramble to adopt what they saw as a new consensus, thrillingly ditching their manifesto commitments on the way.

There have been great successes, of course: the reforms of the 1940s under Attlee are the classic example, as was the creation of the Open University in the 1960s, and much of the Blair/Brown re-provision of public realm infrastructure in the 13 years of Labour power from 1997. But niggling doubts remain as to whether we could have done more. Great issues, like the reform of social care and the regulation of the financial sector, were either fudged or postponed for another day – and that day never came.

Labour has also failed to comprehend the role of political parties in the running of the State. The Conservatives have the pick of those leaving the top schools and universities when they want them, but Labour has failed consistently to understand that it needs to have a pipeline of capable, well-organised people to be ministers and shadow ministers when the need arises, and to deal with the very different problems of running an advanced democracy like Britain in the 21st century.

As has been well documented by the excellent work of King and Crewe, huge blunders have been made in the development and implementation of policy over the last 50 years, under governments of both main parties.

These blunders illustrate the inconvenient fact that decisions in power are getting more complex, not less. They are often based on mining huge datasets which need interpretation, and a basic ability by civil servants and politicians to understand the landscape of a problem, to ask the right questions, and to call out nonsense when it is presented to them.

The pandemic of 2020 is a very modern example of how this is true, and if Labour demands for the replacement of 'incompetent ministers' are to be believed, then they must put their own house in order. All too often over the years I have experienced the 'glaze over' effect as MPs you are talking to face-to-face want to get away as rapidly as possible when anything complex is discussed.

Not only this, but Labour has avoided or ignored the problem of how to recruit bright and sensible working class people as candidates. It has rightly sought to rebalance its councillor groups and the PLP by establishing training for women and BAME candidates, but it has failed completely to deal with the swift erosion of the working class from its own internal power structures. The absence of a modern working class tradition in the PLP especially means that the very significant voices of the abandoned areas have been set aside in favour of the educated tones of the London middle class.

Brexit was the outcome of a lengthy ungluing of the working class areas from Labour and was not the result of a sudden bout of the vapours by loyal Labour voters. The erosion of loyalty between working class voters and Labour has been going on for 50 years as people grew into new jobs or no jobs, and as communities fragmented. But the flaking away began in the late 1960s until, by the 1970 General Election, 89 constituencies – mainly Labour held – had a higher percentage of non-voters than the percentage vote for the winning candidate.[3] Abstention became endemic in working class areas and is still so today. Turnout in the iconic constituency of Bolsover at the General Election of 1950 was 86.2%; by 2019 it had sunk to 61.1%. The Labour vote in Bolsover in 1950 was 34,017; by 2019 this had declined to 16,492 in an electorate that had grown by 54% since 1950. In Scotland and Wales, the ungluing process led to some voters believing that salvation lay in the hands of the SNP and Plaid Cymru. Also, in this period, the Liberals made serious inroads into the Labour vote and replaced it as the party of opposition in much of Southern England, rural areas and some suburbs. But everywhere, whole swathes of working class voters became non-voters because they ceased caring about politics, feeling that Labour offered little for them, and sometimes that others offered more.

The self-inflicted part of the harm was started, in my view, by the policies of the 1964-70 Government after it failed to devalue in 1964, by the disdainful way in which the low paid and public services were treated by the Wilson and Callaghan Governments, and by their foot-dragging failure to hear the concerns of less powerful groups, like women. By the late 1970s attitudes at the top were so bad that some Labour Ministers and advisers wanted to teach their own people a lesson, and by succeeding in doing so they paved the way for Thatcher. The characteristic of

---

3. *The British General Election of 1970*, DE Butler and M Pinto-Duschinsky, Macmillan 1971, page 393

Labour in power in this period was that they appeased the powerful and ignored the weak.

So, we can say that over time the working class has left Labour, in the sense that large swathes have ceased to vote for the People's Party. It is also the case that Labour has left the working class by ignoring the need for working class representation. It has been driven back to urban redoubts and has, by and large, lost the old coalfields and swathes of the legacy industrial areas.

The party founded to represent 'working men' has turned into the party that doesn't. It has, to be brutal, turned into a party of insiders, the party of ex- special advisers and councillors.

There is no way to turn back the tide of demographic change flowing from economic imperatives. The middle class will probably go on increasing, the working class, classically defined, will probably go on shrinking, but new dimensions will emerge. It is likely that millions of white collar jobs will be destroyed by the advance of artificial intelligence and robotics, and the economic pressure on younger generations will continue to be acute.

Fewer of the younger generations will be able to afford a house, or have a decent lifestyle, and whatever you call these groups they will be outside the privileged world that the Conservative party has always represented. Therefore, to argue that Labour just needs to tweak its policies a bit and wait for the Government to implode is a strategy bound to fail.

Labour has also allowed its own structures and decision making bodies at national level to become the playground of sectarian dispute and the neglect of the most basic systems of managing a large and important organisation has been scandalous. No managers have key performance indicators unless they write them themselves, there are no debates that are not seen through sectarian prisms, no one wants to be responsible for decisions and they ensure this is so by copying 50 people in to an email, no system performance review exists, there is no strategic plan and no people plan – all this and more is the evidence of an organisation out of control and acting like the human body's immune system in overdrive, attacking itself.

Political parties do not exist in a vacuum and one of the key findings of this book is that political parties influence the way in which the State itself handles issues, and the failure of the Labour Party to undertake basic governance of itself will inevitably have desperate consequences for decision making in Whitehall if Labour ever wins power.

This book is not a paean of praise for working class life, nor a criticism of it. It explains how Labour broke away from its roots in the working class, and how working people in turn stopped voting, or stopped voting Labour, because they didn't trust the party. It describes how this Long Goodbye has been proceeding quietly for 50 years without many in the Labour Party recognising what was happening. It is not a product of the 21st century.

The book is not a detailed history of the party nor is it demographically determinist: after all, Blair won three elections handsomely with a population and electorate wildly different from that of 1945 or 1960.

I have written this book from my own experiences, and have also taken the analysis far back into history. Some other explanations of Labour's failure stress very recent events, but in my view this is misleading.

My argument is not that individuals failed but rather that the failure is structural, although several leaders of varying persuasions have been negligent in understanding what was going on. The rot set in many decades ago, and the party will never learn its lessons if it fails to deal with the incompetence and out and out corruption at many levels of the organisation as I have seen it.

Labour also needs to understand how bad it is at making strategic decisions, such as the 1970s débacle over low pay and women's rights when an enormous fight had to be undertaken to make the rulers of the party listen. It took decades to put right. Many were opposed to women's rights because they wanted to defend male privilege, and top people were opposed to dealing with low pay because it might infringe powerful rights and bargaining power wielded to retain the share of the pie that they enjoyed. In other words, the Labour Party has in recent times defended privilege and the existing distribution of power rather than challenge it.

Again in 2014, reforms to party membership had vast unintended consequences and caused huge damage to the reputation of the party. Labour, paradoxically therefore, opposes change in many cases and tends to defend the status quo as it happens to be at the time, when it should not reject sensible reform. On occasion it jumps at a new consensus or fad and gets it wildly wrong. It needs also to stop looking and sounding like a Pall Mall members club or the chattering classes at an Islington dinner party.

The choices now are hugely challenging: how to respond to the tsunami of unemployment, public debt, social division, mental health crises, and funding deficits in the public services flowing from the coronavirus crisis and responding to a Conservative Government that has adopted high spending and intervention, at least for now. These challenges will harshly tax the Party's ability to make strategic choices once more. Let us hope it does not fail again.

Why should we bother about any of this? We should, because it is vital in a democracy to have two national parties that can take power and legislate competently. One Party States are bad news. Britain is lucky that it accepts the results of elections, as they are still a key mechanism of consensus building in our society, but there has to be a credible choice of parties to vote for.

Renewing the Labour Party is important in this sense: it is vital that those without power, or access to money and influence, can be heard, and that the floor should not be left only to those who have been born to rule, who have climbed to the top or have landed there automatically.

INTRODUCTION

The Long View

It is not the case that the problems Labour suffers from are the product of decisions taken recently. In the 1960s it was just possible for the Labour Party to win elections as a predominantly working class party. Two thirds of the working class voted for it, along with a relatively small proportion of middle class supporters.

Now it is not possible to win elections on that basis. And the internal power structure of political parties in Britain has suffered major shocks. What has caused this transformation?

Mark Abrams' study, *Must Labour Lose?*[4] argued at a very early stage in the great social changes of the 20th century that there was a problem, and that it could be fixed. His argument was that by better leadership, better focus on middle class concerns, that Labour as the alternative party of government could beat the Conservatives. The apotheosis of this strategy was 1997, and the first of three Labour victories which seemed to prove his point.

However, the processes of social change have continued apace and the whole basis of voting by working class people has been transformed. It is now arguable that Labour will never come close to winning again unless it widens its appeal, retains its now substantial middle class support, and brings back significant tranches of working class voters. Or unless there is a miracle.

However, this is not the first time that the significant decline in the size of the working class, and its changing views, has been identified as a political problem for Labour. Not only was this the basis of the Crosland/Rose argument but it was also the underpinning of the Eurocommunist 'broad democratic alliance' strategy best exemplified by Eric Hobsbawm's

---

4.   M Abrams and R Rose *Must Labour Lose*, Penguin, 1960

important piece *The Forward March of Labour Halted.*[5] This perceptive analysis, implicitly calling for a revised view of tactics and strategy by both the Labour Party and the trade unions, has now been overtaken by events: trade union membership was at its height in 1979, and has now collapsed; and the size of the working class has shrivelled to around 23% of the population. Hobsbawm thought there was a crisis in 1978: the crisis is now a full blown emergency.[6]

Not only has the class composition of the electorate changed radically, and continues to do so, but other factors have intruded. This is not to argue that there is a demographic determinism to electoral behaviour at work. In fact, almost everything that academic political scientists taught their students in the mid-1960s about the nature of political parties has now had to be revised substantially.

The revisions are not just about the basis of voting behaviour but about the structure of power within the parties themselves. It appears that the world has turned upside down; and this book tries to describe how that might have happened – and indeed whether the changes are permanent and are capable of being reversed.

The questions we have to ask ourselves are: have the huge demographic changes in the electorate and the changes to the economy been the decisive force in changing the internal power structures of the parties, or are there other forces at work? In the 1950s and 60s it was argued that the two great British political parties were likely to be dominated by their Parliamentary wings, and some political scientists even said that there were powerful 'laws' guaranteeing this, meaning that in a first past the post, single member constituency electoral system such as Britain's, two dominant parties would always be sustained by that system. Duverger's Law (drawn from the writings of the French political scientist Maurice Duverger), allegedly showed that the electoral system caused a particular kind of party system to develop and be sustained: under a first past the post, single member constituency system two major parties would dominate. Under a PR system, multiple parties would fracture the vote and representation. In practice, the 'law' has been shown to be malleable, less a law than a guideline, operating powerfully in some decades

---

5.   E Hobsbawm, Marx Memorial Lecture, 1978, reprinted as a compendium of articles by Verso, 1981

6.   See the perceptive analysis of the structure of politics in 1983 and of Hobsbawm's contribution in Richard Hyman's piece *Wooing the Working Class* in *The Future of the Left*, ed. J Curran, Polity Press 1984, page 90.

and not so in others if splits developed in one of the dominant parties.

It was also the case that in the 1960s, the role of powerful pressure groups acting on Government for the pursuit of political objectives or for the maintenance of interests was widely recognised. But now, national and international pressure groups seem more powerful than ever – and they appear to be destroying the traditional function of political parties, namely to order and package issues to present alternative visions of government to the electorate.

It was clear in post-war Britain that the National Farmers Union had immense influence over the agricultural policy of the British Government, and Prime Minister Harold Macmillan[7] said that there were three organisations that a sensible government would never offend: the National Union of Mineworkers, the Brigade of Guards and the Catholic Church. It was accepted that such pressure groups were too powerful or influential to be ignored. Now, however, Parties seem, because of the great democratisation of influence created by social media and electronic communication, to be in thrall to outside forces fuelled and propelled by transient and unpredictable grouplets of individuals coalescing and recoalescing around issues as they see fit.

Critically, what is the role of leadership in all this? Is the Labour Party doomed to failure under a succession of mostly fragile leaders who exacerbate the structural problems of winning votes in a permanently declassed society?

In order to start understanding what has been going on, it is essential to review what we thought was true 50 years ago. The key observations used to describe British politics and the Labour Party in the mid-1960s were the following:

A Homogeneous Country

Britain, as one of the most urbanised societies in the world, was politically homogeneous, we were told. Now it manifestly isn't. Scotland, Wales and Northern Ireland have smaller and different political systems from England. Different parties compete in those spaces, and different politicians try and win there. Even Shetland is thinking about separation.

---

7.   The phrase is also attributed to Stanley Baldwin.

Decline of Class

Britain was riven with class distinctions, it was said, and this was indeed true; after social class, 'all is embellishment' in explaining politics, went the argument. Now, other cleavages are perhaps as important as class. Brexit is the most obvious cleavage issue, along with the impact of education and the growth of identity politics. In the 1950s barely 5% of an age cohort went to university. Now it is nearly 50%. In the 1950s and 60s, class identification was linked to party politics in an umbilical way. Middle class voters identified the Conservatives as their Party, and many working class voters regarded Labour as theirs. Now they don't. Attachment to party is now developed by more diverse processes, some of which produce no attachment at all.

Many voters in the 1950s were deferential and preferred the sons of elite parents as Parliamentary candidates and felt comfortable voting for them. Now these features have largely vanished.

Class as a dominant issue faded in other ways too: ownership of consumer durables equalised over the years. In 1958 only 7% of social class DE had a car, and 3% a refrigerator.[8] Also, 48% of households didn't have access to a car in 1971, but this shrank to 24% in 2018. Having a fridge is now almost universal and 98% of Britons now own a freezer. This expansion of prosperity is but one factor underpinning the decline of class based politics and perhaps not the most important, with the most significant being the changes in the sizes of the social classes themselves. Party identification has also collapsed in terms of the strength of attachment people feel to both major parties, and in the degree to which these attachments are felt. People are now prepared to vote for a wide range of party choices that would have seemed incomprehensible in 1970, let alone 1950.

Voting Against your Class

Despite the longstanding and strongly felt class distinctions in Britain, commentators in the 1950s and 1960s were astonished by the working class failing to be solidaristic, and in a 19th century phrase 'discrediting itself terribly.'[9] This continued to be so, because significant numbers of

8.   Abrams, *Class Distinctions in Britain*
9.   Engels to Marx after the General Election of 1868

them in the modern period continued to vote Tory. Typically, about a third of all working class voters cast their ballots for Conservative candidates after 1945 and it was even true that in mining communities about one in four voters chose the Tories.

Deference still existed in the early 1960s but secularised Tory working class voters were growing in number and more elderly deferential voters were dying out.[10] This process has continued apace. Voting 'against your class' has grown in strength and is more complex now than in 1960. Some social groups have developed almost from nothing, are harder to identify, and some occupational groups have shrunk markedly in size. Opinion is complex and contradictory and it is harder for a party to mobilise voters along class lines for a coherent set of programmes.

Middle Class Takeover

The major parties in the 1950s and 1960s had memberships which largely correlated with the demographics of their voters. Labour membership – amongst individual members as well as in affiliated organisations – was overwhelmingly working class with a few clerical workers with administrative skills occupying local officeholding positions and being prominent councillors.[11]

The upper middle class was represented in small numbers through a few individuals like Attlee, Dalton, Cripps, Benn, Wilson and Gaitskell who had either been born into the middle class or who were admitted to it via the gates of the top universities and sometimes the public schools.

Now, the Labour Party has a mass membership which is overwhelmingly non-manual worker, with most office holders at local level, national level and in Parliament being middle class. Finding a manual worker in Labour membership now is not easy.

10. *Angels In Marble: Working Class Conservatives in Urban England*, R McKenzie and A Silver, Heinemann, 1968
11. AH Birch and AH Hanham *Small Town Politics: A study of Political Life in Glossop*, 1959

Parliamentary Dominance

Power inside the main parties in the 1950s and 60s was heavily skewed towards the Parliamentary leaderships of both the Conservatives and Labour. In the Conservative party, elites dominated, and chose leaders through what was described as a 'magic circle' of prominent men.[12] Rose argued that it was not the Conservative rank and file who could be especially militant but that 'the real opposition to change' came from factions which drew support from all ranks of the party, 'from noble Marquesses down to humble voters.'

In the Labour Party, RT McKenzie argued that the leadership was likely to be supported by majorities in the PLP, the trade unions, the NEC, and in both sections of the Party Conference. This, however, was not congruent with Labour mythology about the location of power inside the party but the reality was identified by RHS Crossman who said of Labour 'democracy' that:

[A] constitution was needed which maintained their [the activists'] enthusiasm by apparently creating a full party democracy while excluding them from effective power. Hence the concession in principle of sovereign powers to the delegates at the Annual Conference, and the removal in practice of most of this sovereignty through the trade union block vote on the one hand and the complete independence of the Parliamentary Labour Party on the other.

This seemingly stable power structure, which broke down temporarily in 1960-61 over nuclear weapons, has – it seems from the perspective of 2015 – now completely dissipated.

More recently, a majority of the trade unions supported a radical leadership of the party for five years, for the first in its history. The membership, greatly expanded through the Miliband reforms, supported the radical leadership by at least 60-40. The NEC was under the control of the left elements, leaving the PLP as the only part of the party overall which did not give majority support to the leadership team.

This new balance of power of 2015 has for the moment proved to be unsustainable but the real question is whether modern conditions have undermined the domination of the PLP for ever. It is possible that wild swings in control of the Party are now a permanent feature of Labour life, because the underpinnings of radicalism are still there. McKenzie would be astonished at the transformation that has taken place.

---

12. See *How Militant Are the Militants*, R Rose 1961 and 1962

Bureaucracy no Longer in Control

Set reading for politics students in 1965 were the works of Max Weber and Robert Michels. Both argued that political parties were inherently prone to bureaucratic tendencies which minimised their radicalism and that it was therefore no surprise that the parties became dominated by rather reactionary forces.

They were arguing the same case as McKenzie but from a different angle. McKenzie said it was due to the observance of Parliamentary norms, Michels and Weber blamed the effects of bureaucracy.

In Britain it is possible to argue that the Labour Party was never radical in the sense that Michels and Weber meant. These arguments, that bureaucracy would permanently deradicalize parties, the common currency of political sociology in the 1960s, seem to have been disproved, certainly in the case of the Labour Party in Britain. Here the grassroots has overcome the previously obedient and 'de-radicalised' positions of the leadership and the PLP in a stunning move that has overturned all expectations.

The whole political structure of established parties and consensus politics is also being undermined by anti-establishment populism illustrated by UKIP, the Brexit Party and the *Gilets Jaunes* in France (and other more right wing formations in Germany, Austria, Hungary, the United States, and elsewhere).

So, the Michels/Weber arguments, widely believed in the early years of the 20th century, seem to have been discredited because the forces of change have swept away consensus politicians in many countries. Any deradicalisation that could have been attributed to adherence to Parliamentary conventions and norms has been upended by populism outside, sometimes with a socialist label, sometimes not.

Labour's Approach to Capitalism

We were told in the mid 1960s that it was important for social democratic parties to adapt to new conditions, otherwise they would be marooned on the beach. There had to be a direction of travel to accommodate and adapt to capitalism; what was not needed was reversion to a socialist utopian position. There had already been attempts to accommodate the Labour Party (and others in continental Europe) to new realities flowing from changes in the economic base and social structure.

The first in Britain was Croslandism, starting with the publication of *The Future of Socialism* in 1956, which argued that in the modern world, control of the economy through nationalisation was not required and that key social objectives could be achieved through expanding the economy and using the fruits of higher economic growth to expand public services. This ideology illuminated the policies of 1964-70 and importantly 1997-2010 – but its victory was not decisive.

The second attempt to adapt to new conditions began in the mid-1970s because it was thought that British capitalism in particular had become unmanageable using normal Keynesian policies. It argued that Croslandism was no longer possible because of the growth of powerful companies with their own agendas, and that consequently Labour leaders would give in to these pressures to comply with big firm agendas unless they were made accountable to the party through various constitutional changes and compelled to introduce new kinds of economic policies. Otherwise, leaders would renege on promises and produce few gains of a progressive kind. This attempt at alignment with new realities was led by Stuart Holland (as the key author and populariser of the Alternative Economic Strategy) in the 1970s and centred on crafting a post-Keynesian alternative to Friedman and to respond to the abandonment of Keynesianism by the Labour Government. This ultimately failed, but did underpin the constitutional and political rebellion of 1977-83.

The push for democratisation via the Campaign for Labour Party Democracy (CLPD), which ran side by side with the Alternative Economic Strategy succeeded in part and was then decisively defeated by a fightback by the right wing forces in the trade unions and the PLP which overturned or changed previous Conference decisions. The importance of these democratisation arguments were revived in 2015: it was the dominant ideology of the inner party apparatus under Corbyn.

The point is that powerful countervailing arguments were being used in different directions in 2015-20.

In the early 21st century, the PLP were spectacularly bad at renewing and refreshing the strategic approach to dealing with the economy, and the radical left outside developed a simplistic but effective call for more socialist policies. The heirs of Crosland and Blair (Burnham, Kendall, Cooper) were defeated heavily in 2015 and the heirs of Benn were rewarded, in a complete *volte face* in policy stance for the first time in the modern history of the party. The membership had defeated the party establishment and were now in a position to reshape the Party in their own image, until the electorate removed their credibility and in turn trashed the Corbyn leadership.

Internal Revolts

In the mid-1960s we were told as students that revolts within parties usually fail. Now it is clear that they can succeed, because of changed conditions underpinning political activity. In the period 1950-2019 revolts against the Labour leadership took place regularly, usually with a key Parliamentarian as the figurehead.

Bevanism went nowhere because it did not develop a sustainable rank and file organisation. Benn did have a grassroots organisation but it just failed to get to critical mass, partly for accidental reasons (illness), partly because of personal disbelief in sections of the PLP, and partly because of the absence in that period of easy and cheap communications which enabled the rapid mobilisation of supporters. But Corbyn, the least powerful and credible MP in this group of challengers, had a grassroots organisation unrivalled in any previous attempt to dislodge the leadership because external conditions had changed.

All three major revolts depended on personnel from the top, middle and bottom of the party. They were balanced in different ways at each level on each occasion but the strength of anti-establishment forces has recently been greatly enhanced by social media and information technology.

However, social media determinism cannot be supported. Corbyn only succeeded because he identified changes in the capitalism of the 2015-period which prevented many from benefiting at all from economic growth, productivity increases, and the provision of homes and jobs. The other candidates in the leadership election of 2015 seemed to have no effective programme except more triangulation. All three were former Special Advisers.

The bacillus of revolt clearly strengthened over time, between the height of Bevanism and the rise of Corbyn to power; the experience of the 1976-79 period of Labour Government was probably decisive, as I shall show later. The point is that revolts can now succeed.

Credibility and Authority

Deference ruled in the 1960s and it is certainly true that Members of Parliament were regarded as part of the upper elite. Now, after Corbynism, the expenses scandal, and seemingly endless administrative failures in Government, it can be argued that the PLP is seen as being poorer in quality than before. Some longstanding MPs and former ministers agree with this, and there is serious work to be done in identifying high quality candidates who can serve at all levels of public life. These are not just the views of the disillusioned and jaundiced: they are backed by serious political scientists.[13]

It is certainly true that politicians are less well regarded than any other profession except estate agents. If Labour is to provide an alternative team of leaders, it needs high quality candidates at all levels but there has never been any plan to ensure that this was the case.

The difference between the 1960s and now in public administration is that there is much concentration today on the effectiveness of policies and how they are implemented.

In the 1960s measuring and controlling the effectiveness of policy was not on the agenda in local councils, the NHS, nor in schools, for example. And it was not on the agenda in political parties in the sense that they did not adjust their behaviour to address these problems. Public administration has changed its focus but the political parties have not.

So, there are a great many important questions to be asked.

- How different in reality is this new power distribution in the Labour Party from the past?

- Is the new disposition entirely related to changes in the economy and class structure?

- How much has pressure group politics changed and what has been the impact on political parties as institutions?

- When did the seeds of turbulence start to germinate?

---

13.   A King *Who Governs Britain*, see pages 290-1, Pelican 2015

- Will the unprecedented grassroots movement and revolt survive the electoral defeat of 2019, or will the Party revert to a more traditional, PLP-dominated organisation?

So, has the world inside Labour turned upside down on a permanent basis; have the defeats of the Labour establishment been reversed; and if a reversion to 'normality' has been achieved, what needs to happen to turn back the tide of electoral failure?

Asking these questions is essential. The 'explanations' on offer from the Labour establishment about the electoral débacle of 2019 are wholly unconvincing. The *Labour Together* review,[14] argues that the problem goes back only 20 years in describing the drivers of change, and does not in any way describe the contribution that Labour has itself made to its own failure. It says, correctly, that the electorate can now be divided in to smaller freezer size chunks which have coherent views but are distinct from others. It describes the tensions between these groups, especially on the axes of social liberalism and attitude to Brexit.

But the real problem with the *Labour Together* prescription is the assumption that a series of complex changes can be made to the way the Party is managed and controlled in a short period of time when the very structure of the Party, its constitution, and its personnel, let alone its reputation with working class people, militate against this. It is a form of cross your fingers managerialism based on an incomplete analysis which will probably lead nowhere.

It follows a long Labour tradition of pretending that disasters are not quite as awful as they look at first sight and that things will turn out all right in the end; and in making what now seem extraordinary lapses of judgement. TUC officer Herbert Tracey used formulations of this kind in the monumental three volume series of books extolling Labour's magnificence, to slide over the débacle of the 1931 General Election; he said that the National Government victory, which reduced the number of Labour seats from 287 to 52, was a triumph 'more apparent than real,'[15] on the grounds that turnout was down and that this explained the lower Labour vote. In fact, turnout was up slightly. Others have followed along the same trajectory. The policy lapses are legion but we should remember, as an example at the extreme end of gullibility, that important

---

14. *Election Review* Labour Together, June 2020, published online
15. Herbert Tracey editor 'The British Labour Party', Caxton, 1948 vol. 1 page 183

Labour people were just as bamboozled by Hitler as some members of the British establishment were. The former Party Leader George Lansbury visited Hitler in April 1937 and returned making statements that the great dictator would not go to war.[16] Even more surprisingly perhaps, Oxford don Richard Crossman, later a Cabinet Minister under Wilson, thought for much of the 1930s that Hitler would introduce socialism to Germany, and that he was sincere.[17]

People always make mistakes and errors of judgement. The point about Labour, however, is that it has a founding set of myths that get in its way: that it is the most democratic party in Britain, when it wasn't; that it was continually making electoral progress, when it wasn't; and that replacing Tory Ministers with Labour ones would automatically improve decision making, when those Labour Ministers were just as prone to incompetence and absurdity as others.

This book is an attempt to answer some of the serious questions that must be answered if we are to understand politics in the 21ˢᵗ century, with significant illustrations from my personal experience over the last 50 years. I hope that it illuminates a few dark corners.

16.   TCH Jones, *Diary with Letters*, Oxford University Press London 1954
17.   AL Rowse *A Man of the Thirties*, London 1979, page 4

CHAPTER 1

MANCHESTER IN THE HIGH NOON OF BUTSKELLISM

The 1950s and early 1960s in Britain saw the triumph of Butskellism[18], the belief that there was an agreeable consensus between the political parties about the role of the State, the objectives of social and economic policy, budgetary matters, and even housebuilding targets.

My university tutor Fred Whitemore[19] illustrated the idea by asking his first-year students to guess which party had promised specific policies and pledges at recent general elections. He read out the quotes from the manifestos; and needless to say, it was almost impossible to tell, because the Tories often outbid Labour at election time. This was indeed the high noon of an economic and social consensus and my early life was conditioned and surrounded by it.

Born in 1947 when Attlee was Prime Minister and a year before the NHS came into being, I grew up in 1940s industrial Salford and Manchester when the UK was still talked of as 'the workshop of the world', despite the depredations of two world wars and the obvious decline of influence which accompanies an economy losing competitiveness. However, 1950s Manchester, the first industrial city in the world,

18. The combination of the names of two Conservative and Labour Chancellors – RA Butler and HTN Gaitskell
19. Fred Whitemore, Senior Lecturer at University of Kent at Canterbury, Labour Councillor Canterbury City Council and District Council from 1972 onwards, Lord Mayor Canterbury City Council 2001. Parliamentary Candidate Canterbury constituency 1992. Fred had been at Worcester and Nuffield Colleges Oxford and active in the university Labour Club. He claimed, Inter alia, that the Oxford Club had collected money to buy a machine gun for the Vietcong

still boasted a coal mine in the city centre and scores of 19th century cotton mills employed thousands of workers.

The number of mills in the city had peaked at 108 in 1853 although production rose to a high of 8 billion yards of cloth in 1912; but by 1958, Britain was a net importer. The seeds of steep industrial decline had been sown, not just in cotton but across most of the traditional staple industries, bringing with it – in the 1970s – attempts to reform economic policy. Great shocks lay ahead which would destroy Butskellism.

My family and Other Workers

In my household, history seemed to be constantly present. My father, a stereotyper on national newspapers, and my mother a secretary who had worked in prominent positions for the *Manchester Guardian* and the City Council, used to speak of the Peterloo massacre of 1819 as if it had happened last month.

They were progressive upper working class, sometimes active Quakers, solidly committed to the Labour Party but not politically active in any way. They lived in a society where such alignments seemed natural. They talked of Hugh Gaitskell in the 1959 General Election as 'the next Prime Minister.' Churchill was nothing less than 'a warmonger.'

However, the influence of religion was still strong in many working class areas. The Whit Week Walks, when children progressed under the banners of their chapel, Sunday School or Church were still in full flow in the early 1950s. Near us, the Oldham Road was shut and hundreds of young children – including myself – walked to some purpose. In both Liverpool and Glasgow, and other towns in the West of Scotland, even stronger religious influence was embedded: rabid anti-Catholic organisations stood in local elections and were frequently elected. In Glasgow, Pastor Jack Glass allied himself with strong anti-Catholic forces and worked with Ian Paisley to denounce the Pope's visit to the city in 1982; even Paisley said that Glass was 'a bit of an extremist.' In Liverpool, the Protestant Party stood in local elections and was the third largest Party on the Council and Glasgow had the Scottish Protestant League which garnered a quarter of the vote in the 1930s on a programme of ending state funding of Catholic schools. In the early 1950s, religion still had influence on voting behaviour, but it declined sharply after that and class became even more dominant as the prime influence on who people voted for. Now, religion has almost disappeared as a direct influence and even social class has significantly less power.

The Quakers

However, my parents' source of difference from others was linked to the tenets of Quakerism. My father, Denys, called up in 1940 at the age of 23, had objected to the second war against Germany on the grounds that the State could not order its citizens to kill others in its name: only God could permit slaughter.

He went to a tribunal, obtained the highest form of clearance available to conscientious objectors, and was allowed to work on the land for farmers, the Forestry Commission and then for horticulturalists growing tomatoes. He even (unlike many other Quakers) refused to join the Friends Ambulance Unit, formed to give members of the Society of Friends the opportunity to help the wounded but not to fight. This was, he thought, collaboration with the State.

His experience before and after the war, however, traumatised him. The print workers on the *Manchester Guardian* (where he had been apprenticed to his father, a compositor) refused to work with him because of his views, and eventually his union ticket was withdrawn. This barred him from any job in the print and his sense of injustice and difference arising from this led both my parents to social isolation.

His feeling of being treated differently was heightened later by having to work constantly on night shifts for 30 years after he had been reinstated to union membership in the mid-1950s. It led him to mood swings and bullying, with the constant victim being my mother.

One of the earliest examples of this that I can recall was the day I 'ran away.' I was three. I had been taken on a very long jaunt towards Droylsden by a small child I knew. He said he wanted to see his auntie and would I like to come along? I thought a walk would be nice, so I did.

Eventually, after what seemed many miles on foot, we climbed randomly on a bus (which my friend swore was going in the right direction) and were noticed by an observant and kindly conductor. He stopped the bus and took us across the road to a local police station. My mother had to get a taxi there and back at vast expense as she had no means of transport.

When my father came from work he went ballistic at the costs she had incurred. Shouting and swearing at megaphone levels went on for hours. The poor woman just had to take it for retrieving her child.

Elsie, my mother, was far more intelligent than my father and was forced to stay at home after I arrived in 1947. This followed normal practice after the second world war, when many women were driven back to the kitchen, having undertaken responsible and vital war work.

In some industries, women's employment was common – for example in cotton and wool manufacturing – as they were thought to be more dextrous in handling fragile strands of material than were men. But men had the supervisory and managerial jobs nailed down.

Elsie had been in an editorial role at the *Manchester Guardian* at its old Cross Street offices in Manchester and had also worked in very senior positions for the City Council. She was bright, industrious, super intelligent, and forced after 1947 to be idle, simply because she was a woman. It drove her to distraction and the resentment level rose markedly by the year as she was essentially held prisoner by social convention and my father.

Much later, in the 1960s, I tried to help her re-establish a career by secretly writing to all her old employers seeking references. Those that replied respectfully declined to provide a reference because no one could remember her. These were the days before employment agencies sprung up on every street corner, but it was likely that if she had pushed hard enough she would have found interesting work. Full employment was still the order of the day.

This marginalisation of my mother and women in general helped convince me that women's rights were central to fairness and the successful development of society. It took until 1964 to remove the legal ban on women in employment after marriage in the civil service, and that was a meagre start.

No Social Contact

Life as a child for me in the 1950s consisted of doing your homework and boredom with no social contact whatever. There was no telephone in the house, no television, no alcohol, no playing with other local children (especially if they were Catholics, a hangover of discrimination from the 17th century roots of Quakerism), no siblings or family close by, and constant fear of the next brutal rage from my father.

Although there were few books in the house, father brought home all the national newspapers – usually the *Manchester Guardian, Daily Mail, Daily Express* and any others that had a northern edition printed in Manchester.

In those pre-internet days the newspaper offices exchanged copies with all the others so that everyone had a view about which stories had been prioritised; and this meant that from about the age of 10 I could read most newspapers every day at our kitchen table. I was told that information was power, and I believed that.

My parents were rather odd. I was not a well child. I had to use leg braces early on as I could not walk properly, and had serious asthma and allergies from a young age. This went untreated as my parents did not like doctors and they refused to take me to see the GP to get something done about my wheezing and inability to perform physical tasks like other boys. They did, however, recognise there was a problem and part of the move to Sale was to get me breathing better air. Also, after a while, we were able to afford electric storage heaters in the house which improved my condition a lot with stable temperatures and lower humidity.

In the end, when I was about 14, I decided to take matters into my own hands and sought help from a friendly pharmacist who recommended ephedrine hydrochloride, a bronchodilator – which at the time you could buy over the counter without a prescription. It significantly eased my asthma and this easing went a stage better in 1962 when one of my classmates, concerned about my health, nicked one of the first blue asthma inhalers from his father who happened to be a salesman for a pharmaceutical company. This kind act transformed my life and I soon got one on prescription.

Not Noticing

My parents were pretty unobservant too. When I went to Firs Road primary school in Sale after our move, I landed in the biggest class in the school (well over 40) as the 1947 cohort were 'the bulge', the first wave of the baby boomers. Consequently, we used the school dining hall as our classroom as it was the biggest room.

It was a long wide hall with a blackboard erected at one end. I happened to get placed at the back and shortly after arriving a teacher came up and asked me, 'Race, why have you not copied down the work from the blackboard?' I answered, 'What blackboard, Miss?' At first, quite naturally, she thought I was being cheeky but she then took me halfway down the room and I could just about make it out. Only when I was right on top of it could I discern the writing setting out questions we had to answer.

Her attitude immediately changed and she quickly took me to see the head teacher, who tested my sight and reading in the best way that was available and it became clear to them that I was very, very short sighted. I am forever grateful to their care and professionalism. My parents, however, had not noticed or picked up on any of the clues that must have been obvious.

Looking at the world, I had always failed to understand how people built things like cars – how could they see how to do it, I wondered? Crossing the road was a nightmare because I couldn't see traffic until it was on top of me. I went for an eye test, got my NHS glasses, and I could see properly for the first time ever. The world was there. Another liberation had arrived, thanks to the support given by the public services of education and the NHS. They had dealt with the inherent medical conditions that my parents had hardly noticed.

However, those early years had made me an introverted only child, dependent very much on myself. There had been no one to play with, learn from, or discuss things with, and it made the development of my personality slow and uneven.

My parents disliked the establishment, and bitterness – always a feature in my father's life after his banishment to the Clun Valley in Shropshire as the price of his pacifism in 1940 – was heightened by the Cadbury Brothers' sale of the News Chronicle overnight in 1960, without any notice to the staff.

The paper still had a circulation of over a million but had lost readers because of its opposition to the Suez adventure of 1956 by Prime Minister Anthony Eden. So, my father turned up to work one evening and all the staff were told to go home and it was announced they had lost their jobs. The paper had been sold to the right wing *Daily Mail*, and that was that. No redundancy payments in those days (the 1965 Redundancy Payments Act was still five years away).

My father, though, was one of the lucky ones: a straw ballot allocated him work on his trade as a production printer to the *Daily Mail* at its Deansgate offices in Manchester. He was one of only a dozen or so who landed jobs in 'the print' immediately. My father blamed the Cadbury family for all this – and indeed they did behave disgracefully. There was an immediate ban on Cadbury's chocolate in our house which lasted for many decades afterwards.

Newton Heath

I lived first in west Salford and my key memories as a very young child are of crawling around the front lawn towards white mineral rocks placed round the edge of the sward and looking upwards from my pram to the trees overhead on Radcliffe Park Road.

Then when I was two, my parents moved to a rented shop in Newton Heath, where Elsie, my mother, ran a grocery and attempted to educate the local workers in the benefits of high quality, expensive food and china.

It didn't work. The shop was basically a front room with a kitchen behind, a scullery, an outside loo, a tin bath, and no bathroom. There were two bedrooms and a storeroom upstairs.

Beyond the back gate was land enclosed by the walls of the great Methodist chapel a few doors away. The shop was one of a row, including a tobacconist and a butcher, all now demolished.

My father worked as a gardener at the Brookfield approved school in Cheadle, an extension of his interest as the secretary of the Manchester University Horticultural Society.

Brookfield had vast lawns covered with horse chestnut trees, so autumn meant many conkers arriving at the shop. On each side of Droylsden Road were traditional brick terraced houses, and a short way away Brookdale Park, a huge Edwardian sprawl with bandstands, rhododendrons and grass galore. This was as well, because Newton Heath was a serious industrial area with cotton, railway works and other engineering. Indeed, they manufactured the sections of the Blackpool Tower there.

My first political memory was, I think, the 1950 General Election when a house opposite the park advertised the fact that it was the Labour Committee Rooms.

The entrance to the park, through iron gates and green painted municipal railings was opposite and it was possible to walk through the park to a back gate accessing the Brookdale Park primary school, which I started attending. Years later I discovered that Alf and Charles Morris, two very prominent Manchester Labour MPs, had also attended the school, as had Harold Evans, the highly successful journalist and Editor of the Sunday Times.

Across the Mersey

As the 1950s came to a close, my parents' economic position improved significantly because my father somehow had his union ticket reinstated. So, the rather hand-to-mouth existence in which parents had lived changed overnight to one of modest prosperity on the much higher wages of a newspaper printer.

Consequently, a decision was made to use the inherited money from Elsie's father Stead, and a move was organised from Newton Heath in east Manchester, to Sale, then a salubrious and growing southern suburb of Manchester across the river in Cheshire.

My parents bought a brand new semi-detached house with a proper bathroom and a huge garden on a new development. They loved living in a cul-de-sac and mother liked to pretend that we lived in 'Ashton on Mersey' rather than Sale, because it sounded better and rather posher. Father advanced from a motor bike and sidecar to a Ford Popular. A refrigerator arrived along with a washing machine and a television. Mother bought large amounts of meat to celebrate the end of rationing and rather overdid it.

A slight tremor in this suburban existence occurred in the Suez Crisis of 1956 when she thought that there was going to be another war, although quite how the Egyptian air force would reach suburban Manchester was not entirely clear. She taught me to dress in the dark, and made vast amounts of cake and jam and bottled fruit which were kept under the stairs just in case, until after 25 years of sitting there unopened, but festering, the damson jam caused botulism in the 1980s.

But things were looking up financially, as they were for many industrial workers. Prime Minister Harold Macmillan, at a 1957 speech in Bedford celebrating 25 years of service by Colonial Secretary Alan Lennox-Boyd, argued that 'most of our people have never had it so good.'

These sentiments – of growing prosperity for many, and a feeling in many quarters that class barriers were loosening – were replicated in our household. Much debate was had about whether we were now working class or middle class. Predictably, my father argued that we were workers but my mother, sensing the mood of the times, considered we were middle class.

Part of this desire to be aspirationally different came from her family history. Her father, Stead Broadley, had risen from being a plumber to a water inspector for the City Council and then a lecturer at Owens College (which became the fully independent University of Manchester in 1903).

He had done very well by the standards of the time, and had bought a modern semi-detached house for his son Clifford, and was to leave his own house to my mother. She continued his commitment to a Victorian work ethic and self-help through extensive night school courses in typing and shorthand, winning an RSA silver medal in the 1930s for her performance. When she was working at the City Council she was also the Secretary of the Northern Royal Horticultural Society.

She believed that education and effort were the passport to a better life – as did many others in the working class. But the Janus face was that others who were not as diligent and who indulged in drink and gambling were feckless good-for-nothings. This was especially true, it was believed, of those who lived on council estates.

This was somewhat strange, as my parents had spent the 1930s running camping breaks for slum kids from Salford and Manchester, and they had been leading lights in the International Club, which specialised in providing community support for people from abroad who had landed in Manchester, mainly to study or teach at the University. However, by the 1950s there was an especially strong injunction on me not to walk on to the newly built council estate across the main road. It would lead to no good.

Accelerating Decline

In a sense Macmillan was right. However, the inexorable decline in Britain's industrial performance, although only opaquely visible to the general population, was accelerating. In Manchester – Cottonopolis in local parlance – the glory days of cotton were long gone as had most of the awful living and working conditions described by Engels in *The Condition of the Working Class in England* in 1844.[20]

20. George Allen and Unwin, 1952 edition, based extensively on his own observations in Manchester.

But in the 1950s the Manchester Ship Canal was still full of large vessels bringing in raw cotton and other supplies and exporting finished goods and engineering products from the enormous factories at Trafford Park. The second world war had, of course, disrupted exports and Japan became the largest producer of cotton goods in the 1950s with the industry in India not far behind.

The consequence was relentless pressure on profits, closure of mills and, eventually, the Cotton Industry Act of 1959. This tried to manage decline through subsidised capacity reduction, with employers being paid cash for each spindle taken out of use.

The political effects of this were long term but even by the General Election of 1959 there were flickering signs of unease, and revolt was developing against the policies of the Conservative Government.

The 1959 General Election produced a Tory majority of 100 and the third defeat in a row for Labour nationally, although there were swings to Labour in constituencies such as those in Oldham, Bolton, and Stockport, and in most of the City of Manchester seats. Parts of Glasgow and the West of Scotland started their long slide to Labour at the same time as deindustrialisation took hold. It was the shape of things to come, and the harbinger of the end of Butskellite economic policies and consensus politics.

As a 12-year-old in my first year of grammar school, these events had only a peripheral impact on my life. It was clear that things were changing rapidly and I just happened to be there at the point when very serious industrial decline set in, with consequences for politics that would stretch into the far distance.

I knew how disappointed my parents were at the 1959 election result, with their views becoming especially clear when we were canvassed by an unfortunate local Tory in a gabardine mac and trilby, who inquired of my father, 'Will you support Sir Frederick Erroll, the Conservative candidate in the General Election?' True to form my father replied, completely inaccurately as it happened: 'Fuck off, we're all communists here.' The canvasser fled.

Sir Frederick, Economic Secretary to the Treasury and soon to be a Cabinet minister as President of the Board of Trade and Minister of Power, was returned with a majority of 15,851. Even so, there was a modest swing to Labour in Altrincham and Sale.

If 1959 was the high noon of Butskellism, this was soon to be over-taken by concerns about the long-term erosion of the British industrial base which was, by the 1960s, accelerating. There was deepening concern in the establishment about Britain's declining place in the world, the disappearance of Empire, and the profound changes in economic performance which illuminated the fact that British rates of economic growth were falling short of those in Europe and the Americas and, some said, even in the Soviet Union.

Evidence of this could be seen in the fall in manufacturing employment, the reduction in the number of coal mines, cotton mills, and other plant as recorded by the Office for National Statistics, and by the growth in service employment. ONS data shows that secondary sector employment (mainly manufacturing) peaked in the mid 1960s at about 40% of total employment, falling to 15.1% in 2016.

Looking further back to the inter-war period, the share of manufacturing jobs in the total economy averaged 25% but declined sharply to an average of 9.5% between 2000 and 2016.[21]

The local impact of deindustrialisation was felt strongly in Manchester: the last deep pit, Bradford Colliery in the east of the city, closed in 1968. The site is now the location of the Etihad stadium, home of Manchester City and owned by Arab oil wealth. Scores of cotton mills, and the whole glass industry in Manchester, were shut: one of the most eerie sights even now is the industrial desert north of Ancoats. Many huge cotton mills, now empty or converted, loom out of the mist like deserted hulks representing another era; they were the shining vanguard of the industrial revolution and now are the discarded remnants of a recent past.

However, it was still full employment for some of Lancashire in the mid 1960s: I walked in off the street to a big office in the centre of town in an attempt to earn some holiday money and was recruited on the spot by a Mr Blood of the Manchester Guardian Society, essentially a debt collection agency. It seemed easy.

The Fading of the Working Class

But these downward economic trends, highly visible in parts of 1960s Manchester, were not entirely new and their impact on politics has been highly contested: from the late 19th century onwards, employment in intermediate strata grew slowly, bridging the gap between the 'two nations, perceived alike by Engels and Disraeli, of the manual wage

21.   ONS, *Long-term Trends in UK employment: 1861 to 2018, April 2019.*

workers and the major property owning groups.'[22]

From this early 1960s perspective, the sociologists Goldthorpe and Lockwood argued that the so-called 'embourgeoisement' of the British worker had been exaggerated. They said that earning much higher wages – which some manual workers were clearly doing and which they accepted was happening – did not mean that they were achieving a similar social status, broadly equivalent to some traditional middle class professionals, administrative and clerical workers. This 'status gap', they argued, would keep richer manual workers attached to the working class.

What they did not envisage was what came later: the wholesale removal of manual workers' jobs from the economy by the processes of technological change, divestment of state owned resources in the 1980s, and globalisation.

As they hadn't foreseen this future jobs Armageddon in the early 1960s, they therefore exaggerated the resilience of class ties even if workers were being paid more. But the collective weight of the working class, and manual workers in particular, has been fundamentally altered by rapid subsequent economic change.

This process, of long standing, may be nothing in terms of what is to come. Further changes connected to artificial intelligence and robots are arriving fast: some estimates suggest that half of all existing jobs may be taken from humans in the next 20 years. Even great institutions such as the Bank of England are warning of fundamental changes in the future world of work.

This looming vision of a job-poor, roboticised future is made more likely by the impact of pandemics: if you can't get staff to work in an office, employers will accelerate the move to artificial intelligence where this can be done.

This arid vision of the future is a million miles from the Manchester of the 1950s and 1960s that I grew up in. It calls into question the role of the trade unions, the very existence of a 'Labour' party, and the ability of the State to fund public services from taxes levied on employees and employers. It also raises the possibility of civil disorder and a breakdown in political legitimacy and consent.

The changes in class composition that have occurred since the 1960s are nothing to the changes that are to come.

---

22.   Goldthorpe and Lockwood, *Affluence and the British Class Structure* 1963

The Politics of Croslandism

In the light of what we know now, the revisionist economists, and especially Crosland, perhaps exaggerated the importance of very subtle and small scale changes in the economy, class structure and voting behaviour in the mid-1950s. They developed the proposition that the Labour Party needed to respond to these changes by revisions in ideology.[23]

Crosland went back further in time to justify his claim that Britain was now fundamentally different from pre-1914 capitalism. He said:

almost all the basic characteristic features of traditional pre-1914 capitalism have either been greatly modified or completely transformed.[24]

This can now be seen clearly as wishful thinking, but in the late 1950s it seemed plausible and rather modern, especially as the practical consequence might be that the Labour Party remained electable through modernisation.

My own awareness of these accelerating changes began with the Conservatives, after their triumph in the 1959 General Election, casting around for ways to reverse economic decline. They had achieved a giant majority and had made significant gains in southern England and the West Midlands. But, fearful of the economic future, they started a search for new solutions to the comparative decline of the British economy at a time when the old Empire was being dismantled and the relative advantage of colonial preference arrangements was disappearing.

Their solution came in two forms: first, the beginnings of indicative planning through what became the NEDC (National Economic Development Council), established in 1962, and the Little NEDDIES, which were set up for a wide range of industries. They hoped that these tripartite bodies, which contained representatives of industry, commerce, the trade unions and Government, would improve coordination between industry and policy makers, as well as refreshing and modernising high-level planning and industrial practice. The hope was that these bodies would speed economic growth, develop new industries and narrow the gap between Britain and its competitors.

The plan was that the NEDDIES would get Britain away from the stop-go policies of successive Conservative governments and chancellors which had clearly damaged economic performance by, for example, cutting taxes in April and increasing them in July, as happened in 1955.

---

23. C.A.R. Crosland, *The Future of Socialism*, 1956
24. C.A.R. Crosland, *The Future of Socialism* 1964 edition, p33-34

The second policy initiative was more controversial and consisted of approaches to join the European Economic Community, the predecessor of the European Union.

The Conservative leadership thought that the declining weight of British manufacturing industry in the share of world trade[25] created conditions under which the permanent problem of the balance of payments would affect the value of sterling, worsen the problem of the Sterling Area balances, and create further problems for the British Government in financing its borrowing needs in the open market.

Accordingly, they saw the creation of a wider home market based on the population of western Europe, as guaranteeing higher economic growth and participation in the so-called economic miracle that had been created in Germany, especially since 1945.

They misread the situation in believing that the end state desired by European leaders was anything other than a journey to a unified political and economic Europe with decisions made there rather than in nation states.

They also misread the reasons for the German boom, which was in fact created by the Marshall Plan working to reverse the destruction of capital goods during the War. Andrew Shonfield, in his book *British Economic Policy Since the War*, used figures for the original EEC Six which showed that the highest rates of economic growth had in fact occurred before the creation of the Common Market by the Treaty of Rome.

Labour Leader Hugh Gaitskell, speaking at the Labour Party Conference in 1962, picked up this point and said, 'the rate of expansion in Europe, however you measure it – by industry, by exports, by gross national product – was faster in the five years 1950-55 than it was in the five years which followed.'

He followed this up by arguing that joining the EEC 'does mean, if this is the idea, the end of Britain as an independent European state … it means the end of a thousand years of history. You may say, 'Let it end.' But my goodness, it is a decision which needs a little care and thought.'

The extent of political opposition to the concept of European integration from the 1940s to the 1960s in both political parties has been misrepresented. Ernest Bevin, Foreign Secretary in the Labour

---

25. House of Commons Library Briefing Paper, 5th November 2018, *UK trade 1948-2018* showed that the UK share of world exports was 11% in 1948 and 3% in 2018. In 1922, Britain's share of all exports was 14.9% and of all manufactured exports 28.8%.

Government from 1945 until shortly before his death in 1951, is quoted as saying, 'If you open that Pandora's box, you never know what Trojan 'orses will jump out.'[26]

Attlee was lukewarm at best about the creation of the first European institution, the Coal and Steel Community, and Gaitskell argued convincingly in 1962 that Macmillan had no mandate for what he was doing, as the issue of joining the EEC had not been the subject of discussion at the 1959 General Election. In fact, Gaitskell said that if an application to the EEC was agreed in principle, then there should be a general election at which the will of the people could be tested.

The argument advanced by Sir Keir Starmer in 2019, that Labour has always been a pro-European party, is therefore quite wrong. This opposition and semi-opposition to the European project, continued in a roundabout way by Harold Wilson as Leader until the 1967 application to join the EEC, is striking.

What is also striking is that the subject of European policy was not a public issue at all and certainly not one which had large pressure groups behind it during the 1950s and early 1960s. It was handled almost exclusively at elite level and the issue of Europe was, unlike today, not on the radar of most voters. The pro-Europeans did not at that stage feel the need to develop a public facing campaign designed to woo the citizens. Neither did anti-EEC forces build a significant public presence. Pressure group politics external to Parliament, to build support for a pro- or anti-European policy, was not at that point visible and important to voters.

In any event, President de Gaulle vetoed the British application on 14th January 1963. Speaking under the crystal chandeliers of the Elysée Palace, he said, 'She (Britain) has, in all her doings, very marked and very original habits and traditions. In short, England's nature, England's structure, England's very situation differs profoundly from those of the Continentals.'[27]

---

26.   Sir R Barclay, *Ernest Bevin and the Foreign Office*, Latimer 1965, page 67
27.   Quoted in A Peyrefitte *C'Etait de Gaulle* Vol. 1, 1994

Profumo

So, Britain was changing slowly and the air of impending decline, fuelled by the Cuba missile crisis of 1962, Khruschev's behaviour,[28] the shooting down of the U2 spy plane over the Soviet Union, and the growing sense that the Conservative Government was running out of steam and looking back to the Edwardian era, fuelled my interest in politics.

But it was the Profumo affair of 1963 which was the catalyst for my political involvement in the first place. Profumo, the Secretary of State for War in the Macmillan Cabinet, had been frequenting with Christine Keeler who was also sharing a bed with the Soviet naval attaché and GRU officer Yevgeny Ivanov.

This came out because of rumours and evidence given in court cases, driving Profumo to make a personal statement to the House of Commons in which he said he had done nothing wrong. Later, he confirmed that he had lied to the House of Commons and to the Prime Minister, and eventually resigned on 4th June 1963.

These events seemed to me to encapsulate what was wrong with Britain's government: it was run by a bunch of toffs who did what they liked and were morally bankrupt. Something had to change, I thought, and that meant the election of a Labour Government under the dynamic Harold Wilson, at that time reaching the height of his powers.

Much later, Geoffrey Robertson's brilliant book *Stephen Ward Was Innocent, OK*[29] showed that government ministers in 1963 had connived in the investigation and prosecution of Stephen Ward and encouraged Scotland Yard to frame him for crimes that he did not commit – a blatant interference in operational police matters for political ends – that is, to take the heat off Profumo.

Home Secretary Henry Brooke and his permanent undersecretary Sir Charles Cunningham had in March 1963 summoned the head of MI5, Roger Hollis and the Commissioner of the Metropolitan Police Sir Joseph Simpson, to discuss the Profumo and Ward cases. The Home Secretary clearly encouraged the investigation of Ward in order to get Profumo off the hook and, as Robertson says, 'he wanted Ward put away because he set a rotten example for youth, making young women

---

28. Eg: taking his shoes off and banging the table with them at a United Nations meeting designed to reduce tensions. The Western Press took this incident as an indication that Khruschev was another robust and aggressive Communist.
29. Biteback, 2013

51

available to tempt old Tories … Brooke abused his powers if he directed the police to 'get Ward."

Of course, none of this was known at the time in any detail, but the stench of corruption emanating from the Conservative front bench was apparent to everyone. If I had known the full extent of the decay my actions would not have changed. I would still have joined the Labour Party in the misguided belief that they would be inoculated against such dreadful immorality. It was my Quaker upbringing coming out big time.

The Real Manchester

However, in what passed for the real world, I had to buckle down and do my A-levels. I was taught well in some subjects and less well in others, as is often the case, and so in order to get some peace and quiet and a better atmosphere for reading and revision, I used to travel into the Central Library in Manchester's St Peter's Square on the Corporation bus, usually sitting in the smoky upper deck to get a better view.

There was a lot going on. First, the demolition of the Victorian slums and blackened red brick housing of Hulme (now 'redeveloped' for a second time); spotting the headquarters of the Manchester Ship Canal Company; and noticing that most adults on the bus turned to stare when a black person was walking along the pavement.

The city looked dark, especially in the winter: black slate Manchester roofs shone in the rain and all the important buildings were covered in a grey-black covering of soot and industrial pollution. The magnificent Town Hall was a black edifice pointing to the skies, and the John Rylands Library and the Cathedral – really a large medieval church butchered about by the Victorians – were completely covered in black coal dust and sooty residue from the hundreds of industrial engines in Cottonopolis.

But you could tell that Manchester took itself seriously, with red tarmac outside the Town Hall instead of the regulation black. It was a proper city, proud of its civic institutions and the place it had in industrial and political history. Not only had Manchester been the founding city of industrialism and a great centre of Chartism, its cotton workers had actively supported the abolition of slavery. They supported emancipation, despite the fact that they were starving, with factories closed and evictions mounting as a direct consequence of the Northern blockade of Southern ports in the American Civil War, which meant that cotton could not be shipped to Lancashire's 2,400 factories.

At a meeting in the Free Trade Hall on New Year's Eve 1862, they responded to the crisis by passing a motion urging President Lincoln to pursue the war vigorously, end slavery, and supported the blockade.

In gratitude for their support, Lincoln wrote to the working people of Manchester on 19th January 1863, in words which are now engraved on his statue in Lincoln Square, Manchester:

I cannot but regard your decisive utterances on the question as an instance of sublime Christian heroism which has not been surpassed in any age or in any country.

It is indeed an energetic and re-inspiring assurance of the inherent truth and of the ultimate and universal triumph of justice, humanity and freedom … Whatever misfortune may befall your country or my own, the peace and friendship which now exists between the two nations will be, as it shall be my desire to make them, perpetual.

This was not a trivial political history and I was very conscious of the part Manchester had played in the development of the working class movement. Mancunian workers were different from the ship owners and financiers of Liverpool who sided with the slaver South to support their own ends.

Cotton workers, however, knew that the last hands that touched the cotton they spun and wove had been black, and unfree. It seemed to me that if this city advocated change, anything might be possible. There was a moral force to Manchester.

As I got off the Corporation bus in St Peter's Square to attend the Central Library, the Peterloo Massacre site was to the left under the Free Trade Hall;[30] to the right was the Town Hall, where Prime Minister David Lloyd George had been secretly hidden for 11 days after he contracted the Spanish flu in September 1918. Behind the library, off Albert Square in Brazennose Street, was the Lincoln statue sent there by President Taft, intended to commemorate the role that the cotton workers had played in ending slavery. Important political history was all around.

The Central Library itself, a round white Portland stone building of beautiful proportions, had an interesting history. The foundation stone

30. The Free Trade Hall was opened in 1856 and had been built by the Manchester Corporation to celebrate the repeal of the Corn Laws in 1846. The Corn Laws had artificially raised the price of bread by placing a tariff on imported corn, thus raising the price of bread to the consumer. Manchester is the only City to have a conference hall named after a principle. After bombing by the Luftwaffe in 1941 it was reopened in 1951

was laid by Ramsay MacDonald as Prime Minister in May 1930 and was later formally opened by King George V in 1934. It allowed any school student in Greater Manchester to borrow books and study them for hours. I did this for months and began the process of self-education which I both enjoyed and which has been extraordinarily useful.

The library sits opposite the home of the Hallé orchestra and the centre of Manchester's cultural life. The Free Trade Hall has now been converted into a Radisson Blu Hotel, as solid a symbol of commercialisation as you can get, mirroring the fate of the old Central Station right behind it – closed in 1969 as a consequence of the Beeching cuts to the rail system and now a conference venue when it reverts from being a Nightingale Hospital.

Escaping from the Narrow World

Studying in the Central Library was far easier than being at home. For a relatively well educated and education focused family there were few books in the house and no other stimulation available.

My A-Level subjects were English Literature, History and Geography, and what was then known as General Studies. I was ruthlessly determined to get the best possible grades so that I could go off to university and escape from what I saw as the confined, narrow world of my parents and the lack of focus that living there determined. The choices of university for me were driven by geography and by attractiveness.

At that time the great expansion of university provision was under way following the Robbins report of 1963[31] which had advocated what became the Robbins Principles that education beyond 18 'should be available to all who were qualified for (it) by ability and attainment.'

In 1964, only about 8% of the 18-year-old age cohort went to a university. Robbins meant in practice the rapid creation of brand new universities, mainly on greenfield sites, and the conversion of the Colleges of Advanced Technology to university status.

But it also meant that these new institutions, which began teaching in 1964-65, were completely untested and it was impossible to judge the quality of the courses they would establish, because when my age cohort was applying in 1964 they did not exist, had not appointed key

---

31.   *The Report of the Committee on Higher Education, Cmnd 2154 September 1963*

academic staff, and were in some cases dreams on blueprints.

This did not deter me. I knew this was a critical choice which could have a serious influence on my life chances. But there was little guidance from my school (Sale Grammar School). The so-called careers guidance was weak and run by a staff member who really did not know what was going on. I was told that the best I could hope for was teacher training college. This made me more determined than ever and I set out to demonstrate that they were wrong.

This, together with the need to get away from my parents, meant that I had to look as far away as possible from suburban south Manchester. Many prospectuses were obtained and arrived excitingly through the post. I made application through the new UCAS system to a wide spread of institutions: I thought of Aberdeen, but decided that it was definitely too cold, and gravitated eventually towards the University of Kent at Canterbury (as it was then known), which was being built on a hill overlooking the magnificent cathedral.

In those days some of the universities interviewed all applicants and Kent certainly did so. I went by train, for the first time experiencing the joys of the Southern Region of British Railways with its strange green signs (London Midland had the, to me, familiar maroon) and arrived at the magnificent Westgate, 60 feet high and built in 1380.

Westgate House was a lovely Georgian building where I had a friendly interview and received a sensible offer from the registry shortly afterwards. The only deterrent was uncertainty about whether the place would be built in time. From Westgate House, we were taken on a bumpy ride in an old Bedford vanette, with red leather seats, up to the site. They had completed the access road – unsurprisingly called University Road – and we swept past Beverley Farm, towards the unprepossessing building site.

They were constructing the first of the colleges, Eliot, and the first of the science blocks. That was it. The main conclusion that I drew from the day was that the view to the city and the cathedral was wonderful but that mud would overwhelm everything.

It was raining and grey, a typical January day, and it drizzled. Canterbury did not look its best in the gloom. The mud – of Western Front 1916 proportions – created by heavy deposits of fireclay over the chalk of the North Downs, was so bad that when the installation of Princess Marina as chancellor took place a year later, armies of workmen laid turf over the parts that she would see and when the dignitaries had moved on, took it up again.

Despite the mud, I accepted the university's offer and set aside the others I had received and won the best grades available in my A-levels. I was off to uni – the first person in my family ever to have done so. This was a common feature in a 1960s childhood and many parents were inordinately proud of their offspring for getting that far.

But my generation and I were immensely lucky. We did not realise it at the time, but we were the beneficiaries of the huge improvements to welfare provision and education set in train by the wartime Coalition and deepened by the Labour Government of 1945-51.

We benefited from modern primary schools, free secondary education (chargeable for many before 1939), the NHS in all its forms, well-funded public libraries, and finally by the ready availability of maintenance grants for those of us who entered higher education. I did not enjoy a full grant as my father was earning too much in the print, but I also obtained the only scholarship available from Sale Borough Council – which paid me £50 a year (nearly £1,000 at today's prices) plus sums for the vacations if you applied for them.

Hidden under this veneer of opportunity was, however, a strict hierarchy based on educational selection. The 11-plus was still in operation in Cheshire, but the County Council allowed a rather higher proportion of its 11-year-olds to go to grammar schools than in other authorities. It traditionally allowed about 8% to progress to the much better grammars with the rest going to the much worse funded secondary moderns. But only about 18% of all pupils entered for the GCE nationally in 1965 obtained 'good' grades, and many were not entered at all. Once students reached the age of 16 in the Grammars there was another winnowing process with a significant number going on to jobs rather than continuing in education, and the available opportunities for attending university were heavily restricted before the Robbins reforms kicked in around 1965. In the Secondary Moderns, most left education at 15.

So, I was lucky four times over: lucky to have parents who emphasised education as the most important factor in your life; lucky to have passed the 11-plus; lucky to have entered a grammar school with better facilities, more and better teachers and more funding; and finally, lucky to have got a prized place at university, unlike most of my age group.

What I did not realise at all at the time was what this meant: that a meritocracy guaranteed that there were losers, and in this period, many losers. I had no conception of the poor educational attainment of those in working class areas; no conception except in the vaguest sense of how relatively privileged we were; and, at the point when I went off to university, no real sense of what needed to be done about it. That would change but what I did not know was that the Manchester I had experienced was rapidly disappearing, along with millions of jobs elsewhere, with its huge tax base, a culture of its own, and a tradition.

CHAPTER 2

GLAD CONFIDENT MORNING AND AFTER: THE EMERGENCE OF A NEW MIDDLE CLASS

I arrived in Canterbury in September 1965 as one of the 'first 500' students at the University of Kent. It was an exciting liberation to be away from my parents and the stuffy atmosphere of suburban Manchester.

One of the first important events was the posting of sign-up sheets inviting students to join clubs that had been proposed by the senior members of faculty.

I scanned the array by the bar and spotted that the Labour Club had fewer sign-ups than the Conservative Club. This could not be allowed to stand so I took down the sheet and went round the common room signing up as many people as I could. Large numbers signed, despite the fact that the student intake was overwhelmingly middle class and even more overwhelmingly from the south east. There was hardly anyone from the North. But this was 1965 and there was a relatively shiny new Labour Government in power, albeit with a precarious majority of four.

Because this was the first year of Kent University, there were only 486 students on site. This suited me as I may have felt lost in a larger institution. I had never developed any social skills because social contact as a teenager had been non-existent for me, so I had to learn rapidly. We were given a primitive induction, which consisted of 'don't spend all your grant cheque money at once,' and a blast from the past by the City of Canterbury Director of Public Health, a late middle-aged man in a suit who was obviously agitated at the new arrivals. He warned us in stentorian terms of the 'disease speeding down the railway tracks from London,' by which everyone thought he meant VD. As a DPH in a garrison town this shouldn't have been new to him perhaps, but there we were. He thought we were all going to be a bad influence on the pristine locals.

My learning did not develop through partying: it happened through politics. Although I was very good at my work – at the end of the foundation course I was awarded the highest marks of all the 500 or so students – I began to develop the view that some of them , especially those majoring in literature, were really self-centred and only in it to please themselves. This was terribly bad, I thought, and at the end of the foundation course I changed faculties to study politics and sociology.

There was a great hoo-ha about whether I would be allowed to do it at all, and I had to be interviewed by Professor Brian Keith-Lucas, an eminent Liberal Party supporter whose specialty was the history of parish councils. Eventually I was allowed to switch and that began my formal training in political life.

Everything at the university was gleaming and exciting. I had a good room on the first floor looking over the car park. It was also close to the iron gate which clanged shut at 10pm each night, after which you could only enter if you had the foresight to obtain an exeat, obtainable in each instance from your tutor. And if you were late or hadn't obtained the relevant paperwork, you were literally stuck outside.

However, this presented an opportunity and I did a roaring trade in hauling up latecomers through my window, which was just about reachable from the ground. This service was especially popular amongst the young women who frequented the Hunt Ball. The voluminous evening dresses of the time were, however, an impediment to climbing.

The exeat system did not last long. It was rightly regarded as a ridiculous piece of bureaucracy designed for the 19th century and an infringement of the simple liberty of going about your business. It was soon abolished after considerable agitation by the student body.

The abolition of the exeat system was the first indication of a major sea change in opinion, in about the spring of 1966, reflecting the more libertarian mood of the times. Hair styles changed, clothes changed, students became considerably wilder and some started taking drugs. By 1967 some were dying from overdoses of LSD.

I was deeply unimpressed by the cavalier, live-in-the-moment recklessness of hippy culture and I never went near it. I wanted to do something useful with my life. I did not even have any alcohol till I was 20 and I avoided music like the plague.

Templeman

The university authorities resisted the agitation against restrictive rules and our deeply reactionary Vice Chancellor Geoffrey Templeman was aghast when we started a full scale student union. He had wanted a 'Guild' reflecting the name of the Birmingham University organisation of students. His view was that it would be easier to manage these ghastly oiks if the student body was split between the colleges with a separate Guild in each one.

This was so obviously Divide and Rule that resistance was easy to organise, despite most focus being on the 'Ents'[32] spending for bands. At this point Templeman decided to beard the person who he saw as the ringleader, i.e. me. I was summoned one day, out of the blue, to his spacious office in Beverley Farm. As I nervously entered, he said, 'Race, you are a red revolutionary,' (because I had opposed him). This was pretty far off the mark as I was the most mainstream Labour Party supporter that you could find anywhere – probably a Croslandite, if you had asked politely. I gave as good as I got from Templeman, and we got our union.

First Contact

Internal student politics was, however, not appealing and I spent most of my non-studying time on the University Labour Club. Despite the fact that I had never been to a political meeting, I wrote the constitution, rounded up members, worked with a strong team of leaders, and organised visits from prominent MPs in the news.

This was greatly assisted by the fund that the university had established to provide rail travel expenses to visiting Parliamentarians, at first class carriage rates. 'They must have the ability to work in peace on the train,' said Keith-Lucas. This enabled me to invite many members of the Labour Cabinet and backbench MPs and we had a constant stream of them arrive to talk on topics in the news and to debate with the student body.

This was when the shock dawned on me.

Tony Crosland arrived and drank a full bottle of whisky right in front of me in Fred Whitemore's room. Foreign Secretary George Brown rolled in, and after manful resistance to seditious offers of alcohol by

32. Entertainments, basically loud music

lecturers he succumbed and became dreadfully drunk, making all kinds of inappropriate remarks as he went. Stan Henig (MP for Lancaster), David Winnick (MP for Croydon South), David Ennals (MP for Dover and at that time a junior minister), Terry Boston (MP for Faversham and described as the politest man in the House), Anne Kerr (MP for Rochester and Chatham and most famous for attacking war toys) came and were mostly boring.

Tom Driberg (MP for Barking and a darling of the left) attended, demanded to stay overnight in a guest room, and suggestively argued that I should personally wake him up in the morning. I wasn't having any of this so I told Whitemore that I would only go to Driberg's room if he accompanied me, which he did, and the planned Driberg seduction was averted.

The revelation that came to me – and I was genuinely astonished by it – was that many of these MPs and Cabinet ministers were really not very good.

Always a critical observer, I noticed that some were confused, some were unconvincingly peddling a party line, others were clearly soaks, others again had the Driberg touch. For a suburban 18-year-old Quaker reared boy from up north this was astonishing.

My contact with non-MPs was also disappointing: we invited Jack Dash, one of the prominent leaders of the London dockers and a straightforward member of the Communist Party. He demanded to stay overnight and be put up in the best rooms in the city, at that time provided by the County Hotel in the High Street. He also demanded first class train travel and loss of earnings, which he calculated at an astronomical rate, and which I foolishly paid him out of my own pocket. He was the easiest straw man for the establishment to knock down, and a bit of a clown despite his reputation as a fire breathing leftie.

As time went on and I met further outriders, I decided that the political class as represented by them left a great deal to be desired and that dealing with that problem was critical if we were to get anything serious done. Many of these people were quite useless, I thought in my very young head. Later on – much later in fact – I recognised that some of the prominent MPs I met were in fact far better than the present 2019 iteration of that political class.

There was one clear exception to this string of disappointments when a Cabinet minister in the Wilson Government was invited in 1969, and impressed us hugely. Tony Benn was sharp, intelligent, engaging and determined to listen to the very large numbers of young people who had come to hear him speak.

He was in a steeply banked lecture theatre, and instead of protecting himself behind the long wooden podium he sat on it, swung his legs, and answered questions from the full house.

Tony had only recently dropped the 'Wedgwood' bit of his name and was beginning a tentative trajectory from MINTECH[33] to left winger and was very obviously testing the water to discover responses to his emerging 'crisis of capitalism' position. The teetotal Benn was plainly in a different class to the tired old boozers, no-hopers and intellectually vapid MPs that we had mostly had at UKC. It was a sign of things to come.

I spoke to him and that was the start of a lengthy association.

Unpaid Labour

One of the most important events early on at UKC was a very small meeting held at the behest of the Canterbury Labour Party. Two of the local Labour councillors, Bill Clarke and Jim Coombs, visited the university Labour Club along with the Labour Agent, Ken Elks. Their pitch was simple: help Labour to win Canterbury City Council by going out canvassing.

They thought that if they laid their hands on an unpaid workforce that triumph would follow, as they were adhering to the normal Labour rubric at the time, which was purely organisational: get more of your vote out than the other side.

That meeting was decisive in shaping the future of Labour politics in Canterbury for many years to come. The City Council was the smallest County Borough in England, with full powers to run major services such as education and social services. This was prior to the Heseltine reorganisation of 1974, although some of these powers were devolved to Kent County Council under agency arrangements. In early 1964, just before the university arrived, every seat on the City Council was filled by a Conservative.

The ruling Conservative group was dominated by shopkeepers: Bertie Buckworth the butcher, Porter the chemist, Jennings the printer, and so

---

33. Ministry of Technology. Benn was Postmaster General 1964-66 and Minister of Technology 1966-70, responsible inter alia for the development of Concorde.

on. Behind these small town retailers, which we labelled The Shopocracy, stood what was thought to be the insidious figure of Ted Brown, the Tories' full time agent and the Chair of the council Finance Committee. His writ ran wide and he was also thought to be the author of the torrid anti-Labour 'Diogenes' column in the local paper, the Kent Herald. He was extensively disliked – especially by Conservatives, but also by the many who crossed him. He attempted to bully Labour Candidates in 1967 to withdraw from contests on the grounds that their careers would suffer, and had instructed Tory-supporting GPs not to accept postal votes from anyone if they were brought in by a Labour supporter.[34]

Those who got in his way were punished using the full force of the Council: when the Professor of Politics Brian Keith-Lucas and his wife Mary moved in to a large Georgian-fronted house on King Street, retribution was taken because Mary had just won a seat on the Council as a Liberal. Brown organised council officers to make inquiries about part of the Keith-Lucas's garden, and found that some of it might be said to be a medieval graveyard. He then caused a major planning dispute, with the upshot that the Keith-Lucases were forced to make part of their garden accessible to the public. To this day there is a gate which allows entry, opened at daybreak and closed at nightfall. The public have the opportunity of sitting on a seat in the garden, just a few feet from the back door of the house. This vindictive behaviour could have been used against anyone with a house within the Medieval City walls, as every inch of ground in Canterbury has archaeology running at many levels beneath it. Brown just wanted everyone to know who was in charge.

However, he did not always get his way: a widely publicised disaster[35] involved Brown telling Alderman Jennings, Chair of the Council Education Committee, to organise facilities for a Conservative Central Office film unit to visit Canterbury schools at one day's notice, so they could get stock footage for the coming General Election. Jennings, owner of a large print shop two doors down from Conservative HQ, was, however, rebuffed by many schools concerned about consent from parents and the children themselves. Many pupils revolted, scrawled slogans on the school windows, and refused to co-operate. Reporters from the Labour-supporting *Daily Herald* turned up. Tory Minister Chris Chataway, who was due to visit the Simon Langton Grammar School and

---

34.   In the 1960s postal votes applied for on medical grounds had to be supported by the signature of the applicant's GP
35.   *The Spectator* 3rd January 1964, page 6

be filmed with adoring children, got on the train at Victoria only to be turned around on the Canterbury station platform by a Tory official and sent straight back to the capital. Brown had been beaten by the parents, the kids and the teachers who did not want to be tools of Tory propaganda. This was the height of Brown's powers, the apogee of one-party rule in Canterbury. In six years he would be out of power permanently.

Those of us who wanted to get involved in making political change happen were intrigued by the opportunities we identified.

Canterbury City Council had made the serious mistake of locating large council estates in each of the wards in the city. Some of these had been constructed as a result of the Wheatley Act under the 1923 Labour Government but most had been built after the heavy bombing of Canterbury by the Luftwaffe in the Baedeker raids. Much of the town centre had been flattened but the cathedral had largely escaped despite being hit by many incendiaries. This meant that the council had to rehouse thousands of families bombed out by Hitler and Goering.

In addition, there was something of a residual radicalism in the town. There had been a large Communist Party branch in the 1930s and 1940s, and significant anti-fascist activity, encouraged by the presence of the Red Dean of Canterbury, Hewlett Johnson[36], and the activities of a small left wing bourgeoisie grouped around Catherine Williamson, whose family owned the Tannery – one of the largest private employers in the City. The Williamson tannery provided the green and red leather for the Commons and Lords Chambers and was also the source of immense quantities of noxious fumes because of its use of urine on an industrial scale.

She had been Mayor in 1939-41 and later became a founder member of Sir Richard Acland's Common Wealth Party.[37] Williamson and her

36. Hewlett Johnson became Dean of Canterbury in 1931 and was a fellow traveller of the Communist Party and a fervent admirer of the Soviet Union and of Stalin, even after the Russian invasion of Finland in 1939. He exasperated most of the Cathedral clergy, especially by bringing Mahatma Gandhi to the Cathedral. Gandhi turned up at the Deanery in a Rolls Royce along with his spinning wheel and personal goat. In 1936 after a brief tour of the Soviet Union he penned *The Socialist Sixth of the World*, now thought to be a work cut and pasted from Stalinist internal propaganda. He was not a spy or traitor but was closely watched by the security services from the 1920s. He never joined the CP or even the Labour Party. Source *Open Lecture UKC 2007* by Emeritus Professor John Butler, and his book *The Red Dean*, Scala, 2011

37. The Common Wealth Party contested several by-elections during the electoral truce of the Second World War, and won a series of very safe seats from the Conservatives. Catherine Williamson contested the Ashford by-election

husband joined Labour after 1945 but she ended up, when very old in the late 1960s, as a Maoist.

She addressed a meeting at the university, supporting Chairman Mao and the Cultural Revolution then sweeping China. When asked by Fred Whitemore if there was freedom of speech in the communist state, she firmly retorted, 'You can say whatever you like provided you don't criticise the Government.' Nevertheless, she put up a poster for me when I stood in the city elections in 1970. A long journey indeed.

Perhaps the most revealing evidence of this fading radical mood in Canterbury was the naming of some streets of prefabs on the Sturry Road estate, erected around 1945 and named after the wartime leaders – Churchill, Roosevelt, Truman, and Stalin. This is one of only three examples in Britain of Uncle Joe being honoured in a street name (the others are in Colchester and Chatham – garrison or naval towns as Canterbury was during the 1940s).

For me, the possibility of making change happen by getting involved in local Labour politics was irresistible. I had already organised the first student demonstration in Canterbury (and the first by anybody for a very long time) on the issue of the Unilateral Declaration of Independence (UDI) in Southern Rhodesia. The Rhodesia Front Government of Ian Smith had unilaterally declared independence from Britain in order to preserve all white rule and the all-white franchise.

A couple of hundred students marched through the city centre chanting slogans in support of majority rule. It was a visible sign that Canterbury was not the sleepy market town of the past. All this activity meant, however, that I could develop friends amongst the students and working relationships with real people in the city, something I had never experienced before. But the real challenge of making things happen in Canterbury was daunting.

A Long History of Failure

The history of the Labour Party in the city and constituency had been one of continuous failure since 1945. Looking at local political history

---

in February 1943 but lost by 5,000. The Party was initially chaired by JB Priestley with Tom Wintringham and Sir Richard Acland as leading members. The Party collapsed in 1945 after the great victory by Attlee.

through election data (kindly sourced from David Cowling)[38] Labour's performance in city local elections prior to 1965 was very poor with only five victories out of 120 contests since 1945 (excluding by-elections).[39]

Even at the height of the Attlee wave of support, performance in the local elections of November 1945 was exceptionally poor given that this election was held months after the great Labour victory announced in July.

This was because a shopkeeper front organisation, the Citizens' Defence Association, swept the board in response to the proposals for rebuilding after the 1942 raids which destroyed most of the High Street area from Butchery Lane to what is now the Whitefriars Shopping Centre.

This defeat was followed by a long trough. In the early years after the second world war, there were still Independent candidates contesting seats and sometimes winning them. The Tories frequently did deals with Independents, by standing only one Tory candidate, to ensure that the Independent won

On many occasions, wards in the city went uncontested. The best example was 1955, when there were no Labour candidates anywhere and all Tories were returned unopposed. Five Labour victories out of 120 vacancies between 1945-65 was not impressive. No Labour councillor having been elected, was ever re-elected.

The reasons for this weakness before 1965, in what was essentially a working class city, was that the Tories had developed a hegemonic alliance between the old local middle class and the shopkeepers. There was also a clear feeling amongst anti-Tories in general elections that the local Conservatives were all-powerful and undefeatable in local elections (a view which was largely correct).

In addition, the Labour Party had weak local leadership for most of this period. It was based on some trade union branches (notably NUM Chislet, the railway unions, and USDAW).[40] It had no prominent local figures until the emergence of Fred Rippington, who won Westgate Ward in 1964, and Bill Clarke, who won a by-election in Northgate in 1965.

---

38. Former Head of Political Research for the BBC 1999-2016 and a Visiting Senior Research Fellow at Kings College London.

39. Northgate 1951 (when the Tories and Independents forgot to field a second candidate. If they had done so, the Labour candidate elected would have been defeated substantially); Northgate 1952; Northgate 1958; and Westgate 1964 (two elected).

40. National Union of Mineworkers, Union of Shop, Distributive and Allied Workers

The problem with Rippington was that he did not try and create an ongoing support structure and that he preferred to be a one man band. Clarke did, however, understand this point and reached out immediately to the university Labour Club in 1965. He was the closest thing we had to effective local leadership.

During the 1960s and 1970s the military presence also diminished, a factor marginally helpful to Labour. Also, in this period the Business Vote still existed as a dual franchise and was helpful to the Tories in that it gave an extra local vote to those who owned business premises – and there were scores of them in the city.

In the period after 1945 there was much council house and prefab building in each of the three wards, in what later proved to be a dangerous cocktail for the Tories. But the big post-war estates (London Road, Hales Place, Spring Lane, Sturry Road) were completed and occupied in full only by the late 1950s or, in the case of Hales Place, by 1970).

Some of the older houses on the estates were in poor condition because the council's maintenance was dreadful, and they dumped the most disorganised and most antisocial into specific places. There were households on Querns Road and Vauxhall Crescent that were the victims of this policy.

As a result of these factors and others, the Labour share of the vote in contested elections rose substantially in all wards from 1950 – a year of exceptional national Labour strength.[41] By 1971, Labour was getting 58.6% of the vote in the very middle class Westgate, with Mike Fuller winning 2,669 votes and beating the leading Tory by 787 votes.

But the exceptional weakness of the local Labour leadership in the 1950s and early 1960s allowed a vacuum to develop which the Liberals exploited.

Their first explicitly designated party candidates stood in 1964 (after the Orpington by-election surge) and they won their first seat in 1966 (Dane John). In later years they managed for long periods to turn Dane John (later Wincheap) into their strongest area in the constituency – because of Labour weakness.

This weakness also resulted in the collapse of a Labour branch in Whitstable, the lack of a functioning branch in Herne Bay at any time, and the continuing lack of candidates almost everywhere else.

---

41.   In Northgate, Labour scored 29.6%, in 1950, rising to 47.5% in 1966, and 52.7% in 1971 (figures for the top Labour candidates share of the vote).

Decisive Events

The decisive event for the Labour Party in Canterbury was the arrival of staff and students at the university in 1965, and it was the beginning of the end of Conservative hegemony in the city.

This in itself was a precursor to the development of an educated middle class electorate that behaved and voted differently from the non-university educated middle class everywhere in Britain. It was especially powerful in a small city like Canterbury.

We were beginning to see in the early 1970s what happened much later in university towns and gentrified suburbs elsewhere. Numbers were small at first, and hardly any of the students could vote because votes at 18 were not granted until 1970. But the organisational weight of the student population began to have a significant effect on Labour performance in city elections, starting in 1966 when mass student canvassing by the Labour Club began.

Large teams of students canvassed everywhere in Northgate and Westgate and developed a proper marked register[42] for the first time ever. This allowed the targeting of Labour voters and doubtfuls for leafleting and knocking-up purposes.

Full Reading systems[43] were in use on election day by 1966. In addition, the presence of a significant number of lecturers with exceptional political ability from 1965 made high quality candidates available – people with good planning and communication skills. All these factors contributed to the rapid development of Labour credibility in the late 1960s and 1970s.

The same factors also strengthened the Liberals – their victor in Dane

---

42. A marked register is a record of the voting intentions of individual electors set against their names and addresses on each year's voting register. This enables the leafleting and knocking-up of supporters only, and the targeting of voters who express views about particular issues

43. The Reading System: Ian Mikardo, then MP for a highly marginal constituency in Reading, invented the system, which consisted of multiple carbon paper copies of the knocking-up lists with names written on, of promises made to vote Labour. Each sheet could be torn off and given to polling day workers to be in their hand when in a road 'knocking up.' People who had voted would be crossed off the sheets when returns of polling numbers came back from each polling station, meaning that a record could be made of those who had voted all through the day and that workers were not sent in error to those who had cast their ballots

John in 1966 was the wife of the Politics Professor at UKC.

However, the local party infrastructure was still poor. Membership of the City Party was 34 in 1969, out of a population of more than 20,000. When I took over as secretary, most of them had not paid subscriptions for many years. They were simply names on paper. Despite these positive developments from 1965, the Constituency Labour Party was also very weak and had not paid its mandated subscription to the national Labour Party for many years.[44]

The constituency AGM in 1967 consisted of six people. Its links with the only substantial branch (covering the City of Canterbury itself) were almost non-existent and steps had to be taken to move control of the apparatus into safer hands.

The low point was undoubtedly 1966, when a Parliamentary candidate had to be effectively imposed days before nominations closed because the party could not organise itself to run a selection in time. In that election – the great Wilson victory producing a national majority of 93 – the Canterbury CLP hadn't been competent enough to get its election address into the Royal Mail freepost[45] and was instead delivering the election address to council estates the night before the election. Most of the constituency had no election literature at all.

This level of weakness locally at a time of national Labour strength created the opening for the Liberals to gain substantial numbers of votes in general elections and lay claim to be the true opposition to the Tories in Canterbury.

It is clear from the local election results from 1945 onwards that national political fortunes influenced local results significantly. This is most clearly visible in the 1960s when contested elections had been established for Canterbury City Council, and Labour were usually assiduous in standing candidates.

Despite the presence of the university, Labour support declined sharply between 1966 and 1967 and especially in 1968 in normally contested wards, as it did everywhere in Britain. In 1969 the local Labour Party was so demoralised that it did not nominate candidates at all.

This also coincided with the exceptional weakness of the CLP[46] itself

44. Only rectified in 1970.
45. Each Parliamentary candidate validly nominated has the ability to send one 'postal packet', usually an election address or leaflet, to each elector on the constituency register, without charge for the service. These are distributed by the Royal Mail, whose costs are reimbursed by Government.
46. Constituency Labour Party

and the closure of Chislet colliery[47] which had in the past provided some of the local CLP leadership.

The Great Change

By 1970 the situation had changed again. Labour began standing candidates in Northgate and Westgate and won a seat in 1970, beating the heavily disliked Tory agent, Ted Brown.

Brown countered by causing a by-election in Westgate by 'requiring' the sitting Tory Councillor to resign. It was called in June of that year, and he expected to be returned safely – but Labour won by 33 votes. Mike Fuller was installed, and he later became the Parliamentary candidate.

In 1971 Labour stood four candidates in the city and elected them all, with massive swings against the Tories. In 1972 Labour stood six candidates – including the Dane John ward, usually regarded as the weakest Labour ward – and won all of them.

So, Labour had gone from zero seats in 1969 to control of the Council in two years. Outside the count, held in the Westgate Halls, a crowd of several hundred had gathered; no one had asked them to come or had organised it. City election counts and declarations usually attracted a crowd of zero. They knew instinctively that something big was happening and they were not disappointed. I phoned the Party's regional office to report in on the election results, as you had to in those days, and said, 'six seats vacant, six Labour candidates, six gains, and control of the Council passing to us.' We had won every seat in the City by very significant margins.

The BBC television election coverage was flummoxed as the news came in of our gains and control of the Council. 'That can't be right,' the presenter said – but it was. The *Times* newspaper stated on its front page after the 1972 elections that 'Canterbury is Labour's pride and joy today because it breaks new ground.'

The reasons for the transformation in Labour fortunes in the early

---

47. Chislet Colliery was one of the four Kent deep coal mines, developed later than other coalfields. Chislet provided much of the steam coal for British Railways Southern Region trains and was therefore especially affected by the electrification of longer distance lines in the early 1960s, hence the date of its closure. It was located at Hersden, North East of Canterbury.

1970s were partly political, partly organisational, and partly connected with highly qualified candidates with real credibility. That is, leadership.

At this time, the national political situation was very favourable, with an unpopular Heath Government fighting the miners, introducing market rents for council homes and ending the ability of councils to subsidise their housing revenue account from the general rate fund.

It also attacked middle class subsidies through such measures as the imposition of museum and gallery charges for the first time since 1945. This made it relatively easy to paint the Canterbury Tories as the enemies of decent middle class people *and* of working class people (via the massive hikes in council rents they were proposing).

In addition, there was a rich vein of incompetence in local political decision making which was exploited by us. For example, the council had leaking and inadequate sewers, and the local officers were so angry that they made inflammatory public statements about it. 'You have done no sewerage work for a century,' the City Engineer said.

Organisational factors were also strongly in Labour's favour. From being also-rans for decades, Labour could now deploy the large numbers of students who were willing to spend time canvassing and establishing the records essential for a sophisticated campaign.

In addition, we introduced for the first time in Canterbury the concept of mass poster coverage: 5,000 window bills and 1,000 large A3 posters in red dayglo were ordered each year and almost all of them were displayed in windows. Canvassers put them up for the residents. The effect on Tory morale was profound: one Tory canvasser walked into Sussex Avenue on the Spring Lane estate in 1970 and saw almost every house with a Labour poster in the window. He ran.

Postal votes were organised; pickups on election day were undertaken; polling stations were staffed by our people operating the Reading system; highly efficient committee rooms were staffed by trained people; and we had teams of people knocking up.

Selective leafleting with targeted messages was introduced on the basis of good canvass records. Leaflets were in some cases only delivered to Labour promises and doubtfuls, thus giving the impression to Tories that we were indolent and disorganised. Many of these concepts are now commonplace but were not normal practice then. We had a Rolls-Royce organisation, created entirely by a few people.

The objective was to maximise turnout as well as persuade. And we were successful. In some elections there were queues outside polling stations in city elections in Labour areas. We had persuaded significant numbers of people that going to vote – and to vote Labour – was going to lead to the defeat of the local establishment, and that a victory would result in significant changes of local policy.

All of these factors were influential but they only worked because we were able to mobilise what should have been Labour's working class vote in large numbers and add to that significant numbers of middle class voters who might have voted for other parties.

After elections had taken place and seats were won, we printed and delivered personalised cards from the new Labour councillors with information about surgeries and how to get in touch.

During canvassing we had picked up cases and we referred them to councillors. We also organised a team of researchers to call on council tenants in order to get them to claim any benefits they might be entitled to – there was strong evidence that many were not. Claim forms were completed on the doorstep and submitted for them.

We also watched the election process carefully: on one occasion the Tories had bizarrely called a by-election with polling day on a Tuesday (unheard of). One of our team noticed that the Returning Officer had not posted the official notice outside the council offices, which was a statutory requirement. Representations were made and the polling day was changed to the following Thursday, causing the Tories to reprint their leaflets at significant cost and disruption.

Tory attempts at revenge disruption did not succeed. They tried to get the university authorities to stop me using my university address, where I lived in college, as the statutory contact point on Labour leaflets. That was defeated, as were attempts to stop students putting up window bills in their college rooms where they were registered to vote. The top brass at UKC did not like students getting involved in politics and they did everything possible to discourage us. They simply hated Labour people and in particular upstart Northerners like me. Hadn't been to the right schools.

Making it Stick

The final factor contributing strongly to the victories of 1970-72 was the mobilisation of highly talented candidates and key supporters.

In 1972, not having contested the Dane John ward for five years, Labour fielded two powerful candidates – Alison Ruddock and Fred

Whitemore. We won both seats easily. The sitting, and formidable, Liberal councillor came third. These high-quality candidates could persuade on the doorstep, looked and sounded credible, and were well organised and committed.

Great care was taken, however, not to put university candidates into all seats available and to pair them with locals; and to find well qualified non-university candidates such as Hettie Barber, who became the first ever Labour Lord Mayor of Canterbury City Council[48]

These activities, in which I was highly involved, led to gradual but profound improvements in Labour's local leadership. The presence of new leadership groups had more impact on Labour than on the Liberals or the Tories, and the long-term influence was profound. Without the innovation of the early 1970s in Canterbury Labour politics, and the rapid development of the local middle class, Canterbury would never have elected a Labour MP in 2017 and 2019.

The New Middle Class: First Stirrings

Changing demographics meant that the composition of the local middle class was transformed over time. This process can be seen to be continuing, with families moving out of London to obtain decent housing at lower cost, and with the expansion of the two principal universities[49] driving the recruitment of more staff: there were 500 students in 1965, and around 30,000 today.

It can be argued that the massive expansion of the two universities has created the most unusual demographic in an English constituency. The proportion of students is higher here than in almost any other seat.

This has created both opportunities and problems. For example, the need for constant renewal of registration efforts given that around one in three students leave each year; and the need to motivate them to cast votes, not just in general elections but also in lower-turnout local elections.

48. The City received its first Royal Charter in January 1155 and its first recorded Lord Mayor emerged from a later Royal Charter granted in 1448, in the reign of Henry V1. Hettie Barber was married to a prominent Cambridge economist and was the mother of Chris Barber, described as the 'Godfather of British Jazz.'

49. The second university is Canterbury Christchurch, formerly a teacher training College.

The main takeaway, however, is that the character and attitudes of the middle class has changed beyond recognition in the last 50 years. What happened in Canterbury in the 1970s has been repeated in many other locations in the 21st century, at the same time that Labour was losing mass working class support.

After the local triumphs of the early 1970s, Labour took its eye off the ball in the 1980s, which allowed the various name changed Liberals the political space in which to claim they were the true opponents to the Tories, with the only chance of defeating them.

It is clear, however, that performance in local elections fundamentally follows national trends, mitigated and influenced by effective or ineffective local leadership and organisation. You can't win many local council seats in Canterbury when Labour is floundering nationally.

Bizarrely, the 1970s saga was replayed at the 2017 General Election and produced by common consent one of the most unusual results nationally.

Canterbury was for many years a Conservative safe seat, with the last non-Tory elected in 1868 (when the previous Conservative MP ran as an Independent Conservative and a Liberal was elected for the second seat), and with Labour not even bothering to contest the constituency in the General Elections of 1923 and 1924.

Because of its very specific and rapidly changing demographics, Labour won Canterbury and has its first ever Labour MP, with the Labour share of the vote trebling from 16.1% in 2010 to 48.3% in 2019. This unprecedented result eclipsed the previous highest Labour vote share by Emily Thornberry.[50]

It has also changed the way in which the constituency is seen. It is significant that the Labour appeal in 2017 suited the demographics of Canterbury, and not those in the other eight seats In Kent previously won by Labour – some of which swung to the Tories, and none of which were won by Labour in 2017 or 2019.

The 2017 election result in Canterbury was replicated in 2019 at a time when Labour suffered its most serious national defeat since 1935. History may see it as an accidental consequence of the very particular appeal that Labour built up in 2017. Organisational factors in the traditional sense played a low-key part in the 2017 result, despite claims to the contrary, but the influence of social media may have been profound: it is clear that for the first time the student and academic vote was heavily mobilised in a way that was difficult to spot on the ground.

---

50.   36.1% in 2001

Local Action Works Locally – but Only Locally

In terms of the local effectiveness of political parties winning elections, the experience of 1970-72 showed that it was possible to change the character of election results, at least for a while, by professional organisation linked to credible local leadership and issue-based campaigning.

By 2017, with much poorer election capability, Labour won in Canterbury in a general election largely based on national campaign factors – and with the advantage of a tight fit between the national appeal and the local demographics (one of the largest student and university employed populations).

Interestingly, most local observers believe that the 2017 victory had almost nothing to do with Momentum (Canterbury was not on their go-there list issued to activists). Also, the local branch parties were not explicitly under their control at the time. Had they been, organisation on the ground would have been much poorer than it actually was. Their ability to talk was far greater than their willingness to work.

It is also clear that effective local organisation before the advent of electronic communication was heavily dependent on key individuals, and that electoral success was mainly, but not wholly, governed by national political conditions. It was just possible in the 1970s, in exceptional circumstances, to change the political complexion of a local authority by organisational methods and astute local leadership. But other stories like Canterbury's are hard to find.

In 1970, Canterbury was on the cusp of radical social change as an educated middle class became more prominent in local public life. But the story of mobilising these forces is impossible to repeat. We were not able to do it, for example, in Derbyshire, 50 years later.

It did not seem possible, in that 1970s period, to repeat those local triumphs elsewhere and it was quite impossible to replicate them in national elections in these same specific places where local victories had been assured, and I believe this is still true today, hence the utter failure of the Community Organisers concept imported from the Bernie Sanders Campaign and used by Labour in the period between 2015 and 2019.

The national character of Labour's political appeal in the early 1970s was still generally strong but that appeal was weakest in national elections in the constituencies where the Party was traditionally weakest. However, after the advent of the internet and social media, self-organisation could be more prominent, and in some cases decisive.

CHAPTER 3

THE 1970s BREAKDOWN OF
KEYNESIANISM

The late 1960s saw me leave Kent for a brief stint at Essex University to take a Political Behaviour module in 1968.

Here I learnt a very important lesson.

It was the time of the notorious Revolutionary Festival which was inspired by (and followed the thrust of) the May events in Paris. The local Trotskyist and revolutionary groups went hell for leather – but not without challenge. They occupied bits of the university. Their first act was to desegregate the loos. This was quickly overturned by the women who wanted a safe space of their own and disliked sweaty blokes inhabiting their toilets.

The *coup de grace* for the radicals came, however, when a group of them spotted an abandoned car that some student had left in the car park for months, gently rotting but still intact.

They dragged it into the main square outside the coffee shop and set fire to it, as a 'symbol of the oppression of capitalist property.'

The local workers on the university building site were far from impressed: 'We could have done something with that,' they said to me in anger and disbelief at the antics of the tiny few.

An important lesson on the way in which vanguard revolutionaries become totally detached from working class opinion, as they always do.

I didn't stay long at Essex. The main run of student accommodation was in tower blocks on campus and these, before the introduction of 'suicide locks' on the windows, were notorious.

Some deranged individuals used to refill the used triangular milk cartons bought from the shop and launch them out of the windows onto the path beneath, landing them as close as possible to visitors and students. The cartons were moving very fast when thrown from the 10th floor, and were heavy with water.

They could have done serious damage to heads let alone dignities. There were even rumours that someone had thrown a kitchen fridge out of the window.

It was better elsewhere, I decided.

Jobs

By 1972 I had left UKC for good, having started my Ph.D. on the impact of organisation on the alleged deradicalisation of the Labour Party. In terms of getting a job, I received good advice from one of my lecturer friends, Professor Margaret Gowing[51] who told me to write to all the trade unions as they were recruiting new tranches of researchers to support the more complex wage submissions now required and to work on policy development.

I also saw an advert in the *Guardian* flagging the creation of the first two political adviser posts to members of the Shadow Cabinet. They were funded by the Joseph Rowntree Social Services Trust, a mildly progressive and Quaker founded organisation that gained its funds from the sale of chocolate bars. Accordingly, these posts were known amongst the cognoscenti as 'the chocolate soldiers.'

I applied and was interviewed by a bunch of luminaries from the PLP including the Chairman of the Parliamentary Labour Party, Douglas Houghton (MP for Sowerby). I didn't get it, despite being down to the last two for the post I was aiming for, because – as Houghton said to me in writing afterwards about the shadow minister – 'He preferred the Oxford man.' Houghton was very cross that a well-qualified north-erner with impeccable credentials lost out because of what amounted to Oxbridge prejudice.

So, I did write to the trade unions and received two offers: the first was from COHSE[52] to become the new Head of their Research Department, where I was interviewed by the amiable General Secretary, Albert Spanswick. He welcomed me with the phrase, 'Come on in, lad.

---

51. Co-author of the official *History of the Second World War* (specialising in nuclear policy)
52. Confederation of Health Service Employees now part of Unison

I'm sure you can do the job. When can you start?'

The other offer was from NUPE,[53] to join an existing research department of two people. NUPE had an office looking over the wide spaces of Blackheath and was closer to where I had found a house to rent. It was also a more radical union with a wider membership covering NHS staff, local authority workers, university staff, ambulance crews, along with water and sewerage workers.

The EETPU[54] also interviewed me in the formidable shape of John Spellar, now MP for Sandwell in the West Midlands, but then head of the research department.[55] He asked if it was all right for him to tape the interview, took me into the boardroom, and offered up the information that they taped every meeting of their Executive. They had not long ago been through the trauma of ridding the union of its communist leadership so the level of paranoia was still high.

Despite the fact that I had never been in a left group of any kind, and felt no inclination to join one, John told me (much later) that he thought I might become a Trot. There was no direct evidence of it, he agreed, but it might happen. John is well known to this day for having the best files in the Labour Party.

So, they didn't want me. I accepted the NUPE offer and started in September 1972.

Inadvertently, I had stumbled into what became the cockpit of opposition to the policies of the 1974-79 Labour Government and was able to play some part in the realignment of British political thinking that occurred between 1975 and 1979.

Industrial Unionism that Wasn't

NUPE, the National Union of Public Employees, was an interesting union with a left wing leadership and a very moderate membership – 80% were women, and low-paid women at that. In 1972 the National Executive was entirely male because the branch secretaries all got paid for running their branches and the blokes made sure that they won and kept these jobs. But the union was also an outsider organisation.

53. National Union of Public Employees, also now part of Unison
54. Electrical, Electronic, Telecommunications and Plumbing Union, later part of AEEU and now Unite
55. Later MP for Birmingham Northfield, and then Sandwell.

NUPE's origins lie in the 1880s when it split from what later became the General and Municipal Workers Union to form the National Union of Corporation Workers. The leading figure in the new organisation was Albin Taylor, a believer in industrial unionism. This theory proposed that an organisation would only recruit amongst workers employed in a particular industry – in this case local authorities.

In Edwardian Britain, local councils ran many local industries – the water and sewerage systems, gas and electricity generation in some places, and some hospitals. Nor did the theory of industrial unionism take account of the fact that central Government was liable to change the ownership of particular services by reorganising them, nationalising or privatising them.

A so-called industrial union like NUPE actually had a very diverse group of members, almost as much as the big general unions did. There were also competing unions working within the same space as NUPE who represented different segments of the public sector – usually professionals (like COHSE, founded by mental health nurses) and NALGO[56] (representing white collar administrative and managerial staff).

The result of this late-19th century split was still echoing in the early 1970s. The big unions like the TGWU[57] and G&M[58] disliked NUPE's up-and-at-'em attitude and jealously guarded their lead negotiating positions on national negotiating and representative bodies (such as the General Council of the TUC and the National Executive Committee of the Labour Party).

In addition, NUPE had been led by a succession of left wing general secretaries, especially Bryn Roberts and, in 1972, Alan Fisher. NUPE was also very small. In 1972 it was stuck at around 160,000 members but the opportunity for membership growth was substantial as the public sector was expanding rapidly. By 1979, when I was elected to Parliament, its size had grown to 700,000.

The research department which I joined had been established in the late 1960s by the appointment of Bernard Dix, who came from the TUC, and who was the prime instigator of new developments. The union's journal was modernised, proper work was done to support negotiators on the national negotiating bodies, and the beginnings of policy work started. This was mainly reactive, but the union started to get publicity

---

56.   National Association of Local Government Officers
57.   Transport and General Workers Union
58.   General And Municipal Workers Union

from the so-called dirty jobs strike in 1969, when many local council workers struck for higher pay against the restrictive wage policies of the Labour Government.

The Deaths Column

With Bernard in the research unit when I arrived was Jeannie Drake (now Baroness Drake CBE), a splendid feminist and at the time a member of the Communist Party, who later left to join the CPSA.[59] In 1972, Ian Scott was also there, recruited at the same time as myself, with a later arrival being Judy Mallaber.[60]

My job, sat at a desk overlooking the heath, consisted initially of writing the deaths column for the journal and clipping newspapers for the research files. It was desperately boring. Bernard, it was explained to me, had never found anyone he trusted to do complicated stuff, and we had to work our passage till he was more confident that we wouldn't screw it up.

Office life was enlivened by the regular rows between Jeannie and Bernard about the role of women in society, with Jeannie always keen to support the women but mercilessly goaded by Bernard.

Incessant and compulsory trips to the pub at lunchtime were also a feature of that era. Bernard was a steady drinker and each daily session at the Three Tuns in Blackheath lasted from about 12.30 till 3, when everyone rolled back to work – much to the annoyance of others in the office.

Bernard had had a colourful life. His story was that he and his mate drank the takings from the Co-op milk round that one of his friends did in Woolwich. This eventually landed them in the Magistrates Court where they were given a choice by the bench: join the Army or get a gaol sentence. Bernard joined the Buffs.

He smoked like a chimney despite having had tuberculosis and one of his lungs removed during his tour with the Eighth Army in Egypt, and he was as thin as a rake. His politics were complex: previously a member of the Communist Party and then the Revolutionary Communist Party, he had worked for Rajani Palme Dutt in the 1950 General Election when

59. Civil and Public Services Association
60. Later Chief Executive of the Local Government Information Unit, and MP for Amber Valley 1997-2010

Dutt stood against Foreign Secretary Ernest Bevin. When canvassing for Dutt or speaking in Beresford Square for him, Bernard never used the candidate's first name – Rajani – because the party's view was that the intrepid workers of Woolwich would not vote for a non-white communist. So, Palme Dutt he became and he received just over 600 votes.

In the 1950s, Bernard had become Secretary of Greenwich Labour Party and was present when Dick Marsh was selected as the candidate for the 1959 General Election. 'He only got the nomination because he wore a CND badge to the meeting,' said Bernard. By 1972 Bernard had left the Labour Party in disillusionment.

Eventually I was allocated more useful work than the deaths column and started supporting the national negotiators in the NHS and universities with data from government statistics, and by writing wage claims.

The early 1970s was a time of sharply growing inflation, with the wages of the low paid particularly vulnerable to hikes in food and fuel prices. Inflation at its peak reached 25% in 1974, pushed by the oil price spike stemming from the growing power of the OPEC cartel. Trade unions had to run to catch up.

The main feature of 1970s public sector wage claims were clawing back the effects of price inflation. One argument about the disproportionate impact of the Retail Price Index (RPI) increases on low paid workers pointed out the inadequacy of using general indices of inflation when there should be one for the low paid.

Also, of extreme importance in a union representing women workers, we witnessed the implementation of the 1970 Equal Pay Act.[61] From that point, national negotiators won a gradual movement of women's hourly pay rates towards those of men under the 'equal pay for work of equal value' rule, which caused endless definitional difficulties – and still does.

At one point, women workers in the public sector in the mid 1970s were getting three kinds of wage increase a year: the annual wage adjustment designed to bring wages back to the level of inflation; monthly increases (threshold agreements) when inflation was at its highest, based on the rise in the number of points in the RPI; and thirdly, an escalator increase to bring women's hourly rates closer to those of men in the sector.

---

61. Only granted commencement in December, 1975.

Beginning of the End

Gradually in the 1970s, the Chicago school economists and later the Conservative Party hawks pushed back hard against the burgeoning costs of the public sector, arguing that public spending was crowding out investment and was responsible for the allegedly crippling tax rises for many. The wartime Bretton Woods agreement governing the value of major currencies and tying them to gold, broke down decisively and led to speculative attacks on the value of currencies including sterling, especially when balance of payments and inflation concerns were raised. It was clear that a major attack on the Keynesian consensus was developing, with the days of Butskellite politics and economics disappearing rapidly.

This process in Britain was greatly assisted by the election of Margaret Thatcher as Tory leader in 1975 and by the conversion of the Labour leadership – especially Prime Minister James Callaghan and Chancellor Denis Healey – to the view that 'the party's over.' This was in complete contradiction to the policy on which they had been elected in the two General Elections of 1974, which included food subsidies to reduce the impact of inflation on the low paid and plans to maintain full employment.

By 1975, only a few months after the October 1974 election, Healey had decided that there was a case for substantial reductions in public spending of the order of £1bn, about £8.5bn at today's prices. This *volte face* was the most significant move away from the Keynesian consensus since 1940 and the cause of much political trouble later.

It was not just the Keynesian consensus – which included demand management and the commitment to full employment – that was overturned in the mid-1970s.

The problems of the British economy included: a poor growth rate when compared with others; vulnerability to external shocks; a weak exchange rate subject to speculative attacks; and (it was alleged) poor comparative position in relation to European economies. Establishment politicians attempted to solve these problems with several policies in the period after 1960.

These included the creation of the National Economic Development Council (NEDC) and its individual-industry, little NEDDIES, which were supposed to foster good practice and innovation through discussion and research, and hence build comparative advantage and support higher economic growth.

But this initiative, whatever its intrinsic merits, had not dealt with the fundamental problems. The National Plan of 1965 which was supposed to drive up growth rates across the board and to modernise industry, was a dead letter after the crisis of June 1966. This had the Wilson Government reducing spending on public services shortly after winning a landslide in the General Election in March.

Setting up a specific ministry to encourage productivity growth and the adoption of new technology was tried with the establishment of MINTECH under Tony Benn, then still occupying his centre-right position in the Labour Party. Evidence of progress was patchy, and Benn thought so too. One of his constant mantras was that however good a Minister you tried to be, the fundamental character of capitalism meant that you were thwarted at every turn with the civil service playing an important role in frustrating Labour Governments.

Devaluation was tried in 1967 to make exports more competitive and minimise attacks on the value of sterling. The effect was temporary and by the early 1970s, especially after the end of the Bretton Woods era of fixed exchange rates, it was clear that holders of sterling were likely at the first sign of trouble to sell the currency, especially if the 'trouble' was evidenced by higher public expenditure. It was the balance of payments consequences of changes in the exchange rate, as well as the structural failures of the British economy, which enslaved Wilson and Callaghan.

There were two attempts at joining the European Economic Community, in 1963 and 1967, both vetoed by the French, so the route to a bigger tariff-free home market was blocked. The project was resuscitated in 1970 by the Heath Government which negotiated Britain's entry in 1972.

And last but not least, there had been many iterations of incomes policy since the late 1950s, sometimes with dividend control as well, but they all broke down because working people on weekly wages and with few backup resources could not for very long see prices accelerating and their living standards falling without claiming and sometimes winning higher real wages.

Political reaction to these failures was immediate and profound. The Conservatives, under Ted Heath, toyed with an early version of monetarism and privatisation in 1970 under the policies adopted by the Selsdon Park Conference declaration.

But when they were elected, they reverted to extreme growth measures which resulted in the eponymous Barber Boom, which stoked cost-push inflation and wage demands. It was one of the last attempts at growth-or-bust, and it ran into the sand as the miners' strikes of 1972 and 1974 became victories for the National Union of Mineworkers.

The attempt at trade union legislation through the 1971 Industrial Relations Act provoked widespread demonstrations and anger, especially after the imprisonment by the National Industrial Relations Court of the so-called Pentonville Five. The dockers were released after huge pressure from the unions and this was in some ways the height of trade union influence and power in Britain. However, the events of the next decade were to reduce union membership and that union power close to impotence.

Margaret Thatcher was waiting in the wings and struck in 1975, defeating Heath in a leadership election, supported by the advocates of monetarism such as Sir Keith Joseph.

Labour's Response

The Labour Party had also reacted strongly to the General Election defeat of 1970. Wilson expected to win easily because that is what the opinion polls told him, but a lazy campaign in the summer sun, plus – critically – evidence of higher inflation in food prices and consumer goods, caused some voters to switch in the last few days, creating one of the surprise results of the century. There was also mass abstention in working class areas, for the first time since 1945.

There was furious reaction from the left, both inside and outside the Labour Party. The ultra-left, centred around the International Socialists and the Workers Revolutionary Party, thought that the Wilson Government had betrayed its principles. But the reaction inside the Party was much more important.

The policy sub-committees of the NEC and the then-formidable Research Department started extensive work on a revised party programme in the light of the new circumstances that were thought to exist, and in the light of the economic policy failures of the 1964-70 Government.

The central belief of the left revisionists was that demand management was now incapable of controlling the path of economic development on its own, and that more radical measures were necessary in order to guide the mixed economy. In due course the Party published Labour's Programme 1973; it was, without doubt, one of the most radical and specific statements produced in the party's history.

Benn led the way on this. He was helped by Geoff Bish, head of the Party's Research Department, Stuart Holland, former economic adviser to Wilson as Prime Minister, Frances Morrell as Benn's political adviser from 1974, and Margaret Jackson (now Beckett) who at the time was secretary of the Party's Study Group on the National Enterprise Board.

The key phrase in the new raft of policy proposals was to effect 'the fundamental and irreversible shift of wealth and power to working people and their families.' The specifics included the nationalisation of 25 profitable companies, the creation of a National Enterprise Board, and planning agreements between individual private sector companies and the State in order to influence the trajectory of investment and product development. It is interesting to note that the proposed planning agreements of the 1970s were little more than contracts between central government and individual companies, requiring the company to do specific things in return for taxpayers' money. That principle exists widely today both in central and local government.

These radical policy positions were opposed by powerful elements in the Shadow Cabinet and the PLP and it was with great difficulty that the key planks were included in the Labour manifestos for the General Election of February 1974, which Labour unexpectedly won.

So, by the early 1970s politics had been through several changes of policy clothes under governments of both parties in order to solve the problem of the balance of payments, higher inflation than others, low growth, and growing structural employment.

Britain was increasingly seen as the 'sick man of Europe.' Both parties, when in opposition, had reacted strongly to the growing problems of the economy by turning to radical ideas outside the former demand management consensus and incomes policy. The test of the left alternative came after the February 1974 election when Labour had the chance to see if the new medicine worked – if it was allowed to be implemented at all.

Would the mandate given by voters in the two General Elections of 1974 be allowed to stick, or would the PLP leadership's cautious approach last beyond the initial phase of the Social Contract? This was the attempt at a big bargain between organised labour and the PLP which was supposed to demonstrate that only the Labour Party had the ability to govern in a society where trade unions were a powerful estate in the land.

No one knew, but the answer came soon enough.

The Developing Crisis

Not long after the October 1974 election came calls for cuts in public spending, in order to reduce pressure on the Public Sector Borrowing Requirement (PSBR), and these were endorsed by Prime Minister Wilson and Chancellor Healey. The Cabinet was split but there was always a majority for agreeing to the terms that the markets were seen to be demanding.

The crisis deepened as the consequences of high inflation and rises in the oil price ratcheted upwards, coming to a real head during 1976. The debates in the Cabinet on defending sterling against speculation and the reductions in public expenditure that were thought necessary to defend the exchange rate and maintain ease of borrowing in the markets has been well documented in Tony Benn's diaries.[62]

The saga began on 7th June 1976 when the Economic Strategy Committee of the Cabinet received reports from the Chancellor that standby credits of £10bn had been arranged to prop up the value of the pound if needed. Also, an undertaking had been given that the IMF would be called in, if required.

Chancellor Healey at that point said that further reductions in public expenditure might be needed in July. Further meetings of the committee discussed a paper by Secretary of State for the Environment, Peter Shore, advocating import controls but this was 'torn to shreds' by officials.[63]

A note from Kenneth Berrill of the Central Policy Review Staff in the Cabinet Office argued that a response to the depreciation of sterling (down 25% in six months, pushing up inflation to over 14% at that point), based on import controls and strict exchange controls, would fail because the benefits of a siege economy would arrive too slowly to mitigate the risks and short term costs. Cabinet Minister Harold Lever argued instead that sterling should be linked to the evolving 'currency snake' in the EEC, whose most important currency was the deutschmark, which would impose fiscal and public expenditure discipline without an IMF loan; this argument was rubbished by Crosland who pointed out that the policy would fail because UK inflation was much higher than the dominant snake currency of Germany.[64]

---

62. *Against the Tide, Diaries 1973-76*, Hutchinson 1989
63. Op. cit., page 680
64. Berrill, Lever and Crosland Cabinet papers released by the National Archives December 2020

The truth was that Ministers were arguing over the best response but the dominant voices were always going to be those of the Prime Minister and the Chancellor, who were both ideologically committed to a fundamental change in policy away from Keynesianism. They believed that a fall in the comparative value of the pound could only be dealt with by monetary policies based on cuts in the borrowing requirement flowing from lower public spending.

However, Benn argued for the freezing of the sterling balances, the control of financial transactions, control of imports, and linked all this to new planning agreements with large companies as an alternative to public spending reductions. He later commissioned a strategy paper from his economic adviser, Francis Cripps, and political adviser, Frances Morrell. This advocated economic growth rather than reductions in spending as the way to reduce the PSBR.

On the 6th and 15th July, the Cabinet discussed formal papers from the Chancellor and Joel Barnett, Economic Secretary to the Treasury, which advocated a cut of £1.25bn in spending to bring the PSBR down to £11bn immediately, and £9bn by 1977-78. This was broadly supported, with Roy Jenkins, Denis Healey, Harold Lever and Jim Callaghan explicitly backing the cuts programme.

Papers from Peter Shore and Tony Benn on 15th July opposed these moves and argued for an alternative policy. Benn went so far as to say in Cabinet that he thought the British establishment was infected with the defeatism of Vichy in 1940. The discussions continued in December when the terms insisted on by the IMF became clear: they wanted an immediate cut of £2bn in the PSBR in return for tranches of credit.

The final cuts package adopted by the Government in the 1976 White Paper was £4,595m at 1975 survey prices[65] to take effect in the financial years 1977 to 1979.

These were cuts from published plans but there was also a projected further year of heavily reduced spending covering 1979-80. Excluding debt interest, the reduction in 1979-80 was £1,163m compared to spending in 1976-77.

These were staggering levels of reduction and they involved the near elimination of food subsidies on bread, butter, cheese, flour, milk and tea which had saved an average family with two children 71p a week in

---

65.   Public expenditure was still being counted in 'funny money' – ie a calculated
      constant real terms value in pounds

the summer of 1975.[66]

Assistance to nationalised industries, running at £630m in 1974-75 was substantially reduced, thus passing the burden of costs on to retail prices paid by consumers. There were great reductions in capital expenditure with, for example, the hospital capital programme being reduced from £378m in 1975-76 to £298m in 1979-80, and the personal social services capital programme cut from £115m in 1975-6 to £54m in 1979-80.

Even worse, the current expenditure increase for programmes was only 1.4% on hospitals and community health services. This was way below the level of inflation – let alone the NHS rate of inflation which typically runs at about 4% a year (owing to the increased costs of innovation, medication and treatments).

The education budget was similarly slashed, with capital spending on nursery schools cut from £31.9m to £6m and total planned expenditure reducing from £6,164m in 1975-6 to £5,995m in 1979-80. Subsidies to the cost of school meals were cut in half and overall spending on this service cut by a third, with the cost burden placed firmly on parents and local authorities.

There were many other examples of reductions in public spending on the nationalised water industry, local authorities and on universities. In addition, cash limits were introduced for the first time, removing the odd assumption that the real level of services would be maintained whatever the level of inflation.

Based on Rubbish Data

Whatever its logic, the worst feature of all this was that the cuts programme was based on spending and economic activity assumptions that were completely wrong.

The House of Commons Expenditure Committee noticed in 1976 that the Treasury had cooked the books because it wanted to show that unemployment would come down whilst implementing a highly deflationary policy – an unlikely prospect. The spending forecasts and forecasts for activity and unemployment were structurally unsound.

These forecasts had to assume that the gap in output and therefore in taxes received would be filled by massive 20% increases in the growth of

66. National Food Survey

exports, equally massive rises of 17% over the next three years in private sector investment, and big rises in stock building. These were heroic predictions and were for public consumption only. It is not clear that these inflated assumptions were picked up and challenged by anyone in Cabinet during the long debates over economic policy in 1975-6.

There were several alternative views put forward in opposition to the full IMF programme proposed by the PM and the Chancellor. Crosland argued for one view, Shore for another, Benn for a third, Foot for an indeterminate position. Others were opposed, too.

However, there was no unanimity amongst the opponents of the IMF deal as to what should be done and the alternative positions put forward sound to modern ears amateurish and ill-informed.

It was also clear to opponents that the statistics on which the Treasury were relying to predict the future path of the PSBR were inaccurate (as they had been on numerous previous occasions). Far too little was made of this, and there was no real modelling of alternative scenarios by the Cabinet opponents of Healey and Callaghan.

The alternative plans were almost 'back of fag packet' calculations, and some of them included desperate one-off savings such as the sale of the Government's shares in Burmah Oil which would have no continuing effect on the PSBR and which would in fact increase it a little in future years.

In addition, personal jealousies and dislikes between Crosland, Benn, Shore and Foot doomed any prospect of a united front and it was soon clear that the social democratic right, as Benn called it, would fold in favour of the PM's position, whatever that was in the end.

There was also a disparity in information between those with Treasury information at their fingertips, and who were involved in the negotiations with the IMF, and those who did not have such access.

So, eventually, the Cabinet agreed to an IMF package that had some eerie echoes of the 1931 decisions by the MacDonald Cabinet. Benn had even gone so far as to ask the Cabinet Office for the 1931 Cabinet minutes and caused the Tribune newspaper to print them on its front page, as well as circulating them to Cabinet colleagues. The level of dissent reported in the Cabinet between Benn and right wing figures such as Roy Mason was profound.

The Pivotal Point of Post-War Politics

The July 1976 decisions by the Labour Cabinet and the subsequent agreement with the IMF were in contradiction to the Party's manifesto in 1974 – the industrial policy, and more than anything, the commitment to full employment inherent in every government's programme since 1944. And it came just at the time when the highest unemployment figures since the war had been announced.

In order to mute opposition, Callaghan threatened Benn with the sack if he made a mild statement to his Bristol South East Party about the Cabinet discussions. The essential point, however, was that Benn stayed in the Cabinet despite disagreeing with the new central plank of economic and social policy, even though this was widely criticised by elements of the Labour movement.

Ministers and the PLP were shell shocked. They could see no real way to resist demands to reduce spending in return for access to borrowing rights from the IMF and to enable borrowing on the commercial markets. Michael Foot reported to colleagues that Callaghan had threatened to go to the Queen, resign as PM, and offer his advice to the Monarch to send for someone else to run the show if the Cabinet did not agree to the draconian steps.

In reality there was no worked through alternative strategy that commanded respect from professional economists. Ministers were threatened with the collapse of the Government, the resignation of the PM, and the installation of some other type of government in a partial re-run of 1931.

The Cabinet chose to stay in office in the expectation that this decision would keep the Labour movement together, and no one resigned. So, in 1976 the Labour Cabinet did what the Labour Cabinet in 1931 refused to do – cut public spending sharply in order to borrow money. Benn, like the others, stayed in the Cabinet and chose not to resign, which would have been justified as a result of his profound policy disagreements with Callaghan. His failure to do so weakened his position later and was a mistake, as I told him at the time.

The events of 1976 were undoubtedly a pivotal moment in British politics. They were, however, based on completely incorrect statistics about the Government's borrowing and with no carefully formulated fallback plan which could command a majority in the Cabinet and PLP.

The response outside Parliament was more profound and long lasting than that within the PLP. This response came in a number of arenas: there were demands for increased wages to recoup the loss of value against inflation, and to improve the relative position of the low paid as against those in better paid jobs.

This was also the start of the modern campaign for a statutory national minimum wage. The trade union movement and the wider public began to organise against public expenditure cuts, and in NUPE's case, we worked to increase the union's influence in the Labour Party in order to maximise the chances of alternative policies being adopted.

NUPE's Engagement Plan

This was a deliberate strategy supported by booming subscriptions from new union members who were boosting not only the general fund but also the union's political fund. As the only active Labour Party member in the office, I started arguing that we should raise the union's affiliated membership so that we could exert more leverage over the NEC and the Labour Government.

In 1972, the union's affiliation to the Party was set at 150,000, significantly less than the growing number of members paying the political fund levy. Over time, I persuaded Fisher and Dix to increase it in instalments to 600,000, and some of the victories against the platform at Labour Conferences in the late 1970s and early 1980s were a direct consequence of those decisions.

By 1974, Dix had been persuaded to rejoin the Labour Party and stood for the NEC in the trade union section – the first time that a NUPE candidate had ever been nominated. He lost heavily, but it was progress. These changes also enabled the union's nominations for the NEC to be taken more seriously, and Tom Sawyer[67] was elected to the National Executive Committee in 1981.

Influence in the Labour Party was also linked indirectly to the number of sponsored MPs that the union had, and whether they had influence within the PLP. Our MPs were a distinctly mixed bunch.

The best of them was Arthur Bottomley, a Minister under Attlee and Wilson, a sensible man and a devoted supporter of NUPE. He had been a full time organiser before the war and had a residual influence and

---

67. General Secretary of the Labour Party 1994-1998. Deputy General secretary of NUPE from 1981 and now Lord Sawyer.

prestige as well as a photographic memory for people.

I was walking with him down St Stephen's Hall in the early 1980s and he spotted a man he had last seen at the Rangoon independence conference for Burma in 1947 when a minister. He went up to him, shook his hand, got his name spot on (which was not easy), and conversed with him for some time.

Roland Moyle was, in the 1970s, a minister of state at the DHSS, with the wags describing him as the man who closed more hospitals than anyone else. This was unfair as most of the closures were to locate services in more modern buildings.

The rest were: Peter Hardy, an ex-teacher with little connection with the union; Ken Lomas, a former blood transfusion service worker; Tom Pendry (now Lord Pendry of Stalybridge), the secretary of the NUPE group and a former Services boxing champion and Oxford Blue; and Ted Leadbitter, MP for Hartlepool, a rather eccentric MP from a mining family.[68]

None of them were particularly active on the union's behalf; they took the sponsorship money and that was about it. Fisher, in particular, was incensed at their lack of application given the fast moving agenda in politics. He suspected with good reason that some were hostile to the union's emerging policy positions, and he wanted big changes by expanding the panel[69] and getting rid of some of the dead wood.

So, in the mid-1970s I was given the job of recruiting more candidates and setting tasks for the existing panel. It was decided that they would have to reapply and complete an application form, write an essay on a subject chosen by the union, be shortlisted and attend an interview.

---

68. Leadbitter threatened to bring down the first Wilson Government (which had a majority of four) because the Post Office had erected a telephone pole outside a constituent's house. Leadbitter wrote to Tony Benn, then Postmaster General, and threatened to resign the whip if the pole was not removed. The Chief Whip dressed him down and the pole stayed. Later, Leadbitter was stopped in his constituency by the police for suspected drink driving. They recognised him and let it pass, but Leadbitter then wrote to the Chief Constable to complain that the officers had crushed his grandchildren's' Easter eggs on the back seat by sitting on them, thus reopening the whole affair, to his detriment.

69. This was the union's Parliamentary Panel of sponsored candidates, officially the 'A' List supported by the Labour Party nationally. If on the list, the sponsoring union would agree to find a high proportion of the candidate's election expenses and inclusion on the A List was a considerable advantage to candidates seeking a Labour seat in Parliament.

They kicked up an enormous fuss, indicating that this was *lèse majesté, how dare you, don't you know who we are?* - a typical PLP response. As I had been dealing with large numbers of ministers and MPs since 1965, these threats fell on deaf ears and we completed the process. The two most useless[70] were removed from the panel and we appointed a raft of new people.

The National Minimum Wage

In addition, we started submitting resolutions and amendments to the Labour Party Conference and TUC. This had not always been done in the past, but it was an obvious way to influence policy and campaigns.

I started writing material on public service wages, cuts in public expenditure, and the minimum wage. This was the beginning of the modern agitation for a national minimum wage.

There had in the past been explicit commitments to national minimum wage rates, advocated for example by all sides at the National Industrial Conference in 1919. Then, in 1923 there had been pressure to enact a minimum wage by Dr Arthur Salter (MP for Bermondsey), and a motion passed in Parliament to initiate an inquiry.

But these early campaigns went unfulfilled and the Labour Party's vacuous platform of a National Minimum (never explained, let alone legislated on) was forgotten as many trade unions made headway on collective bargaining during the second world war and afterwards. So, the modern campaign had to be started from scratch and by the early 1980s was gaining traction.

By the late 1970s, NUPE-led resolutions on establishing a national minimum wage had passed the TUC and the Labour Party Conference. By the publication of Labour's policy programme in 1982, plans to establish a Commission on a National Statutory Minimum Wage were in place and it seemed only a matter of time before the Party adopted it formally. This was done in 1985 and embedded in the Party's manifesto for the 1992 General Election.

---

70. Ken Lomas, MP for Huddersfield West from 1964-79, later defecting to the SDP; his only prominence in Parliament was to act as a cheerleader for Minnesota Mining and Manufacturing, makers of material for reflective number plates. And Peter Hardy, MP for Rother Valley 1970-97, later Baron Hardy of Wath.

In this critical development, Tom Sawyer was crucial, and he carried forward the union's policy on the NEC with great skill, eventually becoming General Secretary of the Party in 1994. Many individuals supported the proposals in practical ways between 1980 and 1997 but I am proud to have been there at the start, taking the flak and moving things forward.

When I was elected to the Commons in 1979, I started raising the issue in Parliamentary Questions and speeches, and by giving financial support to the Low Pay Unit. At the time there were only two declared supporters of a statutory minimum wage in the PLP: Jeff Rooker and myself. By 1998, the establishing legislation was on its way through Parliament.

The campaign for a minimum wage across the board was resisted strongly by those organisations with greater degrees of bargaining power. They argued for free collective bargaining as the essential element in relationships with employers. The NUPE campaign was resented by many, and ignored at first by most.

The Endless Problem of Wage Control

The day-to-day process of creating wage claims and arguing for higher standards of living for low-paid workers was bread-and-butter work for the Research Department and was indeed a core part of the role that I had been employed to do.

The central problem was that almost all of the union's members were employed by the public sector and therefore subject to whatever form of incomes policy was in place at the time. As Alan Fisher said many times, 'all Governments have an incomes policy, whether they say so or not.'

Sometimes these restrictions were voluntary ('guiding lights' for example), and sometimes harder edged 'severe restraint' or specific norms set by a statutory pay policy. In any event, public sector wages were controlled for all practical purposes by the public sector financial settlements in place at the time.

There were several ways in which the corsets of financial control operated.

First, through the local authority rate support grant settlement. This worked on the assumptions made in a particular year about the level of inflation and the uplift in funding which Government was prepared to give to councils.

Second, in the NHS, by the year-on-year allocation of funds to health authorities.

In the 1970s, the Government was still controlling costs through annual financial settlements which made planning difficult for employers (three-year settlements were still decades away).

There was the added complication that funding was set in 'real terms' and not cash limits, meaning that the number of pounds that an employer had available to spend would vary from one quarter to the next, especially at times of high inflation, and were not easy to calculate.

This was the landscape and the trade unions had not dealt with it effectively. The issue of dealing with low pay has had a long and ignoble history in the Labour movement. In 1963 the TUC General Council published a detailed policy statement *Economic Development and Planning*. This was designed to incorporate the trade unions in the work of the NEDC, with most emphasis being on wage restraint within the context of 'general agreement on national economic and social priorities.'

There were still two million workers in Britain earning £10 a week or less in 1963, but helping them was not a priority. The unions were embedded in the warm glow of early Wilsonism and his commitment to the scientific revolution – indicative planning and sharing the fruits of higher economic growth.

Unfortunately, this broadly expansionist policy lasted only till July 1966, when the Labour Government adopted deflation, public expenditure cuts, and defence of the fixed sterling parity against the dollar as the main objectives.

However, a further development was that the National Board for Prices and Incomes (NBPI) was now being used to monitor and intervene on wage claims. Legislation granting these powers to the Board was introduced in late 1965. It required that all wage claims be notified to the NBPI with any pay increases deferred until the board had reported on them. The July 1966 measures introduced a six month standstill on incomes followed by a further period of severe restraint.

In response to this, the TUC and individual unions began to change their attitude toward wage restraint and the position of the low-paid. But the impact of the NBPI was profound in that it 'fixed' the solution to low pay as being that of increasing productivity.

In particular, the Board's Report no. 29[71] concluded that the root cause

---

71.   Prices and Income Board, 29 March 1967

of low pay in local authorities and the NHS was low productivity and that any attempt to improve pay for low-paid workers in these industries would have to be based on improvements in efficiency and productivity.

As the Australian economist Allan Fels wrote in a study commissioned by the NBPI:

[The Board] did not regard the alteration of the existing distribution of income as one of the main purposes of incomes policy, unless greater efficiency or wage stability was likely to result.[72]

During the whole period of the Labour Government from 1964, wage restraint of one kind or another was applied with little effort to deal with income disparities. This led to growing feelings of resentment and some hardship amongst the lowest paid. By 1969, some public sector workers were prepared to strike to obtain better terms and conditions.

The first action taken was unofficial. In September 1969, London dust crews (refuse collectors) struck to press a claim for an extra £4/11 shillings on the London weekly rate just when the national negotiations were taking place. At the same time, the unions were ramping up their capability to deal with productivity negotiations following the findings of PIB 29.

Many of the productivity schemes were semi-fictitious in the sense that they relied on major assumptions about savings that could be made from work study[73] and the subsequent efficient adoption of the schemes.

The expansion of the union's Research Department in 1972 was intended to fill the capability gaps that existed on pay research and on policy analysis arising from this new environment. At the same time, the Government was investing in better data collection through the New

---

72. Quoted in Fisher and Dix, page 28.
73. Work Study looks at the characteristics of work, eg how many movements it takes to collect a bin, upend it in the cart, take it back to the house, and how quickly each of those things can be done by an efficient operative. This analysis was then used to determine how many staff were needed to do a job (eg collect 4,000 bins) and over what time it would need to be done. That would then be benchmarked against the number of staff actually employed and the time they were actually taking to do it. In turn, this led the analyst to identify how many staff fewer could be used and what cuts in time could be made if they were working at full efficiency. This produced a 'savings' pot which could in theory be shared between the staff and the employer, meaning that bonus payments could be made to the remaining staff on the assumption they were doing the job in the prescribed way. In many cases they got the bonus payments without actually performing the improved productivity, hence the view that schemes were 'semi-fictitious.'

Earnings Survey but was still arguing that solutions to low pay would have to be found within an imposed 'wage norm' and some statutory powers over wages.

The NBPI had been investigating particular groups of low-paid workers and in April 1971 published its studies of hospital ancillary workers, laundry and dry cleaning workers, and contract cleaners.

This significant report on the *General Problems of Low Pay* claimed that the task of helping the low-paid was 'intrinsically difficult', that there was no experience of dealing with it, that definitions of low pay were not universally shared, and that difficult economic circumstances meant that it was hard to do anything.

This negativity was followed by the low-paid taking matters into their own hands.

The incoming Heath Government abolished the National Board for Prices and Incomes but the reaction of the local authority trade unions was to escalate by submitting a claim in support of the then-TUC target wage of £16.50 per week. After a six week strike (dubbed the 'dirty jobs strike' in the press) they obtained increases which brought wage rates to within 25p of the TUC target.

This first national strike of low paid workers in modern times was historic as it was a break with the past, and it could be argued to be the most significant action by the low-paid since the development of mass trade unionism in the 1880s.

The low-paid groups involved were mainly women in the school meals service, cleaning and catering, although there were some harder nosed groups involved, such as refuse collectors who had significant bargaining power.

With some exceptions these groups were difficult to mobilise and harder still to persuade to undertake strike action. They had to be seriously motivated by economic necessity to agree to take action of any kind.

The Statutory National Minimum Wage Emerges

In the early 1970s, some trade unions were beginning to think of additional methods to advance the claims of the low-paid. These were weak at first, but at least they were a beginning. In 1972, USDAW[74] moved a

74.   Union of Shop, Distributive and Allied Workers

resolution at the TUC which urged the General Council to 'press more vigorously for the establishment of a national minimum wage.'

The 1970s push for a minimum wage was by no means original: the demand had first surfaced in Fabian Tracts in the 1880s and had been codified in the National Minimum, a vague concept embedded in the Webbs *Industrial Democracy*[75] covering factory conditions and public health as well as wages.

They saw a minimum wage as an extension of what they called the Common Rule, that is the function of trade unions to level up working practices and payments which they argued had a beneficial effect on the behaviour of employers and of capitalism generally by minimising cheap labour.

The argument for a national minimum wage was taken further in Fabian Tract 83[76] and in *The Case for a Legal Minimum Wage*.[77] Its most enduring iteration was, however, in *Labour and the New Social Order*, the Labour Programme of 1918 written by the Webbs, which said that:

the Labour Party to-day stands for the universal application of the Policy of the National Minimum, to which (as embodied in the successive elaborations of the Factory, Mines, Railways, Shops, Merchant Shipping, and Truck Acts, the Public Health, Housing, and Education Acts and the Minimum Wage Act – all of them aiming at the enforcement of at least the prescribed Minimum of Leisure, Health, Education, and Subsistence) the spokesmen of Labour have already gained the support of the enlightened statesmen and economists of the world. All these laws purporting to protect against extreme Degradation of the Standard of Life need considerable improvement and extension, whilst their administration leaves much to be desired.[78]

So, the 1970s discussion on the Minimum Wage reflected much older debates. Moves towards it had been further signalled by the creation of the Trade Boards in 1909 covering four low paid industries with provision for further extension where the Board of Trade considered wages to be 'exceptionally low.'

The 1919 creation of Whitley Councils as consultative bodies in low-paid industries was followed by the creation of a civil service negotiating body in 1919. Formal Whitley Councils were instituted as negotiating bodies for the NHS when it was created in 1948.

---

75. S and B Webb, *Industrial Democracy*, Longmans 1897
76. W M Macrosty Fabian Tract 83 1897
77. Fabian Tract 128, 1906
78. *Labour and the New Social Order*, Labour Party 1918, page 3

State support for the lowest paid was developed by the Fabians, embedded in the Labour programme of 1918, and taken up by the Liberal and Coalition Governments of 1906-21. But since the 1920s, trade unions had largely pursued policies of free collective bargaining which did not address the problems of low pay because the widespread belief was that increasing trade union negotiating power would enable the unions to deal with these issues without assistance from legislation.

The 'new unionism' of the 1970s took up where the Webbs and the Fabians had left off. They were developing a case for state intervention to help the lowest paid.

1974 and All That

If industrial politics was changing rapidly at the beginning of the 1970s, so British and world politics seemed to be unravelling.

In America, the Watergate scandal was developing at speed and was about to overwhelm President Nixon. The Vietnam war was to claim the lives of 282,000 US and allied armed forces personnel, 627,000 civilians and 444,000 Vietcong and North Vietnamese troops.

In Britain, the miners had won a significant victory after their national strike in 1972. Also, there was heavy duty industrial action and demonstrations against the Tory Government's industrial relations polices and especially the legal restrictions on trade unions imposed by the National Industrial Relations Court. And finally, in an act of pure folly, Heath had called a General Election in February 1974 to determine, in his words, 'Who governs Britain?'

The second miners' strike of 1974 caused the imposition of a three day week in order to maintain coal stocks and power supplies. This, and the power shortages that accompanied it on a rota basis across the country, provided moments of pure Whitehall farce.

There was the advice to 'brush your teeth in the dark,' uttered by Patrick Jenkin MP, then Energy Secretary. He also told the Evening Standard that, 'Except for a glance at the papers, I can manage my whole morning routine without putting on a light.'

This sage advice was promptly undermined by the *Observer*. They sent snappers to Highgate, where Jenkin lived, and discovered that his house was lit up like a Christmas Tree, lights blazing in five windows and on the porch. Politicians never do well when their exhortations are revealed to be 'do as I say not as I do.'

These were indeed heady times and it felt as if anything was possible and, indeed, likely to happen.

The election of the minority Labour Government in February 1974, followed by a marginally more robust victory in October 1974, raised the temperature further. Wilson had been elected on the central plank of getting Britain back to work, ending the three day week, doing a deal with the trade unions, implementing a social contract between Government and the TUC, and running a form of expansionary economic strategy.

This included price controls, wage restraint, food subsidies, and a National Enterprise Board which would introduce planning agreements with the private sector. It was also planned to nationalise shipbuilding and aerospace, as well as up to 25 big companies.

This was in the context of the highest ever recorded inflation of 25% on an annualised basis caused principally by the hiking of oil prices by OPEC. But it became clear by 1975 that the Labour Government was keen to find ways of resiling from its public expenditure plans and implementing tougher wage controls.

By 1975, the election manifesto commitments were imploding. The impact on living standards, especially in the public sector, was a slow burn. For a time, workers were protected by inflation equalling pay rises, ratcheted extra pay when inflation triggered it, and, for women, equal pay additions to bring their basic rates closer to male rates.

In July 1975 the Government introduced a £6 a week limit on pay increases for most workers, a policy that was narrowly approved by the TUC General Council.

In September 1976, the TUC opposed a return to free collective bargaining with no incomes policy and instead accepted Stage 2 of the incomes policy, more restrictive than Stage 1.

Stage 3 of the incomes policy was a phased return to free collective bargaining; and it has to be said that the policy did contribute to a reduction in the rate of inflation, bringing it below 10%. But then Chancellor Denis Healey made one of the central mistakes of the Labour Government: he advocated a 5% pay limit to operate from August 1978.

5% of Bugger All is Bugger All

The Trades Union Congress overwhelmingly rejected the policy in autumn 1978 and it was then that General Secretary, Alan Fisher, made his famous speech attacking the 5% limit, stating that '5% of bugger all is bugger all.'

However, there were still strong elements of loyalty to the Government in the trade union leadership, epitomised by the comment made to me on the floor of Congress by a very senior official of the AUEW.[79] 'You people have had it far too easy for far too long.' This expressed in a nutshell the hostility and sneering attitude of some of the bigger trade unions for the upstart public sector types who clearly did not know their place. He knew that I was writing Fisher's speeches – or most of them – and wanted to make his point.

The 5% pay policy was wildly unpopular amongst trade unionists who by then had experienced over 10 years of wage restraint and high inflation.

Healey, many years afterwards, recognised that the policy had been a major mistake. He was quoted by Elinor Goodman in a BBC interview in 2007 to celebrate his 90th birthday as saying, 'the government could have got away with a higher pay ceiling of perhaps 10% … It was silly to expect to get it. That was a mistake.'

He was right. The Labour Party Conference of 1978 defeated the platform by two-to-one and urged a return to free collective bargaining. At the same time, and before any public sector workers had struck, the trade union general secretaries were seeing Prime Minister Callaghan in private, urging relaxation of the policy and warning of the anger amongst workers which would be impossible to contain.

Fisher also went to see Callaghan several times in the autumn of 1978 and later during the strikes. We always knew when he had been because he came back looking deeply unhappy.

These events, 10 years and more of unrelenting downward pressure on wages, endless pay policies, continuing low wages, and massive cuts in public expenditure on the social wage, were the midwives of industrial conflict.

Going Outside the TUC Box

The NUPE Research Department was at the heart of these very signif-icant conflicts. Along with my colleagues, I was developing the wage

79.   Amalgamated Union of Engineering Workers

claims, developing the case for the minimum wage set out in *Low Pay and How to End It*,[80] organising the industrial action by liaising with our regional offices and organisers, building public support for our position in the media and with the public, and critically developing the case against the public expenditure cuts imposed by the Labour Government especially from 1976 onwards.

The problem about fighting the public expenditure programme measures was that the TUC was at the time completely inert as an organising mechanism. It was leaden footed, slow, consensus driven, highly bureaucratic, and demanding of vast amounts of time to do anything. So, we hatched a plot in the summer of 1976 to circumvent Congress House, establishing a November 17th Steering Committee to build momentum for a national demonstration against the cuts.

This was preceded by an important practical document: *Time to Change Course*, NUPE's first economic review which I penned from start to finish, and which argued for radical changes from the Healey policy of surrender to the IMF. This energised the Union and was critical in building support within and outside the trade unions for the linked actions that were gestating.

Time to Change Course argued that there were now deep structural faults in the economy which were making it impossible to combine full employment and a reasonable rate of growth with either a healthy balance of payments or an acceptable rate of inflation.

It said that the spiral of decline in manufacturing industry had eroded the tax base and had created strong pressures for containment of wages in public services and downward pressure on the availability of capital expenditure to modernise facilities in the NHS and elsewhere.

It said that the economy was less sensitive to Keynesian demand management than ever before because of the concentration of capital in large firms.

Control had passed from government-inspired demand management to control by the managers of the largest firms, many of which were multinationals. They were working on internal planning systems wholly out of sympathy with the timeframes and policies of the British Government.

Time to Change Course said:

The ability of multinational companies to transfer resources, production, process and investment between countries and different regions of individual

---

80.   A Fisher and B Dix, *Low Pay and How to End It*, Pitman, 1974

nations ... has led to an investment strike and added further twists to the spiral of decline in manufacturing industry.

This identification of what we now call globalisation as the core problem of the modern British economy called for a policy response from progressive forces.

Instead, as *Time to Change Course* pointed out, the Labour Government had emasculated its own policy child , the National Enterprise Board. It restricted its funds, shredded planning agreements as an instrument of policy,[81] and had introduced tax hikes at a time of dropping purchasing power flowing from high inflation.

The consequence of this deflationary policy was a rapid rise in unemployment and of short-time working, coupled with public spending cuts which ate away at the social fabric of the country as well as contributing to the deflationary hole.

The economic alternative consisted of two strands.

First, an emphasis on reflation, limited in its possible effects by the balance of payments deficit which Britain was still running at the bottom of the deepest recession for 30 years.

Second, a commitment to more substantial Government intervention including import controls and controls over multinational companies to restrict their ability to move primary production overseas and import semi-finished components for assembly here.

This policy flowed in some ways from Labour's programme 1973 and to a lesser extent the policies advocated by the TUC and the radical economists of the Cambridge Group.[82] It began as an interventionist answer to a real crisis but quickly became the alternative not just to the Labour Government's policy but also to the emerging core of Thatcherism.

This was a significant break from consensus politics originating from a

81. Only one was ever completed with a major private sector company, Chrysler. The Company unilaterally repudiated the agreement shortly afterwards.

82. The principals In the Cambridge Group were Nicholas Kaldor, Wynne Godley, Robert Neild and Francis Cripps. Cripps had been appointed as Tony Benn's economic adviser and Kaldor had worked for Prime Minister Wilson in the 1960s. They argued for a number of complex propositions including that deflation by Government increased the level of consumer price inflation. They also argued for import controls as a mechanism to restrain consumption without cutting real wages. In that sense the policy was progressive. An important article in the *Cambridge Journal of Economics* (Vol 36 issue July 2012) describes the Cambridge Group's positions in detail and their disputes with the Treasury over time. The CEPG was disbanded in the early 1980s when the ESRC cut its grant.

breakdown in the ability of the economic system to operate in the normal way. The full blown crisis of 1976 was the decisive turning point in post-1945 politics and economics. Nothing would ever be the same again.

Looking back from 2020 it is, however, clear that the Alternative Economic Strategy (AES) had serious flaws.

The principal failing was the assertion that the British economy was more difficult to control through demand management than ever before and that, therefore, greater levels of government intervention were required to ensure price stability, growing investment, and full employment. The evidence for this was thin. It was also the case that academic advocates of some interventions kept changing their minds on the desirability of items such as import controls.

Given the record since then, it seems to be the case that currency volatility was a greater threat than the structure of industry and commerce. The failure of monetarism on broad or narrow money criteria was striking in the 1980s, and in the early 1990s rigid adherence to 'shadowing the mark', entering the 'snake' of European currencies and finally abandoning efforts to stay within money value limits was more connected to overall perceptions of the British economy by the currency markets than anything else.

The Alternative Economic Strategy harked back to 1940s-style physical controls on the economy, which was within the working lifetimes of some politicians and advisers. The reason that it was not adopted was that it was inherently disbelieved as a practical alternative. And then, in the period 1997-2008, the 'great stability' gave the impression that stable prices and growth could be sustained for ever. That was wrong too.

Government Strategy Implodes

After the great demonstration of 1976, the 17th November Steering Committee grew into the National Steering Committee Against the Cuts (NSC). I became its secretary.

This covered most of the trade unions (15 of them) with members in the public sector including NALGO[83], COHSE[84], NUT[85] and the Civil

---

83. National and Local Government Officers Association
84. Confederation of Health Service Employees
85. National Union of Teachers

Service trade unions. The big general unions – TGWU[86] and GMB – stayed away, but the proof that we were on to something had become clear in the response to the call for the 17th November demonstration.

Special trains – many special trains – were hired to bring demonstrators from all over the country and the total entering Hyde Park was estimated at 90,000, the biggest trade union demonstration for decades.

When Alan Fisher climbed on to the platform in the Park he asked me, 'Where have all these people come from?' He was amazed and so were the rest of the trade union leadership, who had not understood the strength of feeling out there in the rank and file.

The Labour Cabinet did, however, contain elements which were overtly hostile and there were reported examples of criticism of NUPE in particular based on a view that we were just 'militants', a ridiculous phrase but clearly intended to link us to Militant,[87] and which none of us were associated with at all. We were advocating an alternative policy at a time when it could have been introduced.

Later, when the full scale of errors in the national accounts became clearer, we felt justified in the campaign we had launched.

It turned out that the Treasury had overestimated the Public Sector Borrowing Requirement by £3,080m in 1976-77 and we believed at the time that similar errors were being made for 1977-78.

Given that the scale of cuts required by the Labour Government's cuts packages in 1976 were of the order of £1bn,[88] it is obvious that the whole exercise was a disciplinary one to bring the Government's policies under control as far as the markets were concerned.

Not only did the Treasury overestimate the borrowing requirement, it also allowed very significant underspends on approved programmes to develop within the year, and these also had serious deflationary effects.

86. Transport and General Workers Union
87. The Militant Tendency was a Marxist/Leninist organisation formed from the ashes of the RSL, the Revolutionary Socialist League. Its basic tenet was that infiltration of the Labour Party was the only way to effect substantial social change in Britain. It had its own full time organisers and branch structure and was funded essentially from sales of its newspaper *Militant* and levies on its members. It gained traction on Merseyside and controlled Liverpool City Council for a few years in the 1980s. The editorial board of Militant and others were expelled from the Labour Party in 1983 and the organisation split again in 1991 when it expelled its most prominent founder, Ted Grant. Militant was regarded as a figure of fun by many people in the Labour Party.
88. £1,033m in July 1976 followed by a further package in December 1976 amounting to £1,016m in 77-78 and £1,513m in 78-79

This disastrous series of errors was indeed continued in 1977-78; the budget forecast was for a PSBR of £8.5bn but outturn was around £5.7bn.

The whole policy of the Labour Government was thus built on scandalously incompetent economic forecasting. Much later, Denis Healey agreed that the PSBR figures were wrong and that it had been completely unnecessary to resort to the IMF loan at all. He said so in an interview with *Observer* financial editor William Keegan in 2006.

But the dodginess of the PSBR figures was known about at the time. Callaghan and Healey used the crisis to impose a policy which they wanted and which they knew would not get through Cabinet otherwise.

Government Nonsense

The underlying argument of the Labour Government was that the proportion of GDP taken up by public spending was too high, having risen from 50% to 60% of GDP.[89] This figure of 60% included, however, all transfer payments such as pensions and social security benefits and was therefore highly misleading –as it was intended to be.

The Government also argued that tax rates and the level of tax thresholds were too high and that millions of workers were being dragged into tax which they had not paid before. But the problem with this was that it assumed that most of the tax take had to flow from the incomes of individuals.

However, the Bank of England pointed out in a Quarterly Bulletin that mainstream corporation tax had in practice fallen to zero as a proportion of company profits, despite the official rate being 52%, thus placing the burden of funding public services almost entirely on personal tax.

The response to this in Parliament was very strong, with the Rooker/Wise amendment of 1977 (to the Finance Bill implementing the Budget proposals) forcing the Government to index personal tax allowances to preserve their value, thus minimising fiscal drag.

Chancellor Healey also argued strongly that high public expenditure, and high public borrowing, 'crowded out' private investment to increase productive capacity. The crowding-out theory, covering the pre-emption of financial resources and staffing resources, was likened by Healey to two

89.   Cmd 6393 page 1

competing buckets going into a pool, one labelled 'public expenditure' and the other 'private sector investment.'

This position followed Bacon and Eltis who argued that the slow growth of the British economy since 1961 was the product of a fast growing public sector.[90] This was taken up vigorously by the media and the Conservatives, as it implied that only by cutting public expenditure could you ensure economic growth and prosperity. It also assumed explicitly that anything done by the public sector where there was no market was inherently less desirable than private sector activity.

A cogent and well-argued criticism of this approach was set out at the time by Terry Ward, Specialist Adviser to the House of Commons Expenditure Committee, who argued that:

Two fallacies of the economic reasoning underlying the Chancellor's statement and IMF letter are that the supply of loanable funds is fixed, from which it follows that the more goes to finance the PSBR the less is available for private industry, and that manufacturing industry is critically dependent on the level of interest rates rather than the level of profits and the expectations of making future profits. In fact, there is little evidence that the level of investment is at all sensitive to the level of interest rates … The very action of cutting the PSBR supposedly to encourage investment reduces aggregate demand for industry's products and hence the desirability of investing in additional capacity, and it is far from clear that a major reduction in interest rates is in prospect.[91]

The 1973 Social Contract bargain envisaged that the central objective of the Labour Government's economic strategy would be to increase output per employee and thereby increase the rate of economic growth. It was a pure Croslandite, pro-Keynesian policy.

By early 1977 at the latest, it was apparent that the Government had abandoned economic growth, the minimisation of unemployment and price inflation, and indeed their side of the Social Contract.

As the respected National Institute of Economic and Social Research said in its February 1977 *Economic Review*, 'Fiscal policy – in the sense of changes in revenue and expenditure designed to manage the level of aggregate demand in the economy – virtually ceased to exist in 1976.'[92]

---

90.   Roger Bacon and Walter Eltis, *Too Few Producers*, Macmillan, 1976
91.   Expenditure Committee of the House of Commons, General sub-committee, Minutes of Evidence, 20th December 1976.
92.   NIESR Economic Review February 1977, page 7

Callaghan and Healey Make the Jump

The deeply shocking truth is that the Healey/Callaghan majority in the Labour Government were content, indeed eager, to argue that Keynesianism was dead, that 'the Party's over,' that public spending should be the sacrificial lamb to resolve economic policy dilemmas, and that it was essential to resile from the pledges and manifesto commitments of the two General Elections of 1974.

This was unlike 1931, when the MacDonald Cabinet had split over quite specific and limited proposals to reduce unemployment benefit and the dispute had occurred over a very short space of time.

The 1976 abandonment of Keynesianism by the Labour Cabinet, undertaken in three separate cuts exercises that year, was more drawn out, even more intense than in 1931, but resulted in no resignations from the Labour Cabinet – but a total reversal of economic policy.

The advocates of the Alternative Economic Strategy in Cabinet simply swallowed it, calculating that it was more important to hang together than to hang separately.

It was not Thatcher that destroyed the Keynesian consensus. It was Healey and Callaghan.

An ancillary problem was, however, that the advocates of alternatives in the Cabinet did not pursue a united or coherent strategy and tactics. Some of them just folded; others went along with the leader under sufferance; and others put forward rather incoherent positions, contradictory with each other, which were not backed by rigorous thinking.

It was a critical juncture and they fluffed it.

The Labour Government had bought the idea that Britain was in secular decline. They believed that the economy would continue to drift downwards, that the trade unions were a principal source of cost-push inflation, that public expenditure was by definition a problem, and that action had to be taken to rectify these issues – principally by disciplining the public sector.

It was a strategy that a radical Tory government could have adopted, and indeed did so after 1979. The policy ignored the declining living standards of sections of the working class and closed its eyes to high unemployment.

Not only did the Healey/Callaghan axis shred Keynesianism, it also advanced arguments that were highly divisive. It said that the public sector was hogging scarce reserves of staffing which were urgently needed in manufacturing industry, ignoring the fact that substantial reserves of unemployed labour existed.

In late 1976, there were 1.6 million registered unemployed. It was unlikely, therefore, that 'bottlenecks in production caused by scarcities of skilled labour are due to the demands made for steel erectors, laser operators and other similar grades by the public sector.'[93]

Further, the growth in exports and economic expansion that the Government was aiming for proved elusive. Following the 1977 budget, the Cambridge Economic Policy Group estimated that to reduce unemployment to well below one million by the mid-1980s would require a growth rate of 5% a year, maintained for 10 years, twice the annual rate actually achieved over the previous 20 years.

In contrast, the 1977 budget officially aimed for a growth rate of 1.5%. The forward projection of reducing unemployment to 700,000 by 1979, made by Chancellor Healey in March 1976 was simply abandoned.

Even the TUC, never an early adopter of radical policy, was driven to agree that the economy was way off target and that neither the Government's nor the TUC's targets on employment were attainable on present policies and within the timescale originally envisaged.

There are those who argue that Prime Minister Callaghan's change of course, and the IMF loan and its associated cuts in spending was tactical, that he really wasn't committed to such a radical policy shift.

William Keegan, at the time a Bank of England official,[94] argues that Callaghan's statements, especially his speech to the Party Conference on 29th September 1976, were purely tactical and designed to ensure support from the White House and US Treasury for an IMF loan to Britain in the context of a 'gilt strike' in the markets (whereby potential lenders were refusing to buy British Government Treasury bonds).

Callaghan's speech was partly drafted by his son in law, Peter Jay, who at that point had espoused monetarism.

Callaghan said at Blackpool:

We used to think that you could spend your way out of a recession and increase employment by cutting taxes and boosting government spending, I can tell you in all candour that that option no longer exists, and that insofar as it ever did exist, it only worked on each occasion by injecting a higher level of unemployment as the next step.

---

93.   R Race, *Breakdown, the Crisis in Your Public Services*, NSC 1977
94.   Previously a columnist for the *Financial Times*, later a distinguished economics editor of the *Observer*, and a long time Labour supporter.

He also said that we had been living on borrowed time; that we should not borrow to support the standard of living; and that 'The cosy world we were told would go on for ever, where full employment would be guaranteed by a stroke of the Chancellor's pen, cutting taxes, deficit spending, that cosy world is gone.'

Listening to that speech as I did at the Blackpool Conference, it was quite clear that it was intended to signal a watershed moment, a change of gear and direction, a continued reaffirmation of incomes policy and reliance on a modified Social Contract to deliver what had become a monetarist policy.

Callaghan was pretending to 'stick like glue' to the trade unions by promoting the Party's Social Contract, but he had already by that stage fundamentally changed the Government's economic policy.

This was not being 'blown off course.' It was a deliberate and substantial shift, and he wanted the audience to know it had happened. The speech encapsulated his change of direction and it was not just tactical for the purpose of corralling the Americans; this was a clarion call to abandon Keynesianism. His view is in marked contrast to the initial actions of the Johnson Government in 2020 when confronted by the need to collapse the economy temporarily to control the COVID 19 pandemic.

Reaction and Counter Reaction

In 1976 these new policies – the cuts in services and capital spending, and constant restrictions on wages – caused a serious reaction in both the Labour Party and the trade unions.

Party members and the unions at local and national level started looking round for a new way of doing things, not just on the kinds of policies that were developed and implemented, but on holding a Labour Government and Labour MPs to account. It was the beginning of serious trouble for the Parliamentary leadership which finally came to a head in the election of Jeremy Corbyn in 2015.

The view that the Labour Government had lost its way and that it was adopting the policies of the financial establishment gained traction quickly and led to countervailing campaigns by some of the trade unions. The downward pressure on real wages radicalised many workers who were not usually prepared to take industrial action in support of wage claims. Real wages fell faster in 1976–77 than at any time since 1945, and Healey actually boasted to the Cabinet that by the late summer of 1977 they would be down by 7%.

The National Steering Committee was one vehicle through which action was taken. In 1977 and 1978 the NSC organised regional demonstrations and spent a great deal of time developing a thoughtful case against public expenditure restrictions on the scale implemented by the Labour Government.

We organised a day conference on the Social Wage, addressed by prominent academics as well as trade union people, and published a major intervention on the secrecy with which public expenditure plans (and economic policy generally) was being developed.

NUPE itself published economic reviews and analyses of what the Government was up to and advocated a North Sea oil fund to invest some of the revenue from oil taxation for the future. It was anticipated that oil taxes would bring in revenues of around £4bn a year by the mid-1980s with Gross National Product increasing by 3% because of oil-related activity.

But it quickly became apparent that Healey and Callaghan simply wanted to use these resources to subsidise the private sector whilst holding down wages. The White Paper on oil revenues[95] admitted that oil would be a major help to the balance of payments (regarded as the major constraint on economic policy since 1945), and that it would provide additional resources to the Treasury.

But the White Paper also argued for a continuation of existing policies on incomes and on public spending and failed to take advantage of the opportunity that had arisen – a genuine windfall opportunity – to build for the future by investing a portion of the North Sea revenues in an oil fund which could attract interest and profits over the long term from dividends in successful companies and reinvestment in bonds.

Norway, which shared some of the North Sea fields around it's West Coast and Shetland with the UK, set up such a fund in 1990 to protect the wealth produced by oil revenues for the future benefit of the Norwegian people. Today it holds wealth of over US$1 trillion in assets, including 1.4% of global stocks and shares, making it the world's largest sovereign wealth fund. In May 2018, it was worth about $195,000 per Norwegian citizen. Britain could have done this in the 1970s, with hugely beneficial effects for the future.

95. *The Challenge of North Sea Oil*, Cmnd 7143

North Sea oil revenues were a big chance to break out of the constraints on public expenditure over time, and the Government completely fluffed it. They were committed to their restrictive policies and that was it. The Healey/Callaghan line was deeply conservative.

Crunch Time: the Winter of 1978-79

By 1978 the Government's wages policy had reached a turning point. In the early months of 1978, ministers made a series of speeches arguing for a fourth phase of wages policy, linked to a demand that national average earnings should rise by no more than 5% in 1978-79.

In addition, the consequences of the 1977 wages policy were being felt not just by workers but also by companies. One of the proposals in the July 1977 White Paper[96] was that companies that reached wage settlements above the norm might be discriminated against in the award of public contracts.

This actually happened, and several companies were blacklisted including Reynolds Tankers, Spencer Engineering, and the John Lewis Partnership. Others, however, escaped punishment because they were too big to take on: the Ford Motor Company escaped, no doubt because it was regarded as too difficult a target.

The reaction by trade union leaders was very strong. Joe Gormley, President of the National Union of Mineworkers, described the wages policy as 'electorally disastrous.' Lionel Murray, then General Secretary of the TUC, said that they were very worried about the activities of ministers who were advocating a fourth stage of wages policy, and that the TUC had no intention of being drawn into discussions about such a continuation of wage restrictions.

Neither Gormley nor Murray were agitators: Gormley himself was identified by the BBC in 2002 as working for Special Branch to identify extremists within the NUM and was one of 20 senior trade union leaders to whom Special Branch was continually talking.

These views, and the explicit decisions of Congress in 1976, were ignored by the Callaghan/Healey leadership. The July 1978 White Paper, *Winning the Battle Against Inflation*, wanted a permanent pay policy where there would be a rolling agreement between Government and the unions about the maximum level of earnings compatible with keeping

---

96.   *The Attack on Inflation* after 31st July 1977, para 16

inflation under control in the next 12 months.

In the pay round beginning August 1978, the White Paper called for a maximum limit of 5% and that any proposed settlements beyond that would be called in and subject to 'very critical' examination. Any proposal to include reductions in working hours would have to be 'paid for' against the 5% limit.

NUPE was very conscious that 1978 could be an election year, or at least the year leading up to an election, and it was anticipated that the Government and the public sector employers would be more amenable to more generous settlements than they had been in the previous three years.

Not only was there considerable reaction in the trade union membership to the prospect of a further year of wages policy, which might continue forever, but there was a growing gap between the wages of some public service workers and the totality of workers.

In April 1970, the earnings gap for men between local authority full time manual workers and full time manual workers in all industries and services had been £5.60 a week. By April 1978 it had grown to £12.06.

Similarly, the pay gap between the earnings of full time male ancillary staff in the NHS and all manual workers had grown from £4.80 a week in 1970 to £10 in 1978.

So, the position of the lowest paid was deteriorating against that enjoyed by similar workers in industry as a whole. And the absolute level of earnings of full time male manual workers in parts of the public sector was parlous.

In April 1977, male NHS ancillary staff earnt £59.11 a week, local authority workers £58.80, and male manual workers in all industries and services were earning £71.50.[97]

Women workers were differently affected in that they had been receiving significant equal pay wage increases on top of their annual wage increases, following the introduction of the Equal Pay Act, and in some cases, this had meant that the pay gap between 1970 and 1978 had not grown.

It was clear by this time that low-paid workers in the public services that NUPE organised were low-paid in relation to the pay of other groups of workers, and to the pay of the average worker, and that one of the reasons for this were low basic rates of pay.

They were also low paid in relation to the social usefulness of their

---

97. New Earnings Survey and DHSS pay survey.

jobs, and when compared to the absolute standards of poverty laid down by the Government at the time.

For example, the level of earnings below which Family Income Supplement[98] could be claimed was £50 per week in a family with two children, and 34.7% of male, full time NHS ancillary workers earned less than £50 a week.

There was also the familiar poverty trap where the payment of income tax kicked in when increases in basic rates and earnings were negotiated. In fact, NUPE argued for a lower rate band of tax below the standard rate in order to ease progression into the tax system, a proposal that was taken up by the Labour Government in the late 1990s.

Testing the Temperature of the Water and Heating It Up at the Same Time

The question was: did the union's members feel strongly about these injustices, or were they prepared to sit it out? The wages campaign developed by the union in the autumn of 1978 was, from Fisher and Dix's point of view, doing two things.

First, it put the arguments to the members directly, face to face and in writing, ramping up awareness of the issues.

Second, it was also taking the temperature of the waters.

It was clear after a few weeks that there was considerable sympathy and support amongst members for the actions that the union was taking, and in Dix's phrase, 'willingness to go for a bundle.'

I personally addressed a meeting of several hundred catering and cleaning staff – almost all women school meals workers – in Gloucestershire, who had been given time off by the employer to attend. It was clear that these part time women workers were pretty determined to confront the Government.

This feeling of 'time to have a go' was enhanced by the effects of Tory amendments passed on the Finance Bill in mid-1978, which had the effect of sharply raising the amount of tax relief given by the Healey Budget.

As a result, someone earning £25,000 a year (an enormous sum at the time) saw an 11.3% rise in post-tax income whilst a worker earning

98. A means-tested benefit introduced by the Heath Government in 1970 to top up low wages.

£1,500 a year saw an increase after tax of just over 1%.

The union's pay strategy in 1978-9 focused on two demands: a substantial increase in basic rates, and a reduction in the working week to 35 hours. The objective was to get as close as possible to the TUC's long held plan for a low-pay target of £60 per week; and the claim for a 35-hour working week was framed unashamedly as an attempt to increase the number of job opportunities in the public services.

After it became clear that the support was there, Fisher went to see Prime Minister Callaghan to warn him that the Government's £5 per week pay policy would not hold.

He listened but did nothing. Other trade union leaders went to see him too and said the same thing.

At the same time, NUPE was actively campaigning in the Labour movement and the general public for an end to low pay. We linked it to the union's alternative economic strategy, and we saw a large number of resolutions being submitted to the Labour NEC and Congress House in support of these objectives.

The fact was that union members and many members of the public were incensed at the failure to address low pay and at the continuing cuts in public expenditure which had undermined the Labour Government's credibility. A perfect storm was developing.

Failures of Leadership

Negotiations with the Local Authority Employers began in October 1978 and there were signs that Government ministers were coming round to the view that low pay would have to be tackled eventually – but not now.

John Grant, Minister of State at Employment, said that low pay could be tackled in the future (Grant was a future defector to the SDP) but reiterated that the pay norm was 5% and the going rate in settlements was 13-19%.[99]

In order to make progress, there were discussions between the TUC representatives on the National Economic Development Council and Government which led to a Statement of Accord. This took note of the

---

99. I am indebted to the splendid book by Stephen Williams and Bob Fryer *Leadership and Democracy, The History of the National Union of Public Employees* for detailed points on the chronology of the disputes

need to keep inflation under control and asked union negotiators to 'have regard' to the effect wage settlements would have on prices. It also referred to the possibility of pay comparability arrangements in 'some areas of the public sector.'

The Accord relied on action through the Wages Councils, through the Fair Wages Resolution (of 1948), and through the application of Section 11 of the Employment Protection Act. But these instruments did not apply in practice to the public sector and they could not grip the problem of low pay in that environment.

The Accord was later endorsed by the Cabinet, and the TUC General Council met on 14th November to discuss it. The expectation in Government circles was that this would square the circle, enable the national negotiators to persuade their members to agree to low wage settlements in return for future pay comparability assessments, and thus avert the possibility of extensive strike action.

This general approach had worked in the early years of the Labour Government in 1974-75 but the prospects were poor in late 1978. Fisher voted against the accord at the General Council and the vote was tied 14-14. Chairman Tom Jackson was forced to use his casting vote against the Accord. The rules said that in a tied vote on the General Council the casting vote must support the status quo.

Jackson was furious and made intemperate attacks on Fisher the next day, and Bernard Donoughue, the Prime Minister's most senior policy adviser, made a statement saying, 'Had the General Council been consti-tuted of personal representatives of Mrs Thatcher, it could not have acted more effectively in the Conservative leader's electoral interest.'[100]

Biggest Wage Shock in Modern History

The developing crisis was seen by the Labour political establishment as one which required loyalty from the trade unions and nothing much from the Government. But real wages had been cut by 13% between 1975 and 1978 and for NUPE members the cut was close to 19%.

What ministers were ignoring completely was that the wage shock caused by the two oil price spikes and rises in inflation in the 1970s resulted in the biggest single reduction in real wages since records began,

---

100. *Prime Minister: The Conduct of Policy under Harold Wilson and James Cal-laghan*, Cape 1987 page 171.

and that record still holds true today. The reduced earnings in the corona-virus pandemic have been less powerful in effect than those of the 1970s.

Answering a Private Notice Question in the House of Commons, John Golding MP stated[101] that the earnings of local authority and NHS employees had risen between 6% and 15.5% less than those in all occupations, which could, he said, be attributable to the effects of pay policy, but that these were money increases before inflation.

There were, however, some Cabinet ministers who had grave doubts about the Government's pay policy: Barbara Castle told Michael Foot that the 5% policy was unworkable and David Ennals, Secretary of State for Health, had told the PM that the 5% limit would not 'stick' in the health service.

Len Murray told Callaghan that he would have 'industrial troubles' if he tried to push it through. Murray said later that he was glad to see the rejection of the Accord as he had 'no confidence at all in those 'intensive discussions.' They weren't really intensive discussions, they were just trying to put some words together.'[102]

However, these wise counsels cut no ice with the top leadership and the instructions to the employers' side were to stay with the 5% pay limit.

By mid-December pay offers of 5% had been rejected by the trade unions covering local authority manual workers, NHS ancillary workers, and ambulance workers. A 9.3% offer to the water workers had also been rejected.

The unions had collectively agreed a national day of action on 22nd January 1979, followed by a rolling programme of strikes. NUPE had used the concept of selective strike action effectively during the early 1970s, with key workers taking strike action, and others affected who could not work because of the selective action being (usually) sent home on full pay as work was not available.

Staff not taking strike action were encouraged to work to rule or ban overtime, which in many instances was very effective. These tactics meant that the union's dispute funds (the Hardship Allowance, in the rather Dickensian term favoured in the NUPE rules) would not be eroded too quickly, and that a more protracted dispute could be carried forward. Many would see this as prudent financial planning.

---

101. Hansard January 30th 1979. At this point Golding was answering in his ca-pacity as Parliamentary Under Secretary at the Department of Employment.
102. R Taylor *The TUC from General Strike to New Unionism,* Palgrave 2000 page 239

At this point the Government had ignored a last chance to reach settlements, preserve its own political future, and deal with low pay in a decisive way. They completely miscalculated the strength of feeling of ordinary staff who were fed up with a decade of declining living standards and reductions in public expenditure.

It was one of the gravest political miscalculations in Labour history and an epic failure of leadership.

The Powerful Do What They Can

Matters were made worse by the breakdown of the 5% pay policy in the private sector. The Government had imposed sanctions against Ford Motors because it had reached a settlement with its workers for a 17% pay rise. The Government then lost a House of Commons vote on the sanctions it had imposed on the company for breaching the pay policy, along with 220 other firms. Vauxhall Motors had also agreed an 8.5% rise for its workers.

After the Parliamentary defeat on sanctions, Callaghan had to put down a motion of confidence in his Government which passed by 10 votes but he had to accept that sanctions could never be used, thus depriving the 5% policy of its only leverage in the private sector. The entire weight of pay policy was now focused on the public sector.

The failure of the sanctions policy emboldened key workers with leverage, especially oil tanker drivers in the TGWU. They began an overtime ban in support of a 40% wage rise in October. Eventually the drivers settled for 15%.

In January the following year, all TGWU drivers struck and picketed oil refineries and ports. Eventually they settled for around 20%.

During all this, Prime Minister Callaghan returned from an inter-governmental summit on the French Caribbean island of Guadeloupe and gave remarks to a press conference at Heathrow. The Evening Standard reporter present asked him what his general approach was, given the mounting chaos in the country. Callaghan demurred, saying that in his view that was an exaggeration. Next day the *Sun* newspaper splashed a front page headline: *Crisis? What Crisis?* with a strap line *Rail, lorry, jobs chaos – and Jim blames Press*. It was a distortion of what the Prime Minister had actually said, but the phrase stuck.

And this was before the public sector strikes began.

1.6 Million on Strike

The national Day of Action on January 22nd 1979 marked the beginning of the pay disputes in the public sector.

An estimated 1.6 million workers joined the one-day strike, making it on some measures the most important industrial action since the General Strike of 1926.

There were major demonstrations in London, Belfast, Glasgow and Liverpool and a lobby of Parliament at Westminster. Against NUPE's advice, London ambulance crews decided to strike without providing emergency cover and there were rolling and selective strike actions in many local authorities.

By the end of January, it was estimated that half of all UK hospitals were providing accident and emergency cover only, with almost all elective surgery halted.

The press was apoplectic and on January 29th the Sun described Fisher as 'the Fuhrer leading his shock troops.'

Frank Chapple, General Secretary of the EETPU, described the industrial action as 'terrorism'[103] and followed this up by remarking to Bernard Donoughue that 'most of his (Fisher's) members have never done a single fucking day's work in their lives.'[104]

Estimates put the proportion of NUPE members that had taken some form of industrial action at 90% by the second week of the dispute. By week three, we announced that action would be focusing sharply on the constituencies of Cabinet members, on the basis that the quarrel was with the Government and that ministers needed to see the consequences of their decisions following them right back to their constituencies.

Half a million local council workers were taking some form of action and local deals between the employers and the unions in individual local authorities began to be struck.

Callaghan himself then caused confusion in a speech in Newcastle on 3rd February 1979 in which he repeated his suggestion for a comparability study and hinted that there might be some movement in the offer of 8.8% provided that the final settlement was in single figures.

David Ennals, Secretary of State for Health, interpreted this as a clear signal and negotiations resumed on the Ancillary Staffs Council on the understanding that 9.9% plus the comparability scheme was now on

---

103. *News of the World*, February 18th 1979
104. Quoted in B Donoughue, *The Heat of the Kitchen*, Politicos 2003, page 309

the table.

However, Callaghan announced in the Commons on February 6th that his Newcastle speech had been misinterpreted and that the Government was sticking to 8.8%. Callaghan, Joel Barnett (Chief Secretary to the Treasury) and Peter Shore, the Minister responsible for the local government negotiations then blamed Ennals for going too far.

By this time the water workers – where NUPE had a minority membership – were in the process of settling as their offer had been increased to 15.9% plus extras. This was because they had very significant bargaining power and could have 'turned off the taps' very quickly had they decided to do so. The employers warned that the cost of the settlement would be nationwide redundancies of around 60,000. It did not happen, of course.

Going to the Top

On February 9th the four general secretaries of NUPE, COHSE, GMWU[105] and the TGWU – Fisher, Spanswick, Basnett and Evans – met Callaghan and senior ministers at Downing Street in the presence of TUC officials. The meeting went on for over 11 hours and ended at 2.15am with a marginal improvement above 8.8% and a reiteration of the availability of a comparability study if a settlement could be agreed.

Considerable pressure was being exerted to reach a settlement as the dispute was becoming a significant embarrassment for the Government with a General Election due by October 1979 at the latest. In presenting itself at the election, the Labour Government could no longer claim, as it had said in 1974, to have a special relationship with the trade unions which allowed them to ensure industrial peace in return for concessions on the Social Wage. By this time, it was clear to many that the Social Wage and public expenditure were being sacrificed, and workers were also being asked to agree to wage rises below inflation and a continuation of low pay forever.

This was how it looked.

In early February the press were in full attack mode in response to the behaviour of the GMWU gravediggers in Liverpool who had refused to bury the dead. It turned out later that this group were heavily influenced by the Militant tendency.

---

105. General and Municipal Workers Union

The incident caused the unions to come together regularly at Transport House to approve branch and regional proposals for industrial action in an attempt to control publicity and remove the ability of hotheads to dominate the news agenda. Here was an excellent example of poor leadership as this should have been done from day one.

By this time the national negotiators were in full retreat with Ron Keating, the NUPE local government lead negotiator, saying, 'We have to live with these people afterwards.'

Rodney Bickerstaffe (later General Secretary of NUPE) anxiously called for a special Sunday meeting of the national officer's team to discuss the offer on the table, which he wanted to accept, and get the dispute resolved. Dix was called from extended sick leave to attend but he was furious with Fisher, and his presence at the Sunday meeting made it impossible to get a united front.

Fisher could not impose his will on the team but nevertheless pursued a settlement based on the headline figure of 9% and stated that he would recommend it to his Executive Council, as did Charles Donnet of the GMWU and Mick Martin of the TGWU.

Fisher Fails to Organise, Callaghan Digs In

Fisher was then humiliated by his own organisation. The union's national committees met on the morning of 22nd February and rejected the offer as it did not represent sufficient progress toward the £60 basic rate. In the afternoon the full Executive Council discussed the proposed deal and voted by 26 votes to nil to reject the offers and the advice of their individual national negotiators to accept.

Fisher had misread the determination of the members; had failed to mobilise National Committee and Executive Committee members to support him; and did not instruct his national colleagues to back him. Some were in favour of the offers and some were opposed. He exerted no authority whatsoever.

At this point a split emerged between NUPE and the other unions with the TGWU and GMWU in particular voicing antipathy to their old antagonists in NUPE on the basis that they were grandstanding in order to win more members. This was unfair but wounding. The motives of the NUPE National Committee and Executive Council members were that they believed they were representing the deeply held views of their members, and they were also incensed at the Labour Government's treatment of public sector workers.

Callaghan had supported a 30% rise for top civil servants in June 1978 and had then failed to impose his will on private sector wages in the autumn of the same year. He was left with the need to impose low settlements on the public sector because that was where the levers of power were strongest.

Lay members in NUPE were also concerned that the comparability study could be stymied by the Government in its written instructions to the Commission defining what factors could be taken in to consideration by them and what could not. As it turned out, the instructions were indeed revised when the Conservatives won power and they changed the orders given to the Clegg Commission in June 1979.

This was a gigantic political failure by both Callaghan and Fisher. Elements in the Labour Government (like Bernard Donoughue) believed on the basis of Treasury studies that public sector workers were not underpaid at all but were in fact overpaid.

Callaghan had joined in the press criticism and had supported Peter Shore when he said that the conduct of the dispute posed 'a threat to democratic society.'[106] The Labour Prime Minister had also urged workers to cross picket lines and had described the dispute as 'free collective vandalism.'

Chief Secretary to the Treasury Joel Barnett said in Cabinet on February 1st that 'The NHS auxiliaries are well paid, unskilled people and the trade union leaders have raised the expectations of people on £60 a week, who do not starve, and anyway 50% of their wives are at work.'[107]

Callaghan clearly believed that macho behaviour would carry the day and help win him the forthcoming election. Fisher's failure was more serious in failing to carry his national leadership with him and failing to prepare the ground for an effective comparability study which would have been in the long - term interests of members.

By early 1979 it was the case that NUPE had developed serious criticisms of the Government's economic policy and public expenditure stance, had proposed detailed alternatives, and was seriously dissatisfied with its inability to get to grips with the problem of low pay and this gave coherence to the union's overall position.

In fact, Callaghan had departed not just from recent Labour policy

106. *Daily Mirror* February 2nd 1979
107. Quoted in Tony Benn Diaries page 450 *Conflicts of Interest*, Longmans 1990

but had forgotten (if he ever knew) the pre-1914 Fabian work on low pay and the 1918 Labour Programme written by the Webbs. They were behaving as post-Keynesian, post-Labour politicians, seeking to mobilise the public against inconvenient truths.

Eventually, membership ballots took place in all the unions involved in the dispute. The TGWU voted two-to-one in favour of the proposed settlement. The GMWU announced an 'overwhelming majority' in favour, COHSE ancillary staff voted in favour, and on March 7th NUPE's local government membership voted by 227,591 to 150,455 to accept. Ambulance members had voted to reject, as had COHSE's ambulance crews.

In the NHS therefore, industrial action continued with both NUPE ancillary and ambulance staff taking extensive strike action. But in late March all activity ceased as NUPE found it itself increasingly isolated on the national negotiating committees.

Why This was Pivotal

Fisher's failure to build support for legislative action against low pay was profound. NUPE had few friends in Parliament let alone the Cabinet. The general unions, who had minority memberships in the NHS, did not support the arguments for a minimum wage at that stage. The Labour Government's policy was to offer as little as possible to end the dispute and to be extremely vague about the prospects for future realignment of basic wage rates. But coupled with their abandonment of Keynesianism, cuts in the social wage, and overt hostility to trade unions, they were creating the conditions for confrontation within the Labour Party and paving the way for the Thatcher victory in 1979.

Other policies were available and possible. Callaghan's failure to call an election in the autumn of 1978 when the opportunity arose was disastrous. So was the dismissal of warnings from a broad based group of trade union leaders, the TUC and Cabinet ministers, about the ability to hold the line on the 5% pay policy. Healey admitted this later.

Callaghan and Healey could have called an election, promised serious action on low pay and comparabilities and a study on a national minimum wage – and done this well before the 1978-79 wage negotiations kicked in. They backed down over private sector wage claims and then felt that they had to hold the line against the public sector. It was both illogical and politically inept.

These events were a pivotal moment in Labour history. They led directly to the growth of the Campaign for Labour Party Democracy and detailed demands for constitutional change to redress the balance between the membership and the PLP leadership – and indirectly to the SDP breakaway in the early 1980s. And it was entirely avoidable.

In terms of my own political thought, I had started the decade as a Croslandite and ended it as a radical in the Party I had joined in 1963. I was enraged at the policies of the Government and knew there were alternatives. Callaghan and Healey had in my view attacked Labour's core beliefs and we needed to ensure that their influence was eliminated.

CHAPTER 4

WORKING IN PARLIAMENT AND THE DEVELOPMENT OF THE REBEL ALLIANCE

In May 1979, I was elected as a Member of Parliament for the Wood Green constituency of Haringey, in north London. For the selection in late 1978, I was able to defeat a more right wing candidate, Bryn Jones, and other leftish candidates such as Mike Ward (later GLC Member for Wood Green) and Pat Hewitt, later Secretary of State for Health in the Blair Government.

I was selected to replace the long serving Joyce Butler, who was retiring after 25 years' service as one of the very few women Labour MPs. Little did I know that my tenure as an MP for that constituency was already time limited, as the Boundary Commission had reported that Haringey did not qualify for three MPs and should be reduced to two. Wood Green had been scheduled for abolition as it straddled the top end of Haringey – from deprived north Tottenham to much leafier Alexandra Palace in the West.

It had been a safe Labour seat from its creation in 1950, with varying majorities, but the ineffective and indolent Haringey Council had failed to canvass for the electoral register with the result that many thousands of families who lived in the borough were not on the register at all. Whole roads had hardly anyone registered, who was still there; and this was particularly the case in the more deprived wards in the centre and East of the constituency.

As Haringey was only a couple of thousand voters short of qualifying for three seats under the population requirements of the Boundary

Commission, this was a big deal – especially for my tenure, as it turned out.

The election in May 1979 installed Thatcher as Prime Minister and the long process of financial liberalisation, accelerated destruction of manufacturing industry, and savaging of public services began.

Becoming an MP in this environment gave me opportunities to contribute to the reshaping of a wounded Labour Party with a jaded and discredited leadership.

Getting Started

The Parliamentary Labour Party (PLP) that I entered was very unlike the Parliamentary Party after the General Election of 2019. There were only 11 women Labour MPs, and no black Members. No one had declared themselves to be gay or lesbian despite the law on homosexuality having been liberalised more than a decade before.

The trade union group was still very numerous, with many MPs from the coalfields and Scotland. Many of them said and did very little. Even some new members, such as ex-miner Ray Ellis of North East Derbyshire, were not happy about speaking in the Chamber and felt significantly out of place because of their class background. There was no induction at all, no one told you what to do or where to go, or where things were. It was sink or swim.

The PLP apparatus was also creaking. For most of the period until 1983 there was no London whip because no one would do it.

The only person who was helpful to me was Dennis Skinner. He showed me where the Table Office was located (where you placed questions and motions) and was generally supportive. Dennis was the son of a pit worker in Clay Cross – a grammar school boy with the most vituperative tongue in the Commons.

He was very funny on a good day, but also had the best analytical mind on working class concerns, thought processes, and ambitions. He was part of the last generation of working class leaders to stay in their area and not go off to university.

Younger leaders disappeared from these communities and never came back, with the consequence that less able people were in charge. Places like Derbyshire, especially in the smaller villages, became like the Marie Celeste: most of the talent had gone. It became clear to me later that it was one of the main problems in the old coalfield and industrial areas – the brightest and best largely disappeared, leaving behind the retired and the disengaged.

I joined the Tribune Group, which I quickly identified as a talking shop, and got on with developing my surgeries and a real base of support in Wood Green.

I made myself some rules for dealing with the Palace of Westminster: don't go in the bars, don't go to receptions, get on and do the work, try and be the best informed person on the subject you're dealing with. Perhaps others found me unclubbable or standoffish, but I considered this as a workplace and one where serious work had to be undertaken.

The Parliamentary Conservative Party was at that time a pretty unreconstructed misogynist organisation, stuffed full of knights of the shires and sleek businessmen. I had no idea how bad they were until I was ensconced in Old Palace Yard, in a room on the first floor overlooking the St Stephen's entrance and with the best view of the State Opening.

Downstairs there were a bunch of Tory MPs and their secretaries and this enabled both Mandy[108] and me to observe them at close quarters. Their behaviour to the captive audience of the secretaries was extraordinary. Robert Adley[109] came back from giving dictation to his secretary upstairs and remarked loudly, 'Thank you, that was wonderful!' whilst zipping up his flies.

Keith Best, the surprise Tory victor in Anglesey in 1979, used to come into the secretaries' room and swing on the overhead heating pipes in a show of macho bravado.

His secretary hated this so much that she joined Plaid Cymru whilst working for him. She also kept a folder of compromising photographs in her desk drawer, the most laughable of which showed Best emerging from a de rigueur underground visit to a Welsh coal mine. He was dressed in a bright white and pristine set of coveralls, but with smears of coal dust on his cheeks. He had rubbed his fingers in the dust and plonked them on his chops. The separate finger marks were clearly visible.

This Parliamentary Conservative Party had equally large problems as the PLP.

---

108. Mandy Moore, my secretary, who had previously worked for Joyce Butler and had been a staffer at Transport House, working for Harold Wilson and the Labour Party's National Campaign Committee.
109. MP for Christchurch, 1974-93

The Patch

My predecessor Joyce Butler had been very helpful before the election and had worked hard for the borough as the MP and as a councillor and Mayor. I was determined to play an effective role as the last line of defence for residents and set about publicising my new weekly open access surgeries.

It was soon clear that there was huge pent-up demand: between 30 and 50 families usually turned up each Friday and the volume of casework quickly became enormous. It was mainly on immigration, housing and social security.

Many of those who showed up were desperate and we were there until midnight on occasion having started at 7pm. Some had been to see councillors who did little or nothing. Many had been pushed away by bureaucrats intent on doing as little work as possible and determined not to exercise what discretion they had.

Working out who to contact, which strings to pull, who was an empty shirt and who was helpful, took time. What quickly became very clear was that Haringey Council was a major problem. The Social Services department refused to answer letters at all, and the Housing department was little better.

On one very wet and cold Friday evening a chap turned up from the Noel Park estate claiming that the council owned flat above him had burnt out, the roof was off, and that large amounts of rainwater were streaming through his ceilings destroying everything he owned.

As I had been given an out-of-hours emergency phone number, I thought I'd give it a go in these exceptional circumstances. I called. The phone rang and rang. After a long time, a voice answered. It turned out that the emergency phone number was a public telephone box outside the house of a foreman at one of the housing depots. I asked politely whether a tarpaulin could be found to protect the council's own property – but the answer was that they didn't have any (a lie) and that anyway it was raining and that nothing could be done.

Later, in the mid-1980s, under Bernie Grant's leadership of the council, there were multiple examples of loopiness such as the decision to erect grass huts, designed as West African conical homes with a thatched straw roof, at public expense in a park in central Tottenham.

Bernie's justification was that people should be reminded of their heritage. The locals, in an entirely predictable move, thought it would be interesting to burn them down, so they did.

Under Bernie's leadership there were also plans to turn the old Tottenham Town Hall into a leisure centre, with no parking facilities. Everyone should come by public transport, they said. This in one of the most congested parts of the borough – narrow roads, double and sometimes triple parking. It was utterly off the wall.

The underlying problem was that inadequate councillors tended to do inadequate things and recruit inadequate officers. Good officers didn't want to work there, and so a death spiral of incompetence and sleaze gradually overwhelmed public provision in what was one of the most needy areas in the country. Reports reach me that the situation has not improved.

It all started with poorly informed Labour members selecting poorly qualified local Council candidates who didn't know what they were doing but who were good at posturing. These highlights in Haringey were my first experiences of the rash, foolish, incompetent, don't-care, sod-the-clients attitude that much of the public services had at the time. It was a real eye opener, and it wasn't the last.

The education service was another morass, helped along by the local NUT branch, strongly influenced at the time by the Communist Party. At one point, Northumberland Park School (where the children were substantially from ethnic minorities) held a fashion show. We went along to show support, as did hundreds of parents, and some of the show was mainstream. But we were utterly amazed at other events on stage.

The girls were described as 'models', the boys as 'escorts'. The black boys were breakdancing, and that was it. The black girls were dressed in cami knickers and bras, short skirts, suspenders and stockings. Male teachers on stage were pretending to kiss girls and the white teachers were portrayed as dominant white males involved with less powerful stereotyped black women. It was truly appalling.

Mandy, who was a school Governor there, heckled the performance and the local NUT branch then passed a motion of censure on her. However, the school had made one serious mistake: they had filmed the proceedings and were offering videos for sale. Mandy alerted the Council's Women's Committee to the outrage and they went ballistic after seeing the video. The school pushed back but then apologised. This was the kind of posturing nonsense that was going on in Tottenham in the 1980s with the radical teacher's defence of their actions being 'that's what they want to do' – with 'they' being the girls and black kids.

Perhaps these luminaries of the left could have been teaching their pupils about the achievements of women and black people in science, politics and the arts, giving a lead to their very young teenage students rather than adding to the racial and gender stereotyping of impressionable kids.

There were also running battles between myself, the council and the social security authorities which led to many victories. I didn't do what other MPs did and just send correspondence off to the bigwigs, with a printed slip attached (helpfully provided by the House of Commons authorities) asking the relevant person to send a reply back to the MP who would then pass it back to the constituent without any real work having been done on the case at all.

Some of my neighbouring MPs (like Norman Atkinson) did this and also refused to deal with local authority cases as they were the job of the local councillors, it was argued. That was, of course, a recipe for nothing being done and the cause of much disillusionment amongst the multitudinous ranks of the put-upon.

Apart from its incompetence and slowness on cases involving individual residents, the council also possessed a mutinous and unmanaged workforce. Some of them had decided that the best way to get through the week was to do as little work as possible.

Major housing developments contracted to the DLO (Direct Labour Organisation) were years behind schedule with poor quality finish and many snags. Refuse collection and street sweeping were extremely poor.

As one example, a young street sweeper and NUPE member approached me to intervene in his case. He had been disciplined and sacked, eventually, by the council. He had been noticed hiding his cart in the bushes on Scotland Green and then going in the pub each day till he had to take the cart back to the depot.

His patch was Tottenham High Road, one of the dirtiest places in the constituency, where you had to wade through rubbish when you got off the train at Bruce Grove. He expected me to wave a magic wand, instruct the council to reinstate him, and ignore the circumstances of his drunken indolence. I didn't do as he asked.

The council's 'wild west' approach to the delivery of public services was in stark contrast to well-run boroughs like Lewisham that had far fewer problems of this kind. Some local authorities have traditions of good service, and some don't.

The very worst example of poor decision-making came after the

Alexandra Palace fire of 1980 when large parts of the iconic structure were heavily damaged by a massive blaze that challenged the ingenuity of the London Fire Brigade. Just months earlier, the Palace had been transferred to the control of Haringey Council from the GLC, and the council approached me to sponsor a Private Member's Bill in the Commons to give them the additional powers they said they needed to renovate the building after the fire. Their key pitch was a promise that the ratepayers of Haringey – who were now the sole payers of last resort rather than the ratepayers of London as a whole – would not fork out a penny for the restoration and that running the vast building would 'cost the ratepayers nothing'.

I did not believe this. By that time, I did not believe that Haringey could run a whelk stall let alone a renovation of that size and complexity, or run it efficiently going forward, so I refused to introduce the Bill, based as it was on a false premise.

Years later, it transpired that the council had overspent on the renovation to the tune of £30m and they continued to make losses each year on the charitable events held there. Even now, they are trying hard to overcome the impossibility of managing such an enormous structure, a genuine white elephant if there ever was one, on the back of a restricted council taxpayer base.

To be fair to Haringey, these were the days before the quality of public service (rather than its volume) had taken hold as a concept in the local authority community, or indeed in most taxpayer funded services.

Only a few local councils had begun the process of managing their services effectively and there was little incentive for them to do so as – until the late 1980s – the more money they spent, the more money they received in grant.

Prudent authorities that controlled their budgets were penalised by the 'grant recycling' policy and almost no one was inspected or regulated. There was no national inspection regime for the NHS and the Audit Commission for local authorities, good organisation that it was, had few teeth and restricted itself to audits of the accounts and the publication of bulky think pieces on pressing aspects of national policy and practice.

Haringey was in very bad company and some of the worst council offenders were in London. I later discovered that in the 1980s neighbouring Hackney had lost a million bricks from its Direct Labour Organisation depots. And the notoriety of Lambeth was well deserved – rating for large amounts and then not spending it.

Social tension was also high in Haringey, with serious friction between the police and the many ethnic minority communities. One Saturday I took the family to the Wood Green Shopping City, and walked out on to the pavement to cross the road.

Down the pavement came two black boys aged about 13, quietly chatting to each other, walking slowly, followed by two policemen. They stopped the boys, threw them against the wall, and proceeded to pat them down roughly. I was shocked and approached, saying, 'What are you at? These boys are doing nothing!'

One of the coppers turned to me and said in the most insolent way possible, 'And who are you, sir?', dragging out the 'sir' to make it clear that he thought I wasn't really a sir at all.

I said I was their local Member of Parliament, and I'd be obliged if they could stop what they were doing and let the boys go.

'Have you got any identification, sir?' asked the coppers, with renewed and even greater insolent emphasis on the 'sir.' Luckily, I did: my House of Commons identification card was in my pocket, so it was produced and that changed the tone somewhat.

One of the boys said, 'What do you think you're doing? They'll arrest you!' They didn't, of course, and justified their actions by saying 'We've had complaints.' This was clearly ludicrous and I told them so. It was a generic fishing expedition against the nearest black people they could find who wouldn't put up a fight.

Eventually the boys left, and went on their way. A lucky escape for them on that occasion, but it exemplified precisely the tension that existed between black people and the police.

Community tensions were extraordinarily high and continue to be so, and the Brixton and Wood Green riots were to follow. The police have an important job to do, and they need our support, but in the 1980s they were acting in a way that magnified tensions rather than reducing them. That was Haringey.

The PLP

It was soon clear from close observation that the quality of Labour MPs was highly variable. I was not naïve about the way they operated, but I was still shocked at what seemed the poor work rate, lack of attention to detail, drunkenness, and failure to perform many elements of the job. Of course, this described a minority, but it set an undesirable tone.

The drunkenness was a real problem. Extreme cases abounded, such as Gordon Oakes[110] who was so drunk during one budget debate that we had to carry him physically through the division lobby and past the clerks, saying his name for him as he could not.

And poor old Ray Ellis (MP for North East Derbyshire) who was nervous of speaking absconded from a committee on a 1981 Social Security Bill in the middle of the night. We were pulling long speeches and working in shifts to make the Government guillotine the bill, and hence gain publicity for its odious provisions. Ray just disappeared, and in a 2am tea break we searched and eventually found him sprawled unconscious on the floor of one of the Members' toilets surrounded by a very large number of House of Commons whisky miniatures.

Extreme drinking was rife. The 16 bars and restaurants still provide to this day endless opportunities for those who want to bunk off real work and the atmosphere in the 1980s has best been described in his diaries by Alan Clark.[111]

In later times, this was followed up by a British Medical Journal and report of 2016[112] based on a survey of MPs, which discovered that binge drinking (defined as having more than 6 units of alcohol in one session) was more common amongst legislators than amongst the general public.

The key finding was that MPs were more likely to drink riskily and down the equivalent of a bottle of wine or more in one session than others. Also, that two thirds of the respondents had not been aware of the support services given by the Parliamentary Health and Wellbeing Service which included advice on reducing alcohol consumption.

It is clear that the place is still a mess and that the toleration of drinking at work is continuing. Everyone knows who frequents the Strangers Bar on a daily basis and who are inebriated most of the time on the taxpayers' pound. The problem with alcohol in the Commons is not about opposing social drinking: it is about not drinking in a workplace when important Parliamentary tasks have to be done.

The attitude of sections of the PLP did not just stem from some having a cavalier attitude to constituents and erratic attention to casework, but also indolence in developing policy, a failure to do proper Parliamentary

---

110. MP for Bolton West 1964-70 and Widnes (later Halton) 1971-1997
111. MP for Plymouth Sutton 1974-92 and later Kensington and Chelsea 1997-99, *Alan Clark Diaries*, Weidenfeld and Nicolson, 1993, see pages 28-32
112. Published in 2020

work in committees and on the floor of the House, and a craven attitude where doing nothing was regarded as an inherently brilliant strategy.

The two-party system and the existence of a large number of very safe seats at that time induced a comatose response to work from some Labour MPs and paved the way for the extensive cull of Scottish Labour MPs in 2015 and Northern and Midlands MPs in 2019.

But it would be wrong to characterise the PLP of the day as a hopeless case: the 1979 intake to the PLP contained bright, sensible and energetic people too – Frank Field, Jack Straw, Stuart Holland, Frank Dobson, and many more – but the collective deadweight of the PLP was depressing. Many of the longstanding MPs were, of course, hostile to the idea of the Party being democratised in any way and they were forcefully committed to the policies of the last Labour Government, which had been defeated in disgrace.

However, some of them were not like this and argued vociferously against the leadership when occasion arose – people such as Willie Hamilton and Laurie Pavitt were fully engaged and determined. However, the culture had not changed much since the 1950s and even the 'old left' – people like Stan Orme[113] – were very hostile to change and thought that all the important battles had been won. Stan was vociferous in arguing that 'you don't know how lucky you are' because there was now a telephone on every Member's desk. That hadn't been the case in the 1960s.

Many of them also looked down on any new policy areas such as women's rights and the minimum wage, and they pooh-poohed attempts by more radical elements to raise them. They were riding for a fall, but this was not a question of personal failures leading to poor performance. There were more fundamental forces at work.

There was also the way in which the PLP leadership looked askance at anything remotely radical. At one meeting of the Parliamentary Party in Committee Room 14, we were earnestly requested by the platform not to attend the picket outside South Africa House, organised by the City of London Anti-apartheid Group, the purpose of which was to increase pressure to get Nelson Mandela and his fellow political prisoners out of gaol.

113. MP for Salford West 1964-83 and Salford East 1983-97 and a former Cabinet minister. A Daily Telegraph investigation based on papers from the Czech intelligence services in December 2019 revealed that Orme had been a close contact of Czech intelligence agents in the 1960s, who wined and dined him and gave gifts of brandy and cigars in return for information on the policies of the Labour Government.

Despite the fact that South Africa was still ruled by a white minority government under an overtly racist Constitution, here was the leadership of the PLP urging Labour MPs not to support opposition to it. The real reason was that the City of London Anti-Apartheid group was disliked by the South African Communist Party, who hated the people who ran it – Dave Kitson's family especially his wife Norma – who were regarded as extremists by the CP. That was enough for the PLP top table to request that Labour MPs refused to attend. I took no notice, and neither did a number of colleagues.

I went several times and you were often given a placard to hang round the neck stating which political prisoner you were supporting that day. On one occasion I was given the name of Ahmed Kathrada[114] but the funniest incident on the picket occurred when Lord Gifford QC, an eminent lawyer and Labour Peer, was in the process of being manhandled and arrested for some minor alleged infringement. One of the radical protestors shouted: 'You can't arrest him! He's a Peer of the realm!' demonstrating that the left were willing to use name dropping when it suited them. The police took little notice.

The real eye opener was that the leadership of the Party was more interested in bending to the will of the South African Communist Party than they were to advancing the case for majority rule in the most racist State in the world at the time. Extraordinary.

Elitism and Control

By 1979 there were clear signs in the Labour Party that all was not well with the relationship between the Party in the constituencies and the Parliamentary Party. The praetorian guard of Deakin, Williamson and Lawther as the trade union barons protecting the Parliamentary leadership was long gone.

This close defensive relationship had been challenged by the Cousins leadership of the TGWU in the late 1950s, and later by the election of Hugh Scanlon as President of the AUEW and Jack Jones as General Secretary of the TGWU in the mid 1960s. The growth of smaller more

---

114. Ahmed Kathrada was one of the ANC leadership accused in the Rivonia Trial, where Mandela and nine others including Kathrada were sentenced to imprisonment on Robben Island. Kathrada was later elected as an MP and became a Parliamentary adviser to President Mandela, dying in March 2020.

radical unions such as NUPE had also diluted the loyalist trade union block vote.

But it was the performance of the 1974-79 Labour Government that radicalised sections of the Party membership and illuminated the gap between promise and performance.

The Wilson administration had been elected on a promise of a social contract with the trade unions, and of a 'fundamental and irreversible shift in the balance of power and wealth in favour of working people and their families.' This was to include the creation of a powerful National Enterprise Board, compulsory planning agreements with large companies, and the expansion of the public services.

It became clear by 1976 that none of this was happening and that, *au contraire*, public expenditure was being repeatedly cut because the Government had adopted a neo-monetarist policy.

The Campaign for Labour Party Democracy

The response to this, tentatively at first but growing in strength with the passage of time, was the creation of the Campaign for Labour Party Democracy (CLPD), one of the most influential rank and file organisations ever seen in the Labour Party.

There had in fact been an earlier revolt against the leadership by constituency Labour Parties in the 1930s as there was no direct representation on the National Executive Committee for them, and there was a considerable agitation by many Divisional Labour Parties (as they were called then) which in the end resulted in the national Party creating a separate section in which DLPs could elect their own representatives to the NEC.

This came about because Hugh Dalton, then Chair of the NEC, became convinced that an accommodation was necessary with the powerful arguments for change that had been advanced by scores of DLPs.[115]

After considerable opposition from the trade unions had been overcome, partly with the assistance of the TGWU block vote, the 1937 Party Conference adopted a series of proposals which established a separately elected constituency Party section of seven seats – which were duly filled in the first elections by five public school boys (one Eton, one Winchester), two university dons and two rich lawyers. Only two of the new NEC members were working class and only one lived outside London.

115. Ben Pimlott, *Labour and the Left in the 1930s*, Cambridge University Press

However, the revolt succeeded.

But paradoxically the new arrangements increased the dominance of the Parliamentary Party on the NEC and injected new talent. The leaders of the Constituency Parties Movement succeeded because they had carefully limited their demands to simple objectives which were supported by a substantial majority of 'fundamentally loyal constituency activists,' as Pimlott argues.

Revolts and Structural Change

During and after the Attlee Government, the Bevanite rebellions of the early 1950s had created fleetingly important, MP-led organisations which did not have a permanent life and which spluttered out when the key individuals in them (especially Bevan himself) accommodated themselves to the leadership of the day.

The original rebellious organisation was the Keep Left Group, working between 1947 and 1950 which concentrated on policy and the creation of a programme for the next Labour Government. Ian Mikardo (then MP for Reading) became secretary and it was advised by several top economists such as David Worswick, Tommy Balogh, and Dudley Seers.

The group's output was extensive, including papers on decontrol in Germany, the State and private enterprise, aircraft manufacturing, and inflation rates for the poorest.[116] It was concerned with medium term political issues rather than the day-to-day business of the House of Commons and was different from the Bevanite and Tribune Group in this respect.

It did not, however, calculate at the time that the structural relationships between the rank and file Party and the leadership and PLP needed to be changed.

There had been some disappointment with the legacy of the Attlee Government, especially on foreign affairs, and there were subsequent rows about the direction of travel on issues such as nationalisation. But there was justifiable pride in the achievements of the 1945-51 administration and no desire to make radical changes.

Keep Left was strengthened substantially after the resignations of Bevan, Wilson and Freeman from the Government in 1951 and had

---

116. See Ian Mikardo, *Backbencher*, Weidenfeld and Nicolson 1988, page 119, for a description of the Keep Left Group's activities

attracted 47 MPs and two peers as group members. The group became, in practice, the Bevanites, and began publication of pamphlets which had a wide circulation amongst Party members.

Later, there were Tribune Brains Trusts, the name plagiarised from the BBC Brains Trust broadcast on the Home Service. They had a significant influence on Party opinion and were partly responsible for the larger number of left wing MPs elected to the NEC in the constituency section in the mid 1950s.

But, despite the influence of the right on the NEC and in the Party leadership, there was no campaign by the left to change the constitutional arrangements of the Party to make it more responsive to rank and file opinion. They sought to influence rather than change the rules.

CLPD, the Original Form

The creation of the Campaign for Labour Party Democracy in 1973 followed public statements by Wilson and Healey before the elections of 1974 that certain parts of Labour's programme 1973 could not be supported, despite endorsement by the NEC. The leading lights in the new campaign were Vladimir and Vera Derer, and they began to collect significant support from the trade unions and constituency Parties. It is common journalistic habit to ascribe CLPD's existence, growth and victories to Tony Benn. The truth is that he had little to do with it until it became a force in the land, and was never involved directly in its internal discussions. He was lobbied of course, as an important member of the NEC, but was not influential in determining the track of the organisation's development. A more significant influence associated with him was Frances Morrell, (Benn's political adviser in the 1970s) who became a leading figure in CLPD, especially at Party Conference, but it was always unclear whether she was an independent figure or whether she was doing Benn's bidding. I incline to the view that she was independent, and she did not always agree with Benn's positions.

The early aims of the campaign had been predicated on the assumption that it would be possible to get the NEC to do this job – to report back quarterly to the Party as a whole, to open up NEC meetings to observers from Constituency Labour Parties (CLPs), to extend consultation with CLPs, and to 'carry out fully its responsibility as custodian of Conference decisions.'

There was in the early days in 1973 no set of demands calling for the election of the leader by a wider franchise, or indeed for the widespread deselection of MPs. It has also to be remembered that annual Conference was, in effect, controlled by the block votes of the large trade unions and that CLPs had relatively little power – so getting the NEC to abide by Conference decisions was in almost all cases a policy which was in the hands of the general secretaries of the big unions. If they wanted to insist on compliance, they could – but much of the time they wanted to fudge it.

In the final stage of CLPD's development, the demands were simple, and they were all focused on constitutional changes to embed decision making on a wider franchise than before. The three main specifics were that

1. The Leader and Deputy Leader should be elected by the Party as a whole and not just by the PLP, which was the case at the time.

2. The agreement of the Party manifesto for a general election be under the control of the NEC rather than the leader (despite the fig leaf of the 'Clause 5' meeting of the NEC).

3. All Labour Members of Parliament be subject to a mandatory reselection process.

One of the contributory factors assisting the agitation was that in the 1974-79 Parliaments there had been several examples of bizarre behaviour by Labour MPs.

There was the disappearance of John Stonehouse, after he had cleared out the whole of his Parliamentary allowance by walking into the Fees Office and demanding it (he later turned up in Australia).

There was the long running battle between the Newham North East Constituency Party and their MP Reg Prentice, resulting in his deselection under the old rules and his subsequent defection to the Tories. There was also, of course, the public rejection of elements of the Party's own programme and its manifesto by the Prime Minister; and the implementation of a monetarist economic programme involving heavy restrictions on wage settlements, especially in the public sector, and of course multiple packages of cuts in public spending, in direct contravention of manifesto promises.

As a matter of fact, there had always been provision under the Party rules to remove an MP who was not fundamentally doing their job, but it had been used very infrequently and local Party members were understandably and quite rightly reluctant to use a nuclear option against their own sitting MP, with whom ties of sentiment and relationship had normally been developed.

The idea of mandatory reselection was, at the time, NOT to remove scores of MPs but to make them all accountable through a rules-based process for the work rate, broad positions, and actions they had taken.

Fundamentally, CLPD was committed to ensure that 'decisions reached by annual Conference should be binding on the Parliamentary Labour Party,' and it undertook to 'secure the implementation of this principle.'[117] If anyone doubts the separation of the leadership from Manifesto commitments, a close examination of Benn's diaries should be undertaken. At the Industrial Development Committee of Cabinet on 9th July 1974 Callaghan is quoted as saying: 'You can't write a Manifesto for the Party in opposition and expect it to have any relationship to what the Party does in Government. We're now free to do exactly what we like'. This was a very different attitude to that of Attlee, who had significant respect for the detail of the Party's programme.

Open Revolt for the First Time

By the end of the 1970s the rank and file of the Party was in open revolt against the leadership and specific proposals had been developed to ensure mandatory reselection, the election of the leader, and control of the manifesto by the NEC as distinct from the party leadership.

I became involved with CLPD when in the mid-1970s they sent a round robin letter to all the general secretaries of affiliated trade unions, inviting them to affiliate to CLPD.

All political material of this kind crossed my desk, and I asked Alan Fisher if I should go on behalf of the union. I was allowed to do so and turned up to an Executive meeting in the basement of the Fabian Society offices in Dartmouth Street. It was clear that these were serious people and not ultra-leftists (whom I already distrusted) so I recommended to the union's Executive that we should affiliate, and they agreed.

That started a political relationship which continued for me until the

117. CLPD Constitution, Appendix 1, Statement of Aims, June 1973

early 1980s. I was very clear that the democratisation of the Party was linked to the urgent need to defeat monetarism and the extensive attacks on the social wage which were in progress arising from the Thatcher victory. In the CLPD newsletter[118] I wrote:

The Tory Government's economic policy is nothing less than a strategy to replace a mixed economy by a market economy, and to reduce the bargaining power of organised labour. Their weapon is monetarism. Monetarism in practice means an overvalued exchange rate, huge attacks on the social wage based on savage cuts in the social spending planned by Labour, increases in unemployment in the coming year of over 400,000; a substantial decline in investment; negative economic growth (despite increased returns from North Sea Oil); and, as the Tories impose their policy of labour legislation, intimidation, cash limits increases below the rate of inflation, and reduced real wages for working people.

For me and many others the task facing sensible radicals was a holy Trinity:

- Change the leadership to a more responsive one.

- Ensure that democracy was much stronger in the Party.

- Change the policies to take account of the Thatcher revolution underway and the changed situation in the economy.

We were not extremists or ultra-left Trotskyists. We were mainstream Labour people reacting to the most abject failure of Labourism in the history of the Party, and the whole strategy was designed to achieve one thing: a greater chance of Labour being elected.

The Party could not go on as it had been: constant cuts packages, constant wage restraint for over a decade, vilification of new ideas, and a leadership that was the diametric opposite of what was required.

Things had to change and quickly.

By the 1979, Party Conference – my first as an MP – CLPD had organised two immense victories and had come close to getting a third over the line.

Mandatory reselection and NEC control over the manifesto had been approved by the 1979 Conference in principle, but the proposal to elect the leader by a franchise wider than the PLP had been narrowly defeated. The AUEW delegation's vote was hijacked by the President's casting vote.

118. May-June 1980, edition 19

With a total of 1.483 million members, President Terry Duffy's vote was critical, and he cast it against his union's own policy. The resolution to elect the leader on a broader franchise was lost narrowly.

By this time the NEC had agreed to establish a Commission of Enquiry, at the behest of the unions and a clear attempt to derail the democratisation movement. It was to look into the issues of democracy and accountability.

Subsequently, a Special Party Conference was held in January 1981 which eventually agreed that the leader and deputy leader should be elected on a wider franchise with the trade unions casting 40% of the votes available, and the constituency parties and MPs wielding 30% each.

This compromise was cooked up at the last minute by the NUPE delegation in conjunction with CLPD because the other options had attracted objections from some parts of the trade unions and would not pass the Special Conference votes.

The 40-30-30 proposal did pass, and what followed was the extended scrap of the deputy leadership election under these new rules, preceded by elements of the SDP breakaway in March 1981.

Special Conference: the Irony of Victory

The great irony of the Special Conference decision was not that it was a victory for the left, which some in the social democratic wing of the PLP thought it was, but that it actually ensured the victory of the right in the battle for the deputy leadership that was about to take place.

When the votes were tallied in the deputy leadership contest, it transpired that Tony Benn would have won the contest if it had been under the third-a-third-a-third rule which some had favoured. Benn received 81.1% of the vote from constituency Parties after John Silkin had been eliminated, but only 34.1% of the PLP vote and 37.5% of the affiliated votes (trade unions and socialist societies).

Healey squeaked in by 0.8% and won by 50.4% to 49.6% of the combined vote.

The other great irony of Healey's victory was that it was in some ways accidental. Both Benn and I had been hospitalised for considerable periods during the campaign – Benn with Guillain/Barre syndrome (a disease of the immune system causing muscle weakness) and myself because my retinas had become detached and I had to have them glued back, lasered shut and hammered into place (three times because they kept getting it wrong). I was out for over six weeks and had multiple operations over the period and felt like a dishrag when I came out of Moorfields.

This was relevant because I was the national Chair of the Rank and File Mobilising Committee, which tried to coordinate very diverse strands of opinion in support of Benn.

In particular, Tony's absence meant he could not speak at meetings and I was not available to control the more extreme elements of the left. It was also impossible for me, because of being hospitalised for three months, to support the campaign inside my own union. The NUPE Executive had decided, on advice from the national officials, to make no recommendation to the membership as between Benn and Healey, and to organise a branch ballot to test feelings amongst the membership.

Balloting was fine, but the absence of any leadership from the top meant that it was pretty inevitable that Healey would win the vote, which he duly did by a small margin. A few branches voting the other way would have clinched it for Benn but the irony was that NUPE had decided to vote for the personification of everything it had opposed during the 1970s.

I had a last go at Party Conference in the union delegation before voting took place, when I argued that the ballot result was only indicative (which it was), that the delegation could decide to do what it liked – and that given our collective experiences of Mr Healey, it could be argued that we should abstain or vote for Benn.

This line of argument, a thin one to be sure, was rubbished by Bickerstaffe at the meeting and the delegation decided to vote for Healey as the branches had indicated. So, NUPE voted for its arch enemy in the ballot and helped to ensure his victory.

However, there were other factors at work: some Labour MPs (13 in total) who voted for Healey in the ballot had delayed their defection to the SDP in order to do this, and they said so afterwards. Also, the soft left plan to get a third name on to the ballot paper resulted, after much discussion, in John Silkin standing and peeling off some MPs and critically the block vote of the TGWU in the first ballot. He knew he had no chance of winning but it was essential for Benn to be defeated, it was believed.

This candidature was based on a quite genuine personal dislike that had built up between Benn and other key figures in the PLP: they distrusted him, thought he was a vote loser, and distrusted his economic and political analysis.

It was always true that Benn's arguments for democracy were stronger than his concept of socialism and he had not fostered good relations between himself and other leading figures in the Government. He could also be acerbic and difficult depending on his mood.

A combination of all these factors – Benn's personal unpopularity, the NUPE defection, and the delayed defection of some Labour MPs to the SDP, all combined to ensure Healey's victory. Benn was, in fact, the ultimate Marmite candidate.

Slow Motion Train Wreck

Looking back at the events of the late 1970s and early 1980s in the Labour Party is like replaying a slow and avoidable train wreck. The Labour Government had lost the confidence of wide sections of the Party and the trade unions because of its espousal of policies diametrically the opposite of its 1974 manifesto commitments. This was not the usual and sometimes necessary pragmatic trimming round the edges. It was total reversal.

In addition, the leadership had met a significant obstacle in that new generations of active individuals had come through. There is something in the argument that these represented the growing part of the population that had been through university and were now occupying the research and intelligence jobs in the trade unions, charities and public sector that were growing rapidly in numbers.

These individuals – I suppose including myself – were not prepared to be foot soldiers for an out-of-touch leadership. The policy choices made by the leadership in Government had been disastrous as they alienated swathes of the population and provoked responses which had never been seen previously – a challenge to the constitutional framework of the Party.

And finally, personal relations within the PLP leadership group had broken down and there was bad blood between individuals and groups in a way that had only existed previously in 1931 and in the early 1950s.

Ultimately, Prime Ministers Wilson and Callaghan had failed to keep the show on the road. In Wilson's case because of steeply declining personal powers linked to the development of dementia, and in Callaghan's case because he became convinced of the case for a monetarist policy close to Healey's.

The left are not immune from criticism either: Benn had failed to carry people with him on the Alternative Economic Strategy and had failed to explain how it would work effectively.

But it is absurd to argue that the crisis came because of mass infiltration of Trotskyists and especially those from the Militant tendency. Some, like Ann Carlton (former Local Government Officer of the Party), drawing parallels between 1981 and 2016, have said that antisemitism was a factor in the revolt against the Party establishment and have blamed the extensive infiltration of Militant for the difficulties the leadership faced.[119] This is wild exaggeration.

Militant was strictly confined to Merseyside along with a few individual constituencies elsewhere and to the Young Socialists. They were not a dominant force at all, were regarded as figures of fun, and could be easily contained.

The trouble was that all those opposed to the leadership's policies were regarded as Trots with no distinction made between them. On the issues of constitutional democracy, Militant played almost no part and were sidelined precisely because the sensible forces in CLPD, who wanted a limited focus campaign, were firmly in the ascendant and very well organised.

Militant's influence was greatly exaggerated and Trotskyist groups in general only thrived when campaigning organisations slid towards irrelevance. That is when they were most vulnerable to takeover and when the ultra-left saw chances to build larger than normal factions. And antisemitism, as far as I can recall, never featured at all in the discussions of 1981 or in the campaign to make constitutional changes stick.

Perhaps the most considered academic analysis of the issues is that by Lewis Minkin[120] who argued that:

[The leadership's] position is being questioned to an extent undreamed of under Gaitskell and Wilson. Their union allies have so far been unable to mount a successful defensive operation. And their continuing disregard for Conference decisions has provoked a powerful reaction – stronger even than that which followed the defeat of 1970. They face a major reassertion of the right of the Party outside the House of Commons to formulate the Party's policy and a mounting tide of demands for more accountability ... it is a reaction which is fed by a belief now widespread within the Party – that the

---

119. *New Statesman*, 10th August 2016
120. *The Labour Party Conference*, Manchester University Press 1978, page 367

gulf between the policies proposed by the Conference and the policies pursued by the Parliamentary leadership must be closed.

No One in Charge

The trouble was that in 1979 there was no one to get it sorted.

The Callaghan leadership was thoroughly discredited and the Foot leadership that replaced it simply did not engage with the forces that were trying to achieve policy change and constitutional reform. They didn't speak to us, did not engage with individuals or organisations, and utterly failed in their leadership roles. You can't build a team if you don't engage with the people in front of you.

Earlier, whilst Wilson was still Prime Minister, he had a tetchy, difficult and distant relationship with Transport House and the Party generally. An outstanding piece of evidence on this was that after the October 1974 General Election, Wilson did not thank the Party's staff for their efforts and had to be strong armed by his press secretary, Joe Haines, into having a cursory meeting with them at No. 10. No drinks or nibbles were served.

In addition, big chunks of the PLP were inherently hostile to change and objected most strongly to the prospect of a reselection process which was always going to have marginal effects – as most constituency Parties would not have wanted to deselect their MP unless they were wildly objectionable or indolent.

As evidence of this we had a discussion in Lewisham West (where I lived in the late 1970s) about our MP Chris Price, who had voted for many of the cuts packages imposed. However, we felt collectively that he was on balance a good MP, did listen to people, and that the effort and confrontation of reselection was not worth it in his case.

But many of the PLP wanted to have jobs for life, the ability to ignore Conference decisions when they wanted to, and to sail along as if the crisis of the 1970s had never happened. Their ability to accept and adapt to change was miniscule. This was in great contrast to the most successful political party in the western world, the Conservative Party, always ready to adapt itself to new conditions when need arose.

The real story of the Labour Party in the 1970s was the creation of a new alliance between elements of the trade unions and the pluralistic and democratic forces which had developed a greater degree of power than ever before when Labour was moving from Government to opposition and back again.

The 'recurrent tendency towards Parliamentary elitism'[121] was mitigated by the development of the most powerful grassroots campaign in Labour history, more powerful because of its broad democratic appeal, which reinforced the controls on the untrammelled power of the Parliamentary leadership protected by its trade union praetorian guard.

This set of controls limited the leadership's ability to determine the policy formation process, control of the Conference and its agenda, and the selection of Parliamentary candidates.

The Absent Issue

The tragedy was that no one at the time thought in terms of improving the quality of the PLP and of local councils and what would need to be done to achieve those ends.

The only end that mattered for the leadership was the triumph of its group – and similar motivations drove the sects and the ultra-left. They thought of the Labour Party as a means to grow a larger factional base and, in the end, to change the Party from a pure electoralist approach to one which adopted elements of Trotsky's 'transitional programme'.[122]

The later failure of the Parliamentary leadership between 2010 and 2019 was based on this. The Corbyn project at that point tested a version of the transitional programme to destruction.

For me the period between 1979 and 1983, when my constituency was abolished by the Boundary Commission, was one of frustration. Great changes had been agreed and then sidelined. The Benn deputy leadership campaign had been decisively defeated and there was no appetite by him to continue at that point.[123]

The great democratic campaign started by CLPD became over time increasingly captured by the ultra-left and transformed into a caricature

---

121. Minkin, op. cit., page 335
122. See L Trotsky, *The Death Agony of Capitalism and the Tasks of the Fourth International*, translated by M Eastman 1973
123. He changed his mind later when recklessly challenging Kinnock for the leadership in 1988. He consulted everyone in sight, everyone said 'don't do it as it will lead to humiliation,' but he did it anyway.

of itself. It was not obvious to whom sensible radicals could turn at national level to perform leadership roles. And, perhaps worst of all, it became clear that the new leadership of the Party after 1983 could not, or did not, wish to distinguish between the hard core ultra-left and those sensible radicals who were not connected with factions.

The year 1982 was pivotal in the defeat of the constitutional changes. I observed earlier in an article I wrote for *Mobilise for Labour Democracy*, the newsletter of the Rank and File Mobilising Committee[124] that elements of the PLP simply wanted to veto any changes at all.

I gave as an example a speech made by a right wing MP at a weekly PLP meeting in which it was said that constituency Parties in the south of England that had never had a Labour MP or a majority Labour council should not be allowed to pass resolutions criticising the PLP or advocate constitutional changes.

For much of the Parliamentary Party, it was as if the policy failures of the 1970s had not happened.

The PLP was dripping with hate and there were plots afoot to marginalise and remove individuals if they didn't play ball with the do-nothings. The favourite tricks were to insert you on multiple standing committees on bills and multiple committees dealing with obscure Statutory Instruments and Private Legislation. They did this with me, as they wanted to curb my many meetings with CLPs in the country, all advertised in *Labour Weekly*.

But the main instrument in the toolbox was the upcoming Parliamentary Boundary Commission report. This abolished a whole string of Labour seats in London and the big cities and it was highly beneficial to the Conservatives. But it was also beneficial to the Labour leadership as the report (based on out-of-date estimates of voters registered) was almost certainly going to mean the elimination of Tony Benn in Bristol and (a much smaller prize, but one I suspect they wanted) myself in Wood Green.

Their tactic was to place all the emphasis on waiting for the Enfield Case, a challenge to the Local Government Boundary Review by the London Borough of Enfield which attacked the Commission's proposals on local government ward boundaries and which had a flow through to Parliamentary boundaries.

This did not report until very close to the General Election and there was therefore little time to seek another constituency. Wood Green was to

124. June 1980 page 6

go, and so was I, despite the fact that I had been unanimously reselected as the Parliamentary candidate if the old seat was to continue.

Hard Graft: Multiple Roles

Members of Parliament have multiple roles – if they want to play them. They are required to play a part in invigilating the Government of the day and in legislating, but they also have roles as representatives of their constituency, linking issues and cases which have arisen in the constituency with the work of the Executive, seeking to change the law where necessary and ventilating issues so that they gain visibility to the public.

In addition, they have the role of dealing with the mountains of case-work from surgeries and the postbag. And, crucially, they have the role of preparing the policy of their Party for Government (if in opposition), and maximising the possibility of their side winning the next General Election.

This constituency advocacy role is relatively new in the form it has now taken. Guy Barnett[125] used to tell a story about his predecessor in Dorset, Victor Montagu (later the Earl of Sandwich). When Guy climbed on the train to visit his constituency for the first time after his by-election victory, the train stopped at the first station after leaving Bournemouth in a place it wasn't supposed to stop.

The carriage door opened and the station master in full fig, with scrambled egg all over the place, said, 'Welcome to the constituency, Sir. It is so nice to see you.' This happened at every station till Swanage. It was because Montagu had apparently visited the constituency once a year at most and this great event was regarded locally as akin to a royal progress.

The choice I made in 1979 was to do my best with most of these roles. The constituency was very busy in terms of casework – and far busier than some Northern and rural seats, according to the MPs for those areas.

The advice bureau generated over 2,500 interventions a year and I dealt with all of these fully and personally. And, of course, as is the case now, public policy generated vast numbers of letters and phone calls. In pre-internet days these mainly came in by post and I received over 400 on the GLC Fares Fair case relating to London Transport.

No one who has ever been an MP or worked for one will find these

125. Labour MP for Dorset South 1962-4 and for Greenwich 1971-86

numbers unusual and in 2020 they would be regarded as modest. This activity contrasted, however, with the actions of some Tory MPs who only saw constituents if they were important: Nick Scott[126] told me in select committee that he had to go because he had an important person going to his advice bureau.

'I'd better go and see him because he's an Admiral,' he said. It turned out that he left most of the work to his staff and only saw constituents if they were a member of the great and the good.

Policy Development

In terms of policy development, I was placed on three important sub-committees of the National Executive as I had an interest and some expertise on them. These were the Finance and Economic Committee, the Health and Social Services Committee and the Women's Rights Committee. The last needs some explanation.

In 1979, there were only 11 women Labour MPs and their influence in the PLP can fairly be described as low. Outside Parliament there was growing agitation from women on abortion rights which had been under challenge from deeply reactionary Tory and Labour MPs. The same was the case on issues like childcare, employment rights, and the sex industry, and in respect of the rights of women inside the Labour Party.

There were not enough women Labour MPs who wanted to be on the Women's Rights Committee, and those who were on it unanimously asked me to join as they regarded me as the most outspoken and reliable male supporter of women's rights in the PLP. This vignette shows the extent of the change in the PLP and politics in the 21st century: it would now be unthinkable for women to have to turn to men for support in this kind of way – and quite right too.

The NEC committee work brought me in touch with the Party's Research Department under Geoff Bish, who was in the process of developing 'Labour's Programme 1982' and who had been secretary of the NEC Home Policy Committee during the development of the Alternative Economic Strategy.

He had a thankless task as he was politely pushing back against the more reactionary elements of the PLP, trying to get them to address the fundamental changes sweeping the economy in the early 1980s, and to

---

126. Sir Nicholas Scott, Tory MP for Chelsea 1974-97

recognise the terrible errors that the Labour Government had made.

We received papers from some of the most eminent economists of the day and it was a forum for exchanging radical ideas. I used the meetings of the Finance and Economic Committee to argue the case for the national minimum wage and got an insertion in the 1982 programme committing the Party to an inquiry into it.

On the Health and Social Services Committee there was a legacy of closed hospitals and a poor hospital building programme that had been severely affected by the cuts between 1975 and 1979. No policy had been developed in respect of the reorganisation of the NHS which the Tories immediately brought forward in 1980, believing that the reorganisation of management would lead to improved efficiency and coherence. Reorganisations never do. And hospital closures went on everywhere.

Low Pay

My work on low pay and the statutory national minimum wage was, it is fair to say, ground breaking in the context of the early 1980s. I sponsored a Parliamentary Research and Liaison Office at the Low Pay Unit, along with Jeff Rooker,[127] and the Liberal David Penhaligon.[128] I wrote and Jeff co-signed an introduction to the Low Pay Unit pamphlet on Low Pay,[129] which argued strongly that the traditional methods of dealing with low pay through collective bargaining had failed. It also attacked Callaghan's position on negotiating a five-year pay restraint deal with the trade unions.

We said:

the Parliamentary leadership would appear to have learnt nothing from their own experiences in 1978-9 ... [a further] five years of wage restraint under a Labour Government would breed deep resentment and a possible explosion of anger and frustration amongst the low-paid which would make the so called 'winter of discontent' look like a picnic ... we do not share the view that the low paid workers brought down the last Labour Government but for those who do support that view, one central lesson must emerge. It could happen again. The Labour Party needs to adopt a clearly different

127. MP for Birmingham Perry Barr, February 1974 – 2001, now Lord Rooker of Perry Barr
128. MP for Truro, October 1974-1986
129. Low Pay Report, October 1980, pages 1-3

policy on low pay, based on a statutory national minimum wage which the trade unions would negotiate with the Government.

These were advanced views for 1980 – and the Thatcher Government were contributing to the attack on low paid workers by 'denouncing' the Fair Wages Resolution, first adopted by the House of Commons in 1891.[130]

The TUC had been discussing the issue for decades and could not get anywhere because of the views of the big general unions. The PLP was still hostile but some nifty footwork and a sympathetic Geoff Bish enabled me to get the commitment to an inquiry embedded in Labour's Programme 1982. After I left the Commons, others took up the cudgels thus leading to the introduction of the scheme in 1999.

Hospital Closures and Public Health

In the constituency there were two important examples of the hospital closure programme that was sweeping the country. The first concerned the Wood Green and Southgate, a delightful cottage hospital that undertook rehabilitation and elderly care work of the kind that is now highly prized.

It had been built largely with money from the philanthropist John Passmore Edwards, had been modernised in 1973 and had 45 beds, but in the climate of the early 1980s it was regarded as too costly to maintain, despite the fact that it was providing rehabilitation that kept patients out of acute wards in bigger hospitals and out of A&E.

The Enfield and Haringey Health Authority decided to close the hospital on 18th July 1979 and I started a huge campaign to reverse the decision. The AHA was forced to reconvene on 3rd August, and reversed its decision to close the hospital and remove the patients, on a vote of 11-1. The Chair of the AHA was Audrey Prime, a former national officer of NALGO who was extremely embarrassed that an effective community campaign had scuppered the plans and those to shut the

---

130. Also, amended in 1909 and 1946, and embedded in the ILO Convention no. 94 on labour clauses in public contracts – an early form of contract compliance. 'Denouncing' the resolution meant that they could distance themselves from the Resolution without withdrawing from the ILO Treaty, a piece of international law, which was a bridge too far even for the Thatcher Government.

A&E department at the Prince of Wales Hospital in Tottenham.

The AHA had been turned round but the Government was another matter, as the impetus for closures came directly from them. I organised a meeting with health Minister Gerard Vaughan on 25th July, taking with me the Hospital Friends, doctors, clinical staff, and community groups. Jeremy Corbyn, then a local authority appointee on the AHA, was very helpful and we continued with petitions, demonstrations and eventually an occupation of the hospital by staff and patients – but to no avail. It was closed in 1983.

The case of the Prince of Wales Hospital in Tottenham – still there today as private flats – was more complex. The hospital structure was in a poor state despite substantial investment in new theatres.

But the main problem was that the medical Royal Colleges were reluctant to keep it in certification for training, and if that happened then medical services and its 200-plus beds would become unviable.

The authorities were intransigent and started the salami-style attack by planning the removal of the A&E department which served one of the most deprived areas of London and in the country. The hospital was (just) inside the Tottenham constituency but as the A&E covered much of Haringey and my patch I was entitled to intervene.

Norman Atkinson, my neighbour in Tottenham, gave the impression of being half-hearted at best and had little imagination and drive. He was also showing the first signs of the confusion which overcame him in deeper form later, clearly shown at a big public meeting to discuss the A&E issue when he started taking at great length about housing, and had to be interrupted by the Chair, John Elkington.

However, we mobilised big sections of the community, ruthlessly used publicity, and persuaded the then-Minister of Health, Dr Gerard Vaughan[131] to visit the hospital. We extracted a promise from him that the A&E would stay open and that it could not be closed until a thoroughgoing plan had been constructed by the Health Authority on the functions of the local hospitals – principally the North Middlesex, three miles up the road in Edmonton.

Although Vaughan was the son of a sugar planter, he was an old school toff who was courteous and had been a practising psychiatrist. The Health Authority was another matter, however. They kept on with their cost reduction programme and eventually came up with a more detailed

---

131. MP for Reading constituencies 1970-1997 and Minister of State at the Department of Health

plan that they believed gave better justification for the A&E closure.

Despite them agreeing to a special meeting of their Executive which I demanded, they refused to change their plans. The result was a significant addition to the work of an already wildly overstretched casualty department at the North Middlesex and the cause of endless misery for patients.

A further example of the financial pressure on the NHS was the closure of the big mental health hospitals, which in some cases had been known to incarcerate people for decades without any just cause or diagnosis.

These great barns of places were usually on the outskirts of conurbations where they would be out of sight and out of mind. They were supposed to close and be replaced by community provision where those with mental health conditions would feel more comfortable and less institutionalised.

Needless to say, it did not happen on the scale required at all, and some of the service users ended up on the streets as homeless. It was dreadful and we have not, in my opinion, overcome the consequences today.

The Black Report

On the important issue of public health, the Thatcher Government's position was scandalous. In 1977 Secretary of State for Health, David Ennals, had established a working party to report on inequalities and the differences in health status between the social classes, to identify causal relationships, and to suggest what implications for policy there were.

This operated under the chairmanship of Sir Douglas Black, an eminent Scot, Chairman of the BMA and President of the Royal College of Physicians.

The report was submitted to the Labour Government before the General Election and promptly buried by Tory ministers after it. Everyone in the health policy world knew that the report had been submitted and I started a little campaign to get it published.

Ministers continually pushed back hard with refusals until the pressure became intolerable, and eventually published the document.[132] It is the only example that I am aware of where an official government committee report has not been produced by the government printer.

132. *Inequalities in Health, Report of a Research Working Group*, DHSS August 1980

The version that appeared was bound in a flimsy purple paper cover, and was not properly typeset. It had no illustrations. The charts were hand drawn. It did not even have a list of members of the committee, and the document was a photocopy version of crude typescript. It was designed to look awful and they succeeded in that. But the real star of the show was the nasty little introduction by Patrick Jenkin[133] in his capacity as Secretary of State. In it he said:

the Group has reached the view that the causes of health inequalities are so deep-rooted that only a major and wide ranging programme of public expenditure is capable of altering the pattern … additional expenditure on the scale which could result from the report's recommendations – the amount involved could be upwards of £2bn a year – is quite unrealistic in present or any foreseeable economic circumstances, quite apart from any judgement that may be formed on the effectiveness of such expenditure in dealing with the problems identified. I cannot therefore endorse the Group's recommendations.[134]

The contrast with 2020 could hardly be more profound. Writing this in the middle of the coronavirus outbreak, it is clear that effective public health analysis and modelling is critical to the control of the pandemic, and to dealing with the differential health outcomes and deaths that have emerged.

The whole thrust of NHS policy now in 2020 is to integrate front-line acute hospital health services with community care and effective primary care, with strong emphasis on community actions to minimise hospital admissions amongst those with co-morbidities. It is almost as if the world has been turned upside down since 1980. It can, however, be argued that too great a reliance is being placed on community care to reduce the need for hospital beds, as can be seen from the assumptions in some NHS plans today.

However, in some ways the prejudice against learning about health inequalities is still there amongst politicians, even those sympathetic to public health programmes.

It has always been difficult, for example, to persuade them that cancer treatment is highly dependent on patients being identified early and treated at the earliest possible stage of the development of tumours, and in appropriate settings. Having said that, it was not as difficult as

---

133. MP for Wanstead and Woodford 1964-87
134. Introduction, page 1

making them understand that some patients from deprived backgrounds and different cultures present late and often in A&E departments, when their tumours are well advanced, and in some cases harder to treat.

When these factually-based arguments are acted on we will have the evidence to say that the Black report has been properly understood and implemented. In fact, we need a new Black report, this time with attention being paid to all the dimensions of inequality and including the impact of ethnicity which the 1980 report did not mention at all.

Patrick Jenkin's snooty, *de haut en bas,* attitude was at the extreme end of lack of understanding and petulance at the time. But it shows what we were having to deal with. His quietus came later as a consequence of our GLC campaign, I am very glad to say.

Abortion

In 1979, the front line in Parliament on women's rights was in respect of abortion. The passing of the Abortion Reform legislation in 1967 did not quell the activities of those who wished to restrict a woman's right to choose and this took concrete form in 1975 with the tabling of the highly restrictive Abortion Amendment Bill by James White,[135] an active Catholic.

His bill proposed restricting the availability of terminations by reducing the time period from conception when women could request a termination from registered medical practitioners. It was also clothed in a smokescreen of concern for the welfare of women through attacks on clinics which catered for non-UK women brought into the country to have an abortion.

The measure was defeated through the usual cross-party alliance between Labour MPs and a few principled Tories, although most Conservatives were strongly for restrictions on abortion, if not downright abolition of the legislation that permitted it.

When the Conservatives won the 1979 election, a further opportunity arose to restrict women's rights because there were simply more anti-abortionists in the House. This attack was embodied in the Corrie Bill (tabled by John Corrie, Tory MP for North Ayrshire) which received a majority of 144 at Second Reading and came out of committee strengthened rather than diluted.

---

135. Labour MP for Glasgow Pollok

The main provision was to reduce the time limit to request abortions from 28 week to 20 weeks and it was estimated that 60% of all abortions would have been prevented by this measure (and abortions close to the limit were known to be requested more frequently by young women and by those from deprived backgrounds).

In addition, Corrie proposed to change the basis on which requests could be made so that it was restricted to only those where the woman's life was in 'grave danger' or where there was a 'substantial or serious risk' to the woman's physical or mental health.

The bill also sought to prevent organisations from providing abortion advice and terminations themselves, undermining the model used by the British Pregnancy Advice Service and others, and sought to encourage 'conscientious objection' by NHS staff where their religious or other beliefs contradicted abortion. This was extremely dangerous and could have set back women's rights for decades.

As we did not have the numbers to defeat the bill on a straight up-and-down vote we had to work out complicated Parliamentary manoeuvres, and I worked with the team led by Jo Richardson[136] to design and implement these tactics.

Disgracefully, 54 Labour MPs had voted for the bill on Second Reading, only 82 had voted against, and 127 abstained or were not present, as this was deemed to be a conscience vote (the conscience of men by and large). Therefore, there was no whip, but the response of the PLP to the most serious attack on a woman's right to choose was appalling. So, at Report Stage we had to ensure that a wide range of amendments were tabled and selected.

Long speeches were made to drag out the time, as there were no restrictions on the length of time that Member could speak except by a general injunction from the Speaker to keep it short.

Several Labour MPs were brilliant in opposition to the bill, especially Jo, but the lawyers also played an important part. Sam Silkin,[137] John Silkin[138] and Alex Lyon[139] were excellent in removing credibility from the bill. But the real test came when the selected amendments were put to the vote. Corrie and his dreadful crew realised that the bill could be talked out by us (that is, it could run out of Parliamentary time) if all

---

136. MP for Barking February 1974-94
137. MP for Dulwich 1964-83 and a former Attorney General
138. MP for Deptford 1963-87 and a former Cabinet Minister
139. MP for York 1966-83 and a former Home Office Minister

the selected amendments were pressed to the vote. Cunningly, he did not put tellers in on specific amendments that were thought to be marginal to the bill's success. In the absence of one set of tellers, the amendments would fall automatically without a division and the bill would progress faster. The key point was that a Private Member's Bill was time limited, and the measure would fall at the end of the allotted time and could not pass – if the amendments were still unfinished.

So, we had to make the difficult decision to deploy two from our side to do the job. Jo turned to John Tilley[140] and myself as the obvious two willing horses to do this, but I did take the precaution of asking for a letter of explanation and support from Jo – because we would be seen to be counted on the other side by those observing from the press and public.

The great merit of this plan was that every amendment taken to a division took at least 20 minutes and probably a bit longer once the deliberate delayers in the men's toilets were added into the equation. We spent glorious hours delaying and delaying through this mechanism until the bill was talked out. As Wellington said of Waterloo, it was 'the nearest run thing you ever saw in your life.'

The forces of reaction had been defeated and the 1967 Act preserved, and the prospect of thousands of women being forced to carry foetuses they did not want was averted.

It was manoeuvring that did it as, I believe, there was a majority for the Corrie Bill in the House. The person most responsible for this victory was without doubt Jo Richardson – a wonderful, lovely woman who it was my great privilege to work with.

That didn't end it, though. There was a sequel caused by utter incompetence.

The magazine *Spare Rib*, clearly on the side of a woman's right to choose, decided to print a list of the supportive MPs like myself who had voted against the Corrie Bill and had fought it all the way.

The only problem was that they didn't print all the names. The sub-optimal journalist who compiled the list stopped halfway through the alphabet – so all those MPs with surnames after 'M' were not listed as having voted against. This, of course, included Jo Richardson as well as myself.

Eventually Spare Rib corrected it, but there was significant abuse – quite understandably – from women who thought that we had betrayed

---

140. MP for Lambeth Central 1978-83

the cause. It took quite a while for them to be convinced that it was a dreadful mistake. On such errors are reputations made and lost.

I then initiated a discussion about how we could counter-attack the anti-abortionists. Many, including Ian Mikardo and Jo Richardson, were initially reluctant and thought that a policy of letting sleeping dogs lie was best. But the women's organisations outside Parliament (especially the Labour Abortion Rights Campaign) were supportive and eventually agreement was reached to launch a Parliamentary initiative.

This was designed to attack the significant variations in TOP (Termination of Pregnancy) provision across the country, linked, we thought, to the numbers of Catholic doctors in the area. Merseyside had particularly poor provision, so we addressed this by drafting a bill which laid statutory duties on the NHS to provide equal provision.

Jo agreed to introduce this as a Ten Minute Rule Bill and as part of the deal I sat inside the Public Bill Office overnight in order to secure the next slot that was being made available to MPs. Good job that I did too, as other MPs turned up early in the morning to grab the slot, but they were too late.

Jo introduced the bill on 1st July 1981 and drew attention in her speech to the wide variations in facilities, saying:

There are wide variations in the availability of abortion facilities within the National Health Service in different parts of the country. For instance, in 1979, 94% of North Devon women needing abortions were treated on the NHS, whereas in the same year only 6% of Dudley women had NHS abortions. It was the intention of Parliament when passing the 1967 Abortion Act that terminations of pregnancy would be available on the National Health Service – some consultants have blocked the rights of women as defined by Parliament and this must end.

We organised a lobby of Parliament on 24th June 1981 in preparation for the bill. It went no further, of course, as most Ten Minute Rule Bills do not, but it was an important step in pushing back against SPUC[141] and their backers in Parliament.

I am glad to say that a similar frontal attack on abortion rights based on the Corrie Bill principles would be difficult to sustain today and it is hard to imagine such a measure getting traction in Parliament.

Some things do change.

---

141. Society for the Protection of the Unborn Child

Women's Rights and the Outrageous Attitude of Some Labour MPs

The position of women was not a popular subject for debate in the 1979 Parliament. Despite having a woman Prime Minister, the Tory benches were full of raging reactionaries on this subject.

In a debate in December 1982, I raised the position of women in the economy and advocated a 12-point plan to address this, including more under-fives facilities, major changes in career structures, a positive action programme including changes to the Equal Pay Act, changes in the Sex Discrimination Act to allow positive discrimination, equal employment rights for part time workers, and a statutory minimum wage which would particularly advantage women workers.

In that same debate two speeches of extraordinary obtuseness were made by Tory MPs. Sir Nicholas Bonsor[142] complained of women making a 'shrieking squawking attack on the male sex' and then capped this by saying that women 'have a primary duty to be at home.'

Bonsor, educated at Eton and Keble College, is now a Director of the climate change denying organisation, The Global Warming Policy Foundation.

Then came one of the few women Tory MPs, Shelia Faith,[143] a hard-line law-and-order merchant. She said that, 'if we must look to the Government in these matters, the Act which did most to liberate women was the Clean Air Act 1956 ... therefore, there was far less dirt and dust for women to clear up.'

However, it was not only Tories who were in that frame of mind. In the mid-1980s the PLP did not have a frontbench spokesperson on Women's Rights (Joan Lestor, the previous incumbent, had been defeated at Slough in the 1983 General Election). So, there was a campaign in the Women's Sections to ensure that a spokesperson was appointed to replace her, but the mood in the PLP bureaucracy was hostile.

PLP Secretary Bryan Davies wrote to the Brighton Women's Section and said that he had no idea who would be appointed, 'but it would seem to me to be excessive chauvinism to suggest that only a woman could do this job adequately.'[144]

Slightly later in 1983, the Women's Action Committee (WAC) of

142. MP for Nantwich 1979-83 and Upminster 1983-97
143. MP for Belper 1979-83
144. Letter to Ms Brenda Wilkinson, 27th July 1983

The establishment arrives: Princess Marina at the first University of Kent Graduation 1968. When she opened UKC two years earlier they laid turf to conceal the mud and took it up afterwards.

Fred Whitemore meets St Nicholas as Lord Mayor of Canterbury, December 2001. Fred was RR's politics tutor and a key figure in the resurgence of the Canterbury Labour Party. He later became a lay member of Chapter.

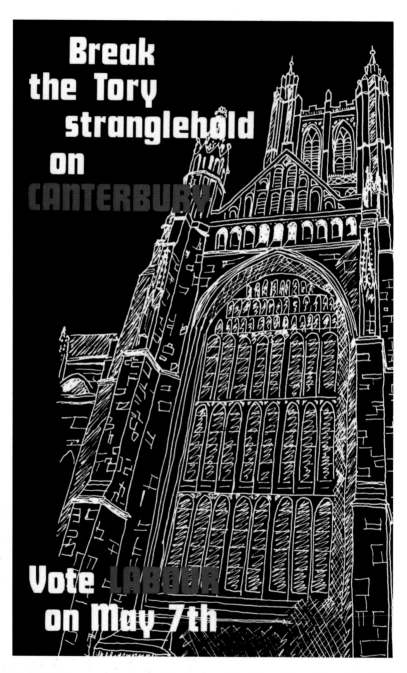

Break
the Tory
stranglehold
on
CANTERBURY

Vote LABOUR
on May 7th

And they did: voters broke the Tory stranglehold on Canterbury. No Labour Councillors in 1970, control of the Council by 1972. The Conservatives were reduced to two councillors.

There will be trouble ahead: Low Pay comes to the boil: Dirty Jobs strike 1969, East End London.

Don't work for Tower Hamlets: a refuse collector gets it on the record, 1969.

The great ungluing starts here: Harold and Mary Wilson 1970. In the 1970 general election mass abstention by working class voters began, with 89 constituencies having more non voters than votes for the winning party – mainly in Labour areas.

Denis Healey, Labour Conference 1976: his speech backed the IMF deal to cut public spending and control wages, based on wildly wrong data about the public finances.

21% of the women Labour MPs lobby for toy safety 1966: left to right Anne Kerr (Rochester and Chatham), Margaret McKay (Clapham), Gwyneth Dunwoody (Exeter), Joyce Butler (Wood Green). There were only 19 women out of a Parliamentary Party of 364.

Jim Callaghan lobbied by fire crews Labour Conference 1977. One of many public sector wage disputes provoked by 25% inflation and the Labour Government's wages policy. Callaghan later described action by the low-paid as 'free collective vandalism' whilst giving large pay rises to top civil servants and private sector workers.

The fight back against Labour spending cuts: NUPE general secretary Alan Fisher with marchers, 17th November 1976.

Head of the march November 1976. 90,000 low-paid workers followed. In picture Dennis Skinner MP, Neil Kinnock MP, Ron Keating NUPE, Bert Spanswick COHSE, Gerry Gillman SCPS, Ken Thomas CPSA, Geoffrey Drain NALGO, and Ernie Roberts AUEW.

Boogying against the cuts: NUPE members create an atmosphere, November 1976.

Tony Benn and Michael Foot. Benn failed to weld together a coherent case against the IMF deal and could not get agreement from others in the Cabinet to pursue a common line against Callaghan and Healey.

Bernard Donoughue, Chief Adviser to Callaghan in 1977. He believed that low-paid workers were in fact overpaid, and said so.

Cuts man: Chief Secretary to the Treasury Joel Barnett MP December 1976. Later, attacking the NHS wage claim, he said that they were 'well paid unskilled people... they do not starve and anyway 50% of their wives are at work'.

Not so matey: Alan Fisher and Frank Chapple at the 1979 Labour Conference. Chapple said earlier that 'most of (Fisher's) members have never done a fucking day's work in their lives' and described the 1979 industrial action as 'terrorism'.

Peter Shore: a former friend of Benn, he described action by the low-paid as 'a threat to democratic society'.

Developing policy: the author speaking at the Labour Party Conference 1979 in favour of a woman's right to choose.

Equalising abortion rights: RR and Jo Richardson MP launch their Bill requiring the NHS to provide equal abortion rights everywhere, June 1981. In picture Sarah Rackham and Jeanette Gould of the Labour Abortion Rights Campaign.

Launching the round-the-clock picket outside South Africa House to get Mandela and fellow political prisoners freed. RR speaking, watched by Ian Mikardo MP (with pipe), Stanley Clinton-Davis MP (with glasses), and Norma Kitson, wife of one of the prisoners. The PLP leadership told Labour MPs not to go.

RR supporting action by CPSA members in Brixton. 1980. The first salami slice against those with little power protecting themselves.

The successful fight to change the laws on child abduction: Seema Waseem and her daughters, Sameena and Rubeena, who were drugged, robbed, left destitute, and had two very young children abducted to Pakistan by her appalling husband.

CLPD wrote to candidates for the Leader and Deputy Leader, and for seats on the National Executive Committee, to ask their views on the five demands made by WAC for reform of the Party constitution to enable women's voices to be heard decisively.

These included the demand for at least one woman on every Parliamentary shortlist and substantial changes to enable women to make their own decisions in the organisation.

The answers to the WAC questionnaire were most interesting and showed the extent to which outdated ideas were still present: Neil Kinnock wrote that he was opposed to almost all the proposals and added in respect of 'one woman on a shortlist' that he was against the proposal.

I think that such a policy would result in the reduction of the number of women selected.[145]

Giles Radice, a scion of the right in the PLP, was opposed to all the proposals. Allen McKay (a whip) said, 'I am not convinced that it would be good for the Labour Party in general for the demands to be met, as it appears to me to be a further split in the solidarity of the Party.'

Roger Stott (Jim Callaghan's former PPS) was against the inclusion of a woman on a shortlist and all the other proposals bar one. Jack Straw was against three of the proposals but was for a woman on each shortlist.

It is clear that opinion amongst many men in the PLP was heavily against supporting the rights of women in the Party and many clung to outdated concepts of solidarity which really meant 'shut up and do what the men tell you.'

Some on the left in the PLP, like Martin Flannery,[146] saw demands for women's rights as a distraction from the class struggle, and said so. Martin did not understand that women faced additional, onerous and highly discriminatory barriers to participation in economic and social life, and personal jeopardy by sexual attacks and abuse, and were often regarded as second-class citizens. For him and other men, the class struggle was everything.

Opposition to change was hard-wired into the top leadership cadres of the Party and amongst many male MPs.

---

145. Letter to the Secretary of WAC 21st September 1983. Details of all the responses are in my papers
146. MP for Sheffield Hillsborough, February 1974-1992

Dealing with the Sex Industry – and the F-Word

It would be nearly 20 years before the great influx of women Labour MPs changed the atmosphere of the Commons substantially. But in 1982, an opportunity arose to deal with the sex industry which I took up and achieved something of a victory.

An unpleasant company called Conegate had decided to market hardcore pornographic magazines, films and other salacious material by opening shops on many streets throughout urban Britain. By February 1982, it had 120 shops, badged as Private Shops, blacked out at the front but located in some places near schools and on prominent high streets.

Women's organisations across the country started picketing them. We had one on Tottenham High Road which we started demonstrating against and raised a great deal of publicity against the owners of the chain.

Two women in Lewisham who had apparently daubed a shopfront (prominently located by the station, a bus interchange and a cinema) were acquitted of causing damage in the magistrates' court and I asked a national newspaper reporter who I knew to visit the shop and take a serious note of what was inside.

He did and reported back that it contained a prostitutes' calling list, prominently on display.

This was good ammunition and in the debate on the snappily titled Local Government Miscellaneous Provisions Bill 1981, I described what was going on.

I read into the record a newspaper report about the Lewisham Private Shop which described the prostitutes' call list, which was entitled 'Phone Them and Fuck Them.'

No one in the fairly well-attended House, nor the Deputy Speaker in the chair, nor the clerks, batted an eyelid because they could see that I was reading a report and not swearing in the Chamber.

However, Speaker George Thomas was later alerted to the words and insisted that Hansard should censor the quote, as can be seen at column 359 of 3rd February 1982. He didn't inform me about the censorship, but his actions played beautifully into my hands because an obscure speech from an opposition backbencher on an unpopular subject gained currency and a great deal of national and local publicity ensued.

It was apparently the first time that Hansard had been censored on the order of the Speaker. The *News of the World* asked me to write a full page article[147] and in it I argued that local authorities were powerless to stop the spread of the porn shop industry as they had no powers to prevent individual kinds of owners from getting a generic shop approval. I quoted Mr David Read, then spokesman for Conegate, who told my local paper that,

Women have exploited their sexuality from time immemorial. Every time they wear make-up they are exploiting their sex and they exploit men by allowing them to have sex in exchange for a new coat or something. The average man is conned by women.[148]

It was clear to me that the industry was simply there to harvest the astronomical profits available by creating a new demand. But more important, it was reinforcing the male view that women were inferior and could rightly be the subject of violence and attack.

In the article I quoted the judge in an Ipswich rape case who said that a raped girl hitchhiker was 'guilty of contributory negligence' because of the clothes she was wearing.

Today, 40 years on, we know that the numbers of rapes, attacks on women, domestic violence incidents perpetrated by men, and child abuse cases are grossly underreported let alone prosecuted, with rape prosecutions falling away sharply and convictions miniscule.

Some argued at the time that the restrictions I was trying to impose were draconian and amounted to censorship and restrictions on liberty. The Conegate owners certainly argued this, but the counter argument was that we should not stand up for the freedoms of the porn brigade but protect the freedom of women, whose rights were being abridged by the industry and by the violent and abusive men who preyed on them.

I had enormous support from a wide range of people, ranging from radical women's groups to Mary Whitehouse's Festival of Light. This was 1982 and not 2019, but I had put down a marker that this kind of industry was not welcome and these kinds of rancid behaviours by men were beyond the pale.

It is a great pity that the advent of the internet has created a space for the further sexualisation of our society and the grooming of young girls and women in a way that no one could have envisaged back then.

We got the law changed to enable local authorities to disallow sex shop planning applications, and that was a step forward. Without my campaign, it might not have happened. For me this was the start of a

---

147. Why I Used That Word, *News of the World*, February 1982
148. See also Hansard 3rd February 1982 col. 360

wider push to deal with sexism: in my *News of the World* article, I said that,

We must defeat sexism in advertising, on television and in newspapers, if we are to ensure that women – who after all are 52% of the population – are treated equally in society and aren't just regarded as mindless morons fit only to do the washing up and mend men's socks.

The Forgotten History of Women's Rights Legislation

The history of women's rights legislation has a long and difficult history. My predecessor, Joyce Butler, along with women MPs on both sides of the House, put up a serious fight in 1968 on the 50th anniversary of the partial female franchise. They argued for an independent board to assess the extent of discrimination against women and to provide for equal pay for work of equal value.[149]

This was some time after the Labour Government had introduced the Race Discrimination Act 1965 to deal with some of the discrimination that was endemic against black people in public places. The Race Discrimination Act was weak in that only civil offences were covered and the Act did not touch discrimination in private such as in housing and employment. But it was a start.

In contrast, the State had for decades legislated to protect women workers. Unfortunately, it had been the trade unions who resisted in some cases (such as that of the engineers) the admission of lower-skilled workers into membership of the Unions, most of them women, during the two world wars.

Both the TUC and the Labour Party had regarded women's rights as a marginal issue at best but in 1968, an alliance between Labour and Tory women MPs argued that there should be a commission to examine the extent of discrimination against women.

This was raised in questions to Harold Wilson when Prime Minister by Joyce Butler and he gave what can only be described as a brush off: 'Send me a paper,' he said, and then made what would be regarded now as sexist remarks about the pleasure of receiving letters from lady Members or even better having personal interviews with them.[150]

Later, Joyce Butler introduced a Ten Minute Rule Bill to combat

---

149. HOC Hansard 7th May 1968
150. HOC Hansard Prime MInisters Questions 7th March 1968

sex discrimination and repeated the introduction four times. Willie Hamilton[151] took over Joyce's bill when he won a top slot in the Private Members Bill 'lottery' and this legislation eventually became the Sex Discrimination Act 1975.

Much of the literature on the development of equal rights legislation ignores the roles played by Joyce and Willie and it is about time that was rectified. It is also worth remembering that the Labour Party in the 1980s was full of people at senior level who were deeply reluctant to move with the times.

Abducted Children and 'Seema's Laws'

A further very distressing policy issue had surfaced in Wood Green with the realisation that the abduction of children was a problem on an extensive scale.

In a few months, three women came forward with different cases, all of them horrific, with the nub of it being that their partners had taken their joint children out of the country without their permission.

The most difficult case of all related to that of Seema Waseem, who was married to a former Pakistani photo-journalist turned shopkeeper and civil servant, who had sold their rather nice house in Winchmore Hill and bought a run-down property in Wood Green.

He then drugged Seema and her two teenage daughters, Sameena and Rubeena, in the middle of the night. He stole their passports, illegally emptied the joint bank account of many thousands of pounds, abducted their two younger children, a small boy and a baby girl, and hightailed it off to Pakistan.

Seema, despite being an internationally recognised poet in Urdu, found it difficult to communicate at times but luckily her daughters were intelligent, highly educated young women and could explain things in detail.

When they first came to see me at the surgery I could not believe my ears, and, of course, the authorities were treating them incompetently and disrespectfully. They had no money, couldn't pay the bills, the house needed radical modernisation to make it habitable, their youngest children had disappeared. All three of them were traumatised.

It took many months to sort the mess out. The money was fairly

151. MP for West Fife 1950-74 and Central Fife 1974-87

easily dealt with as the bank could not justify why they had paid out all the money in their joint account without two signatures to authorise it.

The benefits system was more complex as, true to form, the local DSS were incompetent on numerous occasions and it felt like a running battle to get sensible and correct decisions.

Seema's kitchen, the worst part of the house they were living in, received a one-off grant of £18,000 personally authorised by the then Parliamentary Under Secretary for Health and Social Security, Sir George Young[152] – a thoroughly decent One Nation Tory who was somewhat out of place in Mrs Thatcher's Ministerial Team.

However, stabilising the finances and creating a more civilised living environment could be done systematically, but finding the children was another thing altogether.

Perhaps the worst feature of Seema's experience was that for a while she was shunned by many in her Pakistani community in north London. A woman who had lost her two youngest children through a vile abduction was treated as if it was her fault.

This did not last but was unnerving for us all. I received two death threats for having the temerity to help her, both posted from Pakistan. The real problem, however, was the law: Britain was not yet signed up to the Hague Convention on the Civil Aspects of Child Abduction, which essentially established a procedure whereby States and individuals could lawfully pursue abductors if the second State was also a signatory to the Convention.

The treaty had only just been negotiated and Britain was considering whether to sign: its key objective was to 'obtain the prompt return (of children) wrongfully removed or retained in any contracting state,' and it also made provision for the recognition of British custody law in Pakistan.

However, Pakistan, under Sharia law, resisted accession to the Convention and only did so in 2016. It was the first South Asian Muslim country to accede and only the fifth Muslim country in total. Research in 2011 showed that there were 55 reported cases of such unilateral child removal from the UK to Pakistan, 10% of all the cases reaching the High Court.[153] But in the 1980s there was no legal redress for Seema, in

---

152. MP for Ealing Acton February 1974-97 and then North West Hampshire 1997-2015, now Lord Young of Cookham

153. Figures quoted in E Andrews, Lower Tier Members of the Hague Club Family Law Week, 4th April 2018

Britain – as the husband was long gone out of the country – or under international protocols.

Therefore, getting the Convention ratified by the UK was the prime objective and the Government agreed to do so early on in my campaign. They were concerned about reciprocity, the fact that other countries could demand the return of children abducted to the UK from elsewhere.

My line to ministers who asked me was that abduction was just wrong, and that as a consequence, lawful removals under the Convention of children abducted from other countries who had been hijacked to Britain should be allowed too. It was quid pro quo.

However, it took until 1983 to persuade the Government to introduce legislation to make abduction a criminal offence in the UK and to allow a parent legal aid to fight cases through the courts of another country. Patrick Mayhew, Minister of State at the Home Office,[154] agreed that this should be done, and it was a major victory for my campaign.

In the meantime, all we had was publicity: so, I wrote to every Labour Party in the country, wrote press articles and garnered some money to get Seema and Sameena to Pakistan in a longshot attempt to find the children and get them back to Britain.

A fund was set up, administered by Brian Bullard, Mayor of Haringey at the time, and myself, and it was just enough to get them to Karachi. But there they were stonewalled and returned empty-handed.

Eventually, decades later, the two youngest children returned to Britain when they were adults and were reunited with their family. The appalling husband was allowed to return to the UK – demonstrating that the 'all ports bulletin' of 1981 to apprehend and arrest him had disappeared into the administrative Bermuda Triangle. He died not long after. Seema and her children have rebuilt their relationships, fractured decades ago. It has not been easy for them; but Seema's experience and her campaign prompted two important changes to the law which have helped ease some of the pain of illegal abduction.

Low Pay and Public Service Issues Rumble on

On the day after the General Election, the new Thatcher ministers started wading into the concessions achieved by the low-paid during

---

154. MP for Tunbridge Wells, February 1974-97, later Baron Mayhew of Twys-den

the winter of 1978-79.

This was principally achieved through changes to the instructions to the Clegg Comparability Commission.[155]

The original instructions to Clegg, written by the Labour Government, limited the freedom of the Commission on important technical issues but great damage to the levelling-up of low pay was done by one of the last acts of the Labour Government. It decided that it would not fully fund any pay increases flowing from Clegg to ancillary staff and ambulance crews, and would instead require local health authorities to find £2m from their budgets to fund the pay increases.

The concessions finally extracted from Callaghan and Healey thus proved to be as durable as mist. Then the Conservative Government stepped in and produced new instructions to the Commission which, *inter alia,* prevented 'historical comparisons' as a basis for determining current pay levels.

So, no one could argue that an earlier settlement, reached at a time to bring low-paid staff in line with earnings in other professions or industries, should be uprated in line with inflation or the growth in salaries.

This was not an academic discussion. At the time, the trade union sides of the Nurses and Midwives Whitley Councils were seeking to restore the value of the Halsbury Committee award in 1974 for 400,000 nurses and midwives, and the Staff Side of the Burnham Committee on Teachers pay were trying to do the same in respect of the 1974 Houghton award.

Employers were receiving the same advice from Government and were told that cash limits would prevent them from enhancing offers to meet staff side arguments on low pay. Other instructions from Government meant that only job-for-job comparisons were legitimate and that references to the 'going rate' in wage settlements generally were to be ignored by employers as inappropriate.

Comparisons between one group of public sector workers and staff in other public services, thought to be performing jobs at similar levels of responsibility, were also disallowed. The specific form of words was this:

[the Government] shares doubts over using other comparators from the public sector, and suggests that some of these, and indeed other possible comparators, may turn out to be inappropriate because they are not sufficiently subject to market forces.

On top of this was a requirement that pay increases were to be contingent on the achievement of greater efficiency and performance being

---

155. The Standing Commission on Pay Comparability, established March 1979

achieved before payments were made.

Government also emphasised trade-offs between pay and job security and pensions, saying,

[T]he government is particularly concerned that adequate account should be taken of job security and similar factors, which although difficult to quantify have a very important bearing on the relative attractiveness of jobs.

Unemployment was also to be used as an open method of controlling wage levels, saying in its instructions to Clegg that:

The minimum that must be done (evidence of labour supply) to ensure that comparability studies do not produce results unjustified by labour market considerations

This was a new pay policy with very different outlines to anything constructed before. Our side were supine in the face of this and were embarrassed by people like me who were unearthing documents and making themselves a nuisance.

The truth is they were conscious of their own policies in government and in any event were too indolent to find the ammunition. The trade unions, always reactive, were constricted by their own weakness too, despite the fact that 1979 was the point at which trade union membership peaked in the UK.

Stasis and Indolence

The period 1979-83 was dominated, for me, by the endless fight against the Thatcher Government's innovations in public policy. The destruction of manufacturing industry accelerated, and with the cuts in public expenditure, caused a huge drop in male participation rates in the workforce. In 1911, 93.5% of the male population were in work, but by 1981 this had collapsed to 77.7%. This process drove the alienation of working class men who could no longer work and the alienation of whole communities from politics. Nobody was stemming the tide.[156]

The demand on my time and effort was overwhelming, and it seemed to me that our frontbench was fatally compromised by the previous actions of the Callaghan Government. Nor was there a great deal of evidence that some of my PLP colleagues were making the same effort and had the same understanding of what was going on.

As an example, meetings of the PLP backbench group on Health

156. Central Statistical Office, census of population for the various years

and Social Services were poorly attended and often only three or four Members turned up. As this was the front line of attacks on the welfare state it was pretty staggering to see. Some of my colleagues seemed jaded and were not looking to the future.

The Government had introduced the Health Services Act 1980 which abolished a tier of administration in the NHS saving, it was alleged, millions of pounds. This point I disputed strongly in committee on the bill.

It also enabled new pay beds to be brought into being and crucially – the most important part of the legislation by far – it instructed Health Authorities (Boards in Scotland) through Section 6 of the Act to stay within the cash limit they had been allocated by the Treasury.

It also imposed legal sanctions on health authorities seeking to carry over expenditure from one year to another.

This had direct consequences everywhere. In Haringey by 1982, the Area Health Authority again proposed closing the Wood Green and Southgate Hospital and closing two wards at the Prince of Wales and North Middlesex Hospitals which together produced savings of over £300,000 a year.

A further reason for these plans was that the Government had decided not to fund a third of the annual pay increase for NHS staff and to insist that health authorities fund it from their existing budgets. The NHS policy was therefore to impose a strict corset on spending through cash limits, preventing carry-overs, and not funding annual pay rises.

Compared to policy today, this was draconian.

As further examples of the madness doing the rounds, the North East Thames Regional Health Authority wanted £14m of cuts in services in order to meet the spending reductions from Government and deal with the revenue consequences of opening two new hospitals in Essex.

The Oxford RHA also proposed that patients moving to an area should not receive services from the NHS until a waiting period had elapsed. And when that waiting time was completed, you would have to go back from whence you came to get any kind of treatment at all.

There was never a mention of need, demand for elective care or emergency treatment, service quality improvements or improving the efficiency of the service by improving processes. It was a straightforward cheese press method of squeezing as much cash out of the system as quickly as possible.

Today we have three-year spending settlements (thank you, Messrs

Blair and Brown), full funding of pay settlements (usually) and the ability for front line NHS providers to obtain Treasury loans in-year to offset shortfalls in income or to deal with spikes in demand or changes in drug pricing and technology.

The situation in the 1980s was far worse than under the Cameron/May/Johnson leaderships later. And yet the PLP was ritualistic and sluggish in its response in the early 80s, and it clearly needed a boost of adrenalin. It was like dealing with a wet dishcloth.

The 1982 Wage Dispute

Concurrent with the attack on local provision there was further downward pressure on NHS wages. The 1982 health services wage dispute showed the continuing determination of the trade unions to attack low pay and I was glad to support them and won an emergency debate in the Commons on the ongoing action covering one million health workers, granted by Speaker George Thomas under Standing Order no. 9 (as it was then).

Moving the motion to support the NHS staff, I said:

The basic reason for the dispute is the appalling level of low pay in the National Health Service. Many NHS workers perform filthy jobs. They wash the filthiest sheets in Britain. They wash the sheets of the incontinent patients. They wash the blood-stained sheets of those who have had operations performed on them in NHS hospitals. They also perform dirty and often unpleasant jobs such as stoking boilers in the NHS hospitals. They are often required to work on a 24-hour rotating shift or alternating shift basis. They work unsocial hours, because the whole character of the NHS is that it is a 24-hour, seven-days-a-week, round-the-clock operation.[157]

On this occasion the PLP was united behind my position that we had to support the NHS workers. It was a step towards a more sensible position on low pay generally and pretty much coincided with the change in Labour's official position on the statutory minimum wage, from outright hostility to serious interest, as shown in Labour's Programme 1982.

This movement was greatly assisted by a new frontbench spokesperson on health, Gwyneth Dunwoody[158] who was assiduous and helpful.

157. Hansard 20th July 1982, cols 225-269
158. MP for Exeter 1966-1970 and Crewe February 1974-2008

Although she was on the right of the PLP, she wanted to work construc-tively with Members active on NHS issues.

It was, however, disturbing that the trade unions were lax in their liai-son with Parliament. I contacted my own union (NUPE) after winning the SO9 emergency debate and asked what they might want me to include in my opening speech in the debate. I never received a reply.

The Economy and the Move to Deregulation, Unemployment and a Smaller State

The arena in which there was less agreement between my views and those of the majority of the PLP was on the economy. Initially, many mainstream MPs defended the positions of the Callaghan Government although, over time there developed a more nuanced view that we were witnessing something epochal: a serious attempt to marketise the economy.

This involved a number of measures and strategies:

- Deregulating financial services.

- Managing with much higher levels of unemployment in the new conditions where the exchange rate was underpinned by petropound status.

- Reducing the scale of nationalised industries by removing state support.

- Attacking public spending on the basis that it stoked inflation by raising the money supply.

- Removing support to those dependent on benefits on the grounds that suffering had to be spread equally (the large scale reduction of taxation for the richest groups came later).

This snowstorm of activity by ministers meant that Labour MPs found it less necessary to defend Callaghan, especially after he had departed as leader, and gave opportunities for them to attack what was clearly not a One Nation Tory Government.

The first out-and-out privatisation legislation was in respect of Amersham International. Here was an internationally renowned maker of radioactive isotopes which had started life making radium and material for luminous dials, and was now exporting heavily to other countries from its extensive product list.

The privatisation in 1981-2 produced a share sale which was 24.6 times oversubscribed, and the share price increased from the deliberately artificially low 142p offer price to 188p on the first day, allowing immediate profit-taking after those in the know had 'stagged' the offer.

This was relevant because, during the passage of the legislation to privatise, one of the Tory MPs who shared an office with Mandy in Old Palace Yard came in and told her secretary to buy the shares. They were a steal, couldn't go wrong, and if she didn't have the money she would lend it to her.

This was Elaine Kellett-Bowman, a loudmouth connoisseur of brown crimplene suits, who lived in Norfolk, was a member of the British delegation to the European Assembly and represented Lancaster.

Mandy told me about this, and I raised it on the floor of the House to embarrass the Tory profiteers, but it didn't stop them. Two of us (myself and Jeff Rooker) called for an inquiry and a debate, and we obtained some useful publicity[159] but nothing changed. I suspect that large numbers of Tory MPs benefited from the share sale as they knew it was underpriced, and had instructed their brokers to buy.

Shortly afterwards the ghastly Tristan Garel-Jones, MP for Watford and later a Government minister, approached me to warn me off. He confirmed they were going to stag the shares on launch day, make a killing, then crystallise their gains, and that I'd better stop raising it otherwise there would be trouble. I was being threatened for exposing the insider trading of legislators themselves. It was one of the key features of the Tory privatisation programme: personal profit by legislators arising directly from their Parliamentary duties.

Nothing was done about it, of course. British Gas and other privatisations followed the same pattern: set the price low, encourage stagging and quick profits, and nuts to the taxpayer who had funded these public services for decades.

---

159. *Daily Mirror*, 27th February 1982, article by Roger Beam and John Desborough

Social Security Front Line

Developments also came quickly on the entitlements of the poorest. From 1980 to 1982 there was a new social security bill every few months with the most notorious being the Social Security (No. 2) Bill of 1980.

This stopped earnings-related benefits but not earnings-related insurance contributions. It also reduced unemployment benefit for those over 60, removed benefits from strikers, and struck out the strict obligations to uprate benefits each year.

The official view set out in the Explanatory and Financial Memorandum to the Bill, was that expenditure on benefits would be reduced by about £494m, plus a substantial and variable amount depending on the extent to which the Chancellor failed to uprate benefits in line with inflation. Of this, only £1m was said to be the result of removing the entitlement to benefits claimable by those on strike.

Nevertheless, the BBC described the Bill's principal feature as 'removing strikers' benefits,' which was exactly what the Government wanted it to be seen as.

Hearing this made those paying attention really angry and a couple of us went across to the BBC office on Parliament Street and had a huge stand-up row with John Sergeant, who was covering the story for the BBC. We demanded that they changed their line and stop being a mouthpiece for the Executive.

They changed their tune.

The team that was assembled to deal with the bill in committee was pretty tough on our side and included Jeff Rooker,[160] promoted to the frontbench by Michael Foot, Andrew Bennett,[161] Jo Richardson,[162] Jock Stallard[163] and Willie Hamilton.[164]

There were long speeches, huge numbers of interventions to help each other, and a determination to embarrass the Minister at every opportunity. On the floor of the House, Andrew Bennett and I used 'I Spy Strangers' to mess up the proceedings as we were determined to make the

---

160. MP for Perry Barr February 1974-2001, later Baron Rooker
161. MP for Stockport North 1974-83 and Denton and Reddish 1983-2005. See Hansard May 2nd 1980
162. MP for Barking February 1974-94
163. MP for St Pancras North 1970-83, later Baron Stallard of St Pancras
164. MP for West Fife and then Central Fife 1950-87

Government guillotine the Bill, in other words restrict debate on it.[165]

We succeeded in that, and turned a boring Social Security Bill into something of a cause célèbre. At one point the Prime Minister came into the Public Bill Committee Room and sat in the seats at the end to see what on earth was going on.

One side effect of this was to hammer the first nail in the coffin of Patrick Jenkin, who was dealt with comprehensively later by my team on the GLC Interim Provisions Bill.

These shared experiences helped bind the different generations of the PLP together and after a while people became friendlier after working in concert. But the real consequence of this mountain of legislation was greater poverty and hardship for people on the margins of life. After all, it was the first real attack on welfare provision since the 1930s and demonstrated clearly that we were in new and uncharted territory.

Deflation and Sod the Consequences: Learning to Win Elections with Mass Unemployment

Social security was only one aspect of the economic revolution taking place.

The Government had determined early on to take demand out of the economy, restructure taxes by imposing greater levels of indirect taxes through the rise in VAT, and slash public expenditure to reduce the calls on taxation. The social security measures were just one part of this strategic approach but much of the economy was affected.

By 1982, £992m had been taken out of demand by the rise in national insurance contributions, and the effects of public expenditure reductions, both through cash limits and actual cuts, were staggering. In construction, output was down 22% over two and a half years and there were 400,000 building workers unemployed. The planning assumptions in the

165. I spy Strangers' was a device used by backbenchers to delay proceedings on a Bill they disliked. Members had to stand (the more the better) and shout 'I Spy Strangers,' and if there were enough shouting loudly enough, the Speaker would have to call a division in which the question would be put that members of the public, or strangers, should be excluded from the galleries. Of course, no one wanted to exclude strangers but it was a method of irritating the Government, slowing down proceedings, and getting oodles of publicity on a particularly noxious Bill. The Labour front bench didn't like us doing it either.

Public Spending White Paper based on the Public Expenditure Survey Committee was for a rise in unemployment of 300,000 in 1982/3 over the previous year.

The unemployment total of over three million had only been reduced by persuading 21,000 men over the age of 60 to deregister as unemployed in order to obtain the long-term rate of supplementary benefit, which was higher than the benefits they would otherwise have been entitled to.

The Government did not care if deindustrialisation swept the country. They thought elections could be won with an unemployment level higher than anything seen since 1945 and had scant regard for the quality or volume of public services.

After the Falklands there were few constraints on its actions.

This cluster of policies had local consequences in Wood Green, of course. The most contentious issue was housing. There was enormous pressure because of the size of the waiting list in Haringey. It had reached 10,300 families in 1982 and was to rise to 12,000 by 1983. On the other side of the equation there were just 320 'management voids',[166] about 1.25% of the housing stock, plus a further 800 properties in rehabilitation programmes.

Homelessness was also accelerating quickly. There were about 1,500 referrals to the Housing Emergency Group in 1982, mainly families, many of whom had an automatic right to rehousing under the 1977 Homeless Persons Act.

Because of all this, Haringey had 89 priority-need homeless families living in hostel accommodation in March 1982, compared to only four a year previously. It followed inexorably from this that the perfectly sensible policies of the local council, such as rehousing from the waiting list and the decanting of families with children from tower blocks, could not proceed.

The human cost of this was all too clear at my advice bureau every week. The misery, despair and hopelessness was there *en clair* and it would only get worse. It was the direct consequence of a well-fed bunch of ranting monetarists getting their hands on the levers of power and the only way it could be stopped was by a change in government.

---

166. Homes in the ownership of the Council but unoccupied for whatever reason
    – for example, waiting for redecoration or minor repair

Nuclear Power and Climate Change in the 1980s

By the early 1980s, the unmistakable shape of an entirely new crisis was emerging: that of climate change, coupled with the safety of power generation.

Britain had traditionally relied on coal as its 'base load' fuel of choice. This was mitigated only by the 1950s-designed Magnox nuclear reactors, small amounts of hydroelectricity generation, and a growing group of generators using oil.

There was a genuine mixed economy of power generation, which was thought to be the safest option in terms of fuel security, but there were increasing concerns about the long-term future of oil supplies given the developing political uncertainty in the Middle East and the power of the oil cartel, OPEC.

The Labour Party was confused on the issue and had been for some time. On the Energy sub-committee of the NEC were representatives of each of the power industries, and the official policy was that we had to have a coal fire, a gas fire, and electricity for heating in each home.

They wanted to be nice to the miners, which meant digging as much coal as possible. They wanted to be nice to the North Sea oil producers and give them something of a power generation market. They wanted to be nice to British Gas and, therefore, we all had to have natural gas in the house. And they thought nuclear was OK.

Mandy was a member of the Energy Committee of the NEC and at her first meeting was asked by the representative from the electricity industry whether she had an electric cooker at home.

This illustrated the level of debate and his view as to why she was there.

The accident at the Three Mile Island nuclear plant at Harrisburg in Pennsylvania in March 1979, where there was a partial meltdown of the No. 2 reactor and a significant release of radioactive gases and iodine into the atmosphere, sensitised many to the dangers of nuclear power and raised questions about cleaner, more reliable, sustainable and less dangerous power generation.

The clean-up of the Three Mile Island contamination took 14 years and cost $1bn. However, the full horror of Chernobyl was some years away. But the mixed mode generation consensus was being undermined and the argument that nuclear power would produce electricity 'too cheap to monitor' – the marketing slogan of the time from the nuclear industry – was under serious strain.

These developments did not dissuade the Government from pursuing a new policy, embarking on the planning and construction of what they thought would be a new generation of nuclear plants.

They chose the Pressurised Water Reactor designed and built by Westinghouse and identified a location next to the Sizewell A Magnox reactors in Suffolk.

As part of the PR blitz in favour of the new reactor, I was invited to visit Sizewell and was taken up there by a manager from Eastern Electricity.

The first thing you saw when entering the Magnox reactor public area was a giant board with flashing lights which told you the present output of the station and the cost of production per generated unit. It was, of course, in the low pence.

But they were very defensive when asked whether it included decommissioning costs. I knew perfectly well that it didn't. One of the main objections to the new nuclear programme was that the costs of decommissioning had been stripped out of the cost-benefit analysis supporting the scheme.

Neither had they decided where or how to store the high level radioactive waste which emitted beta and gamma radiation, and actinides which produced alpha particles such as Uranium 234, which has a half-life of 245,000 years. So, Sizewell B was clearly going to be a political decision with huge unknown costs in the future, based on uncertain containment technology for spent fuel at the back end of the fuel cycle, and with the true costs of production of power omitted from all of this.

One problem about challenging a renaissance of the British nuclear power industry was that opinion in the Party and amongst the general public was at that point quiescent. Climate change, and nuclear power itself, did not feature in most voters' minds as salient topics influencing their vote, and therefore it was hard to persuade key decision makers that this was something that should be opposed.

As late as the mid-1990s, prominent MPs such as Dennis Skinner were arguing for the reopening of coal mines, and global warming in the early 1980s was an esoteric subject of interest at that stage only to a restricted group of scientists and academics.

So, my approach in Parliament had to be an attempt to develop the facts for public consumption, and to raise consciousness. It was very obvious to me that warming was real and would develop into a major political and economic issue quite soon. I had always opposed the off-the-wall 'Back to the Stone Age' green arguments put together by people like Ralph Schumacher, who I debated in the 1970s. He wanted to stop economic growth altogether and prevent developing countries from developing further.

This was obviously madness, unsellable and inequitable, so a more sophisticated version defining the problem and what to do about it was necessary.

I developed this by asking pointed questions about the Windscale Fire of 1957 and in particular the release of radioactive material into the atmosphere, which had been considerable. This was Britain's worst nuclear accident and rated 5/7 on the International Nuclear Event Scale. It had produced emissions of the radioactive isotope iodine 131 and estimates were that the radioactive cloud had produced an additional 240 deaths from cancer.

However, there were other radioactive emissions that had not been discussed in the literature – especially polonium. The limited instrumentation in the Windscale tower at the time did not measure the total emissions produced. It was clear to me that the illumination of the dangers of nuclear power generation were crucial in fighting the new programme, so I started asking questions about it.

In this, I was greatly assisted by Professor Colin Sweet of South Bank University, who had published extensive attacks on the safety of nuclear reprocessing and the cost of the nuclear fusion programme funded by the EU.

As is almost always the case, conventional wisdom about the effects of the Windscale fire were revised. A re-analysis of the data by Garland and Wakeford[167] determined that about twice the amount of radioactivity was released as had been previously thought. They included in this revised view polonium, plutonium, caesium and radioactive iodine.

It took till 2007[168] for the revised contamination estimates to be made public. At least I had made a start decades earlier.

The political response to my questions was woeful.

John Moore,[169] the Parliamentary Under Secretary at Energy at the time, got very agitated indeed and started babbling on to me in the lobby about managing the whole fuel cycle and national security. It was clear

---

167. John Garland, formerly of the UK Atomic Energy Authority and Richard Wakeford, Visiting Professor at the University of Manchester
168. Reported by Rebecca Morelle, BBC science reporter, 6th October 2007
169. MP for Croydon Central 1974-92, later Lord Moore of Lower Marsh

that he was both out of his depth and trying to cover up.

What was also clear was that the whole nuclear power programme, based on the construction of 20 new Pressurised Water Reactors (PWRs), would cost £20bn at 1982 prices. So, it was not cheap and arguably not safe, and based on the Central Electricity Generating Board's (CEGB) own projections of electricity demand, it was not needed either.

This was illustrated by the Sizewell inquiry which was then sitting.

It was then revealed that the Chairman of the CEGB, Sir Walter Marshall, had an 'arrangement' with the designers and manufacturers of the PWR, Westinghouse. We know this because the head of the Westinghouse nuclear reactor division said so.

And, indeed, it turned out that Marshall had been working with Westinghouse since 1974. When appointed as Chair of the CEGB, he told the Conservative Secretary of State that he had this relationship with Westinghouse but was advised that this did not bar him from playing an important part in choosing the type of electricity generation systems that would be installed in Britain at taxpayers' expense.

Marshall and city bankers, Kleinwort Benson, were trying to get around US nuclear non-proliferation law[170] which controlled the circumstances under which civil nuclear power technology could be sold to third parties.

If Westinghouse could sell a PWR to Britain, the UK could be used as a base to export US nuclear technology to countries which at that time did not possess it, outside the immediate orbit of the Act. This was important as no new nuclear reactors had been ordered in the US since 1978 as a consequence of Three Mile Island and the Carter legislation.

But the issues had been raised, as they had about long-term storage of nuclear waste. This caused political difficulty for the Government. We never got the promised 20 PWRs nor did we have to spend billions on getting them.

Chernobyl a few years later killed off the civil nuclear power programme for decades but it was resurrected by the Cameron Government after the 2010 General Election, and the new station at Hinkley Point C authorised. But they couldn't get the finances right and the wider programme is still in limbo, waiting for it to be expanded or killed off. The ever-falling cost of renewables may finish it forever.

---

170. The US Nuclear Non-Proliferation Act of 1978

180

Transport: the Attack on Subsidies

A further policy front was opened up by the Government on transport, in which they attempted to reduce subsidies on bus transport and on London Transport generally. The Transport Bill 1982 followed the Labour victory in the GLC elections in 1981 and the subsequent lowering of fares by the new administration, which had been flagged in their manifesto.

This provoked the Denning judgement on Fares Fair (the GLC policy) which followed the levying of a supplementary precept by the Council in July 1981, most of which was to pay for a 25% reduction in fares on London Transport. The London Borough of Bromley took legal action against the GLC on the basis that this decision was not based on what they described as 'business principles.' Bromley lost in the High Court but won in the Court of Appeal, with Lord Denning presiding. The GLC took the case to the Law Lords but lost.

The determinations by the Law Lords were inconsistent with each other, were rambling, and were highly interventionist. They were saying that a modest policy to encourage greater use of public transport was wrong because it had breached their idea – and a contentious idea at that – of public policy.

It is difficult to see how that argument could win in the context of 2020 and knowing what we know about climate change. But in 1982, at the height of the Thatcher ascendancy, it made a strong political statement.

What followed was the new legislation to try and remove the possibility for all time of transport Executives in the metropolitan councils[171] and the GLC to make subsidy decisions beyond what the Secretary of State for Transport determined.

In fact, it nationalised decision-making on local transport and in practice reduced the ability of local authorities to encourage public transport and make private transport, usually cars, less attractive as alternatives.

In the context of big cities and especially London, it was regressive and bound to lead to further pollution. In respect of the London buses, the GLC transport department said that in 1981 buses travelled 2,661 million passenger miles and that the long-term effect of the Denning judgement would be to reduce passenger miles to 1,880 million, a

---

171. Tyne and Wear, West Yorkshire, South Yorkshire, Greater Manchester, Merseyside, and the West Midlands

reduction of 781 million passenger miles.[172]

But the Bill set out a clear stall: reduced public subsidies from taxes to public transport and increased contributions from the fare paying travellers. The victory of Thatcherism on transport policy meant higher pollution, overcrowding, and the elimination of many services. This has taken 35 years to come to its full fruition, but we are seeing the long shadow of the past in this as on other policy areas. It started in the 1980s.

Another modern topic, judicial intervention in politics, was also a key feature of the issues that I raised all those years ago.

The Denning judgement[173] was perhaps the most important legal intervention in politics in the modern era and prefigured the role played by the courts on judicial review and on matters of public policy such as Brexit. Denning made up legal principles as he went along and invented what the law should be, as he decided that the legislation was not clear in its intentions.

Judicial activism really started then.

School Meals and Milk: the Education Bill 1980

Education was not immune from the Government attacks on the status quo, with the Education Bill of 1980 forming the centrepiece.

One of the key moves was to establish the Assisted Places Scheme, using public money to embed disadvantaged school students in fee paying private schools, provided that they scored amongst the highest 10-15% in examinations. I wasn't concerned so much about that as it was peripheral, but the provisions on school meals and milk were appalling.

Soon after I was elected in 1979, we began picking up trial balloons in the press about the abolition of free school milk in secondary schools and fundamental changes to the school meals service. I unearthed the name of the senior civil servant who seemed to be developing the policy, phoned him up, and astonishingly was given a one-on-one meeting at the department.

He explained the whole thing: abolition of the national nutritional standards that ensured a proper delivery of protein and vegetables to children; abolition of the national price for a meal; and abolition of free school milk in secondary schools.

---

172. See HOC Standing Committee A, col 288, 9th December 1982
173. Debated at cols. 573-588, Standing Committee A, 14th December 1982

My particular interest in this was the nutrition of children and the fundamental changes in employment that would stem from the changes. The plan was to inject choice into the system so that kids could eat what they wanted and could afford, and reduce spending by local authorities on the service as prices-per-meal rose. It was another attempt to reduce spending and the size of the State.

Having discovered this plan I then leaked it and got some publicity, and when the Bill was published, the proposals followed what the department had told me. It was clear that over time nutritional standards would fall as kids exercised their choices – and chose the pizza and chips option rather than veg and salads.

It was quite clear that this was going to create a dietary timebomb amongst young children, and so it proved. Some argued later that the pizza and chips option was 'what children wanted.' Part of the rise in childhood obesity seen in Britain since the 1980s is, in my opinion, down to this perverse piece of legislation.

The response to this in the Labour Party was interesting. By early 1980, it was clear that the new frontbench lead on Education, Neil Kinnock, was at best equivocal about the school meals and milk provisions. He had been promoted to the frontbench by Callaghan and was keen to demonstrate his establishment position.

I was getting very frustrated with this so asked Mikardo to raise it at the PLP, as Mik was bound to be called. On 7th February 1980 he did just that, asking for a statement on our attitude to the Employment and Education Bills. When Kinnock got up, he said,

Well, I can't give an assurance that we will repeal the Education Bill. We are committed to ending the assisted places scheme, but we cannot pledge reinstatement of school meals and milk because of the economic situation we shall inherit.[174]

Benn commented that, 'it went down very badly.'

I got up, criticising Kinnock's approach and asked for consideration of the nutritional effects on children and the great loss of jobs that would flow from the policy to be taken in to account when setting our policy, and was followed in support by Kevin McNamara.[175]

Many other Members were agitated at Neil's remarks. There was shouting. The final nail in the coffin came from Jack Ashley.[176] He had been

---

174. Benn diaries 1977-80 page 578
175. MP for Hull North 1966-74 and Hull Central 1974-2005
176. MP for Stoke on Trent South 1966-92, later Lord Ashley of Stoke

passed a written note of Neil's remarks, as he himself was profoundly deaf. He said that it was the most staggering statement that he had ever heard at a PLP meeting. Jack was highly respected because of the way that he handled his disability and the way he related to everyone. He encapsulated what almost the whole PLP thought.

Benn's diary entry continues:

Afterwards the right was laughing itself sick that a left wing frontbench spokesman should have made such a statement and the left was saying, 'This is what happens when you become a shadow minister.' Poor old Neil has taken a knocking.

Kinnock deserved the discomfiture. He really didn't understand the legislation and he thought bluster would deal with the problem.

Eventually the NEC decided to intervene: John Golding[177] moved a motion at the Home Policy Committee on 11th February that the next Labour Government be invited to commit to restoration of school meals, milk and school transport. John was widely regarded as the organiser of the right on the NEC and his motion was carried unanimously. Good result.

The Falklands Crisis

The Falklands invasion by General Galtieri of Argentina created immense political challenges for the Labour Party and was a turning point in the Thatcher premiership.

Before the Falklands, the Conservative Government had been adrift in the polls for much of the time since the 1979 election, first to Labour and then to the SDP. It was pretty clear that Thatcher was going to lose the next election – the question was, to whom?

The decision to assemble the task force and despatch it to the Falklands was a momentous one. After the invasion there had been various attempts at international peace initiatives, such as the Peruvian peace plan, and it was a mark of the ineffectiveness of the special relationship that US intelligence was not cooperating with the UK through use of its satellites.

As I wrote in my Parliamentary Report to the Wood Green Constituency Party on 26th May 1982,

Many concessions were made by both sides during the Haig, UN and Peruvian negotiations ... it is clear that the British Government was prepared

---

177. MP for Newcastle under Lyme 1969-86

to concede sovereignty as a long-term solution. A change of heart only occurred when large numbers of Tory backbench MPs called for 'no sell outs.'

Before the task force sailed, economic sanctions on trade were not followed up by financial sanctions. The Bank of England was still re-financing Argentinian central bank debt (no doubt defaulted on later) and the merchant bankers, Schroder-Wagg, sent their Argentinian order book to Switzerland to evade any sanctions that might be imposed.

Because of the Argentine's low level of reserves and the enormous debt which has been built up, it is reliably believed that financial sanctions could have been highly effective in bringing the Junta to the negotiating table.[178]

There was also a marked lack of clarity about the political objectives of the re-invasion. Some in the Government wanted to reassert sovereignty and then negotiate it away.

There was also concern that any continuation of Crown status would involve a withdrawal of supplies from Argentina which provided much of the food, medical supplies and water used by the islanders. A further option was to create a non-aligned administration, which might have been acceptable to the inhabitants, under the UN Trusteeship Council.

Opposition to the Thatcher policy was low in the PLP but more extensive outside and was the foundation of the later mass movement against middle eastern intervention.

I was personally highly dubious that the task force could be stopped and uncertain as to whether it was desirable to do so. I thought that its presence would be a powerful incentive to Argentinian concessions.

In conversation with Tony Benn, he pooh-poohed these points and stated that once it was sent it was inevitable that it would be used. I remained sceptical but voted with the 34 MPs who divided against the Government on 20th May, and I signed the Early Day Motion calling for an immediate cease fire supported by a larger group of 83 Members.

The gung-ho 'stick it to the Argies' wave that struck public opinion changed British politics forever. The Labour frontbench line was that we were standing up to a brutal neo-fascist dictator and this view was supported by many on the left of the PLP. It did, however, play into the Thatcher line that the greatest weight should be given to the views of the islanders, who it seemed wanted to stay British. It was a fortuitous windfall for the Prime Minister and, in my view, made the result of the 1983 election quite certain.

There were, however, two further developments to the Falklands story.

178. Parliamentary Report 26th May 1982.

The first came when the PM stated – after the sinking on 2nd May of the General Belgrano[179] by the nuclear submarine HMS Conqueror – that the ship had been steaming towards the British task force.

Hansard the next day changed this statement to say that the Belgrano was sailing away from our ships. I was present when the PM made the statement and can confirm that she said the Belgrano was sailing towards the task force.

This controversy rumbled on for years under the brilliant campaigning of Tam Dalyell[180] who was making the point that the Belgrano was not a threat to British ships, was obsolete as it was constructed in 1935 and had inferior weapons, and that the deaths of so many Argentinian sailors should have been avoided.

The second and rather more satisfying development in the end was that, following the description in a radio broadcast of the 34 MPs who voted against the Falklands policy as 'traitors' by the gargantuan Liberal MP Cyril Smith,[181] remedial action was taken by one of our number.

Smith probably thought he could get away with this, but had forgotten that one of the 34 was Leo Abse,[182] a solicitor and one of the Parliamentary awkward squad, who promptly collected £50 from each of the 34 and sued Smith for libel. There was a gratifying out of court settlement in the sense that we got our £50 deposit back, Leo got his costs, and a formal on-the-record public apology was made.

Eastern Europe: Opposing Stalinism and Repression

Despite everything, there were still some in the PLP in 1979 who were deeply sympathetic to the Soviet Union and its allies. There always had been a small group of fellow travellers who were tasked with raising the issues that Moscow wanted to be ventilated, usually on matters of global security and nuclear weapons.

Some of the MPs most sympathetic to communism were, in fact, expelled by the Labour Party in the 1940s, with five forming the Labour

---

179. A heavy cruiser, regarded as obsolete and pretty defenceless against modern weapons
180. MP for West Lothian 1962-83 and Linlithgow 1983 to 2005
181. MP for Rochdale 1972-92
182. MP for Pontypool 1958-83 and Torfaen 1983-87

Independent Group.[183] Some of them stood against official Labour candidates in the 1950 General Election but were heavily defeated. Only Zilliacus was allowed to rejoin the Party later. He, in fact, became MP for Manchester Gorton[184] perhaps because of his nuanced views about Stalin (he criticised the Soviet leadership's views on Tito).

This group were, however, replaced over time with a cadre of fellow travellers who were thought by the press to do the Kremlin's bidding. There was constant debate as to which members of the PLP might be card-carrying communists.

My view was – probably none. The British Communist Party was heavily infiltrated and bugged by the security services who were very likely to pass on to Transport House any information they received.

However, they didn't have to be members of the CP, and some were assiduous about supporting the Soviet regime and its penumbra of client states. Norman Atkinson, my constituency neighbour, may well have been one of them, but it's impossible to say. He was certainly hanging on the words of the Kremlin about the American Star Wars policy, and repeating the Soviet line on other aspects of Reagan's nuclear posture.

Newspaper investigations much later indicated that Stan Orme, Alf Lomas, Barnett Stross and others were the recipients of substantial gifts from Czech intelligence agents in return for information on the policies of the Labour Governments of the day. Others – Stan Newens[185] and Syd Bidwell[186] were members of the Trotskyist International Socialists faction, the forerunner of the Socialist Workers Party, and resigned from it only when elected to the Commons. Newens wrote to Tony Cliff, its General Secretary, the day after he was elected to the House and said that it was no longer appropriate for him to be a member, as he was now an MP.

I was not prepared, in any event, to go down the road of acquiescence to Moscow or to any reheated Trotskyist group. I supported the Eastern Europe Solidarity Campaign (EESC), which organised an annual meeting at Conference, and we were active against General Jaruzelski's war on Solidarity.[187]

We also supported civil rights movements in Czechoslovakia and

183. Platts-Mills, Pritt, Hutchinson, Solley and Zilliacus
184. 1955-67
185. MP for Epping 164-70 and Harlow 1974-83
186. MP for Southall 1966-92
187. The very broad social movement led by Lech Walesa that united Poles against the communist regime and credited with a major role in freeing Poland from the yoke of Moscow.

Hungary and saw ourselves as a counterweight against Soviet influence in the Labour Party and the trade unions (which was considerable).

As part of the campaign, we invaded the Polish Embassy in 1980 and occupied it for a few hours in protest against Jaruzelski. I am quite certain that there were elements on the left of Labour who didn't like these activities and I was constantly described as a tool of the CIA, which was hilarious.

The Americans, however, did try lunching me with a view, I suspect, to gaining me as an informant. The Labour attaché at the US Embassy in Grosvenor Square, no doubt tasked with monitoring the Labour Party, asked me out to lunch. I said no, and instead bought him a cup of tea on the Commons Terrace instead. They went away.

There were no motorcycle trips to East Germany or Progressive Tours packages to Cuba for me either. It was pretty obvious to anyone that the Soviet empire was fading rapidly and could not keep up with western technology and defence spending.

I was most opposed to their treatment of individuals and organisations who were not under the direct control of the local communists, and I am glad that I did what I did. We are better off without State-sponsored repression.

One of my proudest possessions is a full size book of Solidarity posters from the struggles of the early 1980s, given to me by the wonderful Janey Buchan,[188] a fellow activist in support of the EESC, which is a record of what was said and done by Solidarity.

Decay of the Tribune Group and Creation of the Socialist Campaign Group

I joined the Tribune Group immediately after the 1979 election and looked forward to participating in its work. The Secretary was Jo Richardson, who became a good friend, but to say that the group did 'work' was an exaggeration. It discussed events, was entirely reactive, and was heavily focused on Parliament to the exclusion of almost everything else.

The meetings of the group were often thinly attended and desultory, with Members coming and going, drifting in and out as they wished

188. MEP for Glasgow 1979-94

and with little discipline. There was no love lost between some of them. Skinner was very loud in his denunciation of people who he thought had been unhelpful. Les Huckfield[189] in particular was the subject of his wrath.

When Huckfield entered the room where the Tribune Group was meeting, Skinner exclaimed in a stage whisper, 'Here comes Callaghan's spy.'

Further incidents abounded: I had produced a paper for the group in December 1979 entitled *The Political Situation: Wages and the Cuts* which set out the opportunities available to the Thatcher Government to defeat Labour again. Amongst these were rapidly increasing North Sea oil annual revenues, estimated by the National Institute of Economic and Social Research as being £14,067m[190] by 1984, and £21,521m by 1985, assuming only modest rises in per-barrel prices.

These government revenues from oil had risen from £96m in 1975.

The Government could also increase its headroom for fiscal manoeuvre (it said it wanted to reduce the basic income tax rate to 20-25p) by cutting the net contribution to the EEC. Prime Minister Thatcher achieved this in 1984, cutting net contributions by 66%.

By 2017 this rebate, deducted from the UK's gross contributions, amounted to £5.6bn.[191] My point was that there was enormous headroom for the Government to run a low tax economy with mass unemployment and win elections – a fact that was not being factored in by our front bench. They thought that Thatcher would win the election for us – a dangerous delusion and one that was falsified by events.

In this context, I argued, the current vacuum in the Labour movement's policy on the economy, especially on wages and public services, was disastrous. Therefore, work should be done to slow down the Government's ability to implement its programme and by forcing it to change course on a number of crucial issues.

One important area where the Labour movement had some clout was wages, where the covert incomes policy implied a reduction of real wages of 10-15% in the public sector that year.

Despite this strong attack by central government, which might encourage a concerted response from a range of trade unions, I pointed out the idiosyncratic features of public sector pay bargaining. There

189. MP for Nuneaton 1967-83
190. At 1979 prices
191. Treasury estimate

was little coordination between the unions and cohesion amongst them was minimised because settlement dates were scattered throughout the year.

The Labour frontbench was also going along with the Thatcher programme, I said, because statements made by them supported some form of monetarism, commitments to further cuts in public spending, coupled with an incomes policy.

In short, they wanted to continue the disastrous policies of the former Labour Government which had been heavily defeated at the polls in 1979. As action points, I argued for support to workers whose pay had been slashed by inflation and poor settlements, the beefing up of TUC positions on these issues, and for Labour to develop a new programme based on using North Sea oil revenues to rebuild the economy.

This was all too much for one member of the Tribune Group, who leaked it to the press. I didn't mind that at all, but it incensed Ian Mikardo, who employed a private detective to find out who it was.

He reported later that the detective suggested that it had come from an MP close to former Treasury Ministers, based on the typewriter used to send the documents to the press.

I followed this paper up with another in January 1981. This argued for close consultation between the Tribune Group and the trade unions at two levels – the branches and the leadership.

I was concerned that the Government would have real financial freedoms from about 1983 onwards and that we had to rebuild the movement if we were in any way to blow Thatcher off course. Little happened. The group seemed frozen and incapable of looking externally or attempting to build support for its views outside Parliament.

Of course, it came back to the 'prima donna' view of the world which many MPs had. Because you are responsible for your own work programme, working together for agreed objectives was regarded as strange. Perhaps it is different now.

One positive outcome of the row was that the Tribune Group agreed to my proposal for a national conference to deal with the economic policy of the Party and its response to Thatcherism. The conference happened but outcomes were nowhere to be seen, and it became increasingly clear that Tribune needed a radical cutting edge or replacement.

Tony Benn joined the group in February 1981 but that did not deal with the rot that had seeped in. The rot was lack of intellectual clarity of any stripe and no organisational heft. Frankly, it amounted to paralysis.

The Group was a legacy organisation with a serious past but unable to adapt to changing times.

By 1982, replacement was the only policy available and this was agreed by the older generation Tribunites such as Ian Mikardo and Jo Richardson, who were as frustrated as I was.

Its formation was precipitated by the attempts by the Foot leadership to split its opponents by requiring registration of organisations outside the formal Labour Party structures. This was a form of censorship and control, but the origins of the new group were more soundly based than opposition to the leadership on that narrow point.

I went around getting signatures of support and was very successful, but had to force the issue at Party Conference in 1982, in order to avoid the usual backsliding. I suggested to Joan Maynard, who was chairing the Tribune rally, that she should announce the formation of the new grouping from the platform. She did, and the Campaign Group was born.

Writing shortly after its formation, I said:

The Parliamentary Tribune Group performs no useful function at all. It is a talking shop, and an exclusively Parliamentary one at that ... There are many individual MPs in the Tribune Group whose views on a range of subjects deserves the respect and support of the movement. But when real attempts have been made to broaden the base of the Tribune Group by linking up with the left in the constituencies and the trade unions, these attempts have been vetoed.[192]

Our objectives should be both ideological and organisational, I said, and quoted declining support over the previous 30 years for the nationalised industries and nationalisation as a concept among working people, with support for the trade unions declining over the same period, and racism and sexism still widespread.

The only ideas which were gaining traction with large groups of voters were nuclear disarmament and women's rights, both mobilised by groups outside the normally defined boundaries of the Labour movement.

The Party's ability to recruit and retain members, particularly from the working class, was probably lower than at any time since 1945.

I was prefiguring the opportunities created by the explosion of social media from 2000 onwards, but in 1982 it was naïve to think that it was possible to build an external force that would contribute to serious change in the PLP and the unions.

---

192. Left Labour MPs Must Break Out of Isolation in Parliament, *Morning Star* 1982.

Tony Benn in particular disliked my approach, especially as I had ended my article with the words:

[These objectives] can be achieved only by an organisation determined to break out of Parliamentary isolation and ... make a reality of the claim that the difference between the left in the '50s and in the '80s is that we are now LESS dependent on the influence and power of one individual than we were in Aneurin Bevan's time.

He hated this because it was obviously a reference of the dependence that the left had on one person: T Benn. It was unhealthy, and as soon as the head was struck off the chicken after 1983, it was the end of left wing politics in the Labour Party for decades.

Always Getting it Wrong

It was, of course, true that the Tribune campaigns in the 1950s collapsed when Bevan made his peace with Gaitskell. Likewise, in the 1980s, the left were highly dependent on perceptions of Tony Benn. In turn, Momentum have been entirely dependent on support for Jeremy Corbyn in order to build their larger-than-normal faction.

But in the early 1980s, reforming the PLP was not just an obsession of people like myself. Tony Benn and Eric Heffer had produced a short paper on *The Future Work of the Parliamentary Labour Party*[193] straight after the election. which was designed to pose issues for the incoming PLP in an attempt to ensure a more coordinated approach between the PLP and the NEC in particular.

As the left controlled the Home Policy Committee of the NEC and the full NEC itself, it was possible for material to be fed into the PLP from that point of origin. But there was no discussion of the Benn/Heffer plans beforehand. They just 'appeared' and in practice went well beyond the demands of CLPD.

The paper called for:

- A commitment to implement Party policy as determined by the Party Conference

---

193. Dated 19th June 1979

- The Party meeting (that is, the weekly meeting of the PLP) to be in charge of Parliamentary tactics such as the line-to-take on legislation, and on whipping

- The election of the principal Parliamentary spokesmen (sic) and the Parliamentary Committee to be by ballot at the PLP

- Portfolios to be shared with the agreement and consent of the PLP

- Backbench committees to nominate MPs from the backbenches to speak from the despatch box

- Regular meetings between the Parliamentary Committee and the NEC

- No one to be nominated for a peerage

- These reforms to stay in place when there was a Labour Government in power.

This paper went to the NEC on 4th July[194] and was agreed.

Benn presented the proposals at the PLP on 11th July in a debate that spilled over till the next meeting. The proposals eventually just disappeared. This reflected the inability of the 'great men' of the left to propose solutions without including immense hostages to fortune – such as the abolition of peerage nominations, which absolutely no one was asking for at that point, and the unworkable arrangements in respect of portfolios and backbench committees. The paper was undoubtedly drafted by Benn and floated at Heffer for agreement, as it contains issues and wording which were Benn's favourite means of discourse.

The Benn/Heffer proposals were also ridiculous as the Party meeting could not possibly deal with every particle of tactics required on legislation at one meeting. If it had ever been tried it would have failed almost instantly: the frontbench would have been left without instructions from the PLP and would have had to make it up as they went along.

This was such an obvious problem that the PLP would never have agreed to it. But that's what the so-called left leaders were doing at the time – setting up straw men bound to fail, and isolating themselves from

194. See Benn diaries, *Conflicts of Interest* 1977-80, page 517

middle-of-the-road opinion in the PLP and the NEC who would have supported better prepared plans.

It is important to recognise that the left controlled the NEC at that point by a fractional margin, and not on all subjects, and that Benn was pursuing an all-or-nothing strategy there without really discussing it with many in the PLP.

He blew hot and cold on the issue of getting consent from the PLP, especially where his record as a minister was widely disliked by a range of MPs from different traditions. There were times, in a reflective mood, when he recognised the need for consent and a broader political base.

For example, in his diaries just after the election in 1979[195] he says: 'I do realise that I have got to win back the confidence of the PLP.' But in his speeches and personal relations he was sometimes provocative and uncontrolled. He was not a member of the Tribune Group at that point, not that it would have helped him much, and he operated through a kitchen cabinet that met erratically and by invitation only at his house in Holland Park. At the kitchen cabinet the discussions were overwhelmingly about tactics.

His most substantial failure was in not having a strategy to develop hegemonic ideas in the PLP and the senior trade union leadership, and in failure to focus on a limited list of issues.

There were just too many key people that thought him a loose cannon, liable to go off at any moment, and unreliable. He was always trying to push the envelope and didn't listen to the few people who were asked for advice. A specific example was in his first speech from the front bench under the Foot leadership, when he had been made energy spokesman, reflecting his last Cabinet position. He closed for the Labour front bench on 10th November 1981 in a debate on North Sea Oil.

The first half of the speech was a brilliant attack on the Government's policy which drew rapturous cheers from the whole of the PLP because it was indeed a *tour de force*. But then he went too far. He started advocating every micro element of Labour policy, focusing on nationalisation without compensation (a Militant tendency argument which resonated with almost no one else in the Labour Party), did it badly, and the mood soured quickly. He snatched defeat from the jaws of victory. It was clear that his judgement as a front line politician was going, that he was no longer the coming man of the PLP, and that he was clearly yesterday's man.

---

195. Benn diaries, Monday 21st May 1979, page 506

This incident, which I witnessed and was appalled by, showed Benn ignoring Shadow Cabinet decisions, ruined his position in the PLP and in future Shadow Cabinet elections, and was typical of a frequent misreading of events. It was a total failure to catch mood and policy substance in an argument he needed to win.

Another example was on Ireland where he moved a motion at the Home Policy Committee on 11th February 1980 to form a study group to establish a policy on Irish reunification. At this point there was relatively little clamour for it, there was no prospect of agreement with the parties in the North, and a continuing bombing campaign by the IRA was being undertaken.

His proposal was defeated and all that happened was that everyone on the NEC united against him.

So, in these inauspicious circumstances the Campaign Group was born.

After I left the House in 1983, it turned into an oppositionalist and rather sectarian organisation. Its output was erratic and poor, and it did not perform the role that had been envisaged. It published a book shortly after the 1983 General Election which purported to be the bones of a future policy position. It was, with one or two exceptions, awful.

My old friend Bob Cryer[196] said, 'You are the only person who comes out of it well.' Perhaps he was being kind, but there may have been something in what he said. I was invited to attend the group sometimes as a former Member, but it maintained some of the worst features of the Tribune Group: personal hatreds, and a pick-and-mix smorgasbord attitude to issues and campaigns which meant that it did not focus.

Leaving the Place

I left the Commons in 1983 when my constituency – like many others in inner city London – was abolished by the Boundary Commission. Games were played over this as the Party waited 'in hope' (although there wasn't much of this) that the so-called Enfield case would be resolved in Labour's favour. This would have meant that the Commission would have to revisit its findings and that the changes in Parliamentary boundaries would need to be postponed. This did not happen and, despite being reselected unanimously by my constituency Party in Wood Green,

196. MP for Keighley February 1974-83, and Bradford South 1987-94

there was nowhere to contest with any meaningful chance of victory in that election.

Except perhaps in Tottenham, held by Norman Atkinson, where the old Tottenham seat had seven wards moving into the new constituency and I had three coming in from Wood Green. It was a long shot but I had to contest it, and there was some hope because it was widely realised that Norman was suffering healthwise and was not now the most effective MP for the area.

But I lost the selection very narrowly, entirely because the ultra-left Trots and the Communist Party fellow travellers present wouldn't vote for an independent minded bloke like myself who was against Soviet repression and wouldn't take instructions from ultra-left groups. A salutary lesson and not the last time that I had run-ins with that crowd.

The election itself was painful. Labour had got itself into a substantial mess over nuclear weapons policy and the breadth of its manifesto. The ancient form of poor old Mike Foot campaigning in a 50-year-old style did not help.

Rapturous receptions at ticket only rallies did not indicate broad support amongst the voting public, a lesson not learnt in the 21st century by his successor.

Thatcher rode the waves to victory, not just because of the Falklands but as a result of support for her toughness against all comers, and her espousal of change.

The writing was clearly visible on the wall earlier that year when at the Bermondsey by-election the Labour candidate was heavily defeated by the unscrupulous Simon Hughes[197] aided and abetted by the Real Labour candidate John O'Grady, who rode on horse and cart all over Bermondsey smearing Peter Tatchell for being gay.

One unsigned and illegal leaflet circulating in Bermondsey, with no imprint on it, said: *Which Queen will you vote for?* (next to a picture of Her Majesty and Peter Tatchell):

Peter Tatchell is an outspoken critic of the Queen and the Royal Family. He believes that the Royal Family should be abolished... Tatchell is a traitor to Queen and Country. DON'T VOTE FOR TATCHELL!

SHOULD YOU WISH TO QUESTION MR TATCHELL MORE CLOSELY ABOUT HIS VIEWS THEN WHY NOT PHONE HIM ON... (HIS PHONE NUMBER) OR VISIT HIM AT HIS HOUSE WHICH IS AT XXX ROCKINGHAM STREET

197. MP for Bermondsey and then Bermondsey and Southwark 1983-2015

This was the tone which had been unleashed and which had been the result of poor decision making by many. It was appalling, incited violence, and attacked a candidate ruthlessly because of his sexuality. The Labour Party, to its shame, did not deal with these attacks.

I went over there as often as I could, as it was only just over Westminster Bridge, but I can't say that the Labour campaign was inundated with MPs helping the official Labour candidate.

I advised Peter, who was a genuine and, in some ways a sensible activist, to make it clear that he was indeed gay, kick the issue into the long grass, and say, 'So what?' He wouldn't, and I'm sure he regrets it now.

His campaign was also not helped by the behaviour of the press officer, Monica Foot, brought in by Party HQ. She was drunk much of the time. She had a whisky bottle on her desk from which she poured endless libations and when answering the phone to journalists slagged off Peter Tatchell in front of me. It was appalling and the sign of things to come.

On one occasion after canvassing, I went back to vote in the House at 10pm, and in the Members Lobby Chief Whip Mike Cocks spotted me and asked how it was going over the river. 'We'll be lucky to get 10,000 votes,' I said.

He was horrified but I actually underestimated the scale of the disaster. Tatchell actually polled less than 8,000 and the Labour share of the vote slumped by 37.5%. The swing to the Liberals was 44.5%, the largest ever in a by-election.

Much later, Simon Hughes apologised for his behaviour smearing Tatchell; he was himself bisexual, he revealed, but that, of course, was far too late.[198]

The Labour Party was in freefall and was being led by people who didn't know what they were doing. Michael Foot was impossibly incompetent over the whole affair and should have known better to denounce an endorsed Parliamentary candidate from the despatch box and thereby create the space for attacks from anyone on poor old Peter. Which he did.

The most bizarre event for me occurred on the day after the General Election. I had to go and sign on to get unemployment benefit, walked down Tottenham High Road to the dole office, and eventually saw the guy who dealt with new claims.

When he asked me about my former employment and why I'd left it, he blanched when I told him I was a former MP and had not been able

---

198. See the detailed description of the Hughes and O'Grady campaigns in The Battle for Bermondsey, P Tatchell, Heretic Books 1983

to stand in the election. It turned out that he had a dream the previous night about a former MP coming into the office the next day to claim benefit and was flabbergasted that it had actually happened.

He was pretty distraught, and it obviously touched a nerve.

The 1979-83 Parliament was pivotal in that new issues such as climate change, women's rights, low pay, nuclear power, poverty, the slash-and-burn destruction of large parts of State provision, and the destruction of the UK's manufacturing capability, came to a head sharply.

It was the end of the Wilson/Callaghan years, the start of new agendas, and a huge learning curve for the Labour Party. It was slow on the uptake.

CHAPTER 5

THE FAILURE OF LOCAL LEADERSHIP

Immediately after the election in 1983 I had to look for a job. I didn't know what to do and my knowledge of employment networks was woeful and so I started trawling the jobs pages of the *Guardian* to see what was around.

One day, however, I received a call out of the blue from Ken Livingstone, who I had never spoken to, who asked if I was interested in a job at the GLC. It had just been advertised and he encouraged me to apply.

They were very conscious that they couldn't fulfil the programme on which they were elected and had been knocked back on the Denning judgement on Fares Fair and did not have enough capacity amongst the officers to get things done.

So, I applied and eventually went through the interview process, and to my astonishment got the job. I had never worked for a local authority and was, to be truthful, a bit underwhelmed by the idea as my experience with Haringey had been, on balance, negative.

The job, Head of the Programme Office, was a long established post and had been created in the late 1960s in response to the growing requirement for effective management of large local authorities. This was a time when local authority structures were a mess. There were many very small authorities with weak corporate management (if any), and little invigilation as to whether decisions made and policies adopted had the required outcomes.

From the 1960s onwards, both central government and local councils were making heroic decisions which have subsequently proved to be disastrous, for example tower blocks, digging up medieval sites for ring roads, massive area housing clearances, and disruption of communities.

The GLC's response to the perception that performance was lagging policy – five years after its creation in 1964 – was to toughen up corporate management.

They introduced programmes which covered not just one traditional department but a cohort of them which had congruence and 'fit.' The idea was that policies and monies could be managed as a whole, and not in small silos where the officers and members were isolated and did not talk to their colleagues in the slightly separate silo next door.

This innovation was undertaken in the Desmond Plummer administration[199] and was a farsighted move. It was based on the Ford Motor Company system which had been copied by the US Department of Defence. Even in 2020, many local authorities are still working on a departmental basis with no effective performance review: the GLC was way ahead of its time.

The functions of the Programme Office were interesting and strategic, setting the target regime for the whole council, monitoring spending and policy achievement, managing big parts of the council's budget directly, and organising the many mini-budgets and finance reviews.

Ken's failing policies

All these traditional functions were added to after my arrival in September 1983 because the administration's policies were failing. This was because some leading Members were inexperienced at making decisions and others had dodgy competence levels. Because they were not chasing down their officers and being inventive within the powers they had, underspend was extraordinarily high.

This was a ridiculous state of affairs as they were precepting for large cash increases, incurring the wrath of some ratepayers, the press and business, and not spending the cash received.

This was the worst of all possible worlds. The underspend when I arrived in September 1983 was about 66% of the revenue budget for that year. Some of the spending was valid and necessary and some was perhaps indulgent and unnecessary. But that was for elected Members to decide.

199. Desmond Plummer, Leader of the GLC 1967-73

So new functions were created for the Programme Office which included my invention – monthly monitoring. This was where Programme Office staff sat down with committee chairs, departmental heads and the committee finance officer to increase the focus on performance and spending.

This had the effect of driving up spend and performance against target. It removed blockages and led to a better understanding from everyone about the obstacles to some parts of the programme. Underspend came down sharply and the system was widely welcomed.

Another new function was budget planning.

Because of the Government's commitment to abolish the GLC (as set out in its 1983 General Election manifesto) it was obvious that 'normal service' was not going to be sufficient to keep the authority functioning normally, let alone firing on all cylinders. This meant examining the complicated GLC budget system and identifying areas where cash seemed to be sitting for no apparent reason.

I am all for prudence and sensible budget decision making, but in the last year of the GLC rather different processes could be justified. The alternative was to leave scores of millions of pounds which had been collected from the good people of London unused, and identified needs unmet.

Inside this function was constant discussion with the Council's internal legal advisors and external counsel in order to beef up the justifications for expenditure, where this was required.

We became very good at it, and we needed to be because Conservative councils in London had become addicted to litigation: Bromley had done it successfully over London Transport fares and Westminster took over the legal assault as soon as the abolition legislation was proceeding through the Commons.

Abolition: Victory and Ultimate Defeat

A second function which I was newly tasked with was dealing with the massive abolition legislation. This started with the London Regional Transport Bill of 1984 which stripped the GLC of its control over London Transport (which was established only in the late 1960s). Then the so-called paving bill (Interim Provisions Bill 1984). And finally, the full abolition bill itself.

There was no one else in the building with my Parliamentary experience, brief though it was, and so the task of dealing with this fell to me. There was a Legal and Parliamentary Branch staffed by solicitors who were used to dealing with private legislation that the council wanted to pursue but by common consent they were not well suited to deal with high politics stuff like this.

So, I started doing the briefings, building an abolition team, and setting up the links with the Director General himself, the awareness team, and devising the strategy to defeat the legislation. The lead Member for this was Tony Banks, who had just been elected as an MP a few months before, and I led the officer team. We were immensely successful.

The Tories placed abolition of the GLC in their 1983 election manifesto and having won immediately started on the road to abolition via the Interim Provisions Bill of 1984.

The key component of this Bill was to abolish the existing elected councillors and replace them with a new council composed of appointees from the London boroughs. As the Tories controlled a majority of the boroughs at the time it was certain that the replacement GLC would be Conservative-controlled. Political control would have passed from one party to the other without a single vote being cast by the electorate.

This enraged many Tories and neutrals, including Ted Heath, who described it as the 'greatest gerrymander in history' (in a speech I wrote for him and passed through back channels to his desk).

The Interim Provisions Bill was defeated in the Lords on 24th June 1984 by a majority of 46 on a substantial amendment drafted by my team which gutted the Bill and removed its central plank, the change in control of the GLC without a vote being cast. This was after (if I may say so) a brilliant Parliamentary campaign in which we identified the key weak point of the Government's position – gerrymandering.

We only won because I built a team of star lobbyists, with key personnel being Ann Pettifor[200] and Damien Welfare.[201] The strategy was to set out the arguments firmly in the Commons and then work the Lords so that we had a chance of defeating the legislation as a matter of principle – the principle being that London, a world city, needed a strategic authority to enable it to function properly.

---

200. Later a senior economic policy expert and director of Policy Research In Macroeconomics
201. Later an adviser at the Association of Local Authorities, and a barrister at Cornerstone

To be honest, the critical arguments about the need for a strategic authority for London carried little weight with legislators and certainly not enough weight to persuade Conservative peers to rebel against a manifesto commitment to abolish that strategic authority. What mattered with some of them were arguments about unfair electoral practices, which seemed to some to reek of banana republic politics and ran against the grain of traditional Conservative thinking on the maintenance of legitimate institutions.

We were also to pray in aid arguments about the centralisation of power, as many of the Council's functions were to be taken over by the Secretary of State for the Environment – hardly a devolution of power to the London boroughs, which was what was being argued by the supporters of the Bill.

But victory was still a long way off.

First, we had to mobilise the usual suspects who would vote against any Tory bill provided they could be persuaded to attend to vote. Whipping is in many ways light (or was then) in the Lords and a fair number of peers attended infrequently if at all, and then only when pressed – especially the older ones or those in poor health. So, we had to build an effective whipping operation.

This wasn't entirely easy as the Labour Chief Whip (Tom Ponsonby) had insubstantial records of his own Labour Lords – there was a scrappy bit of paper with out of date phone numbers, no addresses in many cases, and some on the list we knew to be dead.

The first task was therefore to build a database which Ponsonby was entirely happy for us to do. He was a gentle soul and referred to as Hon. Tom Pon, to reflect his previous incarnation as the son of a peer and the Secretary of the Fabian Society.

He let us take over his office as a base and we ruthlessly abused his generosity. The toughest nuts to crack were not the Labour side or many of the crossbenchers, usually professional in background, who were familiar with a lot of the arguments. The worst bunch of hardcore uselessness lay on the Liberal benches.

I attended a meeting of their Lords frontbench to lay out the case for a principled amendment on Second Reading to gut the key provisions of the Bill, but they were frozen in immobility. At first, they would not support our plans or, I suspected, any plans on anything at all. They later changed their mind when they saw the extent of public opposition and heard the arguments from their House of Commons colleagues. But they did give a very good impression of why an unelected Upper House stuffed full of ancient people should be avoided at all costs.

The crossbenchers were handled by the lobbying team, very successfully, and recalcitrant Tories were under the jurisdiction of Roland Freeman,[202] an ex-Tory GLC councillor who had recently defected to the SDP.

Freeman knew many people in the deep woodwork of the Conservative Party and we used him to pass on selected speeches and briefings to those who might not welcome them over my name (including Ted Heath).

It was particularly satisfying to hear the Grocer (as he was impolitely known) reading out whole sections of briefing material and speeches drafted by my hand. Freeman was brilliant at the task.

My job during all of this was to marshal the arguments, produce the briefings and speeches, support the lobbying team and the awareness campaign with advice. I had already written hundreds of Parliamentary Questions on abolition for the Commons and the burden became so great that the Table Office stopped accepting them because they argued that it was 'a campaign.'

But I was helped enormously by two people: Tony Banks,[203] who chaired the special abolition team of officers and Members. He was extremely good in giving a wide latitude to my lobbying team and supporting our efforts to rein in the wilder elements in the advertising agency we were using.

We had to stop these people running huge poster billboards showing be-ermined sleeves ripping up the Interim Provisions Bill – precisely the kind of image we did not want in the consciousness of the deeply conservative minds in the Upper House.

Tony backed us all the way.

The second essential and brilliant player was Nita Clarke,[204] Livingstone's media adviser and an important link to the leadership, who had an unerring eye for the key points of argument and a very

---

202. Conservative Leader of Wandsworth Council, GLC Member in two administrations latterly for Finchley, and later Parliamentary SDP candidate for Tonbridge and Malling in the 1987 General Election. He joined the Labour Party in 1990.

203. Chair of the GLC 1985-6, Labour MP for Newham NW 1983-2005, Lord Banks of Stratford 2005.

204. Nita Clarke later worked as a No. 10 adviser for Tony Blair and is married to Stephen Benn (Lord Stansgate), and is the mother of Emily Benn, a former Labour Councillor and Parliamentary Candidate.

diplomatic way of persuading recalcitrants. She was responsible for much of the turnaround in Livingstone's poll ratings and the transformation from revolutionary Ken to newt-loving cuddly Ken in the public mind, which legitimised and underpinned the detailed arguments to save the GLC. Ken could have done with advice like that years later.

We also used the resources of the GLC very effectively, including the fleet of official cars that were used mainly to convey chairs of committees and leaders to meetings and functions. There were a lot of them, and I sent them off to pick up far-flung Lords in the Home Counties who would be reluctant to come in on public transport on the grounds of age. Barbara Castle came in that way, as did Marcia Falkender and some of the other Wilson Peers.

The only recalcitrant Labour peer was Joe Gormley,[205] who hated Ken Livingstone with a viciousness wondrous to behold, and he refused several times on the phone to attend even though it was a three-line whip.

So, I sent a car for him anyway and made him refuse to get in it. I was determined to embarrass the old bombast. Everyone else was seriously cooperative and they were delighted to be getting one back on Thatcher.

One of the only notes of discord was from Tony Benn, who confided that we shouldn't be using the Lords as a way of defeating a government. I disagreed with him and argued that we should use all and every available means of stopping a pernicious piece of legislation that would damage the lives of millions of people, and I'm glad to say that hardly anyone agreed publicly with him.

Defeat for Thatcher and Jenkin

On the day of the crucial amendment, which the Government front bench thought they could cruise through, we hid many of the peers in committee rooms and offices and when they flooded into the Chamber to vote, the Tory whips were appalled.

We had outfoxed them. The fact that it was Royal Ascot and some of the racing fraternity were reluctant to attend a boring session about

---

205. President of the National Union of Mineworkers 1971-82 and a long-term opponent of Ken Livingstone. His main achievement as NUM President was to nail down the productivity agreement which drove up miners' wages but which meant that Areas had different wage rates and the incentive to take unified national action was diminished.

local government reorganisation aided us significantly.

When we won by 46 votes it was astonishing, the first time that a Tory Government had been defeated in the Lords on the principle of a manifesto commitment Bill since 1945. Celebrations were in order and we stole Tom Ponsonby's bottle of champagne that he kept in the office fridge and shared it out amongst the team. He didn't mind, I don't think.

The Bill was emasculated in the sense that its provisions to replace an elected Labour GLC with an unelected Conservative GLC overnight was resoundingly defeated.

The Government had to reintroduce it, removing the key gerrymandering plans, and instead extending the terms of the existing councillors until the end of March 1986, thus giving the Livingstone administration an extra year in office.

There were, however, onerous provisions in respect of restrictions on the letting of contracts: no building or engineering contract worth over £250,000 or maintenance contract over £100,000 could be granted by the GLC without the consent of the Secretary of State. Services to the Council over £100,000 were also controlled under the same rules.

This was an attempt to restrict the GLC's activities and make it much harder for it to fund and carry out the radical policies it wished to pursue. In this, it worked. But we became experts at persuading Department of the Environment officers that projects were desirable for the good of Londoners.

The advice of our crack team of lawyers led by Lord Tony Gifford QC and Robin Allen QC was fundamental in this, as they taught us new ways of defining 'need' and redefining the concept of the Council's duties.

They were very good at it and in the parlance of the day made many items 'judge proof.'

That did not always work, however. The most notorious example of a refusal from the Department of the Environment was on the rebuilding of four Victorian homeless persons hostels. They were awful in their near Dickensian interiors and provided a high proportion of the overnight beds available in London at the time for those unfortunate people who were living on the streets.

Ministers and DoE officials did not think this was important, a waste of ratepayers' monies, and vetoed the scheme.

Because of the Second Reading defeat and the need to re-introduce an emasculated Bill, the then-Secretary of State, Patrick Jenkin, was sacked shortly afterwards by the Prime Minister for his failure. Because the Bill implemented a manifesto commitment, it seemed to be caught by the Salisbury/Addison doctrine of 1945 which in essence said that the Lords would not seek to defeat legislation which had been part of a manifesto on which the Government of the day had been elected.

We overturned that doctrine on that occasion by smart footwork.

The important point for the GLC was that this in practice gave an extra year to the Livingstone administration which had a majority of only four. They had therefore to make choices about what kind of financial regime they wished to run in the very unusual circumstances of being involuntarily abolished.

Money and Who Controlled What

There was, and had to be, daily interface between the Programme Office and finance officers in the Council at many levels. They each had different functions: organising for the precept to be collected and banked, doing the accounting and organising the link with what was then the Rate Support Grant from Government.

Individual finance people were allocated to committees so that they could look after the accounting for that committee budget. Many of the finance officers were friendly and we worked well with them.

However, what the finance function was not doing eagerly was examining their overall financial policies in the light of abolition. They were institutionally small 'c' conservatives (although some of them made it clear they were Labour supporters).

So, each committee had a mainstream revenue budget, a capital budget, debt charges and a revenue reserve which it could dip into when required. The centre held a contingency reserve, a special contingency reserve, and had the capital fund (a mysterious entity they didn't want to talk about).

In the context of abolition and rate capping taken together, this needed serious examination – so this is what we did.

The result was that we found between £100m and £200m of additional resources (above that in a standstill budget) which was available for spending; Members decided how to allocate this as they always did, and spent most of it on re-roofing council houses, re-windowing them, and forward-funding the vulnerable voluntary sector after abolition.

Rate Capping: the Year Zero Pol Pot strategy

The first iteration of rate capping was for the financial year 1985-6 with the Government issuing firm guidance in the autumn of 1984 to the selected authorities about their rate capping upper limit.[206]

In the clear knowledge that this was going to happen, and in the expectation that the miners' strike would drag on, Livingstone and John McDonnell[207] together devised a strategy of 'going illegal.' The plan was to set no precept,[208] which they thought would open a second front against the Thatcher Government.

They won various internal battles inside the London Labour Party to get the Livingstone/McDonnell position adopted, but it was always a policy doomed to failure. The consequences of not setting a precept or rate were that the relevant councillors who had voted for the policy would be surcharged on a crippling and punitive basis and would undoubtedly lose their homes if they owned one.

Personal bankruptcy would also lose them their ability to have a bank account, and they would be disqualified from public office for a period of years (this is what happened in Clay Cross in Derbyshire in the early 1970s when several councillors went to gaol).

The chances of a majority of the Labour group voting to incur these pains and penalties on themselves were non-existent. It was a Year Zero, Pol Pot policy of grotesque posturing.

The thesis developed by McDonnell in particular was that on the basis of his calculations, unsupported by any facts about the actual rate capping limit, there would need to be £140m of cuts in GLC spending.

There would be blood on the floor. There would be mass redundancies. He even developed a little list of horror stories which allegedly flowed from cuts on this scale. It was published in the left wing journal *Briefing*. It was pure nonsense, Halloween shroud waving to frighten the gullible.

Knowing that this crisis was emerging, I wrote to McDonnell in his

---

206. The highest level of rates that an authority could levy without incurring penalties, thus limiting the resources that any of the selected authorities could raise in cash.

207. Chair of the Finance Committee and later when MP for Hayes and Harlington, Shadow Chancellor in the disastrous Corbyn leadership. Active in many ultra-left causes and now President of the Labour Representation Committee, a Trotskyist organisation

208. The monies that an upper tier Council like the GLC could levy on council tax payers.

capacity as Chair of Finance on at least four occasions in the summer and early autumn of 1984, before the rate capping announcement had been made. I identified options for him and quantified the scale of resources that would be available to mitigate and avoid the impact of rate capping.

No replies were ever received.

McDonnell and Livingstone continued advocating the '£140m cuts' argument during this period.

Eventually the rate capping figures arrived and they came into my office. It was immediately apparent that ministers had been very clever: the GLC could spend more than it had the year before, if appropriate actions were taken.

Not a single penny of cuts to services would have to be made.

Peter Brayshaw (the Assistant Director General) and I arranged to see McDonnell, and the meeting happened on 20th December 1984. We gave him the Government figures and a paper from myself which set out clearly that he could have a growth budget. It was our duty to set the facts before him and for politicians to decide.

He was very angry and he told us in the plainest terms to destroy the documents and not show them to anyone else. He said that he heard what we said, but to shred the documents.[209]

What McDonnell was asking us to do was to destroy important public documents, pretend they did not exist, falsify our advice on financial policy to the Council, and all because he wanted to pursue his policy of a second front against the Government.

Civil servants could not in any circumstances be party to such madness. Brayshaw and I stood outside McDonnell's room after the meeting with him and talked in a very clear way about how astonished we were with his behaviour.

Of course, we did not comply with his request to destroy the evidence and immediately asked to see Livingstone as leader to explain the situation. This did not happen for some time and the meeting only took place on 28th February 1985, only shortly before the budget had to be agreed. Livingstone was genuinely amazed at the facts and later he wrote that '…if these figures are right (the Race/Brayshaw figures) we're going to look like the biggest fucking liars since Goebbels.'[210]

---

209. Quoted in Andrew Hosken, *The Ups and Downs of Ken Livingstone*, Arcadia 2008, page 219
210. *K Livingstone If Voting Changed Anything They'd Abolish It*, Harper Collins 1987, page 316

These events have been placed in the public domain by Ken himself[211] and by Andrew Hosken's *The Ups and Downs of Ken Livingstone.*[212]

However, this was not all. For many months after we had given McDonnell this news, he went around London claiming that the £140m cuts requirement was still there and wrote articles about it in an attempt to maintain (as he saw it) leadership of the left.

He knew the facts and chose to ignore them.

Politicians are sometimes criticised for lying to voters. Usually, they are basing their arguments on views which appear to be correct at the time but which are later falsified by events, or by better data, for example.

John McDonnell was doing something else. He continued to mislead Londoners about the financial position of the Council, given to him by civil servants, and expected them to be silent. McDonnell himself argues that the advice from Brayshaw and myself was a plot to stop his policy, but it was not. It was simply placing the facts before him, which he ignored. The great criticism of McDonnell is that even after he knew his numbers didn't stack up, he continued to maintain that it was going to be Armageddon.

If he was prepared to behave in such a way, what would he have done about the national finances if he had ever become Chancellor?

Victory for Common Sense

Eventually my argument about the numbers and the policies that could support spending were accepted and adopted by the majority of the Labour Group and formed the policy for the majority of 1985-6 after Livingstone had sacked McDonnell[213] and Alex Mackay had taken over as Chair of Finance.

This expansion of the budget was made even more possible because of the special circumstances of abolition. Those special circumstances which called for action were as follows:

- First, the fact of abolition would impact on the Council's ability to deliver its programme. Staff would leave to be certain of a

---

211. Ibid. Harper Collins 1987
212. Arcadia Books 2008
213. He sacked McDonnell because he knew that these official documents could

job elsewhere and contractors would worry about programmes going beyond March 1986. Importantly, fewer staff in post meant less money being spent on salaries, creating unplanned underspends which were bound to be significant.

- Second, abolition would affect (as it was meant to) many voluntary organisations of high repute that relied on GLC funding via S137 and grants to their organisations for specific purposes, or as core funding. The expectation was that after abolition there would be closures of organisations or big reductions in their capabilities.

- Third, many London boroughs were reliant on GLC monies to deal with the impact of deprivation, thought especially important after the Scarman report on the Brixton riots. This funding reliance was partly related to the inheritance of GLC functions (housing stock transferred to the boroughs, Alexandra Palace after the fire, for example) and partly related to the expectation that the richer GLC would be able to help them deal with the issues of the inner city in a way that they could not from their flimsier geographically limited resource base.

- Fourth, the GLC's functions (which were very extensive) were being taken over under the abolition legislation by a multiplicity of bodies, especially the Secretary of State himself. The boroughs, who it was pretended would have a far greater control over local affairs, received few new functions or powers. However, uncertainty reigned over precisely what would be given to whom and this level of confusion affected the ability to run programmes in a normal way at the GLC during the last year.

- Fifth, there were very specific GLC-related financial problems which had not been addressed by the Livingstone administration until I was appointed in September 1983. These included massive underspends (60%+ of budget in third quarter 83-4), contributions to a capital fund to defray the costs of

---

not be 'magicked' away from existence and that his credibility with the Labour Group and Londoners would have been destroyed if he had continued to support McDonnell's line.

capital, which were irrelevant in the year before abolition, and other funds lying around in large quantities – contingency reserves, special contingency reserves, and revenue reserves for each programme, for example. This, in theory, gave the opportunity for the Council to unwind some of these provisions and create a legacy for the future.

- Sixth, the GLC was being continually challenged in court by Dame Shirley Porter, leader of Westminster Council and Tesco heiress. She was later surcharged by the District Auditor for illegal behaviour involving millions of pounds after she created a social cleansing scheme by clearing tenants out of council housing to give the Tories ironclad majorities in the local authority wards crucial to her re-election. When the District Auditor's investigation was in full flow she fled to Israel and had in the end to accept heavy fines. However, at one point, the injunctions obtained by her were coming in at the rate of one a week or more and were immensely disruptive – as they were meant to be. The upshot was that the GLC had to become more inventive about justifying schemes and making them as far as possible, 'judge proof.' The injunctions did, in some cases, however, limit the Council's ability to make unfettered financial decisions. And they slowed down the teams that were trying to deal with the consequences of abolition.

- Seventh, there were very specific duties created by the abolition legislation which meant that we had to seek permissions from the Department of the Environment in order to spend any large sums. Yet more time had to be wasted on getting around these controls, which we did on a large number of occasions. But it meant that the profile of expenditure on the agreed programme was slower than expected.

Before the Council had made its precept decisions in March 1985, Livingstone sacked McDonnell as Chair of Finance. After the budget decisions had been made, Livingstone wrote a personal note to the Executive of the London Labour Party, no doubt copied extensively to others.

He described what had happened and identified McDonnell as the man who would not listen to facts. John Carr, a leading committee chair, also wrote a similar eight-page note.[214]

Carr said in his report:

Many sympathetic comrades on the Labour group did feel that important and relevant information was being deliberately withheld from them. Worse, they felt they were being lied to or manipulated or both.

At the Labour Group meeting on 4th March 1985, McDonnell had admitted that the £140m cuts line was a gross exaggeration and that cuts of only £30m would be required to meet the rate cap.

Carr goes on:

However, it then also emerged that John McDonnell had been consistently refusing to work with Reg Race, Head of the Programme Office, to compute an alternative basis for the budget which could not only protect 100% of all existing budgets but also fund £23m of growth.

Livingstone was even more specific. In his report to the Greater London Labour Party Executive Committee after the budget had been set, he argued:

By mid-February it was impossible to discuss these issues. The weekly meeting to discuss the budget was often cancelled, and important issues were not raised. Papers on budget options, which ironically prefigured the alternatives finally put to Council, were not discussed and John McDonnell ordered that the papers should be shredded. In late February Reg Race wrote three times to John McDonnell to resolve these issues. No reply was received.[215]

The finance officers were institutionally conservative and initially did not want to take the steps I advocated to deal with the threat of rate capping, despite the unique circumstances that the GLC found itself in. It was very convenient for McDonnell.

He wanted the highest level of horror, the largest volume of predicted cuts, the greatest amount of blood on the floor to shock Labour people in London. He wanted to persuade them that the choice was 'set no precept and go illegal' or, 'make £140m of cuts'.

After he had been briefed by Brayshaw and me he knew this binary choice was nonsense – but he kept restating the case, even after Livingstone had sacked him.

The rate-capping debate exposed several important features of the

---

214. Report to Hackney South and Hackney North General Committees, 19th March 1985
215. Livingstone paper to the Greater London Labour Party Executive, page 8

Labour Party at the time.

There was a vocal, entrenched, unprincipled ultra-left who were prepared to do anything in order to get their way. Many ordinary Party members in London were fooled by this because they did not have access to the correct information and because they trusted the most ultra-left of the leaders available.

This showed that the old municipal conservatism in Labour had been replaced by a raging fight between two factions. It was at its worst in London, but other big cities were not exempt.

The idea that a clear assessment of the facts was the prelude to decision-making was anathema to many Labour councillors. It was more important to be macho and politically correct. Governing was unimportant; what counted was posturing.

It also exposed the fact that Livingstone had been running the place on autopilot for months at a time. He was interested in getting selected in Brent East, the constituency held by Reg Freeson MP, and was spending lengthy periods absent from the building.

Frances Morrell, the leader of the ILEA[216] (supposedly a committee of the GLC but in fact pretty independent) was unfocused and not on top of things at times, and could not in any event control what happened in the GLC, a separate entity.

Other committee chairs were not senior enough to rap knuckles and get things done and were not in possession of the global picture.

In this vacuum, others 'played' and Livingstone should have taken a grip sooner.

The national Party was also weak in the face of this, and not trusted by some of the rank and file. But the fight was won in the sense that the GLC did not go illegal and did in fact find and spend between £100m and £200m extra in its last year of existence. The Government was unable to do anything about that. However, abolition was certain by that point, despite our best efforts.

If you want to calculate who was right – essentially Brayshaw and Race, or McDonnell – it is important to ask what Livingstone did end up believing, what did almost all of the Labour Group end up believing, and what happened to the budget in 1985-6.

The inescapable truth is that Livingstone, the Group and the finance officers were persuaded we were right and that McDonnell was telling porkies. That is why Livingstone sacked McDonnell and that's why most

216. Inner London Education Authority

of the Group backed Livingstone.

That's why we were able to get the capital fund collapsed and other monies released, because finance officers in the end agreed with us it could be done and should be done.

In addition, Labour leader Neil Kinnock believed me. That's why he sent Labour's General Secretary Larry Whitty[217] to help persuade the Group to vote with Ken's position. He was as appalled as I was at the idea that the GLC could go illegal and it was a victory against stupidity and posturing.

Protecting London

Events after the March budget decisions followed precisely the pattern that I had predicted. We were able to identify very significant funding to do the following:

- Resource the voluntary sector on a forward-funding basis to protect them from the worst effects of abolition for a period of time.

- Fund council house repairs on ex-GLC stock on a large scale. This was done through a vehicle called SATMAN, organised by senior housing officer Bernard Crofton. It enabled reroofing and new windows on scores of council blocks, affecting many thousands of tenants in a positive way (if you spot council houses and flats with 30-year-old roofs and windows, it's probably the SATMAN programme).

- Pay significant sums to borough councils to support specific programmes addressing deprivation (as Scarman had said was important). This was called the Stress Boroughs Programme (offered to all boroughs irrespective of political control). We were able to achieve this despite the best efforts of Shirley Porter. We paid away significant sums before she injuncted

217. Larry Whitty, Head of Research for the GMBATU, General Secretary of the Labour Party 1985-1994. Became Lord Whitty of Camberwell 1996, and a Minister in the Blair Government.

215

the GLC (we had one of the first BACS machines) and we were helped by the fact that she forgot to injunct the boroughs receiving the money, so the money stayed there and was not clawed back.

- Main GLC programmes were increased on a prudent basis for specific needs.

We could not do everything, however. An Inner Cities package adjunct to the Stress Boroughs Programme could not get off the ground because there was no officer time to make it happen.

Everything related to fighting abolition and financing was shoved onto my desk without real regard as to whether there were more than 24 hours in the day available to achieve the objectives.

Some of the people and organisations we were trying to help were quite absurd in their demands. I had negotiated a very substantial package of financial assistance to voluntary organisations which would be hit hard by the abolition of the GLC. This had gone all the way through the relevant committees and was waiting to be delivered.

It hadn't made it out of the door, however, and on the eve of abolition – with less than 24 hours before my powers to act and those of the Council generally were to expire – a bunch of charity bigwigs arrived at County Hall and demanded to see me.

They moaned and whinged about how the package wasn't big enough and demanded a rejigging of the deal. This despite the fact that there was no time to do the paperwork, consult the lawyers, get a relevant committee approval, persuade the Department of the Environment civil servants that it was OK, and organise for the money to leave the building.

I told them to get real: it was 2pm in the afternoon before abolition at midnight, and they were being foolish, I said. 'Accept what's on the table or have nothing,' I had to threaten. Eventually they went away.

The original monies left the building and helped the charities get over some of the worst bits of abolition. But it demonstrated that many of the voluntary sector were amateurs and out of their depth.

They weren't the only ones. A project that was part of the Stress Boroughs package – refurbishment of the Rainbow Theatre at Finsbury Park, derelict for years, and turning it into a going concern – was consulted on, everyone in sight was asked their opinion including all the ethnic minority community organisations in the area the GLC could find, and it was sailing ahead.

One day a man from one of the groups we had consulted burst into my office and accused me and the GLC of being racist because we had agreed the bid from an Asian-led organisation to save the Rainbow. This man's organisation had been consulted and they hadn't replied. He became abusive and threatening and had to be removed. He wanted the whole thing stopped because his particular ethnic minority were not in charge.

It was quite ridiculous to accuse the GLC, of all organisations, of racism on this issue but he was adamant that the Council were out to do them down. That's the kind of nonsense we had to deal with when we were trying very hard to provide a lifeboat for organisations, charities and indeed the London boroughs who were going to be hit hard by abolition.

Stopping the Bonkers Nonsense

It wasn't just the difficult outside organisations that caused trouble. Several leading elected Members wanted to do something really spectacular to mark the end of the GLC and what better, they argued, than to engage the artist Christo[218] to wrap County Hall in white ribbon to make a present of it for the Government on abolition day?

They meant wrapping up the whole building, a gigantic edifice of several distinct blocks. The cost would be many hundreds of thousands of pounds of ratepayers' money squandered on an utterly ephemeral piece of nonsense from which Londoners would gain no benefit whatever.

Christo had wrapped the Reichstag, the gates in New York's Central Park, and the Pont Neuf in Paris and was therefore well known to the glitterati amongst Labour members. But the wrapping of County Hall would have been totally counterproductive.

We had been arguing for years that abolition of the GLC would cause great inefficiencies, would produce a vacuum in London-wide planning, would disadvantage poorer Londoners, and was a vindictive political act. So what better way to alert the public to the fact that the Labour administration was a bunch of profligate wastrels than to encase the whole building in lovey-dovey gift wrap – at ratepayers' expense. It could only confirm all the arguments that the Iron Lady had been using.

It would have been a PR disaster and a shocking waste of money that

---

218. Christo Vladimirov Javacheff 1935-2020 who collaborated with his wife Jeanne-Claude Denat de Guiilebon to produce their work

could and should have been used to put new windows and roofs on council houses (which we did in the end). I stomped on the proposal hard and long and stopped the proposal in its tracks. But the incident confirmed the dilettante tendencies of some Labour Members.

Nor was it the last example.

There was another proposal to dress a whole orchestra of French saxo-phonists in shimmering white and get them to abseil down the sides of County Hall, playing some dirge as they went – again at ratepayers' expense. I managed to stop that one too. This did not make me flavour of the month in some circles and, of course, I was the joyless philistine wanting to stop all fun in a bout of Cromwellian zeal.

But it was the right thing to do, and it spoke volumes about the so-called New Left Labour councillors' links to the culture of the working class let alone middle class opinion.

They were living in a dream world.

Propaganda on the Rates: the Outreach Team

Whilst McDonnell was Chair of the Finance Committee he was also in personal charge of a team of about 12 people known as the Outreach Team paid for by ratepayers. They were ostensibly employed to ensure that awareness of the GLC's policies was spread to all the boroughs.

However, many of them were lefties of various sorts and were running around the boroughs – especially the ones with Labour GLC Members – persuading leading members of the local Labour Parties to back McDonnell's line. They wanted them to mandate their GLC Members to vote not to set a precept. In this, the '£140m cuts' line was critical. They were McDonnell's willing puppets.

This was regarded as very bad by Livingstone and his supporters. After he sacked McDonnell, he gave management oversight of the Outreach Team to me. I stopped them doing it. It was intolerable that ratepayer funded staff were being used openly as agents of a political campaign designed to ensure illegality, and using arguments based on rubbish information.

It was yet another example of political extremism being funded by ratepayers and creating havoc. How this expenditure ever got through committee scrutiny was beyond me. But there would be many more examples of this later in the 1980s.

When I left County Hall just after midnight on abolition day, the Residuary Body had already changed the locks on my office door. I had worked till the very end, spending 18-hour days for weeks on a mission to get everything done.

Almost everything I was tasked with was finished but it was no thanks to some of the politicians who were my bosses. Their minds could be elsewhere, on the latest reselection battle, the latest article that had offended them, the latest cult nonsense infecting the ultra-left, or their personal lives including the need to drink large amounts of red wine.

Some were personally ineffective or incompetent and a culture of confrontation had developed in London Labour politics which was seriously inimical to effective working and the delivery of change on the ground. This, after all, was what local authorities were designed to deliver, for the good of local people.

At the time, my perception was that this was essentially a London problem, but I hadn't met Derbyshire at that point.

However, there was also a group of seriously likeable and sensible elected people and their writ tended to prevail, despite the fact that some of the older Labour councillors went to sleep as you were talking to them.

The officers of the GLC, who were better paid than anyone else in local government, were overwhelmingly supportive and professional but I learnt from the experience that there was an unevenness and competence gap amongst some councillors, and an even bigger competence vacuum amongst rank and file Labour members. It was hard to ignore but even more difficult to overcome.

The membership's grasp of detail and concepts was uneven. They judged personalities and events on the basis of how they fitted with their own prejudices and ideological position (if they had one) and what they were told.

They were not capable in many cases of judging practicality, could not describe desirable objectives and how to get to them in structured ways, did not think in concepts, and did not judge on the basis of outcomes. These are serious charges but born out not just in the 1980s at a time of high tension and conflict, but also much later in the attempts by Blair when leader to engage with the Party's rank and file.

The bottom line was that for the second time in three years I had been 'abolished' by legislative fiat and it was time yet again to find another job.

I knew it wouldn't be easy.

Legislation, Legislation, Legislation

The Government's response to what they saw as the overweening power of local councils was to legislate again and again on finance, powers, and specific restrictions on things they disliked.

Shortly after the GLC was abolished I started doing consultancy work for the Local Government Associations and in particular the Local Government Information Unit, headed by my old work colleague, Judy Mallaber.

My job was to liaise with any friendly forces in Parliament on what was, to put it mildly, not a popular subject – especially on the Labour side. However, the frontbench dealing with Local Government and the Environment was exceptionally strong, being led by Jack Cunningham[219] and supported in a diarchy by Jack Straw.[220]

Both later became Cabinet ministers under Blair, and Cunningham had been PPS to Prime Minister Callaghan and then a minister in the 1974-79 Labour Government. So, the front bench team was experienced, intelligent and in many ways radical. They hated what the Tories were doing to local democracy (and they were doing a lot). It was also the beginnings of the poll tax, the one piece of in-your-face madness which eventually caused the destruction of the Thatcher premiership.

It is now hard to describe the total paradigm shift on local government law and finances that was ushered in in 1979. By August 1987,[221] the Government had reduced the aggregate total of Rate Support Grant (RSG)[222] by £20bn and had created a system of calculating and paying the grant that was so complex that only a handful of people in the country understood it. In fact, the Department of the Environment had to introduce several pieces of legislation to legalise their own illegality.

It turned out that every penny of the RSG paid away to local authorities since 1981 – all £68bn of it – had been calculated on an illegal basis, so said the Attorney General.

---

219. MP for Whitehaven and then Copeland 1970-2005, later Lord Cunningham of Felling
220. MP for Blackburn 1979-2015; Home Secretary 1997-2001; Foreign Secretary 2001-6; Leader of the House of Commons 2006-7
221. See R Race, *Town Hall Finances – Into the Red*, *Capital Issues*, journal of the London Strategic Policy Unit, August 1987
222. The central government grant to local authorities to fund many of their services

This caused the second piece of retrospective legislation in six months to be introduced, to absolve ministers from the consequences of their own illegal actions.

That was not all: they banned all deferred and advance purchase schemes, which had been used to increase capital expenditure by councils on infrastructure. Capital spending by councils had dropped by 41% overall since 1978-9 and by 59.6% on housing, and it was the beginning of the decay of the public realm which is so apparent today.

Ministers had also taken powers to define what was and what was not capital expenditure. Councils had in recent times inventively capitalised repairs – which otherwise would have been regarded as revenue expenditure – to swerve round the controls on revenue spending.

Rate capping was still in place and additional authorities such as Manchester, Liverpool, Hull and Waltham Forest were added to the list of authorities in the frame.

Ministers took powers to treat individual authorities differently from others, thus enabling them to discriminate openly against councils they didn't like.

And the policy of 'flowback' was ended, which previously distributed all available block grant that was spare at the end of the year (in practice, oddly, to those who had spent most) thus eliminating about £270m of cash from local authorities.

Penalties were in place for councils that spent over the limit prescribed by Government but some transitional support was given to London boroughs to recognise the needs of voluntary organisations that had been supported by the GLC as that funding tapered away.

Grant aid from central government was made more specific so that it could not be used for the general purposes of any council, and legislation reduced the amount of 'relevant expenditure' supported by block grant from 60% to 40%.

This whole approach was to 'disallow scope for the existence of independent policies being pursued by local government as a whole.'[223] It would also force councils to cut spending or put the rates up – if they could do so without being penalised.

---

223. R Race op. cit., August 1987

Failing to Deal with the Poll Tax

The looming, seismic change, however, was that of the poll tax.

The Government had wanted to change the system of local taxation for some time, make it more onerous for councils to pursue policies of social mitigation and any semblance of an independent line. They had thus hit on the idea of a per-capita charge on each person in a household.

The theory was that this would induce further control on the spending instincts of local councillors as each individual would be levied with a charge which would otherwise not be visible to many people. The reality was tested at the beginning of 1987 when conversations between Cunningham, Straw and myself led us to draft Parliamentary questions on the impact of the poll tax for individual householders in every local authority in the country.

These were put down in Jack Cunningham's name and were finally answered on 2nd March 1987.[224] The figures were revised somewhat later, but Ridley's[225] first stab at estimating the charge to be levied showed extraordinary results in London and in every conurbation apart from the West Midlands.

In Camden, the household rate bill went from £843 a year to £2,346 for a three-person household, the sharpest increase in the country. It was clear that the new tax would fall most heavily on the boroughs with the most deprivation.

The millionaire's liability would be exactly the same as for a low-paid worker, with the burden falling most heavily on working class areas where properties had the lowest rateable values under the existing system.

The poll tax deliberately favoured the better off who lived in more expensive houses, discriminated against the poor and those on low wages, and had no approximation whatever to the individual's ability to pay. It would hit pensioner couples, working single parents, and the single unemployed particularly hard. The Duke of Devonshire at Chatsworth would pay the same personal charge as a quarry worker in a council house at Wirksworth a few miles away.

This tax was universally hated in the local government world and it had few friends outside the most elevated levels of Whitehall.

---

224. Secretary of State Nicholas Ridley to Jack Cunningham (Hansard)
225. Nicholas Ridley, MP for Cirencester and Tewkesbury 1959-92, President of the right wing Selsdon Group in the Conservative Party, and Cabinet Minister under Thatcher. Created Baron Ridley of Liddesdale in 1992

So, the question was: what would Labour do?

When Jack Cunningham's PQs were answered in March, I couriered them to him in his constituency in Whitehaven. I also got them to Neil Kinnock.

Straw and Cunningham were unequivocally in favour of using the new data in the General Election that was obviously fast approaching (polling day turned out to be 11ᵗʰ June 1987), but Kinnock demurred. His answer to Jack Cunningham, reported directly back to me, was that using the poll tax data 'would remind voters of loony left local authorities.'

The opportunity of savaging the poll tax, probably the most universally disliked tax in British history that later provoked rioting, mass civil disobedience, and the final resignation of Thatcher as PM after a Cabinet revolt, was lost. The leadership was simply not prepared to use it.

It was another example of the failure of Labour to rise to the occasion and adapt to the rapidly changing face of politics. The poll tax changed the way that people protested and undermined the legitimacy of the State in fundamental ways. It was another nail in the coffin of Parliamentary politics as seen by considerable sections of those affected. Millions defied the tax until it was impossible to go on, and this episode of weakness, demonstrating the ineffective way in which Labour reacted to change, showed the inadequacy of yet another leader.

This is not to say that Labour local authorities were shining citadels of common sense or radicalism. Local authorities were and are the local State, and in many areas of Labour control, the Party had no real or public independence outside the council chamber.

As I said in a lengthy article in *Voice of the Unions*,[226]

[The local Party] does not campaign; it does not analyse, it does not act independently – it has been incorporated into the local State. In some parts of Britain this incorporation has reached extreme proportions. There really are local authorities in South Wales where the Party does not even issue an election manifesto, where there are no meetings of the Labour Group, and where policy is made up 'on the hoof' by the leadership at full council meetings.

This was Cynon Valley, and I met similar extraordinary vacuums when we moved to Derbyshire in 1988.

---

226. April 1987, pages 1 and 8

Derbyshire: The Ultimate Horror Show

By the summer of 1987, the Tory tsunami of legislation was beginning to slow down and an opportunity for a more permanent job emerged. This was that of County Director (or Chief Executive) in Derbyshire, a shire county with important education and social services functions and with a declining coalfield in the east of the county.

As a Mancunian, I knew Derbyshire pretty well. On many weekends, my parents had taken me out walking or camping in the beautiful countryside which, in my opinion, is one of the finest landscapes in the country.

I had also had links with the Kent miners during the 1972 and 1974 strikes and we had welcomed miners from the Staffordshire pits to our house when they were collecting money to support NUM members during the 1984-5 dispute, so the wrench from a London environment would not necessarily be a substantial one.

We were also wary of continued living in Tottenham, as we could not let the children walk around the area on their own, especially at night, and our road had been the subject of vicious attack by a band of thugs after the Broadwater Farm riots. This included the smashing of every car windscreen in the road – they ran out of steam about 100 yards from us – and the overturning of a transit van on its side which was then set alight with Molotov cocktails.

One of our neighbours, a lovely Bajan bus driver with London Transport, had to be talked out of defending his car, a pride and joy Vauxhall Cavalier in light blue, if they came near it.

We had also been burgled six times in two years and all of us felt it was time to go. So, after family consultation – as we might be moving 150 miles north to a very different community – I applied for and got the job.

The first stage of the process was an interview with a London-based headhunter employed by the Council, who had been instructed to find someone who was going to introduce more effective processes and who would ensure that the Council implemented its policies as effectively as it could in the circumstances.

I had a three-way interview with the headhunter, Eric Cobb (the incumbent at Derbyshire County Council) and David Bookbinder, then Leader of the Council. The employment specialist pointedly asked Bookbinder whether he really wanted a reformer or wouldn't he prefer a Yes man?

Bookbinder said he definitely wanted a reformer, and on the face of it, it seemed that this was a council with ambition to make itself better, and to focus on what mattered.

In those interviews I met Eric Cobb, the incumbent, who struck me initially as a sensible voice. Eric wanted to retire, his wife was unwell, and he was ready to move on.

Gradually it emerged that the job that I had been given required only one attribute – an obsequious subjugation to the will of the Leader. It gave a very different twist to the requirements of the job I was supposed to be doing. Having started work in January, my first task was to interview the chief officers, find out what their priorities were, where the pinch points were, and start introducing some long overdue reforms into the structures.

There was no central policy function – astonishing in a council covering a part of the rapidly deindustrialising Midlands – no performance review system of any kind, so they didn't know whether they were spending effectively or not; and almost the whole of the politics in the authority was related to malevolence and payback to perceived 'enemies.'

So, I started, and got agreed, a system change so that we would introduce financial and performance reviews, the abolition of some senior posts which were completely superfluous, and initiated appointments to a policy unit which could try and look forward to where we wanted to be in five and 10 years' time. We also needed a structure to deal with the constant flow of new legislation and directives from Westminster.

Even these modest changes, which they felt they had to give me, were given grudgingly and with very little commitment. It was impossible in this atmosphere to get buy-in from officers or Members because they were always looking over their shoulders to see what the Leader was signalling.

There was an attempt to fix the appointment of my PA in favour of none other than David Skinner, one of Dennis's brothers, and a Labour activist in North East Derbyshire. He, as far as I could tell, did not have anything like the skillset required, couldn't type, and was obviously going to be installed as a political fix and a spy inside the office.

I got on well with David and managed to resist this madness, but it was another straw in a wind that was now a gale.

Worst perhaps was the Council's relationships with the media. These had been soured by the endless libel actions and Bookbinder's general truculence with anyone who asked him a sharpish question. This got so bad that I tried to relaunch him by using the issues flowing from the Loscoe explosion (where methane seeping from an old refuse tip had caused an explosion and some considerable damage).

I organised a full scale press conference where he could outline the sensible decisions the Council had taken and to make crystal clear that it was on the side of the residents.

I wrote the script (his comms people were hopeless as well as brutalised), set it all up and paid significant personal attention to how it would work. Came the day and he couldn't or wouldn't read the script properly, and when he was asked questions immediately became defensive and obstructive. It was a disaster and demonstrated to me that he just could not relate to the media. Attempts to get him outside, top level help failed. He was unteachable.

Unreformed Bureaucracy and Libel Actions as Control

The officer-led bureaucracy was wholly unreformed. Papers prepared for the council and its committees were often of poor quality and this came to a head when a report that I had requested from the Director of Social Services was produced. I had asked him to state very clearly where Derbyshire's existing policies on child abuse differed from the recommendations of the just published Butler-Sloss Report.[227]

The draft report to Council wasn't clear at all and I made him rewrite it. He either couldn't or wouldn't produce a report that addressed the complicated issues involved.

Everywhere you looked there were problems. The 'emergency control room', designed to deal with serious incidents or disasters, was a tiny box room with no windows, a 1948-style table, a Bakelite telephone, a wooden chair, and a metal filing cabinet. There was no emergencies officer doing any work. If Derbyshire had been faced with a pandemic in 1988 it would not have known where to start.

The Police Committee was another source of trouble. The committee was composed of councillors and JPs at the time and was absurdly allowed to debate whether a police patrol car written off in a road traffic

---

227. Published July 1988. Lady Butler-Sloss had been asked to report on one of the first child abuse scandals unveiled, on Teeside. A social services authority like Derbyshire had to pay especial attention to the report's important findings.

accident should be replaced or not. It was precisely the kind of issue that should have been dealt with by delegated authority on an agreed basis.

But the committee was not allowed to talk about important things like the hopeless state of computerisation and data in Derbyshire, which meant that the Force could not compile accurate crime statistics (it was still failing to do so in the late 1990s).

All this needed wholesale reform, streamlining and proper research input. But there was none. Derbyshire was a reincarnation of 18th century court politics in the 20th century.

Then there was the not-so-small matter of the libel actions. The leader had initiated a series of libel actions, in the name of the Council itself as a corporate body, and it was said that there were 11 or 12 of them[228] on the go in early 1988. The policy was to challenge anyone who said uncomplimentary things about Derbyshire or its leading politicians, in an attempt to ensure self -censorship by those who took a jaundiced view.

The legal team, paid for by ratepayers' money, was pursuing claims against anybody that had offended, usually local and national newspapers. The tactic was to say that the relevant 'offender' had libelled the County Council as a corporate body, a legal person in its own right for these purposes at the time, as well as (depending on the circumstances), councillors themselves. The hope was to get damages – some of which might fall to councillors themselves.

One side effect of this, which was clearly intended, was to intimidate journalists and show them that criticising Derbyshire was likely to land them in court.

This worked until the *Sunday Times* (under the forthright editorship of Andrew Neil) defended an action on the basis that a public authority like the County Council should not be able to sue for libel.

They won in the end, with a definitive and unanimous decision by the Law Lords[229] stating that public authorities, as democratically elected bodies, had no right to institute actions for libel – as allowing this would restrict freedom of speech. For Bookbinder, that was clearly the point. In all this, the council's solicitors were reporting directly to Bookbinder and cutting out all internal chains of authority and command.

The fun continued as we started to consider the forward look on the council's budget and spending for 1989-90, starting consideration in

---

228. The solicitors at the council couldn't decide whether it was 11 or 12
229. Reported 19th February 1992, decision by Lords Keith, Griffiths, Goff, Browne-Wilkinson and Woolf.

the spring and summer of 1988. It was obvious that further downward pressure would be exerted by Government on councils like Derbyshire through the block grant mechanisms, so we needed a plan to get us through it.

The obvious thing to do was a base budgeting exercise to discover what we were really spending and then decide whether we wanted to do it, or only part of it, and what resources we could free up in order to expand provision in more deserving areas.

I set this in motion, along with a brand new system of Performance Review, setting targets and monitoring them. This was pretty revolutionary for Derbyshire and it was intriguing to see officers and elected Members trying to adjust to this new reality. The District Auditor loved it: 'Music to my ears,' he told me. He'd been having trouble with the Derbyshire accounts for years.

But Bookbinder came up with a new wheeze: why not sell the council's shares in the East Midlands airport? This had been developed as a joint venture in 1964 by Leicestershire, Derbyshire, Derby City Council and Nottinghamshire County Council in an attempt to improve connectivity between the area and the aero hubs of Heathrow and beyond.

Derbyshire, therefore, owned shares in the company that ran it. They could, in theory, sell them if they could find a buyer. However, there were two clear problems about this: first, the sale of shares would be a capital receipt and there would be difficulty in turning this into a revenue sum, given the way that such receipts were treated in local government accounting.[230]

Second, there was a decisive bar in that any sale of airport shares by a local authority had to have the Secretary of State's approval.

As at the time this was chain-smoking ultra-dry, ultra-Thatcherite old Etonian Nicholas Ridley, the chances of this being approved were zero. This was on the face of the legislation – the Airports Act 1986.

I showed the legislation to the leader and he was very angry at being thwarted and he blamed the messenger. It was my fault that the law obstructed him. The airport couldn't be sold, and that was another black mark against me.

---

230. Section 21(1a) of the 1986 Airports Act specifically said that these sums were a capital receipt.

Let's Build a Holiday Resort – in the Soviet Union

The events which demonstrated beyond doubt the alternative universe of Derbyshire politics were related to the plan to build a council-funded leisure complex and holiday resort at Yalta, in the Crimean region of the Soviet Union.

Bookbinder had visited the USSR in 1987 and the council had spent £3,000 on his expenses. He went with his brother Arthur Bookbinder (a travel agent), and Owen Oyston (the former owner of *News on Sunday* and the Miss World titles, and a friend of Bookbinder).

At that time there was great talk of the Gorbachev reforms opening up the country to foreign investors through joint ventures, and Bookbinder was making many foreign visits to sniff out potential opportunities. He also went to North Korea and China.

The justification given to the council was that these were part of the twinning strategy whereby councils developed relationships with similar towns or regions to develop mutual understanding and cultural ties. What interest Derbyshire might have in twinning with Pyongyang was beyond my comprehension, however.

What came out of the Crimea visit was the shape of a plan to develop an absolutely massive £500m[231] holiday and leisure complex. It was to be situated in the area where the Yalta conference of February 1945 had taken place between Stalin, Churchill and Roosevelt and where they had discussed the future arrangements in Europe after the expected German surrender.

When I asked what the justification was for the plan, it was said to be to allow people from Derbyshire to get cheap flights and holidays. The Yalta plan, to dignify it considerably, involved the construction of a marina, two hotels, a golf course and timeshare apartments.

It was not clear how much demand there would be from the former coalminers of Bolsover, Clay Cross and Shirebrook for yacht moorings, but what did I know?

The implication was clear: the benefits to the people of Derbyshire were highly questionable and dubious.

The initial plan was to mobilise the build through a joint venture between the Soviet Government, Oyston, and Derbyshire in the proportions of 50%-25%-25%.

Under their law the Soviet Government had to have a controlling

---

231. Over £1bn at today's prices

stake of at least 50%. But the Soviet system was creaking at the edges and was a tottering structure, riddled with corruption. This was only a year before the dissolution of the Soviet Bloc and anyone with eyes to see could identify this as a major risk in any project beyond the Iron Curtain.

This was to be a council-led project with 'profits' coming back to Derbyshire.

However, in order to deliver something like this you had to have relevant expertise. Although I had more experience than the other council officers and the Members in running large budgets and initiating complex plans, none of the potential UK participants had any discernible knowledge of tourism, major construction or private sector financing options on this scale – let alone experience of working behind the Iron Curtain. And neither did I.

What should have happened, of course, if this was to be taken at all seriously, was to form a project group at senior level, get council approvals, employ serious experts in this kind of project, and assess the options with the associated risks in an objective way.

Of course, there was none of this. The council had absolutely no powers – none at all – to run this kind of project using its mainstream budgets in a foreign country. This was reluctantly accepted and the fallback position then came in to play – using the money from the Derbyshire Superannuation Fund to finance the project instead.

This was also completely mad. The fund collected money from its staff in contributions and paid out pensions to former Derbyshire County Council employees. It was a defined benefit scheme under which pensioners received a set level of benefits irrespective of the performance of the fund.[232]

The scheme had been lucky in recent years, because of the general rise in the stock markets, and was successful in getting good returns on its investments. But it relied on an investment strategy that was supposed to carefully calculate the benefits and disbenefits of particular investments before they were made. It was completely controlled by a small minority of the Labour Group, advised by officers who had been systematically bullied.

Therefore, there was a prospect, so it was thought, of getting the fund to subscribe £125m of its investable income into Yalta.

---

232. In distinction to a defined contributions scheme, whereby pensioners only received what the fund could afford based on the totality of contributions received and the investment performance of the fund.

However, there were problems which anyone could see. Should such a proposal be made it would need to clear the fiduciary duty rules and be able to persuade the public that the financial risks of the project were exceeded by its potential benefits. This would be hard if not impossible to do. The fund could also only invest below a certain money threshold in one project, and Yalta would probably exceed that, depending on its final subscription cost.

There was:

- limited, if any, benefit to Derbyshire ratepayers or staff

- no power available for the council to use its own funds to do it

- no expertise in the council to take it forward

- unwillingness in the council leadership to bring in experts should they wish to pursue it

- very high financial risks

- the likelihood that profits could not be repatriated in hard currency

- no guarantee that commercial law rectification in disputes with the Soviet Government, should there be any, would work

- every sign that the Soviet Union was collapsing with serious effects on the economic and business environment in Russia.

This made the scheme extraordinarily high risk and dangerous for the stability of the pension fund and its ability to continue paying out pensions to retired employees.

That was the balance of advantage in respect of Yalta as I saw it. These disbenefits therefore raised the question of what profits might be generated.

Was there a strong presumption that the good people of Derbyshire and others would flock to a new seaside location in the Soviet Union?

Could it be made to turn a profit? In 1988 the rules on repatriating profits from the Soviet Union were that you couldn't do it in hard currency, only in roubles, which were regarded as pretty valueless in the West.

There was, to be fair, debate on emerging discretions to allow some repatriation of hard currency from the USSR but the rules (if you can say they were rules at all) were opaque. In fact, there was no rule of law in the Crimea or anywhere in the USSR.

And, of course, there could be no assumption that the resort could be made to show a book profit at all. It would require constant, heavy levels of investment if it were to be kept appealing to visitors.

Therefore, a huge resort complex was to be owned and probably managed largely by the Soviets, who were not renowned for efficiency. They might be assisted by one of Oyston's companies, whose core experience was in estate agency and later in football management, although it wasn't clear at the time that this would happen, and by Derbyshire County Council, who had no experience of running resorts, and no authority to act in this sector, or in that country. I suspect that Oyston, an experienced businessman, would have identified the ultra-high level of risk and walked away, leaving Bookbinder in the lurch.

No Governance: Personal Rule

The way this was handled by the Council was also instructive.

There was no proper governance of the scheme. All decision-making powers were in practice invested in the leader and he gave information to different people at different times and excluded people like me from the loop, as he discovered whether or not we would bow the knee to the policy he wanted.

I expressed my legal, practical and governance objections to Bookbinder personally and was supported by the legal officers and by four of the council's chief officers.

The governance was particularly worrying: all decisions were being made by expedited decisions through urgency committees, and this was true generally of most policy developments.

The minutes of these urgency committees were then reported to the Council with little detail and were therefore not invigilated properly. No one could tell who was advising whom, what they were advising, whether the decisions were backed with solid information or not, and what the financial consequences were likely to be.

In addition, the so-called Leadership Group was entirely Member led and met without papers or officers present on many occasions. It was there simply to rubber stamp a predetermined view. These decisions were then sent to urgency committees and eventually to the full meeting of the Council, which took place only four times a year.

It was an edifice carefully and deliberately constructed to conceal and to allow decisions to be made without proper invigilation. It was a world away from the openness and clear decision making of the GLC – with all its faults.

This was so serious that the District Auditor reported on the decisions to invest £305,000 of the superannuation fund in the newspaper, *News on Sunday*. The company owning the paper went into liquidation (unsurprisingly), and the shares were sold to Telemags, a company owned by Oyston. There was then a slew of transactions and the District Auditor records that:

Mr Oyston stated that he agreed to purchase the News on Sunday shares only on condition that the Superannuation Fund become committed to invest £2 million as part of a more comprehensive agreement.[233]

Bookbinder claimed that the sale of the *News on Sunday* had made a profit but the District Auditor went on to say that the alleged profit

does not, however, take into account the simultaneous exchange of cheques for £400,000, and the accounting entry in respect of the cheque drawn on the [Superannuation Fund] which resulted in the purchase of shares in a dormant company having minimal assets.[234]

So, the only real transaction of substance was that the original investment from the superannuation fund had been lost and a paper transaction for an even larger amount had been made in real money from the fund in order to buy shares which were at that time without discernible value.

Two transactions of real money from the pensioners of Derbyshire, two worthless investments and no due diligence about the company concerned.

In addition, the Council superannuation fund could not recover its £2m investment or any profits. This was because the company it was invested in was a deadlock company[235] and such repatriation could not be made without the agreement of the major shareholder – who happened to be ... Oyston.

The District Auditor concluded that:

It is difficult to avoid the conclusion that, in approaching Mr Oyston, it

---

233. District Auditor's report 14th May 1991 page 3
234. Op. cit. page 6
235. Jebwill

was Cllr Bookbinder's intention to disguise a loss arising from the potential liquidation of the News on Sunday PLC ... It is clear that in entering this agreement the Council departed from its usual arrangement of members setting investment strategy and officers implementing it ... It is inappropriate for officers to be placed in positions where it might be construed that their professional judgements could be constrained by the unnecessary intrusion of members into investment matters.[236]

To strip away the verbiage, what had happened – all before I was appointed – was that a loss to the superannuation fund had been deliberately concealed by the Council by entering into another larger transaction of £2m with Oyston, and doing so by sidelining his officers and by using secret meetings, and ensuring that proper reports of these transactions were made invisible.

This was 'investment decision making' Derbyshire style and it was precisely what was envisaged with the Yalta project.

The District Auditor did, however, bottle it and took no action which was pathetic. What he did not consider at all was that Bookbinder was constantly trying to get Oyston to buy the *Trader* newspaper, which was heavily critical of Bookbinder and had a large circulation in the east and south of the county.

This was also at exactly the time he was arguing that the superannuation fund should buy shares in Red Rose radio, owned by Oyston, and thus giving Red Rose a substantial injection of real cash.

The alternative plan that was floated was to get Robert Maxwell, owner of the *Daily Mirror* group and also Derby County Football Club, to buy it.

Oyston offered money to the *Trader* but they wanted more, and the deal did not proceed.

The attempts to silence his enemies continued on a twin track approach: stun them into silence with libel actions, and then buy them out through a third party. The trouble was that third parties are not usually terribly obliging when it's their money being used to buy assets they don't necessarily want on behalf of someone else who wants to silence them. Normally a third party wants to obtain benefit from the transaction.

I had made it clear in the spring of 1988 that I thought the Yalta enterprise was both doomed and wrong. Bookbinder then moved any involvement with it away from me. I was leaving on holiday with the

236. Op. cit. page 10

family in August and before I went, I asked for a report to be written by David Coleman, one of the officer team, about Derbyshire's involvement with Telemags and Jebwill. I was alarmed about what Derbyshire was getting itself in to and thought that illumination was needed.

When I returned the report had not been completed and I have no doubt at all that it was intercepted by Bookbinder.

The Very Worst of Local Authorities

I was very glad to leave the appalling mess that was the top echelons of Derbyshire County Council. The council workers, organised by NUPE, were going to come out on strike in support of my position after they had been briefed by Graham Skinner, but hostilities did not quite begin.

It is important to identify exactly what was wrong with the Derbyshire leadership. They were entirely dependent on one man. Any opposition had been silenced and marginalised – and there was some in the form of Martin Doughty, later Chair of Natural England, and Bookbinder's successor as Leader of the Council from 1992.

Chief Officers had been silenced and were not allowed to do their jobs properly, and there could be free exchange of information and ideas.

A Derbyshire First policy had been followed so that officers were largely recruited from within, a recipe for decay and stagnation. Completely mad controls had been introduced – such as the need to seek the Chief Executive's approval if an officer needed to go outside Derbyshire for a meeting (as many did for case conferences and so forth). I soon put a stop to that nonsense.

The Council had not considered what it did and spent and whether it was performing effectively, and it was in serious legal trouble over the many libel actions that had been started.

The leadership had not seriously addressed deindustrialisation or endemic poverty, especially in the mining villages. It was not behaving as a Labour council should do and exhibited all the worst features of dictatorships everywhere. It was letting down the decent people who had voted for it.

However, the crisis in Derbyshire could not be gripped by either the District Audit service of the time or by the Audit Commission.

The audit service had a tradition of pulling its punches on accounting and financial policy issues and the Commission was only at the start of a process of change which was to move it away from national reports on 'themes' to a more interventionist approach later in the 1990s. The Labour Party nationally was even worse. It simply ignored problems in the hope that they would go away.

When I left Derbyshire, it was important to get the facts on the record. I arranged to see David Blunkett, newly elected as an MP and the leader of Sheffield City Council 1980-87. We told him the story, and he taped it. He was friendly and understanding and astonished at the behaviour of so called Labour members on the Council. We didn't ask him to do anything, but the tape is still around.

Lambeth: a Different Kind of Problem

In early 1989 after leaving Derbyshire, I was approached by Joan Twelves, the Leader of Lambeth Council, to undertake a review of their corporate systems.

Lambeth had been riddled with internal Labour faction fighting for years and was notorious as Ted Knight's Trotskyist bastion south of the river. It had the justified reputation of being the most incompetent London borough with the highest underspend on revenue account and one of the highest rate demands from residents.

Lambeth had a *laissez faire* Chief Executive, John George, who was in the tricky position of having to deal with the shifting sands of internal Labour politics. It is not too much to say that he had rather let go of things. He also, I discovered, wanted to retire which made things much easier.

I started work analysing the structures and processes of the whole council and reported first in September 1989. The report argued that legal advice to the council was poor, that there was inadequate policy advice and no performance review (again), and that the council needed a new Chief Executive.

I supervised the recruitment process for the new CEO and in the end, they appointed the highly respected Herman Ouseley[237] which changed the atmosphere and created an opening for serious change to begin. However, my second report, published in February 1990, laid it on the line. It said:

237. Now Lord Ouseley of Peckham Rye; former head of the Race Relations Unit at the GLC and Chief Executive of the Inner London Education Authority

Throughout the Council there was a culture which tolerated incompetence and failure and which encouraged officers to believe they were not accountable for their actions.

There was a failure to deal with the management and service delivery consequences of legislation (in some cases they were ignoring it). Financial control systems and accounting were in a poor state. The corporate centre of the council hardly existed. The role of the Chief Executive had not been resolved which led the council's management problems to fester.

Corporate issues were not pursued by the management team and were not resolved. The council had a poor self-image and a public image which made it difficult to recruit and retain high quality staff. There was a poor understanding of the respective roles of Members and officers. Finally, there was significant duplication of functions between the directorates and the corporate centre, with some functions being performed twice.

Deliberate Concealment

One problem sitting behind this was that Lambeth had deliberately not responded to CIPFA requests[238] to state the costs of its services and functions – except where it was mandatory to do so. This decision, deliberately taken in my view, made it impossible to benchmark Lambeth's costs against those of a basket of other similar local authorities with similar social problems. There was therefore no practical way of judging relative costs or efficiency but I have no doubt that, had proper accounting been available to make those costs visible, that Lambeth's costs would have been revealed as sky high.

I had known at the GLC, when in charge of the Stress Boroughs Programme (of which Lambeth formed a part), that Ted Knight's council had underspent an even higher proportion of its revenue collected than the GLC – which was saying something.

I was aided in coming to this conclusion by a member of my Programme Office team who had recently worked at Lambeth and who was very well informed. I concluded in my 1990 report that:

The Borough has the worst of both worlds: it has both centralisation and decentralisation, with no clear allocation of responsibilities between

---

238. Made to all local authorities by the Chartered Institute of Public Finance and Accountancy

departments at the centre and departments at the periphery of the Council. This confusion leads to higher costs and lack of management accountability which it is impossible to justify.[239]

I argued that the council should ruthlessly prune administration and bureaucracy, and I gave as an example the process through which a simple request for the payment of a milk bill in a social services home run by the borough was authorised and paid away.

The bill was presented by the creditor and it then went through six checking processes in six different locations within the council before it was fully authorised and paid.

It was clear that the money spent in administering the checking was in many cases far larger than the cost of the bill itself. It also meant that the council could not benefit from the discounts available from suppliers to reward early payment of invoices. And it meant that if anything got lost it often disappeared completely beneath the waves.

They also did not pursue debtors effectively, meaning that money owed to the council went unpaid, and it took excruciating amounts of time to authorise and pay away capital spending which had already been approved and was in the capital programme.

Vast numbers of staff were employed in performing personnel functions. There was £6.8m being spent on 190 personnel officers (plus others in the woodwork). It was an amazing amount for a council of Lambeth's size, and it could have been considered a form of outdoor relief for the indigent poor.

It turned out that Lambeth was splashing 4% of its net revenue spending on personnel function costs alone. As comparison, the GLC had spent 4% of its revenue budget on ALL administrative costs in the year before it was abolished. Ted Knight's raucous claim, *No Cuts Here!* to describe Lambeth's attitude to the Government's policies meant in practice the vast outlay of ratepayer funds on ridiculous and completely unnecessary bureaucracy.

There were also longstanding problems with the council's official accounts. It was widely accepted – including by the Finance Department that this was so – that accountancy standards were extremely low. The District Auditor, in a letter to me dated 25th September 1989, stated:

many of these problems are of long standing (see for example our qualification of the 1984-5 accounts). They have continued because insufficient priority and resources have been attached to resolving them.

---

239. *Agenda For Action*, R Race, February 1990, page 6

The 1988 audit report said:

the 1984-5 accounts were heavily qualified on the grounds of inadequacy of accounting systems, a failure to prepare reconciliations between significant balances and supporting records and inadequate provision for bad debts.[240]

Each department had a multitude of problems. Computer services were still using obsolete punch card driven systems and computer languages that were no longer in public use. There was no IT plan for the whole council, nor any Member level forum at which IT strategy was discussed. Payment of invoices was manual, and there was no head of the Computer Services Department. The list went on, department by department.

Nothing had been done to reform the council for many years but there had been plenty of posturing and large amounts of cash had been taken from local ratepayers with absolutely no regard to how it was spent.

There were 14 directorates, 58 member committees and sub-committees plus the education committees and in addition our old friends, urgency committees. During the previous two years, 3,300 committee reports had been written, 2,800 urgency reports, and 13,000 individual clearances had been sought under the council's arcane and pre-computer age procedures.

Reports did not say what the pros and cons of a course of action might be and it was almost never true that the reports showed which statutory powers were being used to justify a course of action.

The bureaucracy had been allowed to grow exponentially, with no one controlling or curtailing its size or efficiency.

After his appointment, Herman Ouseley started to get to grips with the mess that had been created. However, this was not the end of it as District Auditor Paul Claydon spent two years writing a 93 page report on the Council's failure to manage itself. The annual accounts had at that point not been filed on time for 8 years and he stated in the report that there was an unacceptable incidence of fraud and malpractice; allegedly homeless people had been accommodated for years in council accommodation and had sold the keys to others; £20 m of highways contracts had been improperly awarded; teachers had been overpaid by £3.8m, and so on.

After the elections of 1994, the Council instructed Elizabeth Appleby QC to produce a report which went even further. A new Chief Executive, Heather Rabbatts, instituted cultural change and literacy/numeracy tests

---

240. District Audit Report 16ᵗʰ December 1988

(it was alleged that the Chief Cashier of the day had failed the numeracy test).[241] Through a long process of reform and uprooting of an incompetent and corrupt culture, Lambeth had been changed – but no thanks to the Labour Party, which had tolerated by inaction the scandalous activities of the local leadership for years. A result has over time been achieved and it is greatly to the credit of Joan Twelves that this process was started in a highly unstable political environment where the safest thing for her would have been to do nothing.

Outright Corruption, Brown Paper Envelope Style

The Twelves regime and that of Linda Bellos, was a contrast to the corruption of the Ted Knight period. Bill Brown, Director of Construction at Lambeth 1987-90, brought in to smash corruption by Bellos, insisted on having his own internal audit team. They discovered that £1m was missing from the accounts and they established that it could not be traced.

Part of this undoubtedly went to Knight: his then boyfriend came to pick up brown envelopes stuffed with cash every fortnight. It is not clear whether this was being used to subsidise Knight's newspaper or whether it was for personal use.

Knight was also the director of a small guttering company which miraculously obtained much work from Lambeth before Bill Brown struck it off the approved list of contractors. This was also the case with other incompetent contractors who had been placed on an approved list because of their Irish political connections.

This brown envelope stuff was all witnessed by senior officers on a regular basis and Knight simply got away with it because no one would put their job on the line to challenge the crooks.

Eventually Brown caused legal action to be taken against those who had let contracts against the rules and sacked some directly, including one officer who had presided over 100 heating boilers 'going missing' from the stores.[242]

None of this was known by the adoring left in the Labour Party. Knight could not be guilty because he was on the ultra-left and by

---

241. Quoted in D Campbell-Smith *Follow the Money*, Allen Lane 2008, page 360-362
242. Sourced from interview with Bill Brown 20th April 2020

definition ultra-clean. It was yet another example of ideology trumping all other considerations.

Local Government in the 1980s

The Labour Party was in 1979 and 1983 driven back to its strongest areas and its local authority base in a way that had not happened since the late 1960s, and before that the 1930s.

It is clear from my experiences that the perception of local government as inefficient and incompetent was very true in some authorities. Despite the efforts of individual councillors and some good authorities, many Labour councils were riven with political infighting and exhibited a level of incompetence and disorganisation that should not have been tolerated by any sensible political party.

Haringey was incompetent in patches, despite some good elected Members, and was not a credible organisation to run major projects. Nor did they have sufficient resources to do so.

The GLC was the best of them in some ways. Broadly speaking, they had a higher class of Members and officers – but riven with arguments between different kinds of lefties who were only intent on slitting each other's throats. Despite this, they did introduce some innovative and modern policies – such as on equal opportunities – which are now regarded as mainstream.

On the central task of raising money and spending it wisely, it faltered. But the GLC certainly made a difference for a while as the strategic authority for London.

Derbyshire had a weak Labour Group and some of the Council's officers were at the time poor quality. The authority was oblivious to risk – political, economic, and legal – and its services were leaden footed and needed urgent reform. It was not strategic, was tin eared to the growing signs of deindustrialisation, and basically ignored its working class electorate.

It was also, despite posturing, a stranger to treating different kinds of people equally and with sensitivity. If you were not liked, you were out.

Lambeth was different again: it possessed the most appalling internal organisation because it had just been left to rot. Overlaid on this was the violent posturing of the leadership, for most of the time under Ted Knight.

The basic commonality across all these very different authorities was that the politics seriously got in the way of service delivery, value for money, strategic planning, and decency.

Which faction you were temporarily aligned with and who was winning were the most important things.

The National Response: Tiny

So, what did the Labour Party do nationally to control these blemishes on its brand?

Very little.

It expelled the Militant, not that that did much (and nothing at all in the authorities I knew well). Quality control over local councillors was non-existent, and there was no central invigilation of behaviours. Some Lambeth Councillors were suspended or expelled because of their attitude to the Poll Tax.

In any other organisation conscious of its brand as being central to its consumer appeal, there would have been investigations, retraining, management advice, removals and expulsions. But there was no capacity in the Labour Party to do this. It let things drift because it could.

At the time, many local authorities relied on the majority of its working class voters having a visceral loyalty and a hatred of Thatcher to get them across the line in elections – especially in the Midlands and the North. But those days have gone: voter volatility is now extensive and the Conservatives have tapped into the deep disaffection with Labour at local level that has emerged over the last 40 years.

The electorate aren't daft and Prime Minister Johnson has for the moment reaped the benefit of Labour decay in its heartland local authorities. More fool Transport House, Walworth Road, Southside and the Leader's offices in the House of Commons.

The inadequacy of some in local government in the 1980s reconfirmed the long-established Whitehall view that the centre knew best and that much of local government was not usable as an instrument of policy unless it was absolutely necessary.

In fact, during the 1980s there was a determination to change the balance of central to local powers by beefing up the centre at the expense of the local.

There was also a failure of quality improvement by the State at the time. School standards testing was still years away, and the role of the Audit Commission at first slid past the key issues for individual local authorities.

The Audit Commission undertook 'theme' reporting on issues but did not study individual councils in depth, nor did it offer objective advice to officers and Members on how they could get from a point of departure to a better place. Many argued that the district audit staff were too close to the Councils they were supposed to be invigilating.

The Commission did, however, standardise the collection of data, enabling councils to be compared on a uniform basis – something that was only informally and patchily possible before 1983. After that date it was avoided by some councils afterwards, as we saw in the case of Lambeth.

Established in 1983 by Michael Heseltine in the light of concern about professional standards and the competence of some authorities, the Audit Commission raised the possibility of standard setting in public authorities, and its relation to inspection and regulation.

This reached fruition in 2002 with the introduction of CPA (Comprehensive Performance Assessment) which focused not just on assessing the quality of services but on corporate governance.

It is true that the Lambeths and Derbyshires of this world would not have been allowed to behave in the new millennium in the way they had previously. However, the incoming Coalition Government abolished the Audit Commission in 2010 as it was seen to be getting in the way of the new policies of the Coalition Government.

So, progress was made to deal with the mavericks of Labour leaning councils, but the Labour Party itself contributed very little to this sea change in attitudes. It resisted the Audit Commission as Thatcher's hammer, and many councillors did not believe that effective management was a public duty.

The break with the Fabian tradition could hardly have been more stark. The pragmatic, non-conformist-influenced tradition of public service, and doing the best for your community as a duty, had been replaced in some authorities with the cult of ideological purity or personal enrichment in a small minority of cases.

The Labour Party as an organisation did nothing to monitor the excesses of its own councillors and bring them to heel.

Reforming the Local State

Looking at the local State's relations with the central institutions of government, it is clear that the criticisms of local government in the 1960s and 1970s were well founded.

These critical approaches said that local authorities had failed to adjust to the modern world. Many of them ran highly departmentalised structures which made them less capable of rational policy and resource planning. They failed to conceive of policies in the round and failed to coordinate them.

They were incapable of running an integrated programme to support the social and economic improvement of their area. They had made little attempt to use flexibility and imagination and to implement long-term planning and policy making, or to have systematic monitoring and review of implemented policy.

There are still some smaller authorities like this today, as I discovered when living in Canterbury until 2019 and it was certainly true in Derbyshire and Lambeth and Haringey in the 1980s.

The GLC was a very significant and positive outlier on these issues, with a strategic vision for London (such as flood prevention through the means of the Thames Barrier and continued plans to extend the Underground system), effective performance review and resource planning, and high calibre officers for many years who had the intellectual heft and resources to carry through these system invigilation policies. That was one of the reasons that Prime Minister Thatcher wished to abolish the GLC: it was her most informed, well-resourced and well-organised critic.

The remedy, for those who wanted to reform the local State, was to create management structures which formulated objectives clearly, examined alternative means of attaining them, and then made a careful assessment of the effectiveness of chosen policies.

Redcliffe-Maud[243] argued for one tier, large unitary authorities covering all functions and with substantial resources, incorporating, in effect, the urban and rural district councils and the county councils together. Bigger authorities, it was said, would be more strategic and effective; and the Bains[244] report three years later argued the revolutionary concept of

---

243. cf the Maud and Bains Reports: *The Royal Commission on Local Government*, established June 1966, Cmnd 4040
244. Bains Report HMSO 1972, further analysed by the Institute of Local Government Studies, University of Birmingham

having one team of officers running the show, with the Chief Executive and others chosen solely on merit.

The Labour Party as a political organisation in control of large sections of the local State, never bought into these concepts in many parts of the country.

The problem with the corporatist approach and unitary reorganisation was that it did not address the most difficult problems of local and central State relations, especially if a radical like Thatcher was in charge who wanted to shrink the claims of taxation and reduce State functions in order to do this.

The corporatists failed also to emphasise structures and processes which would enhance council Member control of the local State as well as making that State more efficient. Nor did they address the relationship with the local electorate. There was both a bureaucratic and political failure.

The challenge posed by Thatcherite central government and Tory councils against any form of sensible progressivism took the overriding form of reductions in public expenditure. Although these were presented as technical 'adjustments', they amounted to a radical challenge to the level of public services.

These 'adjustments' came in the form of changes to the Block Grant regime, rate capping legislation, and changes to inner city policies to bring structures like the Urban Programme more directly under the control of Whitehall.

In London alone there was a loss of over £4bn in block grant between 1979-80 and 1986-7.

The standard literature on local authorities[245] describes the functions of councillors but says nothing about what happens when things go badly wrong. Byrne describes the functions of councillors as being representatives, ombudsmen, community leaders, managers and policy makers.[246]

What had happened in Derbyshire was that a powerful leader had isolated other elected councillors who, for a quiet life, let him get on with it. There was little if any interest in managing the Council as a corporate body and they did not attempt to develop policy. They were content, most of them, just to be there.

---

245. eg Local Government in Britain, Tony Byrne, Penguin, sixth edition 1994
246. Op. cit., pages 186-7

Malevolence in Action

In Lambeth it was far worse. There was a group of councillors who were actively seeking to use what power the local State possessed to put spanners in the works of any reform, any efficiency, anything remotely close to the basic collection of taxes and debts. They were using the local State as a platform for their political views to the exclusion of almost anything else.

There was, in my view, a complete breakdown of democracy in both authorities and no one inside that political system, whether they were senior officers, Members, or people inside the Party's own accountability structures, could sort it out. The Labour Party did absolutely nothing about Derbyshire and waited until the mid-1990s to do anything about Lambeth.

To be fair to the PLP leadership in respect of Lambeth, I know that they were waiting to see what was in my report on the Council and afterwards they held back to see whether the council would have the bottle to implement any of it.

They also, I am quite certain, organised more sensible people to stand for the council through the selection process, and ultimately to take it over.

In Derbyshire and Lambeth the level of understanding on local government issues inside the Party was very low and the only reaction was sloganising and the removal of anyone who wanted to introduce reforms.

Nationally, Labour, as a political party, was a bystander in respect of ensuring that the quality of local councillors, their commitment to reform, and their ability to do the job, was present. The PLP frontbench knew perfectly well what was happening in some of the councils and was an intelligent force.

But the degree of change required amongst some Labour Groups and Labour local leaders was ignored. They could have ramped up training, increased the seriousness of selection processes, issued firmer guidance, and imposed deeper sanctions against extreme behaviour. They did none of those things and had no appetite to do so.

This spilled over into a political problem in deprived areas: how to inform and persuade the public that local government was relevant to their needs when it could do less and less.

Where local economies were collapsing because of changes in technology and deindustrialisation there was a need for very different kinds of Members and officers. There was a need for people with expertise, a commitment to intervention where possible, commitment to wide involvement in decision making, and the capability of managing and organising complex programmes and companies.

Instead, what happened was a collapse of confidence created by the intrusion of sectarian political debate into the Labour sphere, coupled with non-intervention by the Foot and Kinnock leaderships on any widespread basis. They intervened in Liverpool and later in Lambeth but it was too little too late. There was no guidance from the top and a terrible failure of leadership.

I argued for these changes of approach at the time. This is not *post hoc* rationalisation.

The Last Benn Initiative

There were those who sought to change the terms of the debate, rather than address these problems, which they were insensitive to.

Tony Benn's initiative in mounting the Socialist Conference movement organised large scale discussion meetings in Chesterfield and Sheffield (in which I played an organising role for him). These demonstrated, if there was any doubt, that the wider Labour movement inside and outside the Party was riddled with sectarianism and an inability to research, understand, and act on information, let alone set a direction which the electorate would follow.

Trying to organise a successful series of conferences that would actually amount to anything was extraordinarily difficult. The academics (and there were a lot of them) were often unreliable and a great deal of their output had to be rewritten. The trade union policy group met far too late to get anything on paper and their contribution had to be inferred by others. The philosophers, who said they wanted to be taken terribly seriously, were woolly and unfocussed and late.

Some propositions, for example, on electoral reform, were very controversial and, in my view, unsupportable. There was a lot about poetry.

Some papers written for the Socialist Conference were absurd:

[A]ll forms of health service should be delivered according to NHS formula. This does not mean a lot more money (probably a 50% increase) and other

health service issues are subordinate.[247]

The author, Hugh Lowe was a former Communist Party member and then a member of the International Marxist Group. He should have known better than use these kinds of vague propositions, as he worked for the Medical Research Council for much of his life.

Apart from the small issue of 50% not being a large number, and the concept of 'NHS formula' being unknown to anyone except the author, this paper showed a marked lack of understanding about the breadth of health challenges facing the UK. Lowe thought that everything would be fine if much more money was spent on it and it was under 'democratic control' (another unspecified concept).

There was inadequate time to rewrite this garbage and I was embarrassed by much of it in the 1987 publications. The unevenness was striking and about half of it should not have been printed at all. Later Conference documents were much better and more coherent internally, but the approach being taken was simply not credible.

Twin Track Strategy, Failing

At the time there was no prospect of building a socialist movement in Britain before the internet, and to think it into existence was merely that: wishful thinking.

As I said about the creation of the newspaper *Socialist* after the first conference, it was not a question of filling a gap in the market. It was about knowing whether there *was* a market in the gap.

There was not.

These experiences solidified my already strong feelings that the broad Labour movement was riddled with people who simply didn't know what they were saying, had not thought seriously about issues, and were in fact driven by a bunch of outdated prejudices.

This wider group were also disorganised and quite unlike the cream of the working class organisations in the trade unions at the time. Inside the Socialist Conference there was a serious cultural rift between the Labour movement types and the independent, middle class, often academic, people. And then again, there were the various Trotskyist groups swirling around the periphery waiting to pounce.

---

247. Hugh Lowe, Interlink Special Issue no. 8 June 1988, page 34

The ultra-left all sent whipped delegations to the Conferences and we spent large amounts of time preventing the Conferences being taken over by points of order and internecine rows by people who just wanted to disrupt and build a marginally bigger sect than before.

One of the problems of coherence was that Tony Benn, so much the leitmotif of the left in the early 1980s, was at that point becoming more sectarian himself. He had been the opposite of that ten years before; now he was less interested in the Labour Party as an organisation and, in fact, dismissive and alienated from it.

He was also less credible. His ill-judged challenge to Kinnock in 1988 was a disaster and he never recovered from it. He was also – although this was not known at the time – ill.

Therefore, his credibility and weight could not be used to fence off the disrupters. So, this attempt to create a new movement (purposes really unknown) foundered under the weight of its own inability to say clearly what it wanted. Never mind the absence of a plan to get from where we were to where it wanted to be.

I suspect that the objective in the minds of some was to split the Labour Party and create some kind of new organisation centred on themselves. Many of them had emerged from the New Left, itself a product of the Cold War and the resistance to orthodox Stalinism and repression.

The official position of the Socialist Conference was to have a twin track strategy – of work within the Labour Party and work outside it to build greater support for left wing ideas.

The reality was that the Labour Party work was sub-contracted to the Campaign Group (not a well organised operation at this point), and the Socialist newspaper made little attempt to cover Labour Party issues. Friendly and intelligent people though many of the Socialist Conference folk were, some of them were dilettantes and it was never going to be possible to build any kind of alternative movement with them in charge.

They did not realise the efforts that had to be made to marginalise the ultra-left groups, or to build a coherent policy position, or to win people in the working class. They disagreed with the salience of electoral politics in the Labour tradition *and they did not do the work*.

Because of these forces, every part of the Socialist Conference eventually fell under the dark sway of tiny leftist organisations and, of course, died.

Independent minded people like myself and Mandy were marginalised having done a great deal of the organising work, with no one else to take it over, and then it fell into the grave. Happy days. The ultra-left never learns how to win, and neither do the academically focussed middle class. The importance of leadership cannot be underestimated.

CHAPTER 6

BLAIR/BROWN AND THE TRIUMPH OF CROSLANDISM

As a political party, Labour often underreacts to changes in the prevailing social and political paradigm. It does this for long periods and then adjusts, gradually or slowly. So, the long reign of Neil Kinnock as leader was a slow slide to acceptance of a market-led economy and the elimination of large sections of Labour's programme that had been envisaged in 1982.

The policy review of 1987 kick started the process, and when Kinnock retired after the 1992 election, it was anticipated that John Smith would continue the soft leftish position that Kinnock had supported.

Smith was an extremely affable man who got on with the vast majority of Labour members and his victory in the leadership election showed this, winning 91% of the vote overall. John was kind and interested in everyone and it was a tragedy when he died well before his time in 1994. What really mattered in the broader context, however, was that social change was accelerating fast.

As so much nonsense has been written about these facts, it is important to set out what they actually were.

Social Change in the 1990s: The Influence of Social Class and other Variables on Social Attitudes

By the mid-1990s society was indeed changing rapidly and there had been important changes to the economy, class structure and attitudes.

These have been so profound in my view as to change the way in which discussions with the electorate had to be conducted.

So, what were these changes?

Changes to social class structures flow essentially from the structure of industry and employment, and of technology.

However, the impact of class on politics is also produced by alterations in social attitudes and changes in opportunities, the best example being the breaking down of barriers to the employment of women since 1918 and especially with the 1970s legislation on equal pay and sex discrimination. Interestingly, despite the profound changes in the economy between 1960 and the mid 1990s – and today – most people still believe they are working class.

The British Social Attitudes Survey (BSAS)[248] showed that in 2012 60% of respondents considered themselves to be working class and 40% middle class, with the proportion considering themselves working class being unchanged since 1983. Evans and Mellon went on:

Many reputable sources have catalogued the decline of the working class in modern Britain. According to the Office for National Statistics and numerous academic analyses, the working class has been shrinking to a fraction of its former size.

Official statistics make clear that what they call 'routine and semi-routine workers' no longer form the largest group in society. This change is, perhaps, not surprising given the dramatic decline of Britain as a manufacturing powerhouse and the rise of China and others as the suppliers of goods.

In the advanced economies of the modern globalised world, manual workers in manufacturing industries are an endangered species. But the number of manual workers in Britain today is only part of the picture. There is another working class: what we might call the working class of the mind.

Though working class occupations are usually thought to amount nowadays to only around a quarter of the population … 60% still claim to be 'working class' when asked to express a class identity (Heath et al., 2013). There is a big difference between being working class as defined by officials and social scientists in terms of occupation and being working class as defined by people themselves.

Not only has objective and subjective social class identification changed significantly over the period, so has party identification by class group:

In 1984, managers and professionals were twice as likely to support the

---

248. NATCEN, various dates, authors Geoffrey Evans and Jonathan Mellon, Nuffield College Oxford. Data taken from BSAS 30

Conservatives as to support the Labour Party (around a half compared with around a quarter did so). By contrast people in the manual working classes were twice as likely to identify with Labour as with the Conservatives (again, around a half compared with around a quarter). In 2012, the professional and intermediate classes are actually more likely to support the Labour Party (38 per cent) than to support the Conservatives (29 per cent). The identification of the manual working classes with the Labour Party has shrunk considerably (to around 40 per cent), although it remains well ahead of their identification with the Conservatives (which is around 20 per cent). Perhaps most strikingly of all, the proportion of all classes who do not identify with any party had risen substantially since 1984: for instance, in 2012, a third (31 per cent) of people in the semi or unskilled manual working classes does not identify with a particular party, compared with seven per cent in 1984.[249]

The BSAS has analysed a set of questions asked in the early 1980s and the same ones used in the 2012 survey.

It found that in 1984 social class was strongly connected to attitudes towards the welfare state, with more working class respondents (as measured by socio-economic group) being more positive towards it on four of the five questions related to spending by government.

Other measures of social class such as education, current economic activity and trade union membership were also linked to attitudes towards welfare spending. The BSAS concludes:

Overall, in 1984, social class appeared to be significantly more important in structuring most attitudes to welfare than our other social cleavage measures.

However, by 2012 social class enjoyed a less dominant role in associations with attitudes to the welfare state and spending.

BSAS states:

People's attitudes to welfare are less strongly related to their social class (measured by someone's socio-economic group) and other measures of their social position are somewhat more significant. People's housing tenure, economic activity and educational attainment are all more important now to people's attitudes to welfare than they were in 1984, having statistically significant associations with four of the five welfare attitudes questions.

Religion, sex, age and ethnicity are all more important now too. They have statistically significant associations with four of our five welfare attitudes, whereas social class is associated with three, income with one, and trade union membership with two. To this extent, there is some evidence that social

249. British Social Attitudes Survey 30

class has become somewhat less dominant in structuring welfare attitudes in the past 30 years to think that class (objectively measured by socio-economic group) was predominant even at this period in the 1980s of apparent class polarisation.

In the early 1980s, there was a differentiation between welfare attitudes, which generally appear oriented on a left-right axis in which class, housing, economic activity, and trade union membership were important, and liberal attitudes, which were more closely related to age, education and religion. However, class and class-related factors such as economic position come over as the most significant predictor of attitudes across the board at that time – so to this extent we can usefully talk about socio-economic position being a fundamental driver of attitudes in the 1980s.

However, BSAS found that over time the strength of feeling amongst trade unionists that the Government should increase spending and taxation had weakened significantly.

In 1984, 53% of trade union members said that spending and taxation should be increased; in 2004 this had fallen to 39%. But the study went on to find that neither measures based on income or socio-economic group have significant relationships with social attitudes, and that it was a more limited set of variables such as trade union membership and unemployment which did.

Overall, says BSAS, there is powerful evidence that social attitudes have changed slowly and in a limited way and that there is only minor evidence that the influence of social class has declined in terms of attitudes towards the State and personal freedoms.

The changing Size and Shape of the Classes

If the influence of social class is somewhat diminished in relation to other variables such as religion in influencing political and social attitudes, it is also true that the size and composition of the social classes has changed very significantly since serious attention began to be paid to this in the 1950s.

When I was a student it was customary to sort the population into AB, C1, C2 and DE social classes, which were essentially based on occupation. There were further analyses based on the influence of particularly solidaristic occupational groups such as mining and deep sea fishing on political attitudes. But the big changes in the size of occupational groups were more important: it is possible to compare the size of particular occupational groups between the 1951 Census and that of 2011, as Figure 1 shows (key Occupational Groups1951-2017).

A Nation of Shopkeepers at Last

As can be seen in Figure 1, some occupational groups of significance in 1951 have now virtually disappeared. Although there are many discontinuities in the classification of occupations between the two censuses, it is clear that some classifications thought to be important in 1951 are not reported separately in 2011. Textile workers have disappeared as a separate category by 2011 because of the decimation of the cotton and woollen trades.

But what is striking is that Britain in 2011 is precisely the society that Napoleon allegedly described in the early 19th century, a 'nation of shopkeepers'.

Whoever originated this phrase (and multiple candidates have been suggested), they had in mind the small family shops of that time. By 2011 this had become reality: the great manufacturing workshop of the world had been transformed into a nation where the single largest group of employees were workers in the wholesale and retail trades (4,736,000), by far and away the largest occupational sector.

If we go further back to the height of the industrial evolution in the mid 19th century, the decline of industry is even clearer: manufacturing, the largest sector of the economy in the period between 1841 and 1871 at just under a 40% share of output, had declined to around 10% in the census of 2011. In contrast services accounted for 30% of output in 1851, but 80% in 2011.[250]

In the 2011 census, the next largest groups of employees after Retail and Distribution were Health and Social Work, and Education. Britain has become a country which specialises in services and in support systems for the population rather than in producing things for export or home consumption.

In the 1951 census it was also thought helpful to segment those in work into broad categories such as Employers and Managers (1,876,650), Operatives (17,679,325), and Own Account Workers (the self-employed) (1,914,900).

---

250. ONS, decennial census

But as Figure 2 shows (% Manual and Non - Manual Employees in Total Occupied Population), by 1981 the numbers of non-manual workers had overtaken the numbers of manual workers, in the long march to a non-industrial economy. In the early 20th century however, routine occupations, many of them manual, were almost five times more prevalent in terms of the number of jobs as employers, managers and the self-employed put together. This was industrial Britain, but already morphing into its 21st century form, slowly at first and then more rapidly; and this was the environment in which the Labour Party was born. That environment has now dissolved.

Political Generations

There was also, in the 1960s, the development of other work on the influence of propinquity, with evidence unearthed by Butler and Stokes[251] about the seeming influence of location on voting behaviour by region and in the most working class areas and, more importantly, the influence of 'political generations.'[252]

This concept, based on the fact that voters are influenced by the political events occurring in their youth (and especially in the period between the age of 14 and 25) seemed to explain in part the long decline of the Liberal Party after 1918 and its replacement by Labour. But they also argued that there was a powerful transmission belt between the political views of parents and the influence these views had on their children.

To this extent therefore, political generations were created by external events and transmission belts; but Butler and Stokes also thought that there was

evidence that party allegiance has followed class lines more strongly in Britain than anywhere else in the English-speaking world.[253]

They prayed in aid studies by Alford,[254] and Robinson, Lipset and Rokkan,[255] but all these studies, including that of Butler and Stokes themselves, were based on research into attitudes and class structures at the end of the 1950s and the beginning of the 1960s. This was when

---

251. *Political Change in Britain*, Macmillan 1969
252. Butler and Stokes op. cit., page 44-64
253. Butler and Stokes op. cit., page 65
254. *Party and Society*, Chicago, 1963
255. *Party Systems and Voter Alignment*, 1967

the working class, however defined, was still very large in Britain and when social stratification was based on a typology of two main classes – according to the subjective views of respondents themselves.

They did not argue that there was straightforward alignment of class and Party and showed conclusively that partisan self-image was strongly linked with class self-image.

So, in their fieldwork of summer 1963, 79% of middle class identifiers identified as Conservative supporters. And 72% of working class self-identifiers identified as Labour supporters. They also showed that when a more granular self-image was used based on a seven category class breakdown it showed that Conservative support fell continuously from upper class to lower working class with the most substantial differentiation being between the lower middle class and the upper working class.[256]

In a separate analysis they also showed that the same pattern was visible when occupational status was used as the variable to analyse class party support.[257]

Butler and Stokes also examined a number of models of class politics, including:

- Politics as the representation of opposed class interests, with parties attracting support by espousing those interests.

- A variant of the 'opposed class interest' model in which parties do represent class interests, but in which interests are not necessarily opposed.

They thought the most persuasive model was a classification of beliefs by voters which showed that in the Conservative-identifying middle class far fewer of these voters expressed their beliefs as the representation of opposing class interest or of simple class interests, with the clear majority (65%) expressing no interest related or normative content to their views at all.

In the Labour supporting working class, however, a different picture emerged. Almost all viewed politics as the representation of opposed class interests (39%), with a further 47% seeing politics as the simple representation of class interests.[258]

Therefore, politics was much more likely to be seen in opposing class

256. Butler and Stokes op. cit., table 4.7, page 77
257. Op. cit., table 4.8 and 4.9, pages 79-80
258. Op. cit., table 4.13, page 92

terms by the working class than by the middle class. Butler and Stokes said that:

The Conservatives' appeal as a 'national' party, the governing agent of a stratified social order, has helped keep the middle class strongly Conservative since the rise of the Labour Party. This image is indeed one that holds considerable appeal for working class voters as well.[259]

Butler and Stokes did not think that class attachments to political parties were static. They pointed to the rise in the number of non-manual occupations and the size of those cohorts as being a significant advantage to the Conservatives as time went on.

They also showed that children rising to non-manual occupations from families where the parents were in manual occupations were quite likely to ditch their families' voting identification with Labour, and also pointed out that in any event individuals who joined non-manual occupations were more likely to come from Conservative inclined families in the working class.

They also rather dismissed the embourgeoisement thesis that working class voters who had become better off and had obtained cars and refrigerators were likely to imbibe Conservative voting attitudes, and they examined the impact of changes in housing tenure. This demonstrated a small movement towards middle class identification in those people who moved to owner occupation.[260]

The paradox of working class Conservatives was found to be, they said, a product of generational differences: the older generations were far more likely than younger working class generations to be aligned to the Conservatives, and they were dying out.

But one crucial fact emerged from their research. They showed that where class was not salient to an individual, Labour's distinctive class appeal was likely to fail, and that the growing affluence of the country undermined the idea of politics as a zero-sum game in which gains for one class were seen as losses for another.

They also pointed to the emerging volatility of the electorate as a new factor, and the weakening of Labour's identification with distinctively working class goals to the steep decline in turnout in working class seats after 1951, and to high swings against Labour in by-elections, especially after 1966.

So, their conclusions were striking:

259. Op. cit., page 94
260. Op. cit., table 5.6, page 103

- Class was the primary factor in determining voting behaviour.

- Images of class conflict or more consensual feelings were linked to party identification.

- Upward social mobility was beginning to have a small effect on voting behaviour, although they dismissed at that point embourgeoisement as a powerful factor.

- Other factors, such as religion or nationalism, were insignificant in importance compared to class.

In addition, they showed that the influence of trade unions was heavily linked to Labour partisanship amongst the working class. Trade union members were much more pro-Labour than non-trade unionists were, in every social grade.[261] Trade union families were much more pro-Labour than non-union families, even after controlling for the different class positions of union and non-union families.

Following Butler and Stokes, twenty years later, the most important book published was *How Britain Votes*[262] which produced helpful breakdowns of voting by social class over time.

The tables they produced[263] showed that at the time of the 1945 General Election, the broad manual and non-manual groups were a mirror image of each other, with non-manual workers breaking 63% to 28% in favour of the Conservatives and manual workers 62% to 29% in favour of Labour.

It was the much larger size of the manual worker population which, at the time, produced the significant Parliamentary majority for Attlee.

Over time, however, and taking both dominant segments together, the non-manual Tory vote and the Labour manual worker vote declined from 62% of all voters in 1945 to 47% of all voters in 1983, leading the authors to state that, 'by 1983 less than half the voters were supporting their natural class party.'[264]

They then went on to make the crucial point that the composition of the 'manual workers' group was changing significantly over time. They said:

---

261. See table 7.4, page 156, op. cit.
262. Heath, Jowell and Curtice, Pergamon 1985
263. See table 3.1, page 30, op. cit.
264. Op. cit., page 31

Self-employed manual workers are much less likely to vote Labour than the working class proper. But they have also been increasing in number in recent years whereas the working class has been contracting. The internal composition of the manual category as a whole has thus changed, and its declining relative propensity to vote Labour will be, at least in part, a consequence of this change in composition.[265]

But the most telling points of all in their analysis were in relation to changing class sizes.

They criticised, quite rightly, the commentators who had focused on 'class dealignment' (in other words people voting 'against their class'), which seemed to have been growing in some elections.

Heath, Jowell and Curtice said tellingly:

In focusing on class dealignment political scientists have concentrated on minor rearrangements of the furniture while failing to notice a major change in the structure of the house. Britain has been transformed from a blue-collar society to a white-collar one.

Whereas in 1964 the working class was nearly three times the size of the salariat, constituting nearly half the electorate, in 1983 the two classes were of almost the same size.[266]

Since then, of course, this process has continued and speeded up. Looking over a longer period, we can see that in 1960 the working class constituted about 70% of the electorate but in 2019 it had shrunk to about 23%.

Uncontrollable Change

This means that when political parties assess the nature of their appeal and how to improve it, it is the inexorable changes driven by technology and globalisation, impacting on the kinds of jobs available and the incomes attached to them, which determine the size of the component groups that the parties are appealing to.

There is little if anything that parties can do to modify the impact of these changes. They are driven by powerful underlying forces removed from political influence. Even the introduction of the National Minimum Wage and the Living Wage have done little to restrain the growth of job insecurity and income inequality between the very top of the income

265. Op. cit., page 34
266. Op. cit., page 3

distribution and the bottom quartile.

Change is driven by markets and finance rather than by conscious political choices based on ideology in one very small corner of the world. However, parties can adapt quickly or slowly and choose the types of response they have to trends. It is fair to say that the Labour Party has adapted slowly and has sometimes been very poor at making choices that render electoral victory more likely.

1997 and After

Blair and Brown understood very clearly the diminishing size of the working class, however defined. The shrinking of the trade union base because of the externalisation of manufacturing and the loss of competitiveness, meant that Labour had to appeal to wide swathes of middle class opinion outside its natural home.

This had been recognised as early as 1950 by the pragmatists who wanted to restrain further significant extensions of nationalisation. Also, having a broader appeal, and not 'frightening the horses' was the keynote of the Blair/Brown approach before the 1997 General Election.

The ultimate note of caution was the commitment to adopt the Conservatives' final two years of public expenditure levels with no increases in taxes, as the leitmotif of the General Election campaign, and to restrict the specific commitments to the electorate to five pledges on a card to be given out to voters.

This was political minimalism carried to its ultimate conclusion, but there was great anxiety in the Labour high command before the election that overpromising and subsequent underdelivering should be avoided at all costs. In practice, they need not have worried and the landslide victory even became apparent to the most sceptical on election day.

Mandy and I were staffing our usual committee rooms in the Arkwright Centre on General Election day 1997 and organising knocking up and leafleting when in walked our old friend Dennis Skinner. He still thought we were going to lose – even after double digit leads in the opinion polls for months and years.

But as we had organised the only proper canvass of any ward in the Bolsover constituency (as usual, I might add), with all our Reading Sheets fully visible, it was easy to point out to him that the Labour vote was coming out strongly, especially in tough little Arkwright. As significant, nobody was voting in the rural Tory parts of our ward (and yes, there were some).

No one was voting from Sutton Spring Wood and the people voting in Sutton Scarsdale, where we lived, were known Labour voters. Even Dennis was convinced. The count came at a rickety public hall in Bolsover later that night. You could actually see through the floorboards into the cellar in multiple places through very large and scary holes.

The District Council had in its usual unhelpful way refused to bring in a television so that the counting agents could watch progress. However, one of the women activists had brought in a telly from home and the scale of the victory gradually dawned on them. There were many puzzled Labour faces as people expected, as usual, to lose.

I was asked whether winning Hove and Harwich was good or not. I explained that we had never won them before, and that they would likely never see another night of victories like this in their lives. There was some scepticism, but the count went on so long in the disorganised death trap that morning was breaking and Blair was off to the Festival Hall to the final sounds of *Things Can Only Get Better* before Dennis's increased majority was announced.

He said the briefest of perfunctory thank-yous and the Tory candidate was not allowed to speak at all. The Returning Officer turned off the microphones and told everyone to go home.

This was victory Derbyshire style.

Preparation Low

In policy terms the Blair/Brown Government continued the harshness of Ken Clarke for two years and then gradually unwound the purse strings. This caused difficulty between the rhetoric and reality on the ground (the word 'transforming' was significantly overused).

They also had major problems with the Machinery of Government until they got properly organised with the Prime Minister's Delivery Unit. And then there was a tendency to over-bureaucratise the monitoring targeting and control systems.

They had few experienced former ministers (in fact hardly any at all after 18 years in opposition) and had not prepared the Shadow Cabinet effectively for the task.

This had also been an error in 1964, the last time that Labour had won after a lengthy period of opposition.

There had been some attempt at preparation for the Shadow Cabinet but, as Harriet Harman daringly reveals,[267] this had left her cold.

The session, organised as a day school at Templeton College, Oxford in early 1997, failed to interest her, and perhaps others, in the Machinery of Government, the role of the civil service, how a minister should work through issues and get an agenda through, and the role of a minster's private office. She says:

At Templeton, former Labour ministers who'd been in government nearly two decades earlier were brought out of retirement to speak to us. They seemed like creatures from a different planet ... The former ministers talked about what sounded to me like irrelevant, ancient history and the academics spoke as if they'd studied politics but never been part of it. Former civil servants spoke in jargon about a world which seemed so alien I couldn't take it in ... It just underlined to me that, whatever they were expecting a secretary of state to be, it wasn't me. I left the day's training none the wiser. I regret not realising at the time how much I could have learned from the people there.

If Templeton in its minimalism and for some of the audience was a failure, Blair in particular felt that the PLP was pretty hopeless and that there would have to be strong central direction from No. 10 if his Government was to be a success.

However, even longstanding and intelligent MPs who had become ministers, like Frank Dobson,[268] were floundering when they were appointed, especially as they had been given no instructions at all by the PM (Frank told me this directly).

He had no agenda flowing from the pledges, or the manifesto, to steer the first years of office, other than in his case a promise to reduce waiting lists for elective surgery by 100,000 by 'reducing red tape' (method unspecified), ending the internal market and measuring in some way the effectiveness of patient care.

These were very broad objectives and, according to Frank, no work had been done on making these promises operational. Shortly after the election, I had arranged a meeting with Frank, with whom I had shared an office in Old Palace Yard, to talk about the data we had collected from the NHS over the past ten years, which I thought could help him and

---

267. Harriet Harman, MP for Peckham 1982- , *A Woman's Work*, Allen Lane 2017, page 188-89
268. MP For Holborn and St Pancras South 1979-83, Holborn and St Pancras 1983-2015, Secretary of State for Health 1997-99

which I was sure no one had taken any notice of.

When we met in his room at Richmond House he was accompanied by several top civil servants. Our A&E data demonstrated that there were inordinately long waiting times to be seen in some hospitals and on occasion patients were waiting over two days in the department before being admitted to a bed. During that discussion one of his top team chortled, 'I thought we'd solved that when Barbara was Secretary of State.' That was a reference to 1974.

Well, it hadn't been sorted, along with a myriad of other issues that I raised and which were significant hurdles for patients to overcome.

The truth was that we were opening a window on reality in the NHS where processes and bureaucracy got in the way of effective patient care. The patients' voice organisations, whatever they happened to be called at any one time, were under-resourced and erratically led at local level. There was also an enormous gap in the patients' needs for information about their condition and treatment and what they were actually told.

Frank hadn't been given an action agenda by the PM, there was very little policy in place and he had no new resources to deploy other than bits of underspend which he applied to winter pressures and setting up investigations like the long overdue Bristol baby deaths inquiry.

We told him that he had to do two things. One: get on top of the processes which were throttling the NHS with bureaucracy, notorious then and now. And two: listen to patients, who would provide him with information that would be like a test card running through the system.

The Department of Health had no data from patients to establish how the service was doing, and therefore the usual information that private sector managers had – sales of products and price margins in a market economy, absent in the NHS for good reason – was matched by a dearth of information about how the service users were feeling it had performed for them.

From our own surveys of NHS patients in 120 hospitals, there was in fact great patient concern about waiting times in A&E, in outpatient clinics and for elective surgery.

But the really stunning point was that huge numbers of patients, between a quarter and a third in most hospitals, were given too little information about their condition and treatment – and if they were given any (by sometimes snooty doctors), many could not understand it.

Frank was surprised and a bit chastened and to his eternal credit introduced the compulsory National Patient Survey programme which started in 2002 and which has been providing top quality data ever since. He was far better than the shadow health secretaries of the earlier 1990s, with whom we had tested out this data. He listened and acted – their eyes had glazed over with boredom.

But he didn't address the bureaucracy.

Governing Blair Style

The governing style of Blairism was loose policy steer in year one, coupled with more central control later. The general economic direction was modern Keynesian with monetary decision-making decoupled from politics through the independence of the Bank of England, announced by Brown on 7th May 1997.

The argument from the ultra-left during this initial period of the Blair Government was an I-told-you-so dismissal of anything that was done, a complete lack of faith in the ability to develop policy and loosen up finances as time went on.

It was often off-beam moonshine: the Blair Government was regarded as an extension of Thatcherism by many including Red Pepper, the organ of Hilary Wainwright[269] and friends. They coined the term 'Blatcherism' because of the way in which Blair initiated modest privatisations, retained some trade union legislation, and allegedly kept monetarist or economically neo-classical models of the economy in its thinking.

This mindset, of slamming anything that wasn't out-and-out, red-in-tooth-and-claw expropriation and nationalisation, demonstrated finally that the ultras were wholly out of touch with the electorate and that there was no way back for them. They needed their own party if they were going to behave like that.

Lapses of Judgement – and Very Good Luck

However, this is not to exonerate the Blair/Brown Governments

---

269. Hilary Wainwright, an author and daughter of the Liberal MP Richard Wainwright. She said that joining the Labour Party as a registered supporter to vote for Jeremy Corbyn 'was a waste of three quid' and thought Corbyn could only be viewed as a figure paving the way for a post-Parliamentary future.

completely. The picture was more complex than that. There were some serious lapses of judgement on individual policy items, such as the 75p rise in pensions in 2000, which they were warned not to do by MPs with their ear to the ground like Dennis Skinner (one of the best readers of working class opinion in the Party). Blair didn't listen to that.

But the really big mistakes were ones which were not at all visible immediately. With the largest Parliamentary majority Labour ever had, they missed chances to solve longstanding problems such as social care, a public/private mixed system of service delivery and payment which had grown up in that way accidentally and which was failing to keep up with the needs of the steeply rising numbers in the older population. So, the unwillingness of government in the Thatcher/Major years to address social problems was continued. To leave this difficult problem, as actually happened, to Andy Burnham, the last Health Secretary under Brown, was quite wrong and doomed to failure at a time when the opposition had their tails up and thought they were going to win the next election.

What was entirely new and extraordinary in British terms was the amount of constitutional tinkering that took place after 1997, without any real debate inside the Labour Party and without prominence in discussion at the General Election, save for devolution to Scotland and Wales.

The definitive modern work on the British constitution[270] cites 15 major initiatives after 1997[271] which not only introduced devolution but also changed the balance of power between the elected Commons and the courts, introduced new tests of legality through the Human Rights Act, reformed aspects of local government, introduced Freedom of Information requirements, entrenched the use of referenda in respect of political decision making, introduced various forms of proportional representation into some elections, and began the regulation of political parties.

This was a remarkable list of reforms, much of it little debated in public, fragmented and uncoordinated, and (with the exception of Scotland and Wales in terms of devolution), not on the radar of the public. If one had asked voters before the 1997 General Election whether they were voting Labour in order to secure a proportional list system for the European Assembly elections, most would not have agreed.

This basket of initiatives, many of them highly contested in elite

---

270. *The New British Constitution*, Vernon Bogdanor, Hart Publishing 2009
271. Bogdanor op. cit., pages 4-5

political discussion, broke decisively with Labour tradition in that they abandoned the idea that the British constitution was something that was best left alone. These changes were, however, entirely peripheral to the electoral successes of the Blair Government.

The constitutional adventures post-1997 also illustrated the ossification of the Party's policy making system from the grassroots. After 1945, a central Labour myth was that an individual member could move a resolution at their branch, get it passed up to the constituency and then Conference, and the essence of it could be adopted there as Party policy, and then implemented as actions by a Labour Government. This myth was exactly that – the process was subject to porosity as elements of the original were watered down or transformed, and at Conference the process of compositing resolutions was such that much original content was lost. If a Labour Government were conveniently elected, then it could simply ignore or sideline proposals that did not suit its central message.

It was also the case that constituency and then Conference resolutions and Party programmes for general elections were subject to 'holes', places which appropriate policy guidance had not reached, as Crossman found out to his cost when appointed as Housing Minister in 1964.

The myth was based on evidence such as the resolution moved at the 1944 Party Conference by none other than Ian Mikardo, which was passed in the teeth of opposition from the platform but formed the core of the Attlee Government's legislative programme.

However, the constitutional experiments after 1997 demonstrate clearly that initiative on major issues had passed to elite levels. There was no clamour for much of the constitutional agenda except from the Westminster bubble, journalists, and lawyers. The Party's grassroots did not count in these circumstances. What a Labour Government did by way of major actions was now determined almost entirely by the elite in charge. The point is that the old myths had been shunted into a siding and the PLP leadership and its friends were now firmly back in charge.

But the reason that Blair was able to cruise along largely untouched by the Conservative opposition was that the economy was growing continuously, with low inflation and falling unemployment, for most of the period between 1997 and 2008.

This had started before the 1997 election but it became an accepted feature of the economic landscape and there were those in the economics profession and in politics who developed the line that the West had discovered a way to combine growth, jobs and low inflation unlike anything before. It was a new paradigm, they argued.

Brown, like other finance ministers in the West, favoured rules-based monetary and fiscal policies which seemingly limited the growth of public spending and political influence on interest rates. But the so-called 'great moderation' in which all the key economic indicators were set fair was based on an illusion.

The financial liberalisations of the 1980s had almost abolished controls on capital flows. Behind the scenes, financial behaviours were becoming more and more extreme.

Brown recognised this himself and accepted that it had been a mistake to accept 'light touch regulation' of the banking and financial systems. In the British case, they were supervised by an ineffective body separated from the Bank of England and the Treasury and acting as one part of an unbalanced tripartite model.

This was, in the British context, a very significant error – but that error was being repeated across the western world under the guidance of the hegemonic views of Alan Greenspan, then the Chairman of the US Federal Reserve.

Greenspan's line was that financial risks had been minimised because modern financial markets had almost abolished the risks of a meltdown by diversifying such risks into new products spread internationally across the ownership of many banks and institutions.

The phrase 'this time it's different' became the mantra of the smooth operators who believed that they really had found a new economic nirvana.

The problem was that precisely the opposite was true. These new products, Collateralised Debt Obligations (CDOs) and derivatives, entailed bundles of debt obligations being tied together and given a price by the markets. Taken together with the use of ultra-loose lending criteria by US banks in the sub-prime mortgage market in particular, they were understood by hardly anyone.

Nonetheless, the debt bundles were rapidly packaged and repackaged across borders using the modern financial flows across the world now linking financial systems. Thus, CDOs and derivatives turned up as 'assets' in previously staid lending institutions.

Few knew the risk level of the securities they were trading or buying, and Greenspan's argument that spreading the risk meant lower risk was utterly wrong.

It meant wider contamination when the slide started in the UK with Northern Rock, followed by the Lehman Brothers collapse and the failure to bail out US institutions. There was also extensive shorting of banks like RBS by hedge funds and their allies, which drove down the share price and made their collapse inevitable.

Light touch regulation failed because it could not grip these risks including the transmission of shocks across borders, and the regulators did not understand the severity of risk arising from acute financial engineering. This led ultimately to a situation where crashing asset prices and losses on bank ledgers in turn exposed banks to droughts of cash available to support their borrowing.

It became clear that banks all over the world had extended their borrowing way beyond the ability of their capital base to support it, and the enforcement of strict capital-to-lending ratios was long gone.

In the end, the State had to step in with nationalisation of all or part of some UK banks and building societies, as the 'lender of last resort.'

William Keegan ends a section of his book on economic crises by quoting Conservative MP Jesse Norman[272] who said:

I can tell you precisely what was responsible for the crash. It was because bank leverage, which was twenty times capital in 2000, went up to fifty times in seven years.[273]

What Norman fails to say, however, is that a few active players in the financial markets took decisive action to bring down banks such as RBS, because it would make them money.

Blair was, however, very lucky. His time as Prime Minister was at precisely the moment when great expansions of the labour force occurred in two areas, mainland China and Eastern Europe, after the collapse of Communism. This meant that huge numbers of workers were added to the world labour supply – 240 million in China and 209 million in Eastern Europe, integrated in to the world trade system for the first time since 1945 in the case of the European post-Communist states, and arguably for the first time ever in the case of China.

This increase in the availability of labour, the most significant 'labour shock' in modern times, drove down the price of labour everywhere in the West, drove up world trade by 5.6% a year between 1990 and 2017, and enabled globalisation on a much larger scale than before. At the time, the economic effects in Britain were benign for the owners of

---

272. MP for Hereford and South Herefordshire from 2010
273. William Keegan, *Nine Crises*, Biteback, 2019 page 181

capital in terms of controlling prices and reducing the bargaining power of labour, and negative for those dependent on selling their labour in the marketplace.

The short term effects for Blair were economic stability, a quiet time for economic problems until 2008, after he had left office, but longer term angst for employees and the excluded as capitalism failed to ensure rising living standards for the first time since 1945.

Labour people often assume that it was the Thatcher reforms to trade union law which caused the decline in working class purchasing power. It was not – the largest effect was caused by the expansion of the world labour force.[274]

Cassandras and Failure to Take Note

This is a well-known story but there were Cassandras of various types who believed that things were getting badly out of hand. Margaret Reid, in her book *All Change in the City, The Revolution in Britain's Financial Sector*,[275] was very concerned about excessive deregulation. She pointed out that the amount of cash washing through the currency markets was now about 30 times the scale of underlying trade and invisibles business. Modern capitalism had morphed into classic arbitrage, taking advantage of sometimes miniscule differences in price between two markets, and even before the big bang she was arguing in respect of the secondary banking crisis in the 1970s:

Abundant credit in a liberalised financial system led by a government hell-bent on growth provided a hot-house atmosphere for a breed of self-styled financial entrepreneurs … Their reign was brief, foundering in a mix of political chaos, currency crises, rebounding interest rates, over-investment in property and the inevitable and dramatic change in that most fickle of ingredients – confidence.[276]

By the mid-1980s the City of London had become the centrepiece of world financial trade in almost every sector, and capital movements

274. This point is argued convincingly by Charles Goodhart and Manoj Pradhan, *The Great Demographic Reversal*, Palgrave 2020. They say 'Especially in advanced countries, a fall in real wages has seen the economic position of un-skilled labour as well as semi-skilled labour suffer relative to capital, profits, and managerial and skilled labour remuneration.' Page 5
275. Reid op cit, Palgrave, 1988
276. Margaret Reid, *The Secondary Banking Crisis 1973-75*, Macmillan 1982

each day really did eclipse real movements for investment.

But it was not only *Financial Times* journalists, as Reid was in the 1970s, who identified an emerging crisis of credibility and nascent danger. There was a similar analysis on the ultra-left, in the shape of a CLPD initiative which created *Beyond the Casino Economy*.[277]

Almost every leftist in sight contributed ideas but it was an extraordinarily sterile document. It argued for the replacement of the 'Casino' with

... the planned development and expansion of a group of core industries of the future that could provide Britain with a secure economic base for the 1990s and beyond.[278]

They wanted a regulated foreign exchange system, 'joint venture polices' and more cooperation with the developing world.

So, they had noticed the new arbitrage economy but were reheating the Alternative Economic Strategy (AES) from the freezer in the hope that serving it up 15 years later would make it more credible. They wanted investment of taxpayer funds in new nationalised industries and in effect an economic policy insulated from that of the West.

Their prescription showed clearly that the old left journalists and trade unionists had no idea what an alternative would actually look like, especially when 'international capitalism' could destroy an incoming Labour Government in an afternoon should it choose to do so (and could certainly eliminate in one month a Government's ability to borrow, if it engaged in a gilt strike).

This dull prescription was set out before the advent of the internet and ultrafast market trading which depended on micro-seconds of advantage being gained in order to turn a microscopic arbitrage gain. But it is significant that some of the proposals, such as 'paying' for the costs of nationalisation by issuing government bonds formed the centrepiece of the Labour manifesto in 2019.

The book ends with what they thought was a neat formulation: 'As the people move left, the left moves right.'[279]

They really thought that advanced capitalism had generated an automatic radicalisation of the people in large numbers, a point followed by Corbyn and indeed to some extent by Miliband in the period 2010 to 2019.

But they hadn't.

---

277. Nick Costello, Jonathan Michie and Seumas Milne, Verso 1989
278. Op. cit., page 11
279. Op. cit., page 279

The people moved right as the left moved to the ultra-left, bringing to a deserved culmination the link between leftist hubris and electoral nemesis.

The point was that both the ultra-left and specialist financial commentators had noticed the same thing: there had been a failure to exert anything but the most minimal of financial oversight and effective supervision, which in a system of free capital movements could cause disaster if the risks were not mitigated.

The failure to act was certainly a strategic failure of the Blair/Brown Governments as was, of course, Iraq. I will not add to the ink spilled over that series of fateful policy decisions.

Important History Lessons

The conclusions that we can reach over the 1997-2010 period of Labour Governments is that they in reality followed a Keynesian economic policy, tried to make the public services more efficient, made some significant errors in not dealing with festering policy areas like social care, and failed strategically to control market capitalism in a way that was possible for them and which would have reduced risk across the world.

It was not entirely in their gift to do this, but the efforts to intervene internationally which were made were too little and too late on regulation and were ultimately ignored after the 2010 election.

The principal failure was, however, to believe the propaganda that a new paradigm had been created. They failed to adapt away from it, just as previous Labour governments in the 1960s and 70s had failed to grip the issues of low pay, and just as the ill-fated Ramsay Macdonald Government of 1929-31 had failed to adopt available options such as the abandonment of the Gold Standard in order to deal with the financial crash of 1929. They were all in the grip of groupthink.

The advantages of leaving the Gold Standard were well known by 1929. Leaving meant that adjustment mechanisms like changing the exchange rate itself, or the ability to use fiscal measures to boost the economy, or the ability to cut interest rates to improve demand, were on the table and would have been very helpful in adapting to the slump in employment caused by the stock markets crash.

Instead, the Labour politicians of the day failed to understand that alternatives to maintaining the Gold Standard were available, despite Keynes's widely publicised dissection of Churchill's policy,[280] and Mosley's later espousal of a kind of Keynesian response to the crisis whilst still a Labour minister. They just accepted the logic of the scorched earth deflation after the First World War, caused by the horror of the establishment at the large debt mountain created by that war. They accepted that cuts in government spending and higher taxes ought to be the order of the day, whatever their vague and ineffectual Party programme said.

They resolutely set their minds against challenging the status quo, the paradigm of the day. They behaved in 1929 in the same kind of way that Labour did about regulation of financial institutions in the 1990s, and in the way that the Wilson/Callaghan Governments failed to adapt away from incomes policy as the leitmotif of economic policy in the 1960s and 70s.

There is a pattern here, and it involves an unwillingness by all three Labour Governments to challenge temporarily dominant ideas, and their acceptance that alternatives in economic policy were very limited.

It is, in fact, one of the major characteristics of Labour in power – a deep conservatism which limits policy options.

On the Ground in Derbyshire: the Divine Right to Rule

Our personal experience in the 1980s and beyond was in experiencing politics in a very different culture. Mandy and I had landed in north Derbyshire in 1988 and bought a lovely farmhouse at almost the same price as we obtained for the sale of our terraced house in Tottenham, such are the vagaries of the regional housing markets.

The children were growing up and at various points we had rescue cats from the Cats Protection League and escaping hens from the farm opposite which didn't want to go back. We also had a bunch of old Derbyshire Redcap hens that wouldn't return to their refuge at night, preferring instead to roost in the tallest trees they could find and who were accordingly and inevitably picked off by the local foxes who thought it was Christmas. Spurs the tortoise lasted for a while and then didn't come out of hibernation. And, of course, we joined our local Labour branch, the Arkwright and Calow Labour Party.

This was a culture transformation from north London and I

---

280. J M Keynes *The Economic Consequences of Mr Churchill*, Hogarth 1925

recommend it to anyone who believes that modern metropolitan politics are to be found everywhere. As a Mancunian I thought north Derbyshire was a bit southern, but the very working class branch we joined was just three years out from the miners' strike of 1984-5 and the wariness of anyone resembling an outsider was palpable.

They had had a hard time at the hands of the Metropolitan Police during the strike and there was a general feeling that Londoners, who by definition we were despite everything else, could not be trusted or relied on.

Their coal, grafted at enormous personal cost, had beaten the Kaiser and smashed Hitler and they were very proud of their heritage. For generations they had been under the impression that they were central to the British economy. Their world was creaking at the edges and about to disintegrate, and they were fearful of the future. Jobs for life down the pit had been replaced with whatever you could find that week.

Our first branch meeting was a revelation: when we entered the room absolutely everyone was smoking (unheard of in Tottenham). There was no agenda. There were no minutes. There was no planning for the future.

They looked at us out of the corners of their eyes as if to say, 'What the fook are they doin' in our branch?'

Of the two local district councillors one was an Independent (in practice a Tory) and the other was Labour but was disorganised and useless. The Parish Council of 11 was completely in the hands of the squirearchy and people who thought they should have been in the squirearchy.

The County councillor was Labour but from another and much bigger village (which was bad, it was said). And, of course, we had a Labour MP, Dennis Skinner, then in his eighteenth year of representing the constituency, having won six general elections at that point with some ease.

No one did surgeries in the ward, there hadn't been any canvassing for generations, there were no Party records, or if there were, they were in boxes in a long forgotten loft, and another four years at least of Tory Government shimmered ahead of us.

The truth was that Labour in north Derbyshire, everywhere, thought they had a divine right to rule. They were there. They were Labour because they were working class and for the working class. They had no discernible policy or objectives except to be against the Tories, and they defined themselves against the Tory Government as distinct from having a mind of their own.

They could also be vindictive when they wanted to be and ran decision-making on a personal basis.

One young woman in Calow, the daughter of an ex-miner and Party member, had got herself into difficulties and needed a home for her and the new baby. When the local Labour District councillor was asked to help secure accommodation, he wouldn't lift a finger because he didn't like the family and said so. There was no points system for housing allocations and it was all done on 'Member recommendation' – a recipe for corruption if there ever was.

There were even reports from one of our local Labour MPs that if you were a young woman, you got a council house by sleeping with the local Labour councillor.

There were in effect several cultures in the Labour Party in the 1990s. The most prominent were a soon to be out-of-touch, middle class, liberal elite, strongest in London; and a separate, traditional male working class regional culture in areas that were in steep employment decline, sometimes with overtones of corruption.

You can, looking back with perfect rear-view mirrors, see the oncoming disaster of the 2019 General Election in the mindsets of 1990.

At the 2019 election, Bolsover went Tory, North East Derbyshire had gone Tory in 2017 and stayed that way, the County had gone Tory twice, and the North East Derbyshire District Council had just gone Tory for the first time in nearly a century.

Chesterfield had just been saved by strong campaigns by an effective and hardworking MP, Toby Perkins – but there were now only two Labour MPs in Derbyshire.

In 1997, at the first Blair triumph, there were nine.

Earlier, in the mid 1990s I wrote a paper for Skinner arguing that the Derbyshire coalfield seats were travelling in one direction, away from Labour, and were following Bosworth in Leicestershire, South East Derbyshire (Erewash) and others in to the Conservative camp. This was because of lower working class turnout, I said, disillusion with local Labour politicians, social change, and sometimes dozy MPs. Unless Bolsover upped its game and a different kind of active, responsive politics was mobilised, Bolsover and North East Derbyshire and the rest would follow down that road. Skinner was horrified and ranted at me on the phone: 'Do not distribute this!' he screamed.

He didn't change his modus operandi, neither did the constituency Party, and disaster followed in 2019. Adopting my proposals, raising serious money, regular surgeries everywhere, proper attention to casework, mass leafleting, regular canvassing, training for key workers, might have delayed the process of change at the margins and stopped Skinner from defeat in 2019. But it was too much trouble, and too foreign: the divine right to rule in the coalfields was still thought to be operative. The old ways, focused on Dennis being driven round in a car at elections and then shouting at voters through a loudspeaker, was 1940s campaigning and didn't work anymore. It was too late for Dennis to change, and the result in December 2019 was predictable and was predicted. Figure 3 shows the catastrophic decline in the Labour share of the vote.

Neighbouring Nottinghamshire was no better, and the anti-Labour swing – and it was that – was enormous. Ex-mining seats that had been Labour for generations now have Tory majorities of southern Home Counties proportions. The effect was at its strongest in the constituencies of small towns and industrial villages that ran down the eastern edge of the Pennines. Labour had been driven back to the big cities and the occasional redoubt.

Trying and Failing to Create an Infrastructure

That was the future. When we arrived in February 1988 the local pit, the Arkwright drift mine, was on the verge of closure but maintenance and recovery was still ongoing. The dark green British Coal buses were still wending their way between the villages to bring outlying miners to work.

By this time a lot of pits had been shut. There had been two in our tiny hamlet of Sutton Scarsdale, but they were long gone. The Calow Main pit had been abandoned in 1873 but there were shafts and drifts all over Calow, and the Arkwright pit had been earmarked for closure some years before.

It was a drift mine which for many years boasted the purest coal in the world. The pit had been sunk in 1898 and there were five drifts connected with cross measures which together produced 750,000 tons of coal in 1975.

Arkwright Town consisted of three streets and a few modern council houses. There was a posh house for the colliery manager, a post office, a chippie, the Miners Welfare, a pub just in case you got thrown out of the Welfare, a county Primary school, allotments, and a St John Ambulance Hall to train the first aiders who were required in the pit and elsewhere.

It had no reason for existence other than to service the pit, and had been built with that in mind, taking families from the Markham, Bonds Main and Calow Main collieries a little way away when it was built.

Outside privies were the order of the day until 1974 and conditions inside some of the houses were Victorian. Many had been modernised but they were essentially two-up/two-down with the main entrance being the back door.

They were of the type to be seen in every Victorian mining area in Northern England, Wales and Scotland, with a great similarity in housing style between Arkwright and Wansbeck, Northumberland.

There were about 300 people living there in the mid-1980s, and British Coal had divested itself as the landlord in 1977. After closure and salvage things started to fall apart pretty rapidly.

Great trepidation occurred when the lights were turned off in the pit yard. The local businesses – always hand to mouth – went into steep decline.

The Welfare in particular suffered as thirsty miners didn't go in after their shift. The chippy opened infrequently and almost when they felt like it. The school had been threatened with closure because of falling numbers and had been saved by a local campaign. The Post Office was obviously stretched.

But it was a very tight community, with all the strengths and weaknesses that meant. Great feuds existed between families because of personal behaviours in previous generations or in previous strikes (when locals referred to the Strike, they often meant 1926). The Post Office was threatened because someone ran off with someone else's wife. You certainly felt as if you were treading on eggshells.

It was still a place where on a Sunday morning you could see whippets being led through the streets by proud owners and women in dressing gowns flitting across the streets to the next row. The most inconvenient feature of all was the suspicion of folk from the next village, let alone anywhere else.

When eventually we tried to get the Labour branch meetings to rotate between settlements, it became immediately clear that the Arkwright members wouldn't go to Calow (one mile away) and the Calow members wouldn't go to Arkwright, and when Holmewood (two miles away) was included in our branch because theirs had collapsed, nobody would go there at all.

It was also clear after a couple of meetings that the feuding went on between levels of local government too: the Parish hated the District, the District despised the County, and vice versa all the way up and down the line.

Often it really was personal: the hard bitten ex-WRP[281] leader of the District Council, David Nuttall, an out-and-out Stalinist who treated his group and the local Labour MP with contempt, hated the Skinner family because someone had allegedly done something sexually inappropriate in the 1940s – and so it went on.

The mafia concept of separating business and personal was unknown. And you were supposed to know all these things before you said anything.

So, we began with pretty much a blank canvas and began the process of recreating a viable Labour machine. The first step was to capture the Parish Council. This was a do-nothing black hole but had considerable powers including the ability to raise whatever precept it wanted without restriction, and to defeat the Independent District councillor.

The chance came shortly after we moved there. I organised a slate of 11 candidates for the Parish and we put up two candidates for the District seat, and did a lot of organising and canvassing. There were bright red dayglo posters everywhere. We issued election manifestos and lots of leaflets, knocked everyone up and treated it as if it were a general election. We did this everywhere in the ward.

Arkwright itself was incredibly solid and we found only two people who claimed to be Tories, and one of them may have been kidding. In the election 97% of electors in the village actually voted and 10 of the 11 Labour candidates were elected. The one who wasn't had thumped someone in the Welfare the previous week, and that ensured that he was not flavour of the month. But our District candidates sailed to a good win. This all turned out to be very useful as important events were about to unfurl.

Huge Fight over Methane

On 11th November 1988 a retired collier, late at night, noticed that there were strange blue flames burning in his open hearth. These were still the days of concessionary coal for ex-miners but it was a good job

---

281. Workers Revolutionary Party. Nuttall openly promoted and sold WRP leaflets and pamphlets at Party meetings in the 1980s, when he was a leading Councillor.

that it was noticed by a sensible family in Arkwright.

At first, it was thought to be a straightforward gas leak from the mains, but tests were carried out and a major methane ingress was diagnosed coming from the just-abandoned mine workings.

The whole village was evacuated and residents housed in far-flung church halls until they had pumped enough gas out of the workings to make the streets temporarily safe. Monitors were pinned to the walls of houses to measure gas content.

There was then the issue of what to do about the village. As methane is colourless and odourless and highly combustible, the residents had had a lucky escape, but there was great trepidation about future ingress.

There were essentially two options. First, to raze it to the ground, compensate the families so that they could buy fresh accommodation and accept that the community would be no more. Second, to relocate Arkwright, move the villagers, recreate new and better community facilities, and as a *quid pro quo*, opencast the surrounding area which contained four million tons of high quality coal, according to professional estimates.

Option one did not appeal to many villagers as they were strongly opposed to their community being abolished. Option two was, however, more expensive and the compensation for the coal owners would only be recovered over a period of time through open casting.

Some in Arkwright made it very clear that they didn't want that: they had had enough, they said. They very sensibly wanted trees, footpaths, streams and hillocks. They wanted a rural paradise from the ashes of the coal industry, and they felt they were owed it.

The political complications of doing anything – and there were many – started at national level. At precisely this time the Thatcher/Major Government was intent on privatising the remnants of the coal industry, with its few deep pits, considerable property and land assets, and significant numbers of opencast sites or potential sites.

So, traditionalist British Coal managers were going to be replaced by Lord-knew-who private companies with different priorities and values, who would certainly not be bound by the sometimes paternalistic British Coal mentality, or commitments made by them.

The second problem was that cooperation between the Labour-controlled Derbyshire County Council and the Labour-controlled District Council was thin to say the least, and they were all unimaginative and hidebound at both officer and elected-Member level.

The third problem was ultra-local. The residents, good people though they were, were going to be eaten alive by the officials and by the privatised owners. Their interests were going to be last in the queue when decisions were made, because none of them had any experience of lobbying for their rights outside the pit, or being forward-looking to get results. They had no framework to fall back on.

This was compounded by the fact that British Coal, still in charge in 1988, rejected the calls for compensation to the villagers and claimed that it was not their workings that the methane came from. This was, of course, ludicrous but it set the context for a battle royal.

There was some local talent: Ged Briddon, an electrical fitter from the local pit who was now on development work in the new (and never opened) Vale of Belvoir coalfield.

Roger Watkinson, who eventually became our County councillor, who was one of the many taxi drivers, and Suzannah Rockett, a young woman who had spina bifida, had educated herself and gone to university, and who still lived in the village. She was to become our District councillor and eventually a trainer of social workers in Barnsley. Finally there was the formidable figure of Norma Dolby, a refugee from Dagenham, who was a leading figure in the Miners Wives Support Group in the 1984 strike, who penned a remarkable book on the dispute[282] and later become one of our District Councillors and Chair of the Council. Norma was tough, kind, and shy and married to the stroppiest ex-miner in Arkwright.

So, there was a core group, and I formed a plan to build on their local credibility and experience to create circumstances in which British Coal and the new owners would be obliged to agree to relocation because the alternatives were too embarrassing and expensive for them.

Constructive Threats

The only way to compel British Coal and its successors (which turned out to be RJB Mining) was to threaten them with legal action to enforce compensation.

I wrote instructions to counsel, selected the environmental lawyers Leigh Day to do the work, got the backing of the local Party branch and the Parish council, and so Ged, Roger and Suzie went off to see the

282. *Norma Dolby's Diary, An Account of the Great Miners Strike*, Verso, 1987

lawyers, who did their job very well.

British Coal at first dug their heels in but eventually – much later – we had persuaded them that moving the village was far better than a long and expensive process of litigation. Especially as it would be followed by even more expensive compensation for 174 families who had almost been blown up by the methane from the mine workings they owned and were responsible for.

Not only was there legal action: I ensured that the Parish Council employed planning consultants Ward Hadaway to ensure that British Coal could not run away from its obligations.

In the drafts of the critically important Section 106 agreement which set out the obligations of British Coal (BC) in return for open casting privileges, there were frightening gaps. There was in fact no obligation to build the new facilities and homes, and BC could in fact have taken the coal and not moved the village.

This was utter incompetence on behalf of the Labour-controlled District and County councils who had been parties to the draft.

We also ensured that restoration of the site was high quality and not the Russian Steppe look that characterised many opencast schemes at the end of their life. We ensured that 'fall behind' clauses which would have allowed BC to fall behind the timetable and walk away from construction of the village were removed, and the new clauses also ensured that BC would have to stick to the strategic plan unless specifically authorised to deviate from it.

We ensured that the County and District councils would have to step in and complete the scheme in case BC or its successors reneged on the proposals. Thanks to these actions, the Parish had ensured that the scheme was legally watertight. It was quite typical of the poor quality of Labour representation at District and County level that we had to step in.

The village was relocated across the main road with a thick imperme-able layer underneath it to prevent methane ingress. Every family got a new house or bungalow. There were special units for the disabled. Each family received £2,500 in moving compensation. The primary school was replaced and a new nursery built. The chippy and Post Office were recreated. A spanking new Miners Welfare was built together with a crown green bowling area. Football pitches were rolled out, and a new community centre was built to be owned and run by the Parish Council.

St John Ambulance also had a little hall attached to the community centre. There was a meeting room for the housing association tenants, and there were trees and a lake. You couldn't have created more different conditions if you had tried.

And that was part of the problem of acceptance.

Some of the old stagers resisted accepting this. There was one ex-collier, Rusty, who was particularly obstreperous about the move and was threatening to stay despite the bricks and mortar demolition soon to take place. He was waiting for me one day when I was canvassing Chesterfield Road down the back ginnel, sitting on a wall and adjusting the rake of his flat cap in the sunshine.

When I got to him he really let go, effing and blinding and saying it was a betrayal and they'd have to carry him out. Then his wife emerged from the back door and said: 'But Rusty, the kitchens are lovely.' That was the end of that.

It was the case that many were relieved to get the proper bathrooms, a choice of kitchen fittings, proper cookers (which some didn't have), stairs that weren't perilous, and money to fit out their new place in the style they wanted.

But others were nostalgic for the old community and didn't like living a distance away from their neighbours (in semi-detached splendour as distinct from a terrace). But the most serious problem was allocating units in the new village. There were, of course, three or four families who no one wanted to live next to for various reasons, and there was a lot of agitation about that.

But eventually the great day came and the whole village formed up and marched across to the new community centre behind the banner of the Arkwright NUM lodge, which had emerged from storage somewhere, and families moved into their new homes.

The village was ceremonially opened by the three local Labour MPs, and Stephen Benn, Tony's eldest son (now Lord Stansgate), splendidly wrote an Arkwright Anthem, an original piece which was played by a brass band.

£26m Victory

It had gone well. By my reckoning the project cost British Coal and RJB Mining about £26m, expressed through the Section 106 agreement sitting behind the permission to opencast. This was an enormous sum of compensation, and RJB received their due in the form of extracted coal from the opencast site, one of the biggest in Europe.

The company behaved pretty well, despite great misgivings from the more suspicious villagers, and the land has now returned to nature and looks significantly better than it did before.

It was a triumph. But there were some sour notes.

When it became clear that the project was going ahead, a group of unscrupulous Labour councillors on North East Derbyshire District Council, acting on an insider trading basis, decided to try and buy up a few of the empty houses that existed in the village, get the new homes, and sell the new replacements on to make money. It was a scam and I'm glad to say they were stopped. But it made visible the corruption of parts of local Labour politics.

Mandy and I spent thousands of hours and years of our lives making sure that the new Arkwright happened and, despite the aggro, it is one of the best things we have ever done. But the hassle was enormous. Life felt like swimming through treacle and there were many times when we wondered whether it was worth it.

The Labour Establishment

There was a postscript to the victory.

At one point a district election was coming up and I suggested that we might actually have a selection meeting to decide who our candidates were. This was greeted with incomprehension by the old timers, but it went through, and the day of the conference arrived.

Nominations were taken – our two sitting councillors were nominated, and Suzie Rockett, who had expressed an interest.

What happened next was classic: Ian Beresford, a sitting councillor and ex-miner, was called on to make a 10-minute speech to make his pitch but he refused. 'If you don't know me by now, I'm going,' he ranted, and walked out of the room.

The other sitting councillor, Pat Kerry, made a short contribution as did Suzie and those two were selected. No one had planned to get rid of Beresford but his arrogant behaviour had scuppered him. Four years later he stood as an Independent candidate and got elected, to our chagrin.

When Suzie Rockett reached the council, she was treated with contempt by the Labour Group, like so many women in local government. She was the only councillor in a wheelchair, the only Paralympic medallist,[283] and one of the very few women.

But she was a pariah according to the mafia that ran the council and it was made very clear to her that she had intruded into the old boys' club and should leave at the earliest possible opportunity. She did.

The quality of the District Labour Group continued to amaze. Before one election, I asked a senior sitting councillor to give me a list of the policy achievements over the last four years, and what the election key points for the future were.

He didn't know. He said he'd go and ask the officers. He came back with a scrappy and inadequate piece of paper. As I was, as usual, writing the election address, I had to interrogate him again and again on what was meant, and eventually we got something that was half reasonable.

But the real revelation came when we discussed recycling, where the council had one of the worst records in the East Midlands according to official figures, but had made some progress. What were the actual increases achieved, I asked in a fit of madness. He went away again to ask the officers and came back with figures for paper an $x\%$ increase, glass a $y\%$ increase, metals a $z\%$ increase and so on.

Then he used the classic formulation of adding all the percentages together to make a figure which came to more than 100%. He was adding the percentages together to make nonsense. 'So that's what we've achieved,' he said proudly. I felt rotten pointing out the basic arithmetical error.

He was Chair of the Finance Committee.

These tribunes of the people were also quite hopeless at doing anything for themselves, like canvassing in support of their own candidature in an election. Our District and County councillors refused to do it until I made them at a closely contested District election, but they insisted on going together to every front door in case anyone leapt out with a carving knife.

After a while, I went across Rectory Road, Duckmanton, to get them to split up but they refused again. They couldn't grasp the fundamental point that if you wanted to get elected it was courteous to ask people for support, and it helped you understand their concerns.

They couldn't do much except drink cups of tea, and if you asked them to comprehend the Reading System (the records of who had promised to vote for you in order to knock them up to get them to vote on election day), they were lost.

---

283. Suzie won a Silver Medal in fencing at the Seoul Paralympics of 1988.

What you could do quite easily in Canterbury in the 1970s was utterly impossible in working class Derbyshire. In Canterbury we had established a deep rooted, systematic method of organisation which survived and was embedded and which helped change the political complexion of the city for ever.

In north Derbyshire this was the stuff of dreams. The Labour Party's modus operandi there was that they hated everything – especially the cuckoo-in-the-nest Blair – and they said so, but they couldn't organise anything, campaign, work out what to say, or do simple sums.

A Limited Talent Pool

The County Council wasn't much better. During the Blair Government, Mandy was put in charge of weeding the approved list of candidates for the next County election to sort the real duds from those with some talent. She was focusing on general ability and awareness of equal opportunities policy, which was by then long established and not controversial in civilised society.

With two other panel invigilation chairs, she interviewed a small selection of candidates including sitting councillors. She and her colleagues came to the conclusion that the marking scheme they had devised to create a minimum threshold was set way too high.

They revised it downwards, so that it was only if someone expressed hostility to equal opportunities that they were struck off the list.

Almost none of the people in front of her knew what equal opportunities were, no one had done any research homework to get them up to speed for the interview (not an absurd idea) and many of the candidates had unreconstructed male chauvinist views.

Eventually a panel was created, but her experience demonstrated that the political culture of the ex-mining areas was at the time a million light years away from that of the metropolitan conurbations.

The problem in the 1980s and 1990s was that two cultures and variants of them existed in the Labour Party. One was introverted, backward looking and class focused, decaying and removed from the modern world. Having said that, it was at least connected to deprivation and the need for opportunity. The other was ultra radical, often incompetent, sometimes corrupt, frequently isolated from broad working class opinion and increasingly dominated by concerns about identity politics. Neither culture was what was needed.

Corruption and incompetence flowed across both these cultures like poison in a way that has been quite ignored. My old work colleague Hilary Wainwright argues that there were in the late 1980s just two Labour Parties: a progressive, largely but not exclusively London-based New Left with new ideas and a commitment to openness; and another one, the Party of Wilson and Callaghan, modified by what she regarded as the opportunism of Kinnock.

The problem with her typology was that it ignored other cleavages, such as the gap between the PLP and others, and the appalling incompetence of many at local level in both metropolitan and more rural areas. And it was far too rose tinted about the prospects for radicalising the Labour Party and winning an actual election.

This was tested to destruction twice: first in the late 1980s by the failure of the Benn initiative at the Socialist Conference to develop a joint twin-track campaigning organisation inside and outside the Labour Party which could form the basis for radicalising the Party by vaccinating it with new ideas and people. The second problem was the idea that the Party could win an election on the basis of a radical programme. Ultra-left leadership was destroyed completely by the Corbyn experiment between 2015 and 2019.

She ends her book illustrating these points[284] with a quote from Steve Riley, secretary of the 3,000 strong Dagenham TGWU branch, where he says:

There's no party that workers can turn to, in a dispute or just to make sense of things.

She then argues that there needs to be a left Party present in every factory, office, hospital and community where the radical left can produce the impetus and confidence amongst people to 'create socialism.'

It is a classical transitional programme approach and wildly overstates the appetite for radical change amongst voters, the ability of popular agitation to persuade those voters to grasp change, and the willingness of large numbers of activists to do serious month-in-month-out work.

In fact, one can argue that the legacy of the radical era GLC, where Wainwright and I both worked, is strong on equal opportunities but almost non-existent on anything else. And she completely underestimates the dreadful record in power of the radical left which she espouses. Culture is vital, but her typology did not grasp the essence of the multiple

---

284. *Labour: A Tale of Two Parties*, Hogarth, 1987

cultures inside Labour, or the cross-cutting cleavages that exist in political parties.

Fissures and Factions

At the beginning of the 1990s, Mandy and I decided to abstain from any involvement in national political life and to concentrate on building our business, which was more than a full time job in itself. We had never been members or supporters of an organised left group and took, always, a jaundiced view of such organised leftism. But we were still involved to some extent in local public life, partly in order to protect the Arkwright community but also to buttress our local MPs, who deserved support.

The MEP after 1989 for north Nottinghamshire and Derbyshire, covering almost the whole of the East Midlands coalfield was Ken Coates, a former member of the Communist Party who had also dallied with Trotskyism and was a founder of the International Group, the forerunner of the International Marxist Group.

He had been a Bevin Boy after the war and was a luminary of the Bertrand Russell Peace Foundation. He used the platform of the European Assembly to raise issues of pollution in a way that would seem ordinary now but was novel in the early 1990s.

However, it became clear that he was pursuing a course which would undoubtedly lead to splitting the Labour Party. We could not tolerate that. Supporting candidates from other Parties in elections has always been the rock on which discipline was maintained, quite rightly, no matter who you were.

We first heard of the plans via John Powell, who worked in Ken's office and was worried at the trend of Coates's thought. John eventually became the Deputy Leader of Derbyshire County Council and was a Labour loyalist. He had warned us for many months that Coates was planning a breakaway and it became clear that this was so when he issued leaflets to all Party members in the area asking if they would be interested in forming a new organisation, free from the shackles of Blairism.

Coates was particularly vituperative about some of the new women MPs elected in 1997 describing them as those 'black women' because some of them wore black clothes on occasion.

Eventually I got him expelled through the good offices of my old colleague Tom Sawyer, who was then General Secretary of the Labour

Party. He phoned me up, asked if it would be more convenient if Coates was expelled before the meeting of the European Constituency Party that night, and I said it would be incredibly helpful.

He was expelled by fax. He complained about it, but in a carefully prepared case I got the European Constituency Labour Party to support the expulsion, which they did almost unanimously. That was the end of the splitters.

Charges Withdrawn and then Reinvented

The atmosphere was also sour at national level in a different way. Joan Twelves (I had worked for her briefly as a consultant at Lambeth in her attempt to make the council more efficient), had been threatened with expulsion from the Party. A case was to come before the National Constitutional Committee (NCC) – which Mandy also happened to be on, elected by national Conference for six years.

The case against Joan was, in fact, thin but voluminous in size, as they were throwing everything at the wall to see what stuck. I helped her get together a detailed rebuttal based on documentary evidence.

We sent this to the NCC and then turned up to the hearing, scheduled to take place at the London Labour Party headquarters.

As we approached the front door, out strode Larry Whitty, then General Secretary of the Party, who for some mysterious reason had decided to attend. He said, 'All the charges have been withdrawn and we are now photocopying new charges upstairs.'

He wouldn't say what they were. Eventually we received a copy and were then immediately hauled in to see the NCC panel which was being chaired that day by Dianne Hayter (now Baroness Hayter of Kentish Town, a former Chair of the Party).

I asked if we could have an adjournment as we had only just received the new charges and obviously had had no time to read them, let alone be in a position to respond.

She refused. They had a vote, and by a majority decision decided to proceed with the hearing.

We were then asked if we wanted to stay or leave. We decided to stay as heaven knows what rubbish would have been produced if we had left. It was the most brazen refusal of the basic right to a fair hearing and of natural justice that I have ever seen, and if it had been perpetrated in a

Labour's victorious pro-Europe lobby: Vic Feather frazzled, Shirley Williams distant, Tony Crosland bored and David Ennals in full flow during the Common Market referendum 1975

'Porn does for sex what Russia does for socialism': Pickets against sex shops mush-roomed across Britain as in Oxford 1981. RR persuaded the Government to change the law to limit their spread, despite the Speaker censoring Hansard to cut words from the author's speech.

Let's negotiate: RR on a Falklands peace march with Harriet Harman, then legal officer of the NCCL, Summer 1982.

Newt fancier Ken: Livingstone at the Camley Street Natural Park when leader of the GLC. Successful efforts were made to change his image to cuddly newt-loving Ken.

End of the road for the Miners: January 1985 march by the Women's Support Group from Markham colliery to the Arkwright drift mine in support of the doomed strike.

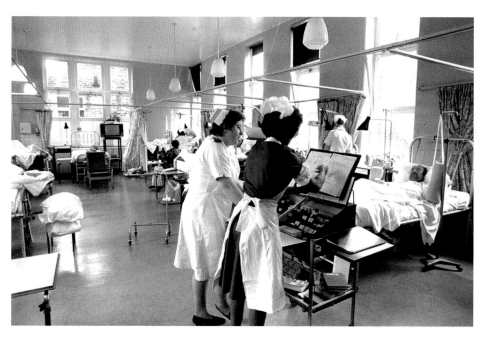

Nurses on a Nightingale Ward at Bradford Royal Infirmary 1985. Staff costs were 80% of the NHS budget and were attacked by Thatcher to make room for tax cuts.

Mandy Moore consulting with Jo Richardson MP and Joan Maynard MP at Labour Women's Conference, Rothesay 1986. Mandy was elected to the National Executive there in shadow elections organised by the Women's Action Committee. The male dominated trade unions refused to recognise the result of the elections and the right of women to elect their own representatives to the NEC.

Creative destruction: demolition of Arkwright Town 1995 after a massive campaign to get the villagers rehoused and moved to a new site. British Coal and RJB Mining paid £26m to rehouse 340 people, build a new school, miners welfare, community centre, and provide money for each household. A great victory.

The decisive defeat: Benn's failure to win the 1981 Deputy Leadership election was terminal. Some of Benn's foot soldiers left to right: Richard Balfe (now a Tory peer); Nigel Williamson, later editor of Tribune and a Times journalist; Stephen Benn, Tony's son; Mandy Moore; RR; Glenys Thornton (now a Labour peer).

YOU HAVE TILL 5 O'CLOCK TODAY TO SAVE LABOUR:

ACT NOW!

Britain is in crisis. We need a Labour Government, soon. We need a credible new leadership for the future. We can't write off a generation.

Labour has a proud record:

- Created the NHS
- Built millions of council homes
- Provided free education
- Created the welfare state to HELP the poorest
- ACHIEVED full employment, tax credits and the National Minimum Wage
- PASSED laws to stop discrimination
- Scrapped Section 28 and introduced Civil Partnerships
- Banned fox hunting
- Created devolved Government in Scotland, Wales, and Northern Ireland.

These are serious achievements. But THERE IS so much more to do.

We need a Labour Government to house the homeless, CREATE MORE AND BETTER JOBS, build huge numbers of affordable homes, save the NHS and Social Care, boost the former mining and industrial areas, give HOPE to young people, INCREASE opportunities for all, outlaw hate crimes, and attack rising INEQUALITY. And much more.

That's why Labour needs a powerful, competent leadership. And we don't have it now. The present leadership of the Party is timid, disorganised and amateur. **Jeremy Corbyn must go.**

There is now a leadership election in the Party, and YOUR voice needs to be heard loud and clear.

You have till 5pm TODAY to register to vote. **Go online to labour.org./leadership** and donate £25 to vote in the leadership election. It's your investment in the future of our country.

Let us Face the Future Together

#SavingLabour

Produced by Saving Labour, in the interests of democracy. www.savinglabour.com

Saving Labour, or trying to: fighting back against Corbynism, 2016. RR organised the campaign to thwart the takeover by extremist forces and was proved right about the consequences of having Corbyn as Leader.

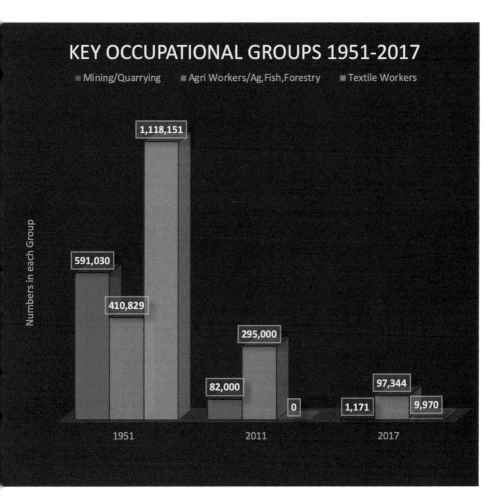

FIGURE 1: Key occupational groups 1951-2017

Source: Census of Population *

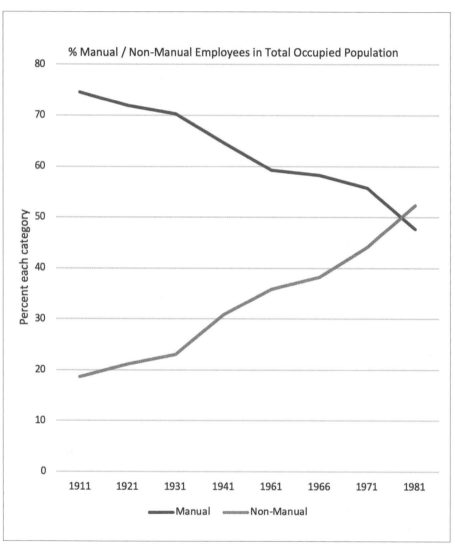

FIGURE 2: Percentage Manual/Non-Manual Employees in Total Occupied
Population

Source: AH Halsey, G Bain, and G Routh, updated by census of population.
See AH Halsey British Social Trends Since 1900, page 163

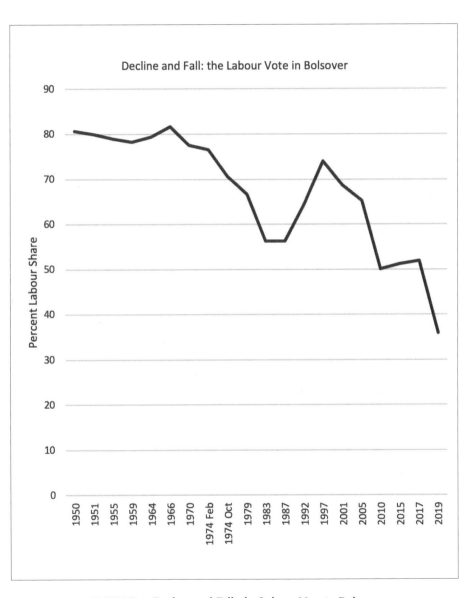

FIGURE 3: Decline and Fall: the Labour Vote in Bolsover

Source: Labour Share of the Vote in General Elections, Nuffield Election Studies

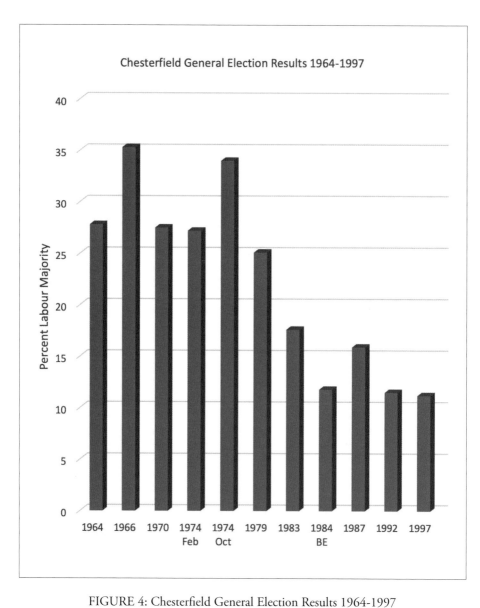

FIGURE 4: Chesterfield General Election Results 1964-1997

Source: General Election Results Chesterfield Constituency 1964-97, Nuffield Election Reports *

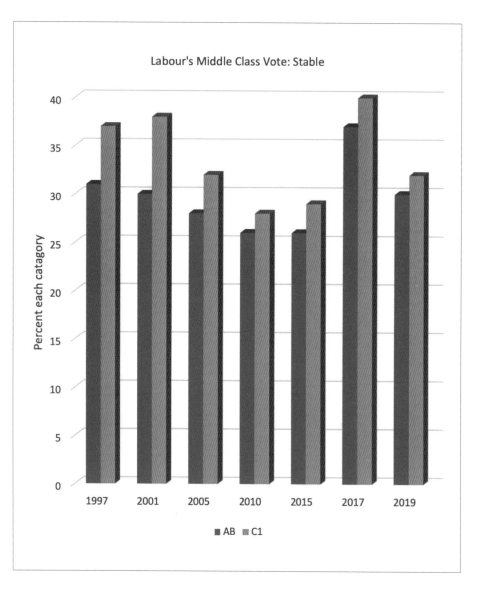

FIGURE 5: Labour's Middle Class Vote: Stable

Source: IPSOSMORI post election surveys, AB and C1 social groups

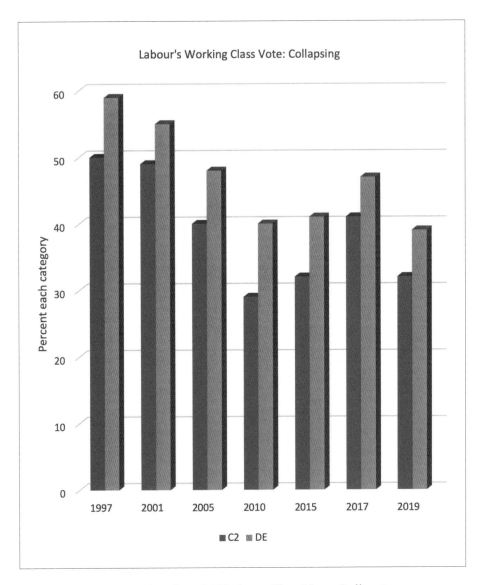

FIGURE 6: Labour's Working Class Vote: Collapsing

Source: Ipsos MORI post-election surveys for social groups C2 and DE

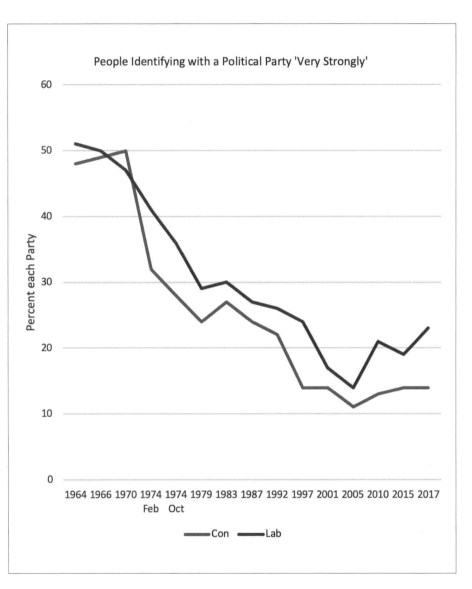

FIGURE 7: People Identifying with a Political Party 'Very Strongly'

Source: David Cowling analysis of polling data, British Election Study

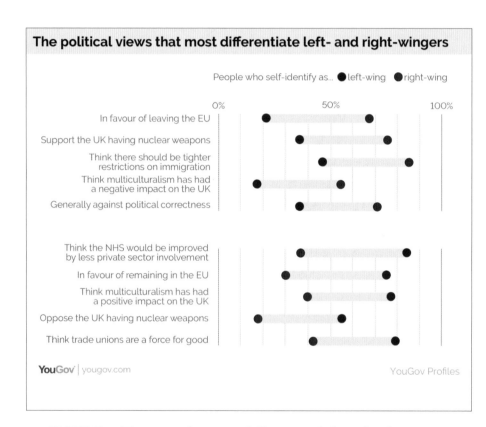

FIGURE 8: The views that most differentiate left- and right-wingers

Source: Data from 2018 YOUGOV poll

court, Hayter would have been the first to complain.

All the charges were photocopies of newspaper reports, many of them inaccurate (why wouldn't they be?). But they were enough for their purposes. In the end Joan received a one-year suspension from membership whilst others in Lambeth were summarily expelled.

In my opinion, Joan was a moderating influence in a Labour Group that was both ridiculous and ultra-left. The Party should have thanked her instead of suspending her, as she had averted many bizarre decisions being made.

This was an example of the policy at the time, which was to cleanse anyone who was disliked by the leadership, almost irrespective of their views.

The Kinnock leadership could not distinguish and did not want to distinguish between people who disagreed with them and others who were ultra-left, deranged or corrupt.

Mandy's experiences on the NCC buttressed this view as there were many cases where extreme decisions were taken to deal with minor infringements. Mandy usually voted to expel active or prominent members of Militant as they were clearly a Party within a Party. But the excesses kept rolling in.

There was the case of a 16-year-old schoolgirl from Bexley whose father was a 'Millie', and who had been asked to book a community hall for a Militant jumble sale. That was the only thing she had done, but they expelled her anyway.

Then there was the case of the Brighton councillors, most of whom were Christian Socialists and one of whom was the brother of Bishop Colin Winter, Bishop of Namibia, a strong supporter of migrant workers' rights and a colleague of Nelson Mandela. They were not in a group, they were just concerned about the impact of the poll tax on the poor, and refused to pay it when it was levied.

For that they were hauled to the NCC and suspended.

However, when a prominent right winger, Michael Cocks (the former PLP Chief Whip) was brought before the NCC because of his overt and well-documented support for the SDP in the 1987 General Election, Mandy had to argue for half an hour in order to get the mildest slap on the wrist for Cocks. The truth was that he should have been expelled in five minutes.

Although a political party has the right to defend its boundaries and to determine who can join and who needs to be outside the fence, the disciplinary policies of the 1980s and 1990s were arbitrary and disgraceful, and they showed the ultra-left what to do when they happened to be in temporary control of the national Party under Corbyn.

The policy between 2015 and 2019 was to lose cases in the woodwork – especially antisemitism cases – and only expel the most egregious anti-Semites and fruitcakes who had come to light. The EHRC report in October 2020 established clearly what was going on.

A case in point was a reference I made to General Secretary Ian McNicol in 2016, when a Corbyn supporter had published photographs of London Mayor Sadiq Khan adorned by Stars of David all over his body with insulting slogans attached. This person was plainly a Corbyn supporter as there were Corbyn-supporting 'twibbons.'[285]

McNicol refused to refer the matter to the police, as I had asked him to do. He said it was my job. But one woman who was asking for money to troll for Corbyn and had a PayPal account on her website flagged to do just that, was expelled as it was impossible to look the other way. This was just the tip of the iceberg, however.

During the leadership campaign in 2016, using sophisticated software, we identified 5,000 individuals who were trolling for Corbyn in the most pernicious way, clearly showing that the internet and social media have enabled nasty people to vent their spleen and have an audience. They are overwhelmingly in the extreme fringes of the political spectrum, and there is a sense in which the elevation of Corbyn emboldened and enabled them. These people need to be dealt with, on the basis of evidence, and independently of the factions on the NEC.

The 2001 Election: the Benn Factor

During the first term of the Blair Government both Mandy and I decided to have another go at contesting Parliamentary elections. We both applied through the long process and we were, of course, subject to special attention from the Party bureaucracy.

I attended several candidates' briefing and interview sessions at Harold Wilson House in Nottingham and in the end was given a formal interview by none other than the Chair of the Parliamentary Labour Party, Clive Soley. I suspect he had been drafted in to give me a grilling.

I had always got on well with Clive, and I don't know what instructions

285. Microsites used to facilitate a campaign

he had been given, but he was perhaps trying to find grounds to refuse entry to the approved list.

One of the questions he asked was whether I would support the Government's policy on the Euro and recommend entry to the currency – and do so to my constituency Party if I had been elected as an MP.

My response was that the Government's policy was not to enter the Euro but to 'prepare and decide' on the basis of the five tests set by Chancellor Brown. He looked a bit crestfallen at this point but in the end I was allowed onto the list, but Mandy was not. It is her belief that she was arbitrarily struck off the list by top bureaucrats at head office who had fallen out with her decades ago.

For me, the obvious constituency to go for was Chesterfield, two and a half miles from our house, with wards that butted on to our own local authority ward of Sutton.

I knew many people in the Party there but there was an issue: Tony Benn's deep unpopularity with voters. Perhaps my first inkling of this face-to-face was on the eve of polling day 1997, just before Labour won its best ever victory.

We were delivering Dennis Skinner's last minute leaflet *You Know It's Time* (which we had written and designed), to streets in Sutton next to the Brimington South ward of Chesterfield. Brimington was mainly classic 1950s and 1960s suburbia with some council housing, and a swing ward in the borough which had sometimes been won by the Liberal Democrats.

It was a beautiful balmy evening, the kind you always want when campaigning. Residents were mowing their lawns in the early evening sunshine and some were having cups of tea or a glass of wine. Then out of nowhere it came: one middle aged man rushed out of his house, pointed an accusing finger at me and said, 'I'm not voting for that bastard Benn!'

My response was easy: 'You're not in Chesterfield, you can vote for Dennis Skinner because he's your Labour candidate.'

That immediately closed down the argument with him, but others stormed across the cul-de-sac and said pretty much the same thing.

What they were angry about was that Benn was in the local papers only about two things, they said: Ireland, and Iraq. To them, he didn't seem to care about anything else and they didn't agree with him about either of the subjects in question.

Benn had championed opposition to the Gulf War and was in favour of a united Ireland. Indeed, he was in support of talking to Sinn Fein which at the time had not finished bombing mainland Britain (it had ended one of its ceasefires in 1996 and was still actively attacking targets).

These voters, classic Labour, in the safest Labour seat in the East Midlands, were so angry about Benn that they would definitely not have voted for him under any circumstances had his name been on the ballot. This was disturbing but not a surprise. Tony had been edging and then running away from the Labour Party for some time and was openly contemptuous about its leadership and direction under Blair. In his conversations with me, he described the Party as having been taken over in a coup.

Close examination of the General Election results in Chesterfield also confirmed this deep personal unpopularity. Since the by-election in 1984 when Eric Varley[286] resigned, general election results had been very bad for Labour in a situation when in all those general elections Labour support had been improving. The figures spoke for themselves (see Figure 4).

The 1997 result rang alarm bells for anyone who was listening. The Chesterfield result was almost the worst in England in a Labour-held seat, at a time when Tony Blair achieved a Parliamentary majority of 179.

There were a few exceptions only. In Bradford West, clan politics ensured the biggest drop in the Labour vote anywhere, and in Bethnal Green and Bow, the Conservatives put up an Asian candidate in a heavily Asian constituency and nearly doubled their vote.

Cardiff South and Penarth was an outlier too because a candidate styling himself New Labour won over 3,000 votes (9.3%), which contributed significantly to the fall in the official Labour vote tally.

A very small number of seats in inner city Manchester, Liverpool and in Barnsley, with huge pre-1997 majorities, swung hardly at all to Labour because there was no-one else left to swing.

If you discount these few exceptional results for exceptional reasons, Chesterfield was the worst. It was clearly going to be a problem and at the extreme end of risk in a situation where the Labour Government was likely to lose votes at the next election.

In contrast, neighbouring seats right next door to Chesterfield had big swings to Labour in 1997.

Amber Valley achieved an 11.7% swing; Bolsover 9%; Derbyshire North East 12.3% and Tory held Derbyshire West saw a swing to Labour from the Conservatives of 11.6%. But Chesterfield swung 0.3% to the

---

286. Labour MP for Chesterfield 1964-1984, later Lord Varley of Chesterfield

Liberal Democrats on the day of the biggest Labour victory ever.

Benn already had 'form' on unpopularity. In Bristol, where he represented Bristol South East from a by-election in 1950 until the constituency was abolished in 1983, his percentage share of the vote declined from 65.0% at the 1951 General Election to 45.4% in 1979, the last time the constituency was contested, a precipitate decline of around 20 percentage points. All the other Bristol seats enjoyed much smaller falls in the Labour share of the vote over the same period, with different Labour candidates of left, right and centre contesting them over the same period.[287]

Benn was extremely unpopular from around 1970 onwards as he switched violently leftwards, and this in the end led to his defeat in the not so different Bristol East constituency in 1983. His diaries confirm this; he was told by shop stewards that everyone at their workplaces thought he was a Communist.[288]

His political antennae had ossified, the press nationally and locally had worked to destroy his credibility, he had chosen to work on extraordinarily unpopular issues, and in the end he just didn't care as his dislike of the Labour Party intensified over the years.

So, Chesterfield was the ultimate outlier and Benn's personal unpopularity was ruthlessly exploited by the Lib Dems who fanned those flames. It was also clear to me that there were big internal problems inside the Chesterfield Labour Party.

At the 1997 election, Benn's agent, Tom Vallins, had phoned me in a panic a few days before the closing date to get the election address off to Royal Mail for the freepost delivery made available to all Parliamentary candidates. Benn hadn't written anything, there were no pictures, and no one had discussed themes, so would I take it on as an ultra-quick turnaround favour for an old friend?

So, I had to write it, get it approved, find some themes and some pictures (there was almost nothing), get it designed by Mandy, and find a printer (they didn't have one lined up). It was all very unsatisfactory and flagged the shambles that was the Chesterfield Labour Party at the time.

There were some extenuating circumstances.

Caroline, Tony's wife, was ill with the cancer that would lead to her

---

287. The Labour share of the vote in Bristol North East dropped by only 1.4 points over that period; Bristol North West by 6.6 points; Bristol West by 5.9 points; and Bristol South by 6.3 points.
288. Benn diaries, *The End of an Era*, page 253.

death in 2000. Tony himself had multiple health problems which were not openly discussed at the time. Consequently, there had been a diminution in energy and definitely in commitment.

The fact that the Conservative vote had already collapsed into the arms of the Lib Dems was very dangerous. The Lib Dem line was to vote for them because only they could ensure the defeat of the hated Benn, and they were right.

It was also true that Benn's appearances in the local newspaper, the *Derbyshire Times*, were often slagging off the Labour Party (and after 1997 the Government) and the only copy that he initiated was indeed about Ireland and Iraq. And a picture of him on an electric bicycle.

Selection and Payback

The alarm bells continued to ring after I had been selected.

My principal opponents in the selection had been a local councillor, Terry Gilby, and Liz Kendall.[289] The local council group thought it was their exclusive right to sort the selection out and they had decided to run Terry. He was a tax collector and a decent guy but argued consistently that as a local lad he and only he could possibly defend the seat.

The politics of localism were in full play and there were various attempts to try and make me identify with a section of the Party. At one open meeting in Staveley in a freezing hall, Terry Gilby's partner Tricia asked me, 'Are you a Bennie or a Blairite?' I replied that I wasn't anyone's 'ite' and that I would plough my own furrow.

In the end I won the ballot with Liz coming second. The main problem, however, was that the NEC had intervened several times in the process with the result that it had taken a year to select the candidate. This was quite wrong and whoever had been chosen would have no time to get organised and project any kind of image. The underlying chaos was not entirely visible.

The day after I was selected we went into the Labour Club on Saltergate to organise the office. This proved difficult. We picked up the key and went upstairs and tried to open the door. We couldn't. Eventually we got two strong blokes to ram it open and discovered that the whole room was waist high and more in black plastic bags, with rubbish of all kinds in them.

---

289. Liz Kendall, MP for Leicester West, 2010-

We had to spend hours taking the bags out and disposing of them. We couldn't see where the phone was. Behind a desk, of course, which we discovered when we used a mobile to call it. There was no computer, almost no canvass records of any kind, with most of what was there being material from the 1984 by-election 17 years before, no money, and no people.

Across the corridor from Tony's main office, which he can't have used for a very long time, was a tiny room that had once been used by Margaret Vallins, his Parliamentary secretary. The main feature of this cubby hole was an ancient answerphone which had this message on it: 'If you want to leave a message for your MP, don't leave it on this number.'

Nothing else, no signposting to another phone or location, no information on where to find surgeries or write to him, nothing at all.

It was scandalous. And evidence that the office was indeed the Marie Celeste kept mounting as every day went by. What was appalling was that Tony had allowed it to happen, and the local Party officers had floated along just allowing the situation to fructify.

Even worse was to follow. The externalities in the constituency were going negative very fast.

Chesterfield had long had a significant engineering and industrial base. But in the early months of 2001 every single factory of any size shut down within days of each other.

Dema glass, a landmark manufacturer right in the middle of town, shut. Tubies, which made cylinders for the engineering trade, gone. Thousands of jobs were being shredded and Benn would not allow me to go with him to meet the trade union stewards who were resisting closure in each case.

Then, at the May Day event organised by the local Trades Council shortly before the election, he was speaking from the platform. Again, I was not allowed up there until David and Graham Skinner intervened and compelled the Chair to allow me to say a few words. It was there that Benn uttered the immortal words, 'Whoever you vote for in this election, make sure you vote.'

He was speaking to a crowd of several thousand as the Chesterfield event was one of the biggest in the country, and that crowd was full of trade unionists and their families and local political activists. His phrase was a green light to vote anything but Labour on polling day.

After working with him for more than 20 years, this was beyond unpleasant and highly damaging: he could not bring himself to turn around on the platform and say that he'd known me and worked with me for a long time, that I was a decent person, and worthy of support. I was beyond anger. It was chilling.

Then there was football. Chesterfield FC had been under the control of one Darren Brown and there were great irregularities on transfer dealings. Brown tried to refuse to pay Chester City the agreed transfer fee for a player and eventually Chesterfield were deducted nine points for this behaviour, and further evidence emerged of significant debts run up by Brown. These forced the club into administration, and a rescue by a hastily organised supporters' group. Brown was later imprisoned for four years for false accounting, theft, and furnishing false information after a Serious Fraud Office inquiry.

At this point the Labour Sports Minister, Kate Hoey, intervened out of the blue with no need and while the SFO were digging around. She commented that Chesterfield should be automatically relegated from the third division as a result of their behaviour, or rather the chairman's behaviour, and fans were incandescent.

She made these comments in the middle of the election campaign and we had to react quickly. I issued statements and a leaflet at the next home game, but the damage was done. Hoey had shafted whoever was the Labour candidate. Fans on their way to the home match where we were leafleting were not impressed. I faxed her and remonstrated, but never received a reply.

Chesterfield managed to get the final automatic promotion place to Division Two and luckily the Football League took no notice of Hoey. Tony Benn, still the MP for Chesterfield, said nothing.

Then there were the councillors.

As part of team building to run the campaign I had asked John Burrows to be my agent. Johnnie was a leading member of Derbyshire NUM and an elected representative alongside Mandy on the National Constitutional Committee of the Party. He was rightly regarded as a safe pair of hands with a substantial degree of skill. He had supported Terry Gilby, a fellow councillor, in the selection and was aggrieved that Terry had not won. He wouldn't do it. So, I had to recruit another councillor to do the job, who was not as competent.

And then there was the decision by Chesterfield councillors to advertise the fact that they might place a travellers' camp in Inkersall – a solidly working class ward where feelings were running high that Labour was ignoring the wishes of voters.

This was publicised a couple of weeks before the election and the doorstep reaction to this piece of craziness was profound. The announcement could well have been made after the election, as this was only the announcement of a short list of sites and there was no time pressure, but they wouldn't do it.

It was kamikaze politics.

There was more of that from one of the wards in the west of town who were also fed up that their candidate (in this case Liz Kendall) had been defeated in the selection. They refused to distribute my election material or canvass for me. So, they went around posting the County election leaflets through doors and I had to send a separate team round with mine.

It was insane, and counterproductive at a time when person-power was short.

The ultra-left had also mobilised as they thought that the legacy of Benn was a good opportunity to build their factions, and they had two candidates in the field who garnered 732 votes. Benn was, of course, silent about them.

Nothing to Go On

With few helpers, no canvass records, no equipment and a highly unpopular MP, the election was really about doing the best you could in a very unpromising set of circumstances. The doorstep reaction was dreadful and it struck me that the real Labour candidate in the election was a Mr T Benn rather than myself.

About one in four that I spoke to explicitly raised the question of Benn's behaviour and the reaction to him was almost universally negative, and boy how negative.

He was toxic and many were going to vote Lib Dem in protest at what he had been doing. Two weeks out from the election I told the Party's regional press officer that I wasn't at all sure we were going to win (an understatement) and he was horrified.

The regional office was helpful in providing a computer and printer and a full time organiser, who was very good.

Jack Straw, Mo Mowlam, Andrew Smith and John Reid kindly came and did what they could but it was noticeable that when Tony Robinson (Baldrick in Blackadder) came, he remarked that the town did not seem to be in the same place as the national politics, where Labour was expected to win with a handsome majority.

He was right. A lot of the time I was on my own on the doorstep because no one would do that work. The fundamental problem was that they did not believe that Labour could lose, and indeed the night before the election Johnnie Burrows predicted that we would have a 5,000 majority.

We lost by 2,500 and it could have been worse. The behaviour of the local Labour establishment at the time was that Labour had a right to win, it was going to win, and that was that. Turnout in the Chesterfield election dropped by 10 percentage points to a post-war low of 60%.

It was the typical Derbyshire combination of arrogance and incompetence. At the next borough council elections Labour lost a large number of seats and the Lib Dems gained control of the council on a big swing. Labour lost the 2005 General Election there too, with a further swing to the Lib Dems. The legacy of Tony Benn was assured. He had wrecked the Labour Party in Chesterfield and it took a long time to recover.

Benn himself knew perfectly well what had happened and his role in it. Afterwards he phoned me on his way to Leeds from a train and was very upset. He said that he had burst in to tears when he passed the crooked spire on the train that day, and he was sorry.

My engagement with electoral politics was over, and so was Mandy's. We built our business up, employed a lot of people, and gained national status as the providers of high-quality data to the NHS. It was much more satisfying.

CHAPTER 7

THE ACCIDENTAL LEADER EMERGES

The end of the Blair/Brown period of Government in 2010 gave the Parliamentary Party a period of reflection in which to reinvigorate itself and reassess its intellectual underpinnings. By the leadership election of 2015, after Ed Miliband resigned as Leader, it was apparent that this rethinking had not gone very far.

The events of summer 2015 were extraordinary in the Labour Party. The premature and foolish resignation of Ed Miliband brought forward the choices that the membership had to make. This happened before a point when serious leadership could have emerged and strategic analysis undertaken about the development of society and two swingeing election defeats.

In fact, what transpired during the nomination process was a series of errors made by senior members of the PLP which have proved to be disastrous. She was not by any means the only participant in the madness, but it is widely known that Margaret Beckett described her nomination of Jeremy Corbyn in these terms in a BBC interview on 22nd July 2015:

Ex-Labour Foreign Secretary Margaret Beckett has described herself as a 'moron' for nominating Jeremy Corbyn for the Labour leadership contest.

'At no point did I intend to vote for Jeremy myself – nice as he is – nor advise anyone else to do it,' she said.

'We were being urged as MPs to have a field of candidates,' she told the BBC.

Ex-adviser to Tony Blair John McTernan had said MPs who 'lent' their nominations to Mr Corbyn to 'broaden the debate' were 'morons.'

He made his comment on the BBC's Newsnight on Tuesday.

During an interview with BBC Radio 4's World at One Mrs Beckett was asked if she was, as Mr McTernan put it, a moron for nominating Mr Corbyn. She replied: 'I am one of them.'

The normally controlled and focused Beckett, mischievously called 'Princess Anne' by the Transport House staff when she worked there, was not the only one duped by the siren calls to 'widen the field' and 'enable a debate.'

It is a fact that Tom Watson, standing to be the Deputy Leader of the Party at that point, and later an ineffective opponent of Corbyn, telephoned a number of MPs and urged them to nominate Corbyn, and for good measure stood outside the committee room door where nominations were being made, urging MPs to nominate Corbyn – and himself. The result was that Jeremy just sneaked across the threshold of nominations and would be on the ballot.

Anger and Vacuum

The election itself was very instructive. I started doing a little work for Liz Kendall and attended a number of meetings in Derbyshire on her behalf.

These, as I wrote later, were more like a lynch mob than normal Labour Party meetings. One of the ones I attended was Derby South, with Margaret Beckett and her husband Leo. She was crystal clear that she wasn't going to vote for Jeremy despite nominating him, but her members did that anyway.

Another meeting, chaired by the cadaverous vegan and former MP Chris Williamson was much bigger and boiling with anger. They also voted overwhelmingly for Corbyn.

By the middle of the summer it was clear that the tumbrils were rolling and could be unstoppable. At this point I went to the Commons in a rare visit as I was doing some work for Natascha Engel[290] and ran across Dennis Skinner taking the sun on the terrace with his face towards the river and his eyelids closed.

I broke the reverie and started discussing the leadership election with him. He let slip that he had been to see Jeremy some weeks into the campaign and had suggested quite strongly that it was time to stop.

Dennis's long-held view was that Jeremy simply couldn't do the job, and that it was all bound to end in tears. His body language was very

290. MP for North East Derbyshire 2005-17 and a deputy Speaker at the time

telling: he was confiding in a friend that this was a bit of a joke and that the umpires had to draw stumps. I know, because he told me, that he had voted for David Miliband in the previous election and that competence, he said, was a major consideration when selecting a leader. He was right, of course, but didn't say so publicly.

In the end, as Liz's campaign was marooned, I voted for Yvette Cooper, as did Mandy, because she struck us as being the most intellectually honest of the remaining candidates.

So why didn't I want to vote for Jeremy?

My contact with him had started in about 1975 and lasted until the mid-1990s, before the election in 1997, when he became embarrassed at what we knew about his life, and he broke off contact with us.

The Unsupportable Friend

The first real discussion between myself and Jeremy was when he applied for one of the new organiser jobs that NUPE was advertising during its rapid expansion in the 1970s. The union went from about 160,000 members to around 750,000 at its peak before the merger with NALGO and COHSE to form UNISON.

Naturally, it needed more field organisers and this is what Jeremy applied for (the official title was Area Officer). He made application and was interviewed by a committee of the Executive Council and was appointed.

At that time, it was obvious that he was an active member of the Labour Party, as were most applicants. The interviews were held at the Charing Cross Hotel and I was in charge of creating a longlist and screening applicants for duds.

Jeremy had been selected as a longlist candidate because he had already worked for the Tailor and Garment Workers and the AUEW and, on paper, he looked promising.

He turned up for interview with the all-male sub-committee of the Executive Council who favoured jackets, suits and ties, and in some cases Brylcreem. They were typical working class 'made good lads' who had done difficult jobs and were now enjoying a little prominence on the Executive.

They were quite radical on economic issues but socially conservative in manners of dress and deportment so when Jeremy turned up on the committee room corridor in a crumpled, creased shirt and no tie, and a beard, I advised him to go on to the Strand outside the hotel, buy a tie, and wear it. He did, and was appointed along with many others.

Appointment meant that he was given a 'patch' in inner London. The union had a substantial membership there in schools (caretakers, school meals staff). His appointment was to the lowest rung of full time work in the union. He did the job competently but without great fanfare. He was just like many other of the organisers appointed at that time: idealistic, a bit naïve, committed.

In 1974 he was elected to Haringey Council for the first time and met his first wife Jane Chapman in the election campaign. Living in Hornsey, which had a long tradition of leftish activity (including a big Communist Party branch, a big CP vote from 1945-66, and the legacy of the Hornsey College strike) exposed him to one of the most unrepresentative demographic areas in the UK.

It was unrepresentative in the sense of being multi-ethnic (Greeks, Turks, Afro-Caribbean, Asian, and some remaining Jewish population although declining rapidly in numbers). Unrepresentative also in that Haringey contained some of the most expensive and affluent wards in London (Highgate, Muswell Hill, Crouch End, Fortis Green), so the contrast between the two worlds was striking. One part of the borough was clearly the inner city with all its issues – the other was pretty exclusive.

Many radical organisations existed in this space. There were ethnic minority 'let's get together and support each other' groups. There were others arguing against injustices – such as the Turkish invasion of Cyprus 1974, Biafra, immigration problems and lack of housing. Many of these were legitimate self-help or lobbying groups. But it also proved a fertile breeding ground for left activity, including the ultra-left with some leading Trotskyists also congregating there.

In Haringey, it was pretty clear that you had to engage with some of these groups in order to get street credibility. This is what Jeremy did, par excellence, partly because it was useful to him and his colleagues and partly because he was sympathetic to those from developing countries who had grievances.

It was regarded as a 'hot' area by the security services – remarkably, they had a senior operative in place on the Wood Green Labour Party Management Committee from the early 1970s.[291]

Jeremy was operating in this arena to win elections, specifically to win

291. Ex-Fircroft lecturer and TUC staffer Harry Newton

the Hornsey seat (which Labour did in the 1981 GLC election, for the very first time, the candidate being Tony Hart of the moderate left and Judith Hart MP's husband).

But he was also rubbing against issues which he was fundamentally interested in, arising from what he would call imperialism and American policy, especially in Asia and Latin America.

It is important not to forget that the US actions supporting the right in Chile, the overthrow of a legitimately elected leader, and the invasion of Grenada, were fresh in the memory. And even Thatcher was angry about the invasion of Grenada, a Commonwealth country, undertaken without warning by the Reagan administration. The memory of Vietnam was only a few years in the past.

Jeremy may not ever have been a member of any of the left groups, nor the Communist Party when it was something of a power in the land, especially in the trade unions. However, circumstances, and especially the circumstances of London politics, drove him to ally with people and groups who undoubtedly had a radical view of the world as distinct from a reformist or social democratic view.

Many who know him say that his strength is not in analytics, and it is obvious that he has subcontracted much of his thought to others who have been delighted to fill the vacuum.

His geographic position in Islington as a backbench MP has made him a very distinctive outsider, different from anyone else in the Labour Party and very different from leaders who represent or grew up in Midlands and Northern communities where they have to operate in a distinct and different culture.

The London Labour politics culture is utterly different from anywhere else, with its 57 varieties of Trotskyists, and the variegated communities of London – political, ethnic and class – have nothing similar elsewhere in politics even now.

The closest comparator to north London politics is in some ways Merseyside, but with far fewer ethnic minority groups, a dominant Militant tendency and an outsider culture which has bred distinctive humour and attitudes and politics. So, it is entirely possible that this particular setting of north London governed Jeremy's thought processes at first: how can I survive and prosper in this landscape, he may have asked himself.

Not Learning

An interesting question to ask is what impact did NUPE have on him and he on NUPE? His impact on the union was very limited, as most area officers' impacts were. He moved on from it at the earliest opportunity (the Parliamentary boundary changes of 1983).

Being a trade union officer and then an MP gave him money support and broad opportunities to engage in politics in a way that a job in another sector would not have done. However, being a trade union officer, even at a time of great turbulence, usually influences people's view of the world in a certain way.

One key influence is to reach accommodation, how to know when a deal is the best that you can get in the circumstances, how to reach a deal with the employers who you have to live with in your daily work.

Alan Fisher used to say it was important that negotiators 'have an escape hatch through which they can disappear,' and this is often the mindset of a negotiator as distinct from that of a faction organiser, community activist, or policy wonk.

The second distinct influence and cautionary impact that trade union officials experience is the conservatism of the members of their union, whichever one it is.

Most of the time, whatever the circumstances, the members are sensibly concentrating on having a decent wage, tolerable working conditions, bringing up their families and enhancing their leisure time. They are normally a significant check on the radicalism of their full time officials, especially if (as in the case of NUPE in the 1970s) most of the membership are low-paid women workers, many of them part time, who in that era were not by and large radical.

Being a full time official in London provided a lesson for him in the inherent limits of industrial action and the deep conservatism of members, but these normal constraints seem to have had little impact on him over time.

Also, the performance management of area officers in NUPE was very loose and you had to be a right dingbat to get sacked. Alan Fisher was most concerned about the state of the union's cars when they came to be changed over: 'Can't they run them through a car wash occasionally?' he used to demand.

Corbyn's impact over time has been to give solidarity to others rather than be pace-settingly intellectual. He has never produced a book as far as I know, and his written articles and speeches have never argued consistently for a distinctive position different from the world view of his Party on the central issues of economic or social policy which happened to be fashionable at the time on the left. He has not debated the difficulties of winning a majority when manual workers have in large part disappeared from the economy, nor has he addressed the future world of worklessness which we probably face. He has always been interested in expressing support for existing organisations, struggles, causes, and campaigns rather than trying to change the nature of the argument. He is a 'list reader', ticking off the virtues of positions, and by extension himself, as he speaks. In comparison to Tony Benn, who was by no means a thinker of the first rank, but who enabled great issues to be debated and who was taken seriously by some until he was destroyed, Corbyn was a footnote.

He is in contrast the accidental leader. Accidental because he never created the conditions for his own success by demonstrating intellectual rigour, and accidental primarily because the experience of Party members in the Blair/Brown Government was such that they would vote for the most anti-establishment candidate possible in order to get away from New Labour and the record that they saw on Iraq.

In 2015 the anti-establishment left in the Labour Party wanted revenge, and if that meant the authentic Corbyn – ill-disciplined but reliably on their side, so be it.

So, without the gunpowder trail of 2003 and beyond in the Middle East, we would probably never have had the accidental leader.

The PLP Candidates Fail

And yet.

A necessary but not sufficient condition for his victory was the inability of the British economy in the early years of the 21st century to deliver rising living standards. The great lack was in investment in housing and public services to enable broad sections of the population to think that they had a stake in society and to expect a decent life, and rising incomes from steady jobs.

Corbyn, to his credit, was the only candidate in 2015 to state that this was impossible to accept and that there was an alternative, however inadequate that alternative seemed to be as described by the thin rhetoric he used.

The reason for this vacuum of ideas was the failure of the leading elements of the PLP to construct an agenda for the 21st century, separate from Blairism, while recognising the changed circumstances of the economy. What all of them offered, to a large degree, were micro measures based on managerialism and a reheated Blairist/Brownist politics which was seen as just more of the same.

Many of the candidates were quite as bad as Corbyn in their failure to articulate a coherent strategic view. The state of the Labour Party now after the decisive defeat of 2019 is partly due to the failure of the PLP to develop these coherent alternatives at the right time.

Jeremy operated on the basis of the 'no enemies to the left' policy, which left him vulnerable to extremist opinion, and to influence by specialist pressure groups that represented concerns a million miles away from the issues on the radar of the electorate as whole.

He seemed to learn little from the constraints of trade unionism and the lessons it gives in crafting solutions that will be acceptable to large numbers of people. Nor did he have any influence on the union he served, as he was by definition too marginal and too junior. He was more interested in the diverse north London communities he lived in, which he found more congenial than any other, and he clearly did not understand the very different culture of the Northern and Midlands working class.

He never set an agenda, and was a reactivist politician par excellence – in contrast to his mentor Tony Benn, who tried hard to move issues in to consideration and up the agenda. However, like Benn he had a tin ear on what turned the electorate off; but he followed Benn in regarding endless meetings as proof of his commitment and of his politics.

He was lucky in that he gained a break with the collapse of the Blair Government's reputation over Iraq, an issue which enabled Corbyn to mobilise large forces – the foundation of his later success – at a time when Benn was a spent force, out of Parliament and unwell.

But, to his credit, he was the only candidate in 2015 who was articulating an alternative message and putting his finger on issues which were of serious concern to many.

He was also a lucky politician: lucky in that he ran into a collectively second-rate group of PLP leaders, who dismally contributed to the vacuum of politics that Corbyn readily filled.

It is also important to consider the impact of technology on his luck. Without the internet and social media, he and his friends would never have been able to mobilise large numbers of people to his cause. His leadership election luck was dependent on Bill Gates and Steve Jobs rather than Marx, Engels and Trotsky. Without the technocrats he could never have won.

So why did I oppose an old acquaintance who I had been friendly with for 20 years? It was complicated, and it wasn't because there was personal animosity. I have a confession: I like Jeremy Corbyn – he's funny, and self-deprecating, even if he is utterly disorganised and unfocused, and sometimes proved to be petulant when leader.

That was the problem: both Mandy and I had had far too much exposure to the eccentric side of Jeremy's political and personal life. The history and the levels of disorganisation were decisive in our view, and meant that although he was no doubt an effective constituency MP, he could not be considered as a serious candidate to be the Leader of the Party.

So, what was our specific experience of Jeremy that was so decisive in forming a negative opinion of his abilities?

In the mid-1970s, after the formation of the 1974 Wilson Government, he was involved in activity supporting strikes, against cuts in public expenditure, and against the National Front which was very active in Haringey. Anti-Front activity was usually led by the Labour Party there with Jeremy as a significant supporter.

Corbyn, however, played little part in the re-evaluation of Labour policy and little in CLPD at that time, and none whatever in the development of the so-called Alternative Economic Strategy, which was essentially created by non-establishment economists, with Benn arguing for it in Cabinet, but being helped only intermittently by Crosland and Shore. Benn was himself regarded as a lightweight by the ex-Oxford dons, with Crossman stating that Benn was 'philosophically non-existent' and 'intellectually negligible', and Crosland telling him that in order to lose a reputation as an intellectual, he would first have to acquire one. Corbyn was in a far worse position than Benn with an intellectual hinterland gravely compromised by his lack of educational attainment.[292]

Corbyn was floating along like a cork on the tide of organised Labour leftism.

---

292. Also, with allies at times such as Crosland and Shore, supported outside Government by distinguished economists such as Stuart Holland and those in NIESR and the Cambridge group who were deeply sceptical of monetarism. Crossman and Crosland quotes are from *Labour People*, KO Morgan, Oxford University Press 1987, page 304.

In the 1978-79 public sector strikes against the 5% pay policy, Corbyn did argue for a local settlement in Haringey to match other local settlements being made elsewhere, and did this as a local councillor.

He supported the campaigns to keep the Prince of Wales and Wood Green and Southgate Hospitals open but in all this he was a follower not a leader. As a former close colleague and Corbyn staffer says of him, 'You can't expect leadership from Corbyn.'

By 1982, he had been selected in Islington North, which required a new Labour candidate because of the defection of the sitting Member to the SDP.

He was elected in 1983 and became active in the Campaign Group and was secretary of it, giving him access to a wide range of organisations lobbying for change, and especially anti-war groups.

His main political relationship was with Benn rather than the older stagers who had left the Tribune Group, many of whom hated each other. Heffer hated Atkinson; Skinner disliked Benn; and the general attitude to the women members of the group was awful. At one point in the late 1980s they all walked out and resigned. This meant that initiatives were partly seen through the prism of personalities.

By the General Election defeat of 1987, it was clear that the Kinnock leadership was losing with the public and winning inside the Party. This led to the disastrous campaign against Kinnock by Benn in 1988, which everyone he consulted told him not to do, but he went ahead anyway. That overwhelming defeat made Benn turn to other ideas e.g. trying to unite the insiders in the Labour Party with the outsiders in community groups and left organisations. Jeremy supported this but was peripheral to its development and organisation. This initiative had petered out by around 1990 when there was disruptive activity as usual by ultra-left groups who took over its bureaucracy and immediately destroyed it.

During the mid-1990s and especially after the intervention in Iraq, Corbyn was able to work with large-scale organisations outside the Party – such as Stop the War. These degenerated in to front organisations for ultra-left and Communist sympathiser groups with a few others. This was eventually the foundation of his 2015 leadership campaign top cadre.

This is a very broad-brush view of the Corbyn trajectory but it is also important to consider what he did not do. Like many in the Tribune Group and later the Campaign Group, he was far more sympathetic to the Eastern bloc than he should have been.

There were Labour organisations such as the Eastern Europe Solidarity

Campaign (EESC), which I strongly supported whilst an MP, which campaigned against the Soviet repression of trade unions and citizen groups.

At each Labour Party Conference, the EESC fringe meeting was addressed by the same people: Phillip Whitehead MP; Ron Keating, Assistant General Secretary of NUPE; and myself. Jeremy was never involved and most of the so-called left wing MPs thought we were CIA stooges. We wanted freedom from repression and dictatorship and the right to form free organisations separate from the clone trade unions linked to the Eastern bloc States. This was too controversial for Corbyn.

In 2015, the view we had clearly formed about Jeremy was that he was never an out-and-out Trotskyist group organiser. He had not been prominent in national industrial disputes nor was he intellectually engaged with developments in Party policy. He was a foot soldier feeling his way, developing credibility with a London crowd which had different politics and views from almost everyone else in the country.

And then, almost by accident, he became the focus of attention.

He wasn't at all competent. He got himself into serious trouble in his personal life. He almost ran from meeting to meeting and his day-to-day existence was chaotic.

Chaos and Inertia

It had become clear to us that his life was so shambolic that it could not possibly survive exposure in a leadership position.

One aspect of this was the financial chaos where we had first-hand experience. Before the 1997 General Election, Jeremy approached me directly and personally by telephone, as he knew that we did analyses of systems and processes to improve quality and performance and that I had run the largest policy and performance review system in Europe at the GLC.

My response to his request was to say that we would be happy to do it *pro bono* as he was an old friend. No payment of any kind was received by us, and none was expected.

Jeremy pitched the problem as making arrangements more efficient, because he had a small office at Westminster which, of course, all MPs are entitled to – he had one in Dean's Yard, the most inconvenient place of all on the Parliamentary estate.

He also had a substantial suite of offices at the Red Rose Club on the Seven Sisters Road located above the bar area. It was immediately obvious that his offices at the Red Rosé would be inherently expensive because a) they were large; b) the building was large, with common areas; and c) business rates and heating/lighting/telephone overheads would be substantial.

His liability for these would, of course, be set by the Club Committee and he would have to pay them from his Parliamentary allowance, as he wasn't a rich man and didn't have his own resources to apply to the problem.

This was obviously, and clearly, a substantial resource problem – by definition. It became clear much later that he was being charged over the odds by the Club Committee, because they could, and it was difficult for him to refuse.

The office problem had arisen in this fashion because Jeremy had made a promise at his initial selection for the Islington North seat in 1982-3 that he would have an office in the constituency.

This may sound odd given that Westminster and the Parliamentary estate was only about five miles away, but the context is important.

No doubt Jeremy made the 1982 promise in good faith to maximise his chances of selection, but also to indicate to the electorate that he was a different kind of Labour candidate: not aloof, concerned about them, hardworking. All this would have marked a strong contrast with O'Halloran, who was probably the defector the SDP didn't want.[293]

---

293. His predecessor in the constituency, Michael O'Halloran, had defected to the SDP as had most of the Labour councillors in the borough, making it the only SDP-led council in the country until the London borough elections of 1982. O'Halloran was widely regarded (and correctly so from my recollection of him in the House of Commons) as a bit thick and completely incompetent. Indeed, a friend of mine who was a delegate at the selection conference in 1969 when O'Halloran was selected as the candidate, tore up her Party card when leaving the building because she was infuriated at his inadequacy and stupidity. The old-style, right wing leadership of the Labour Party in Islington was notorious for being autocratic and pretty Stalinist. It was so bad that Denis Healey's key economic adviser when Chancellor, Adrian Ham, who was moving from south London to Islington, was told by the borough secretary when he applied to transfer his existing Party membership that the party was full. This was the background to the origins of the SDP in Islington and, of course, all three sitting MPs (O'Halloran, John Grant, and George Cunningham) defected. The Islington background was therefore of Stalinist, ineffective Party apparatchiks and public representatives with (by

However, it has to be said that the commitment to an office in the constituency was not closely or carefully defined and was an elastic concept. It could have been what I had: a room in the Party HQ in Wood Green which I used for my surgery on Friday nights, with other surgeries in a community building in north Tottenham.

This involved almost zero expenditure from my Parliamentary allowance and generated absolutely no criticism from Party colleagues in the constituency. What they were concerned about was work rate, cases covered efficiently and competently.

So, Jeremy could have opted for this arrangement, met his commitment, and sailed on without the difficulties that he later encountered.

I know that Jeremy wanted to make a good impression on these issues and to do the right thing because I discussed with him how he should operate if elected. He was keen to be a constituency workhorse – and good for him.

The old-style model of Parliamentary representation, by leaving much casework to Councillors, was in my view absurd. It was especially so in London, where so much housing was council owned and where local authorities were utterly incompetent at doing simple things – and where there were large numbers of complex immigration cases to deal with.

Many constituents came to you after having tried and failed to use the council machinery, or the civil service bureaucracy, to get something done. You as the MP were in many cases their last line of defence, and I know that Jeremy agreed with this view.

But he didn't take the obvious route and he therefore became embroiled in an avoidable and unnecessary set of expenditures which, of course, he had to try and cover from his Parliamentary allowance (at that time, much more limited than now).

Also, he wasn't in control of the outgoings because the Red Rose Club was relying on him to cover off a significant chunk of their growing running costs, and he would have felt obliged to go along with it. As we all know, bars can be notoriously subject to losses and theft.

In addition, one of his staff became ill and was on long-term sick leave for two years and Jeremy decided to retain her on full pay. This was extremely generous, but also fraught with difficulty. Other members of his staff might have developed expectations about what would happen if they became ill (and certainly his behaviour would have had consequences

---

and large) patchy local reputations; and there was then after the defections a corresponding reaction from those who wanted democratisation.

311

for what was defined as normal practice under today's legislation on equal treatment). He therefore had to cover this salary from the Parliamentary allowance and any additional staff cover that became necessary.

In a very busy constituency there was always pressure on resources. I was doing 2,500 personal cases a year in 1983 in Wood Green, and he must have been doing the same or more – a relentless and growing level of pressure from detailed casework, thus provoking tension in his life.

So, the decisions made in 1982 led to poor choices of how to implement the office pledge. An agreement to go in with the Red Rose Club as a key component of its financial support; a decision not to seek cheap rooms for his surgery from a sympathetic council after 1982; and escalating costs that he could not meet from his Parliamentary office allowance.

These were not sensible organisational or managerial decisions and stemmed from his lack of experience.

Also, at that point technology was advancing rapidly and it was possible to link computer systems and telephones more effectively together at physical distance. Jeremy was not alone in being behind the curve on these issues.

Accordingly, the report that we wrote for him advocated:

- Linking his Commons office telephone lines with those in the Red Rose, were he to keep that office.

- Linking computers and printers together in a networked system so files could be shared and commands given over the network whatever the location.

- Reviewing fundamentally his commitment to the Red Rose Club in the light of the escalating financial costs and instead to use the free office facilities at the House where much equipment was also free to use (such as the large printer in Dean's Yard) and where telephone calls and computer networks were free.

It slowly emerged during the review that we conducted that Jeremy had run up serious debts in an attempt to maintain the existing office arrangements. These debts, we were told, were in the form of financial support from banks, taken out as loans and based on the collateral of his personal income as an MP.

It was not clear how he would pay them back over time and he had

312

several such loans, it emerged. This was at a time when he had a family of five to support and a mortgage on a relatively expensive house in the sense that most houses in Islington are expensive in any decade.

The most explosive discussion about these essentially very simple proposals occurred at Jeremy's house, with both Jeremy and Claudia[294] in the room. It emerged that Claudia had insisted that we were brought in to review the situation – because she said so.

When we discussed the written report, Jeremy was silent and embarrassed. Claudia entered the discussion with mounting exasperation bordering on anger, and she talked openly about the amount of money owed (we thought it was about £30,000 at 1990s prices).

It was clear to both of us that the consequence of these decisions had been to denude the family of money to do normal things that families want to do together, and that, despite her best efforts, things were very shaky both financially and emotionally between them. The financial pressure was obvious because they couldn't afford to go on holiday, and so we offered them a chance to have a break at our house in Derbyshire, which we were glad to provide.[295]

In the end Jeremy said in a mumble that he wouldn't implement any aspect of the report, because he felt he couldn't, having given promises to his constituency Party. At that point Claudia became very agitated. It was clear that a breakdown was coming.

We felt desperately sorry for all of them and we could not think of other ways of making the problem go away (other than getting vastly rich people to write off the loans, which was a non-starter). And if that option had been feasible, the same behaviours would have happened all over again.

So, the outcome was that we left the meeting and never discussed the issue again with Jeremy or Claudia. When their separation and divorce came it was obvious to us that money had played a significant part in the dissolution and had caused a breach of trust between them. There was nothing further that we could do.

---

294. Claudia Bracchitta, from a Chilean refugee family, escaped from the September 1973 Pinochet coup in Chile.
295. The tension and pressure were only what we inferred, of course, but it was made plain by the body language.

The Disappearances

In retrospect it is obvious what happened. Jeremy took on commitments which he could not meet, paying them out of his own pocket and making the family finances highly problematic. The tension was exacerbated by Jeremy's erratic behaviour.

Because they had no money, we invited Jeremy, Claudia and the three children to have a week with us in Derbyshire where they would have the run of the place and could go on day trips. Claudia arrived at our house, boys in the car, but no Jeremy. We asked where he was. Claudia didn't know but he had said there was a meeting he had to go to. He arrived with us two days later.

These events also demonstrated a number of things. He was inflexible in not adapting to changed circumstances. He did not listen when representations were made about it by his own family. He did not feel able to take a lead with his constituency and say 'Look, times have changed. I can't afford to do this anymore.'

By this point he was well entrenched as the sitting MP and there was little prospect that he would be removed because of it. He was scared, we think. He reacted weakly, could easily have gone to the leadership of the Council and asked to use public buildings for surgeries (which he did later at Durham Road).

The whole episode showed clearly that he had poor management skills, poor decision-making capabilities, and made bad choices even when his whole life was going to be turned upside down by his inflexibility. Nor did he react well to competent advice from friendly sources.

These are not good characteristics to have when you are a leading politician. We kept quiet about all this for many years whilst Jeremy was just a backbench MP. But when the prospect of him becoming Leader emerged, it could no longer be kept hidden. People needed to know background and track record when really important choices are to be made.

We were very sad when Claudia and Jeremy split up. In a sense, we felt responsible and that we had intervened in a personal matter, despite it being their request that we give advice.

Definitely Not Planned

Some authors have argued that Corbyn planned his own political rise with the clear objective of winning the leadership of the Party and exercising ultimate control over it. It is said that the whole thing was a deep plot and that he was intent on a bid for the top of the Party from the very beginning.

I don't believe this for one moment and I think the argument implies a rationality and ability to plan which is adrift from the reality of his life. In fact, he discussed with his closest friends whether he should retire as an MP before the 2015 General Election and at one point in that series of discussions he seemed in favour of it.

It is also at variance with evidence from his friends about extraordinary behaviour. Tony Banks, personally friendly to Corbyn, told a relevant story about Jeremy's failure to deal with his responsibilities by describing a day when he walked in to the Central Lobby and saw Jeremy's wife Claudia, with the children in tow, camped out on the green benches. She was in floods of tears. 'What's wrong?' asked Tony.

'Jeremy was supposed to meet me here two hours ago and he hasn't appeared,' she replied. The small kids were being understandably difficult in the circumstances and were distressed, so Tony went off round the building to collar Corbyn and get him down.

Eventually he was discovered in a committee room talking about some abstruse issue and was dragged down to deal with his family. He hadn't even told Claudia that there was a family room where she could wait with the kids, in some better degree of comfort.

This kind of behaviour, with endlessly similar examples of thoughtless, silly disorganisation, meant that we could not possibly contemplate him being considered as a potential Prime Minister. He had to be stopped. The correctness of our position can be judged by reference to the vast number of incompetences, failure to make decisions, poor judgements or no judgements at all, failures to deal with egregious acts of anti-Semitism, failure to manage or instruct people in his office, laid out in excruciating detail by Pogrund and Maguire.[296] (The book mostly covers the period 2016-19, the experience of Corbyn as leader of the opposition). Our take in 2015 was that Jeremy would be an utter disaster, was a danger to himself and to others, and could not be allowed to sit on the front bench in any capacity.

---

296. G Pogrund and P Maguire, *Left Out*, Bodley Head 2020

So that was our take on the political trajectory that Corbyn followed and the organisational chaos which followed Corbyn.

When the leadership election of 2015 started, Mandy and I had to decide what to do. It was clear that we couldn't support Jeremy. Once he was elected there was then a question of what to do about it, and we could not remain silent.

It was clear there was an existential threat to the very existence of the Labour Party and it was essential to build opposition to the Corbyn project, which we knew might be terminal for Labour unless it was ended by internal opposition or a decision by the electorate.

Analysing the Corbyn Problem

In September 2015, Corbyn was indeed elected as Leader with a substantial majority and started his tenure on the frontbench. It was a horror show and I described it in detail in a paper I wrote for Parliamentarians and former ministers in January 2016. It was titled:

The Strategic Opportunity.

We need to get on with this and stop talking about it. There is no perfect plan. Of course, we have to maximise gain and minimise collateral damage, and this is a big target. But it is doable.

It won't be possible for team Corbyn to maintain their present level of support within Party members, amongst trade unionists, and on the NEC. Reducing their level of support in all these arenas is important. Events will change perceptions (poor election results as time progresses); a growing realisation that they are not going to get into Government, and that therefore the interests of trade union members are unlikely to be protected (inability to promise with credibility changes in policy which will help); and that the key players in team Corbyn are more focused on factional and personal influence rather than the greater good of the Party (infighting, factional disputes, personality clashes, inability to craft credible messages and policies because they don't have the skills). The passage of time will help us, but there is not much time available.

Is this a Rerun of the 1980s?

In my view it is not. The shape of the problem is different, the character of the opposition is different, and the balance of forces is different.

What has changed since (say) 1980 is this:

1. The trade unions are significantly smaller, in absolute size and in terms of their membership component, with far fewer members in the private sector and manufacturing and proportionately more in the public services. That means that the unions that remain are more susceptible to arguments about the need to get a Labour Government in place than was the case in say 1980 (e.g. the need to ensure a fairer pay/incomes policy for public service workers). There is less of an automatic praetorian guard pro-Labour leadership group than before, but the members on the ground still have significant influence over national decisions by their union. The best way of changing the decisions of the remaining national unions is for members to say: 'We want a Labour Government, and we need to have sensible policies and leadership which will maximise this possibility.' In the end, trade union general secretaries, national officers, internal committees and branch secretaries are all dependent on member decisions, and they will not want to undermine their own livelihoods by ignoring member opinion completely. The debate in the unions over Trident is but the precursor to a wider discussion.

2. The membership of the Party is different: it is bigger, more middle class, and more concentrated in London and middle class areas such as university towns. Many of them have joined/rejoined because they think that the Party has not addressed the goals they support, wasted the opportunity of very large Parliamentary majorities, and intervened militarily when they think it should not have done so.

It is important to realise that this growth of membership, and this degree of influence over the affairs of a national governing Party, is most unusual and runs against the decline in mass parties since 1945, which has affected all kinds of parties in western countries where mass membership parties were once the order of the day. Political scientists would argue that the Corbyn surge is testing to destruction the theory that mass membership parties are dead and that the structure of power in British parties is pretty much the same (cf. Robert McKenzie, British Political Parties etc.). Something has to give.

Activists in political parties (whether Labour or Tory) have always been more middle class than have been the members as a whole and have been more likely to take radical positions. This has been known about since the 1950s.

My view is that a proportion of these new or returning members are transient. Many of them have moved in and out of membership before and it will not take much to disillusion them again. The evidence of high levels of churning is confirmed by senior Party officers with access to membership data.

3. The issues that the Party members care about are different from what they were, partly because different political problems have presented themselves and partly because these new members care about different things than did previous generations of members.

However, it is important to note that some of the policy areas that they are concerned with are of entirely legitimate interest. The continuing and changing impact of globalisation, the funding of key public services in an era when tax is harder to collect and where yields are declining, the generational unfairness as between the young and the old, the growing inequality between top earners and the middle – all are legitimate, all have not yet been addressed by the Party. Many of them feel alienated and separate from the plans and strategies of the ruling elites and many have seen their relative incomes fall and opportunities evaporate. We cannot ignore these issues and assume that a reheated Blair/Brown approach will do. This brings a significant opportunity.

They are exercised about foreign policy and security. If we are to defeat JC we must concentrate more on domestic policy, where the opportunities for conversion are higher.

In policy terms members of the Party think that their views are very similar to those of the electorate as a whole. This is wrong, has always been wrong, and we don't talk enough about it. Party members are highly distinctive in what they care about, and the intensity of feeling that they display. Some of the new members think that because they are enthused, the electorate is also enthused. Evidence will disabuse many of them on this point.

4. Nostalgia is present. Totems are discussed (rail nationalisation for example), which are really 10th order issues. This is all linked to the idea, now widely accepted amongst the membership, that the PLP is an alien pox on the face of the Party which must be purged – a curious view seeing that these MPs were selected by the Party members themselves. It has always been true that the Parliamentary Party has relied on a small group of intelligent, forward looking and competent people to plan and develop strategy and day-to-day tactics; that has been my experience since 1963, and I'm pretty sure is right. A careful watch of PMQs after the Corbyn victory endorses this view. In the long term we must reform the way in which potential candidates are recruited and trained. The feelings of antagonism and hostility towards the PLP are far greater than ever before and have been enhanced by the baleful influence of social media.

5. Society is fundamentally different. In 1960, 75% of the electorate were

318

manual workers; it was 25% in 2003 and is still dropping fast. This is not clearly understood. Less well-informed Party members still think that it is possible to mobilise 'the working class' and win an election. This was only just plausible in the 1960s and is impossible now. The structure of the class system has changed too and is now more diverse and fissiparous than was the case before. All these things reduce the hegemony of Labour ideas and make it more difficult to win elections.

So, we have a Party membership that thinks it is like the electorate – and the electorate of 50 years ago – and an electorate that has fundamentally changed, with different concerns and focus and ambitions than before. These facts pose serious dangers for the continued functioning of a left-of-centre political Party and this confluence is a recipe for disaster. We should be clear, however, that this collection of bizarre views and prejudices have not been created by a small tightly controlled bunch of extremists. It is more complicated.

Strengths and Weaknesses of Team Corbyn

JC and the people around him were lucky. They were able to build on a wave of protest, a yearning for nostalgic certainties, an anti-establishment tsunami of formidable proportions. Team Corbyn did not expect it or plan for it, and that is the best indication that it was not 'constructed' by the small groups of the extreme left diaspora. But they have taken advantage of it in order to do what they always do – try and build the biggest faction possible.

It has been widely reported that JC was approached by a longstanding left MP to drop his candidacy at the point in the leadership election when it became clear that he might win. This was almost certainly Skinner (as stated by DS himself).

Despite being pretty sure by mid-summer that they could win, they were unprepared for the event when it happened. The low-level incompetence of the first few weeks indicates this. Examples are: turning off the phones and on to voice mail in the Leader's Office, to prevent anyone in the Speaker's Office, No. 10 or the Tory Whips from getting through; the attitude to PMQs; failure to have a competent team to run the office from day one; and failing to take up media invitations in order to get the message across.

Now, having spoken to some longstanding Corbynites, the situation is this:

- *They know and accept that there are conflicting 'teams' with different agendas. The obvious ones are JC/McDonnell/Livingstone. There is concern about these tensions and who is doing what to whom. The tensions are all based on longstanding factional differences, and longstanding tensions from rate capping in 1985.*

- *They are really concerned about the polls. They thought they would be more popular than they are. That is why they are using Oldham West (the Oldham West by-election of 3rd December 2015, following the death of Michael Meacher) for all its worth and the evidence of Thanet (the Newington ward by-election, where a narrow Labour victory based on 288 Labour votes cast, removed the UKIP majority on the council.) Newington actually demonstrates that there was a two-party swing of precisely 0.7% to Labour from Conservative from May 2015, and a Labour share of the vote of 37% – compared to a share of 66% in the same ward at the 2011 District elections, the year after Miliband became leader. As we all know, the data on JC's personal approval ratings is disastrous, and we are ahead on individual issues only on the NHS, and that by 2 percentage points. As one leading Corbynite said to me, 'We know we're fucked.'*

- *Some Corbynites are really worried about Momentum, and think that it is going to be riven with factionalism (true) and prone to breakaways and disaffection (almost certainly true).*

- *There is then the evidence of policy incompetence which is making team Corbyn look absurd. The best examples are from the Marr interview last week (four hostages to fortune in 10 minutes – the Falklands, Trident subs without nukes, return of sympathy strikes etc.) and the ludicrous Right to Buy whenever a company is sold. Even senior Corbynites do not know where the money would be coming from to do this, how it would work, or what the difficulties would be in implementing it.*

- *JC's own personal incompetence is known about. His failure to deal with personal issues effectively (as discussed) is devastating evidence of his unsuitability for office. It is clear that the bullishness* of the first few weeks is wearing thin, even for this group of highly committed henchmen. Outside of the leadership group, many pro-JC members say that all this has been got up by the press and their PLP fellow travellers. Time will erode this view.

These are considerable weaknesses and they will be mitigated only at the margins by experience. The team does not get along with itself and there is actually little respect for JC's ability to run things – which is why they are all scrabbling around for influence.

There are also important objective weaknesses, such as their attitude to women and their inability to craft competent alternatives. They also believe, fundamentally, that many people in Britain will respond positively to a voter message considerably to the left of the Miliband project; the empirical evidence on that proposition seems to have been ignored.

The only strengths they have are 'the mandate', a declining asset; individualism and fear in the PLP limiting the ability to organise effectively; and lack of a coherent alternative in the form of an organised anti-Corbyn Parliamentary leadership or an individual who was clearly taking the lead in opposition to him and becoming a focus of resistance as a polar opposite.

Risk Profile

In saying that Team Corbyn are vulnerable and inadequate, we don't assume that they are simple to remove. There are considerable risks in what we need and want to do and in factors related to timing. These are:

- Damage to the Labour brand is already considerable. The longer this goes on, the worse it will get. If we can remove the JC team in 2016, we have a fighting chance of changing perceptions before the next election. If it's later, or if it is clear that attempts to remove him have failed, damage may be terminal. The Tories may respond to this opportunity by organising a surprising dissolution and snap election – which has already been mooted. The consequences of this would be calamitous. There is therefore a time pressure to prepare and act.

- We challenge at the wrong time and lose. This can happen if we mislead ourselves about the state of public opinion and Party *opinion, so the imperative is to poll Party members ACCURATELY and make judgements. It's not just about polling on trust and competence, and on belief in JC: it's about whether people are going to renew their subs or not, and who they might support if JC isn't on the ballot paper.*

- *The May 2016 election results aren't bad enough and give the Corbynites the opportunity to say they are on the up rather than being on the way down. Expectation management is part of this. Ruthless exposure of local government by-election failure is another.*

- *There is no credible single challenger around whom people can coalesce. At present there is a long list of potential candidates, some of whom won't do it (Alan Johnson) or probably won't (Hilary Benn). Others have significant disadvantages which we discussed and others are policy and presentation light (in my opinion). In 2015 one of the reasons JC won was because of the weakness of the other candidates, who had little to say and sometimes said it badly. But we need to settle on a candidate and a team and put in place all the support mechanisms needed. Soon.*

- *The economy moves into lower growth and/or recession in late 2016/early 2017. This is widely expected in financial circles, with predicted declines in M&A activity, lower growth in real incomes, declining manufacturing sales, lower investment in infrastructure and capital goods because of the China/developing world readjustments, and the overall impact of the oil price decline – let alone a financial shock caused by asset price changes. These events, after a period of time (six months or so) will affect the Government's standing by blowing apart the assumptions on which deficit reduction was founded, and make JC, if he's still there, look more like a prophet than a scarecrow.*

- *There is a considerable risk in not having a considered policy alternative. This cannot be reheated policies from the 1990s, as circumstances and needs have changed: and it must be seen as a serious attempt to address the problems of 21st century society. Anything less will be immediately dissed as an establishment stitch* up – and it will be defeated in the selectorate. The policy alternative does not have to be a complete, costed, absolutely hard wired set of policies that have been scored and tested with focus groups. It needs to be good enough, seriously good enough, to win over the selectorate.

These are considerable risks, but many of them are capable of mitigation – by developing policies and messages, identifying a leadership team, doing the polling, encouraging splits and dissension amongst the Corbynites, and planning carefully but with determination. The major thing we can't control is the trajectory of economic events.

Who are the New Selectorate?

There is now something of an industry on this subject. My own observations, partly based on personal experience with them but also partly on information from Party officers at national level, is that the profile looks something like this:

- They are overwhelmingly middle-aged and not young; they are geographically concentrated in London, middle class areas, and university towns. They are not by and large in Scotland or Northern/Midland industrial seats; they are overwhelmingly white in most areas

- They are overwhelmingly public sector and not private sector, definitely not white van man or industrial workers. There are some creative types and some professionals but it would be wrong to class them as intellectuals, as a group

- They are, in relative terms, mainly comfortable financially. Because of their occupational background, they see their world as under threat

- They think that the last Labour Government was a shocking failure and was a wasted opportunity, and sided with the wrong sorts, insofar as they remember it accurately at all

- *They think that they are rather like the electorate as a whole, and certainly don't understand the differences between themselves and swing voters or people in different sorts of constituencies*

- *They think the PLP as a whole (mitigated only in so far as they like their own MP where they have one) is hopeless and confused and obstructive*

- *Many have been members before but many have not, and a lot of them will have no tradition of political activism in their families (an important recruiter of political leadership groups). Their connection to Corbyn's Labour is personal and possibly temporary. We know that churning amongst the membership is very high, with only about 50,000 people continuously in membership between 2010 and 2015 (officially from Brewers Green/Southside).*

Therefore, the risks of doing nothing are extraordinarily high. We need to stop talking and start acting. There is a considerable hope that we can do it.

Key Objectives

Winning back the Party: Organisational Priorities

- *These functions have to be carried out discreetly with plausible deniability*

- *Best to be silent on organisational matters and make few bravado announcements*

- *Someone needs to coordinate. We should not just be originators of action but – crucially – having a coordinating function with the diverse groups who have common aims*

- *The key to this is organisational sustainability and that means winning donors to provide finance for the short and medium term*

- *The key functionalities are: defending existing MPs who want to remain; create a panel of candidates who are sensible and* well informed and selectable; plan the selections; train potential candidates

- *Developing day to day arguments on the need to have a leadership capable of winning an election, and the strategic messaging necessary to convince target voters. First thoughts on this are: the urgent need for a Labour Government in order to take the decisions required; the growing evidence (clearly specified) of incompetence and lack of focus and common sense; and in due course the failure to win elections as practical proof that JC cannot win in 2020.*

- *Encouraging the fissiparous tendencies and jealousies of the competing teams in the JC group*

- *Commissioning/analysing polling data, to ensure that the point at which the LP electorate loses faith with JC et al. is clearly understood*

- *Understanding the demographic of JC support*

- *Developing a narrative on Party democracy that avoids the Manichean PLP bad/members good divide. Ensuring that the argument is not between left wingers and perceived right wingers by making clear that many radical people in the Party are dismayed by JC and his team*

- *Monitoring the Labour Party year and intervening on resolutions for Conference; getting delegates selected and there; opposing negative rule changes and supporting our own*

- *Supporting disruptive ops when required.*

The Narrative

- *This strand of work is not just about developing policy – crucial though that is – but developing a rationale for the direction of travel, a narrative, for both the Party's consumption and that of the electorate.*

- *The contours of society need to be described so that they are clearly understood. That there is no way of reconstructing the Attlee or Wilson coalitions of voters, because society has changed: 75% manual worker in 1960, c. 25% in 2003. It is simply not possible to win elections by relying on working class voters and a few middle class déclassés to defeat the bulk of establishment/business/professional/middle class opinion. Labour Party members need to understand that the trade unions will not be rebuilt to their former size and influence because of the decline of traditional manufacturing industries where unions were strong, and the reducing size of the public sector, together with the impact of stopping check off etc. It follows that a new coalition needs to be constructed.*

- *We also need to describe and explain the new challenges facing progressive movements in Western developed countries. These are: continued globalisation and its effects of spreading productive capacity to BRICs and beyond; the impact of disruptive technological change and robotics, the extent of which is hard to predict; the different divisions this is producing in society, namely the division between young and old, with young people being denied access to stable jobs, middle class incomes, affordable housing, and the ability to construct families of their own. This is a generational shift which has some commonalities with the mid 1960s, when 'teenagers' were invented and students were radicalised against a reactionary establishment (but there are differences too). It is important not to get on the wrong side of this divide.*

- *We need to establish what the size of the State should be and why; what are the big challenges facing a left progressive Government by way of areas of need that require vastly greater state spending, and how we fund that. These areas include Housing, where there is chronic market failure and an illiterate planning system leading to desperate lack of social housing; an NHS and social care system urgently needing £30bn a year extra (in 2016) to stand still and continue to provide what it does now; providing educational and personal support to the growing number of young people in an underclass with no hope; and using the powers of the state to grow*

326

businesses, increase the trend rate of growth, and vastly increase productivity. The rapidly growing profile of inequality between top earners and middle incomes has to be addressed.

- *Developing an 'offer' for the trade union membership and leaders which will split them from Corbyn et al.*

- *We need to answer how you get more cash to spend. The answer must be to increase the trend rate of growth and it must say openly that the key is a vibrant and growing business sector. It is the only way to reliably increase tax buoyancy and protect yield and increase the pool of resources.*

- *Taxation must be addressed. The yield of corporation tax is falling as against other taxes, and we must consider what taxes on production and profits need to be enhanced to ensure that business pays a fair and sensible proportion of total taxes. Hypothecation, to give a clear link between need, tax levied, and tax spent, should be seriously researched and considered. This would be particularly easy to advance in the field of NHS and social care.*

- *The purpose must be intellectual, narrative, and policy renewal. Michael Heseltine was famously asked recently when Labour would win again. He said, 'When it wants to.' He is right. Our key task is to make Labour want to win and give it the intellectual and organisational tools to do so.*

Coordination and Action

This detailed analysis of the Corbyn problem, written in early 2016 before the Brexit vote in June, was followed by a first positive to emerge which was vital coordination between those who opposed the destruction of the Labour Party as a serious force.

I had been working with senior Party officials for some time and this partnership gradually turned into something else: the beginnings of an organisation that would challenge Corbyn's hold on the Party and organise for the defeat of the ultra-left project.

It started with meetings of former donors who were all very concerned about the wild swing to the left and who wanted to talk about what they wanted to do.

This first took shape as The Centre for Inclusive Prosperity, a name chosen from an Ed Balls team up with US centre-left economists, with a formal company established by Gary Follis, a former Chief of Staff to Ed Balls when Shadow Chancellor, and Simon Franks, the tech entrepreneur and Labour supporter.

I met with them a few times but there was insufficient direction and it clearly wasn't the vehicle for mounting a challenge in whatever form and at whatever time that might come. A more substantial team was required and so I set out to find one.

The paper quoted above was my first pitch at getting the group together and I met with Peter Mandelson first as one of the most senior figures available. I had never met him before and initially he was very suspicious of my motives, but I drafted the paper without being asked and sent it to him.

This immediately loosened things up, as he described it as 'brilliantly perceptive', but I insisted that we should have a coordinating group of individuals and organisations who would try and pull things together. This gradually happened and it included the organisations Labour First and Progress together with a number of key MPs and trade union figures.

We met frequently in the early months of 2016 and I insisted that our challenge should not just be organisational but also policy and strategic. This was never allowed to emerge as there was reluctance to get involved at creating an alternative plan which would challenge Corbyn's hegemony of ideas, and it was a considerable failing.

I was prevented from discussing strategic policy papers I had written as I was told that 'these would emerge from existing organisations.' This was obviously never going to happen and was simply a way of kicking the issues into the long grass. But on mounting an organisational challenge inside the PLP there was more traction.

The idea of a rolling programme of resignations from the Shadow Cabinet and junior shadow ministerial positions came first from Ian Austin.[297] Austin's plan was detailed and involved the whole of the frontbench resigning (as far as was possible), others refusing to replace them, not turning up at Prime Minister's Questions to leave bare Labour benches behind Corbyn, and electing a separate leader of the PLP. All

---

297. MP for Dudley North, later to defect from the Labour Party and now Baron Austin of Dudley.

these proposals, apart from individual resignations, assumed that MPs would act collectively and not just in their own interests, which is regrettably the default position of many of them.

Austin's note to Peter Mandelson describing the plan stated that, 'It is difficult to see how he could survive a motion of no confidence and wholesale resignations,'[298] but this did not take in to account Corbyn's inability to make decisions about anything, including his own resignation, and the fanatical resistance of the miniscule team whose job it was to protect 'the project.' To be fair, Austin regarded this as an incremental process but he underestimated the tenacity of those at the top who knew perfectly well that Corbyn was the only chance of fulfilling the dream of a leftist Government in power in Britain.

I challenged the assumption that these actions would undermine the Corbyn project, and said that they might indeed strengthen it. It was clear to me at the time that there were only two ways that Corbyn could be removed: first by a sufficient number of people in the PLP who could sideline him and remove his credibility, and that meant a majority of the PLP moving ship behind another Labour leader in Parliament; and second by the electorate as a whole voting in a general election.

The chances of getting a majority of the PLP to jump ship were, it seemed to me, fanciful. It was not just their sense of loyalty to the Party they had joined that was at issue here, it was their sense of self-preservation: moving to what would be a new Parliamentary formation would energise the Momentum and ultra-left activists in many of their constituencies and improve the chances of them being deselected. And retaining their position as an MP was always a key motivator in behaviour.

Indeed, the only way that Corbyn could be removed as the Leader of the opposition, a formal position, of course, was if the Speaker could be persuaded to recognise someone else as that Leader.

A great deal of flannel was talked about this, so I went through back channels to discover what the attitude of the Speaker would be to 'recognising' another person as Leader of the opposition. The answer was that someone other than Corbyn would be recognised under certain conditions: first, that they had more MPs supporting them than Corbyn.

Second, that the organisation replacing Corbyn's faction would have to be a registered political Party; and that this position could be confirmed from the Chair if a point of order was raised where the subject had been flagged to him in advance.

---

298. Paper by Ian Austin to Peter Mandelson, Spring 2016

This gave an opening and there was discussion of using the Co-operative Party as a vehicle as it was already registered as a Party and some Labour MPs were in fact Labour/Co-op MPs in an arrangement that went back decades. But there was strong practical and political opposition from within the Co-op Party to be approached in this way, and the idea went nowhere.

The real problem, however, was psychological: although many MPs were very determined to get rid of what they saw as the alien incubus of the Corbyn faction, which amounted to no more than a tiny rump in the PLP, there was great loyalty to the Labour Party as an institution and significant reluctance to leave it, even for this purpose.

This point was proved beyond doubt when the Independent Group for Change was formed in 2019, with few MPs signed up, a disastrous launch in February, a fizzling away of traction, and eventually dissolution in December 2019 as all the few remaining MPs lost their seats in the election.

Destabilising

It was always clear to me that if an elbowing away of Corbyn was going to be done it needed a majority of the PLP to defect, and it was difficult to see the circumstances in which this could happen.

It was also important to recognise that the moral authority of Corbyn needed to be destroyed, and this could only be done by one of two things: the votes of Labour members in a leadership election, or the votes of the electorate as a whole destroying the Party at a general election.

My own view was that the second option was inevitable and that the first option might work, provided there was a credible challenger and a determined organisational effort, backed by significant money as was always required in a leadership election, and based on a clear alternative policy that would appeal to many of the people who had joined the Party in frustration at what they saw as the failure of the Brown premiership and the flabby weakness of the Ed Miliband leadership.

So, the Austin Plan was mobilised, essentially through the efforts of Chris Leslie[299] and the first to leave the front bench were Heidi

---

299. MP for Nottingham East 2010-2019 and for Shipley 1997-2005

Alexander,[300] and Hilary Benn,[301] shortly after the referendum on the EU had delivered the vote to Leave on 23rd June 2016.

The pro-EU members of the PLP were very agitated at Corbyn's failure to engage with the referendum campaign as they saw it and wanted to act fast to rid the Party of him. They thought he was a traitor for not supporting the Party's policy on Europe, but I did not share their views as I had voted to Leave and was delighted by the referendum result.

It was typical that they couldn't craft an alternative strategic policy position but that they were having a serious love-in with the Euro-bureaucracy and did not realise that the European project was way beyond Delors, Mitterrand and Kinnock.

They were trapped in the past and it was a weakness that the basis on which they were challenging Corbyn was that he wasn't pro-EU enough. However, 21 members of the Shadow Cabinet resigned between 26th and 29th June, forcing Corbyn to appoint replacements. One of them was Paul Flynn, 81, the oldest person ever to be a shadow minister since Gladstone.

On 29th June, the PLP held a vote of no confidence in Corbyn which was passed by 172 votes to 40. Unsurprisingly he refused to resign.

Saving Labour

Immediately after the Leave vote was announced on 24th June 2016, a small group of MPs and supporters had quite separately begun crafting a response which had the objective of saving the Labour Party.

I knew some of them and had good connections through the donor network with them too, and I was pretty quickly roped in to do some of the hard slog organisational work.

The organisation that was crafted, called Saving Labour, was directed at removing Corbyn, destroying what remained of his credibility with the membership of the Party, and paving the way for a more sensible and competent leader to emerge.

So, I set up a limited partnership, registered with the Information Commissioner, established banking arrangements, and started raising money. Luckily at that point, many people in my networks were still active and wanted to be kind to a new organisation with these objectives.

---

300. MP for Lewisham East 2010-May 2018
301. MP for Leeds Central 1999-to present

However, there were significant obstacles to the tasks: a massive membership at individual level, many of whom had joined to elect Corbyn.

There was also a large cohort of 'Registered Supporters', a new concept in the Party and one introduced by Ed Miliband. They were thought to be overwhelmingly on Corbyn's side.

Finally, an uncertain position in the trade unions, with Unite vociferously on the leader's side and the swing union of Unison under a leadership that was lethargic and unresponsive.

The NEC was moving more firmly under Corbynite control and the membership – at least in 2016 – were unknown in their demographics and views.

In this context, the view from many members of the PLP was that there should be a serious campaign to try and recruit moderates to become members of the Party. No one knew whether there was a significant group of people out there who would respond to a sensible pitch to join in order to recapture the Labour Party, whether you called that pitch 'moderate' or 'sensible radical', as I did.

In the periods before the advent of email and social media, the barriers to mobilising large numbers of new members of whatever kind would have been very significant, not to say insurmountably high.

But in the world of internet-driven politics, a very large pressure group had been created to take over a major political party, sideline its Parliamentary wing, and build an extra Parliamentary wing capable, it was thought, of mobilising new tranches of voters to win a general election under first past the post.

This strategy by Momentum, under the able and experienced leadership of Jon Lansman, had managed to create something unique in British politics in the 2015 leadership election.

A large cadre of active members, many of them tech-savvy, had defeated the establishment of the Party by taking advantage of an opening that had been gratuitously created for them. Ed Miliband changed the rules to allow the completely off the wall concept of Registered Supporters which resulted in 150,000 new people entering the Party.

At the time, Miliband did not consider the impact that the growth of the internet and social media could have on the outcome of a leadership election by enabling a mass influx of 'supporters.' The warnings given to him about the necessity of ensuring that the PLP still had control of the nominations process went unheeded. The so-called Collins[302] review was to get Miliband out of a hole he had himself constructed. It was either rescue Ed or sink Ed.

Collins was not involved until after the St Bride speech[303] and the contents of it had already been briefed out before Collins was asked to work on the review. For Miliband, changing the constitution of the Party was essentially a public relations exercise and it seems that he did not understand the consequences of what he was doing. Collins's attempt to maintain the PLP's nomination threshold for Leader at 20% of the PLP were rebuffed by Miliband and he pushed it downwards thus enabling the Corbyn nominations to succeed in getting him on the ballot paper in 2015.

Later, when the review had been published and accepted by Conference, the Collins proposal for an implementation group was abandoned and the suggestions for lengthy freeze dates to stop a flood of new 'supporters' being eligible to vote almost instantly were abandoned too.

So, the new registered supporters had been 'sponsored' to join by the Miliband leadership, were to be allowed to flood in without restraint, and allowed to overturn the power structure of the Party, despite the warnings given by the former General Secretary, Ray Collins. They then took the bait and routed the PLP establishment. Lansman had been enabled to walk through the curtain wall and had brilliantly taken the opportunity to do so using a playbook that was familiar to me from the Benn campaign of 1981 and later the Socialist Conference.

The difference in 2015 which made the Momentum thrust unstoppable was not just the advent of social media and the internet, but also the legacy of what was seen as abject failure over Iraq and the view from the grassroots that capitalism had stopped delivering for large swathes of the population. Both these factors were new and both were necessary but not sufficient conditions for the success of a leftist coup against the Parliamentary Party.

Nothing like it had ever been close to success in the Labour Party, but in Corbyn there existed a principled and believable standard bearer who despite his obvious faults, could be seen to be a clean pair of hands with

302. Ray Collins, Lord Collins of Highbury, General Secretary of the Labour Party 2008-11. Coincidentally, Collins' politics tutor at the University of Kent was Fred Whitemore.
303. Miliband speech to the St Bride Foundation, July 9th 2013, in which he made clear that changes to the rules on affiliations by trade unions to Labour were the result of the Falkirk selection battle.

a track record of opposition to the Party establishment which endeared him to the tranches of largely middle class recruits who flooded in.

Nothing could have been done about social media and the internet except counter it in 2015 by an even better operation than Momentum's, but the political failure – and it was a strategic failure of devastating consequences – was that the candidates of the middle ground and right in 2015 had very little to say except to repeat the nostrums of triangulation and of reheated Blairism and Brownism which were stale in 2015 and versions of which had been decisively rejected on two occasions by the electorate in general elections.

There were sufficient interesting things to say in 2015 from a non-Corbyn perspective, but no one said them coherently.

This was the context in which Saving Labour was born. The midwife of its creation was the referendum and Corbyn's perceived unwillingness to campaign enthusiastically and energetically for the Remain cause.

But the logic behind the Saving Labour concept was that there might be a huge reservoir of moderate people who would respond to a call to join, and place the Party back into some kind of winning position with the electorate.

I was always dubious about this because of my background in voting behaviour analysis but thought it worth exploring to see what could be done. It was also clear to me that oodles of high profile advertisements and social media work to mobilise moderates would also mobilise Corbyn supporters, and it was difficult to know where the balance of advantage would fall. But it had to be tried as an option.

The other important job of Saving Labour was to counter the ideological nonsense flowing from Momentum and the small Corbyn cult in the PLP. This was both to protect, as much as possible, the brand loyalty to Labour that still existed in quite large sections of the electorate, and hopefully to develop new strategic visions for the Party. To do any of this we needed resources.

Decay and Poison

There were weaknesses in the Corbyn/Momentum cult which were clear from the beginning. It was very weak in the PLP with only a limited number of vocal MPs on their side. Their rank and file membership were quite capable of political overreach at the drop of a hat.

This was also the start point of a tidal wave of antisemitism and sulphurous campaigning which their innate righteousness loved and demanded. And it has to be said, there were many willing to listen to the garbage. Corbyn himself may or may not be an anti-Semite, but he certainly enabled the movement. It flowed from a desire to support Palestine and morphed into a need to carpet bomb Jews in the Labour Party by threats, smears, bullying and thuggery. It was allowed to get completely out of hand.

One sincerely delivered sentence of stern rebuke from Corbyn, and automatic expulsions for those who transgressed, would have stopped it in an afternoon – but he wouldn't do it. This weakness destroyed the reputation of the Labour Party with wide sections of the electorate and, of course, with the Jewish community. Tragically, it had little effect with the mass of new members and supporters that had joined.

However, the threat of deselection by the membership worked like a fast acting dose of Senokot on the PLP. This was further enhanced by the publication of a list of all Labour MPs with a rating attached to each name, ranging from hardcore pro-Corbyn to hardcore antis. This was pored over by individuals and although some were enraged at not finding themselves in the most antagonistic group, many were disturbed at the thought of being thrown out before the next general election.

Another list was then produced of 70 deselection targets and this included the Deputy Chief Whip,[304] several former ministers such as Hilary Benn, Alan Johnson and Ben Bradshaw, and the Chair of the Public Accounts Committee, Meg Hillier.[305]

The list contained the names of about 25% of the whole PLP and it was ambitious to say the least. My view always was that whatever the noise made, Momentum would find it very difficult to unseat a hard-working MP with a good constituency record.

This was especially the case after the Momentum-backed mandatory open selection motion was lost at the 2018 Party Conference and the Corbynites had to retreat to the much less powerful means of reducing the threshold for triggering a sitting MP and forcing a selection.

The facts speak for themselves: more MPs retired or left the Labour Party because of intimidation by antisemitic or Momentum thugs than were deselected in an open way.

At least two women MPs left because of intimidation and 11 joined

---

304. Alan Campbell, MP for Tynemouth 1997-
305. MP for Hackney South 2005-present

other Parties, created one, or left to get jobs outside Parliament.

Others were defeated in the 2019 General Election.

The only trigger ballots to be lost by sitting MPs were by Roger Godsiff, Margaret Hodge, Diana Johnson, Emma Lewell-Buck, Kate Osamor and Virendra Sharma.

Osamor was a supporter of Corbyn who had featured in an intemperate battle with reporters and had employed her son, a convicted criminal, in the Commons. Godsiff had been fighting a battle with Asian Party members in his constituency and was not young. Hodge was a leading critic of Corbyn. Johnson was anti-Corbyn and sat for a constituency with large numbers of university lecturers and students in her Party. Lewell-Buck's and Sharma's local parties were either suspended or had been in special measures.

Not one of these MPs was actually deselected. Godsiff left the Party after losing a number of ward trigger ballot votes and contested the 2019 General Election as an Independent, losing his seat.

This was therefore a complete failure of the Momentum programme of bending the PLP to its will, and it is likely that a few of the MPs who left would have retained their nomination if they had slugged it out. Some of them, however, could not face the prospect of endless rows and months of disruption.

The 2016 Leadership Election

No sooner had Saving Labour started mobilising than a leadership election was called in the Party.

We had no influence whatever over the selection of the candidate who would challenge and there was some embarrassment as various potential candidates' names were bandied about and then discarded. At one point, it looked as if Angela Eagle[306] would run but during her launch news conference information came through that others were moving forward and that she would not be getting the expected support.

It was all very unsatisfactory and disorganised and the PLP did not do itself any favours over that incident.

Eventually Owen Smith[307] contested against Corbyn having secured more PLP nominations than Eagle.

---

306. MP for Wallasey 1992-
307. MP for Pontypridd 2010-19

Saving Labour was not in a position to endorse him as we had not been set up to support a specific candidate, but instead we worked hard to engage with potential new recruits to the Party and encouraged many to join as registered supporters.

To do this I wrote a large number of press adverts which we were able to place in many national newspapers. There were news releases and interventions to discredit poll findings which were based on poor sampling (and at least one polling organisation changed it's sampling frame in response to our criticisms). And we used a prominent firm of digital campaigners to target potential recruits in specific geographical locations, industries and social groups.

However, life was made considerably more difficult by the fact that no one wanted to go on the record: there were many MPs supporting us but none of the most prominent felt able to be quoted.

The result was that Corbyn won 61.8% of the aggregated votes but lost in Scotland, had little support in the PLP or among Labour councillors, and was weakest amongst full Party members.

He won because those who had supported him in 2015 were not yet ready to say they had been wrong, and the result certainly strengthened him for a while. However, we were not able to mobilise enough moderate people to join as registered supporters and it demonstrated that attempts to mobilise centre-ground voters are probably always doomed to fail – as I thought might be the case. People interested in politics are not a 'tap' that can be turned on and off at will; they have to be motivated to join organisations and the motivation to join Labour to make it electable again was weak at that point. Crucially, there was no 'standard bearer' around whom people could unite.

But Corbyn's record with the electorate was appalling and it ended in precisely the way that Saving Labour said it would: with the worst defeat in a Parliamentary election since 1935.

It is worth examining Corbyn's record in some detail, and it shows that his record became more damaging over time: by September 2019, Corbyn registered the lowest approval rating for an opposition leader since records began in 1977: -60%.

In the European Parliament elections of 2019, Labour came third in England and Wales and fifth in Scotland with the lowest national share of the vote (14.1%) since the General Election of 1910.

Many councils were lost and hundreds of local authority members were defeated.

In Parliamentary by-elections, Labour lost seats like Copeland that it had held for nearly a hundred years and retained others with much reduced vote shares. On the doorstep it was relentless anti-Corbyn feeling that was the cause of haemorrhaging votes.

The polling day 2019 survey by Opinium showed that the reason for not voting Labour in every region of the country was overwhelmingly that of Corbyn's presence, and not Brexit, as his cheerleaders said. Internal polling by Labour in the 2019 General Election campaign showed that Brexit was a low priority for most voters, even for 'Labour Leavers', where only 7% of this group ranked it first on their priority list of issues.

Inversion of Power: Permanent or Not?

The real questions about the leadership elections of 2015 and 2016 are about these things: how was it possible to mobilise a very large group of new and returning members to the Labour Party?

Why did these new members vote predominantly for Corbyn rather than other candidates and why did they choose to abandon a Corbyn-backed candidate in 2020?

What did this mean for the traditional view of the distribution of power in political parties? And finally, is this inversion of power inside a major political Party repeatable in other parties and in other circumstances?

Mass parties were created by the expansion of the franchise in the late 19th century in Britain and most political scientists believed by 2015 that 'the age of the mass Party has passed.'[308] After the Corbyn insurrection this proposition must be re-assessed.

First, let us look at who these members were, a necessary analysis before we can answer some of the question posed above.

Luckily, we have detailed information from two surveys of Labour members undertaken by the Economic and Social Research Council (ESRC)[309] in 2015 and then again in 2016. They ask the central question as to whether the new members differed from the old in terms of social composition and subjective political positioning.

Older members were defined as having been a member before the May

308. P Mair, Parliamentary Affairs, vol. 602, 2005.
309. Monica Poletti, Tim Bale and Paul Webb, *Party Members Project*.

2015 General Election and new members as those who joined between May 2015 and January 2016 and were therefore able to vote in the 2016 leadership election.

Broadly speaking, they found they did not differ very much: they were NOT more working class, or younger (average age was 51 in both groups and 76% of 'old' members lived in a household where the chief income earner was in the ABC1 category, 75% amongst new members).

There were more women in the new intake (52% new to 38% old). The new and the old were very similar in terms of social class and educational achievement, but more of the newer members had incomes below the national gross household income of £35,000 pa (34% of old members had incomes below this level but 41% of newer members did).

As the authors said:

Corbyn, then, does not seem to have attracted a very different type of crowd in many socio-demographic respects, except insofar as it is slightly less well-off and more gender-balanced.

However, on the critical issue of whether Party members were similar to the electorate in their political view, the answer is an emphatic no.

The overwhelming view from both old and new members was that they were in favour of redistribution (in favour: 91% old members, 94% new members), whereas the electorate is far more divided on this subject.

On other measures Labour members new and old were overwhelmingly in the place one would expect them to be. For example, on the issue of whether public spending cuts had gone too far, almost everyone agreed with the idea that they had.

On their own perceptions of political position, however, there were clear differences between old and new members. Old members placed themselves slightly to the right of new members and Momentum members (in a separate category) were the most left wing of all. The research authors said that 'the new members see themselves as something of a leftist vanguard.'

They were also more socially liberal on measures of teaching children to obey authority, censorship, and stiffer sentences for criminal behaviour.

The most crucial difference, however, was in the kind of activism they were involved in: new members were much more likely to be just clicktivists whereas old members were much more likely to attend public meetings, leaflet, display election posters, or – most strikingly – canvass. 36% of old members had canvassed compared to just 9% of new members.

Momentum members were an outlier too: they were in some respects just as involved as old members in traditional election rituals such as leafleting and canvassing but were way ahead of everyone else in using Facebook and Twitter.

A further hint as to their political position was given by the answers to the question on reasons for joining Labour: 76.5% of the new members said they joined because of the political position of the leadership.

Finally, the ESRC study posited that many of the new members felt 'left behind' in terms of relative deprivation and they concluded that:

The new members are confident that the new leadership respects them and this is something that distinguishes Corbyn from most other politicians in their eyes.

Finally, there is some evidence that the educated left-behinds might have been particularly moved to place new hope in Corbyn. How long they keep the faith, and what that means for the Labour Party, remains to be seen.

We can correctly say that Corbyn was able to mobilise significant numbers of people to join or rejoin the Labour Party, perhaps in a way that no other candidate could have done. It is also worth pointing out that many of these joiners or returners were of an age when they might remember or have participated in the great campaigns by Tony Benn in the early 1980s, and some may have been re-radicalised by the emergence of Corbyn.

However, the main fault of the new members was that they believed their own attitudes were also shared by the wider electorate, and that therefore a radical Labour Party was only prevented from being born by the reactionary views, as they saw it, of the PLP. This was not true, but the new members did not understand that what they believed was true could be falsified by evidence that already existed. These members, and especially the ultra-left, were operating in a world where they insisted that their reality was the correct and only one. But the electorate were always in a different universe.

It is entirely possible that Corbyn's exit from national politics will crystallise a desire to leave the Party they joined, as appears to be happening in 2020.

We can also be clear that the new members were overwhelmingly middle class rather than working class. The days of a mass working class membership for the Party seem to be long gone.

The data from the ESRC study also confirms what many have long thought: that the new members are far more likely to be internet warriors rather than the door-knockers and leafleters that are frequently to be found amongst the old members. The group of Momentum members within the response group were more like fully-rounded political activists than the bulk of the new membership.

Some of the new members were ultra-left activists in other political parties who dumped their identities in myriad organisations to support Corbyn.

Some of the groups, such as Respect, which split from the Socialist Workers Party in 2007, supported Corbyn as did other splinter groups such as RS21 (itself a split from Counterfire, which in turn was a split from the SWP after serious allegations of sexual abuse were uncovered amongst the SWP leadership) and TUSC,[310] a coalition of Trotskyist organisations put together to fight elections without having a real identity of their own.

The fluctuating size and composition of the groups and their tendency to split, re-split and coalesce is well known but what is clear is that many of the first-tier activists in these groups joined Corbyn's Labour to support him and to try and expunge the Labourist elements, especially in the PLP.

Now that Corbyn has gone and his project has been defeated, at least for the time being, it is likely that many of these people will return to more isolated political activity in sects or to nothing at all.

Embourgeoisement – or Not?

At this point it is worth revisiting a very old concept, the embourgeoisement thesis (the idea that working class voters would change their political allegiances over time because of increased affluence and greater contact with middle class lifestyles), and how it relates to political activism in the 21st century.

Having spent three books discussing, and largely rejecting, this proposition, Goldthorpe, Lockwood et al.[311] settled on the idea that it was change in the occupational structure in Britain rather than affluence

---

310. Trade Unionist and Socialist Coalition. RS21 is one of the many bewildering splinter groups from the Socialist Workers Party

311. JH Goldthorpe, D Lockwood, F Bechhofer and J Platt, *The Affluent Worker: Political Attitudes and Behaviour*, Cambridge University Press 1968

itself which might revise the political attitudes of working class voters.

Given the extensive disappearance of manual worker jobs in Britain between the end of the 1960s and today, it is tempting to agree that these changes have unglued party identification on a very large scale.

They put the argument in this way from the vantage point of 1969:

The long-run trends for white collar employment to expand more than blue collar work and for women to take up an increasing proportion of white collar jobs must mean that more manual wage earners will have siblings and wives (sic) who are middle class in terms at least of occupational status... it is precisely such changes in the occupational structure, rather than affluence itself, that must be regarded as possibly the most influential factor in encouraging the spread of middle class values and lifestyles among the working class.

On the political level, this could, of course, mean a decline in support for the Labour Party with underlying causes that are more systematic, if less widespread in their effect, than those which have been held to be associated with working class prosperity.[312]

What Goldthorpe and Lockwood were really saying was that affluence *per se* did not seem to influence party identification and voting behaviour a great deal (despite all the necessary caveats one can make about the very small size of their survey sample), but that ongoing increases in the size of the blocs of middle class jobs might have more influence over time.

They thought that growing contact by working class voters with more middle class people in their families might effect change over time in party identification. What they cannot have envisaged exactly at that point was the wholesale elimination of manual worker jobs in Britain that was to take place, arising from globalisation, technology, and changes in consumer preference that were to sweep over the jobs market from the 1980s.

As Dick Scase remarked in his book *Britain in 2010*,[313]

More people now work in Indian restaurants than in shipbuilding, steel manufacturing and in coal mining combined.[314]

So, what do we make of the emergence of Corbynism, his triumph in 2015 and the endorsement of 2016? Was this the last hurrah of a dying generation of activists, enabled by the internet and social media, or is something more going on?

---

312. Goldthorpe et al., op. cit. page 81-2
313. Capstone Publishing, 2000
314. Scase op. cit., page 37

It's Not the Ultra-Left Wot Won It

The Corbyn victory in 2015 indicates that a lot more was going on than just an infiltration of tiny numbers of leftist radicals, and this is an important lesson for the Labour Party in the future.

Despite social media and the internet, these small groups could not have recruited vast numbers of new registered supporters and full members without several key components being in place.

In my view these were:

- Having a candidate who was thought to be untainted by compromise and centrism;

- A growing feeling that capitalism as understood in Britain was not delivering for many people in respect of jobs, housing, income security and public services;

- The presence of establishment candidates in the 2015 leadership election who were collectively unimpressive in their inattention to broader social trends and who looked tired and unfocused against the old-time religion of Corbyn;

- And perhaps – and it is only a perhaps – the impact of austerity on specific social groups in the public sector who, it is known, joined in large numbers in 2015.

It is this combination of push-factors which mobilised thousands to support Corbyn and not the operationalisation of some longstanding personal plot to insert a Marxist into Downing Street, as has been suggested by some serious commentators.

And we must remember the fading afterglow of Bennism – I suspect that many who joined in 2015 were doing so having been cognisant of the battles of the 1980s.

It is the failure of the Corbyn-supported candidate in the 2020 leadership election[315] which makes consideration of these influences important: it is possible that these push-forces may strengthen again if the fiscal consequences of the Coronavirus result in revisited austerity to deal with a massively inflated tax deficit. It may then be possible that forces radicalising an internal Labour electorate will re-emerge if such an austerity

315. Rebecca Long-Bailey, MP for Salford 2015 to present

path is in place, necessitating at some point frozen wages and salaries, cuts in public spending and increased taxation.

What is remarkable about the 2020 leadership election result, however, is that a significant majority of new members and supporters abandoned their previous position and accepted a much softer approach in the shape of Sir Keir Starmer.

The extant British culture of support for a Parliamentary regime capable of winning elections – or at least theoretically able to do so – reasserted itself.

This is interesting because it implies that there is still a residual societal agreement, even within the new joiners to the Labour Party motivated by a more left wing analysis of trends in British society, on the importance of a two-party Parliamentary system with at least one opposition Party being capable of winning elections and governing in a competent way.

Joiners to Labour in 2015 may have thought that Corbyn did not challenge this fundamental structure but were dissuaded that this was the case by the clear electoral failure of 2019 which persuaded enough of them to resile. Corbyn was good enough to fit this typology in 2015, but Corbynism was not good enough in 2020 to ensure the election of Long-Bailey.

A Very Large Sub Culture

But a reversion to acceptance of a two-party status quo is not the same thing as an acceptance that normal politics has returned. It is almost trite to say that Blairism/Brownism had run its course in 2010 and that Miliband's policy of believing that opinion had moved somewhat to the left after the financial crisis was found to be wanting as a winning strategy with the electorate.

However, one of the reasons that Corbyn won in 2015 was that there proved to be a sub-culture in society of very significant size, that believed the Miliband/Corbyn message to be true.

They were somewhat left-behind sufferers of relative deprivation and believers that the capitalism that had once delivered for them and their families could not be trusted to do so in the future. The PLP leadership candidates in 2015, excluding Corbyn, constructed a reality that was far away from the beliefs of this sub-culture.

One could argue that they almost believed in the Fukuyama thesis, that history had ended with the triumph of capitalism, and believed the technocratic societies sketched out by many thinkers about that future.

As Scase says:

[The technologists] rarely question their own assumptions about the values of those for whom their technologies are intended… (they fail) to recognise that the world does not consist of undifferentiated individuals. They ignore the significance of social structures, social institutions, cultures and values for shaping and nurturing similarities and diversities in lifestyles.[316]

What the PLP candidates in 2015 failed to grasp collectively was that the very pressures that created an advanced capitalist society created large groups of people who thought that something like Corbynism was an answer to the problems they believed were overtaking British society.

That very significant minority view had constructed their own distinct social reality and they thought that it was close to the identity seen as reality by the electorate as a whole. They, of course, were wrong, as any examination of the views of the Corbyn-voting members shows in comparison to the much more moderate and nuanced views of the electorate.

So Corbyn was in truth the accidental leader, the man who almost blindly and certainly unexpectedly discovered that there was a sub-culture of support that could be mobilised against the PLP candidates' orientation, which was in itself failing to grasp the decisive size of the sub-culture mobilising against it.

And the Corbyn voters did not know Jeremy well enough to recognise that the pattern of unusual behaviours which he displayed over decades made him toxic to the electorate generally.

What does this mean for the future? It probably means that the sub-culture of alienated, leftish potential Labour members is there, because economic conditions have not changed, but is it mobilisable again?

It is impossible to know – but probably not in the near future.

For the bulk of the PLP there is also a lesson to be learned – the importance of understanding the alienation of 50-something public sector workers, and also the separate deep alienation of large sections of what used to be called the working class especially in the Midlands and the North, peeled away from Labour by decades of being ignored (as they would see it), culminating in the great alienation of the Leave vote in 2016 and the Johnson victory of 2019.

---

316. Scase, op. cit., page 113

CHAPTER 8

THE DESTRUCTION OF WORKING CLASS REPRESENTATION AND THE ULTIMATE TRIUMPH OF PRESSURE GROUP POLITICS

In the mid 1960s, there was a settled view of the nature of political parties and the power distribution within them, and why this was so.

In Britain at least, Parliamentary parties dominated even though Labour and the Conservatives had significant mass memberships. Academic opinion held that the very stable conditions of the 1950s and early 1960s were likely to continue.

As far as Labour was concerned, the balance between the powers of the Parliamentary Party and the Conference, the trade unions and the membership was settled – and very different from the position in the early years after the creation of individual party membership in 1918.

At that point the direction of travel that the Party would take was problematic: it had received a boost in votes and seats in 1918 and was to get a more substantial one at the election of 1922. But it is clear that at the outset in 1900 or 1906, whichever measuring point you want to use, the Party did not possess the kind of Marxist or programmatic radicalism which some theorists such as Michels believed would be undermined by its own organisation and bureaucracy.[317]

The growing importance of the Parliamentary Party during the 1920s and 30s was broken by several periods of membership growth and criticism of the Parliamentary leadership. The first, in the period 1911-20, led

317. See Robert Michels, *Political Parties*, reprinted by the Free Press, New York 1962

346

to the constitution of 1918, the creation of individual membership and official commitments to the nationalisation of the means of production as well as the creation of (for that time period) a comprehensive Party programme, *Labour and the New Social Order*.

Uncertain Start and Searching for a Role

The challenge to the relatively weak Parliamentary leadership during this period should not be underestimated.

The shop stewards' movement of 1917-20 supported demands for increased control of production and higher wages under war conditions. The Russian revolution of 1917 also posed questions about the kind of political party that was most relevant to British conditions. And attempts to 'bolshevise' the Party only really ended with the failure of the left at the ILP Conference in 1921, when the far left splitting to form the independent Communist Party.

For a time, up until 1929, the separate Communist Party ran candidates with Labour support, notably in the case of Shapurji Saklatvala in Battersea North,[318] where he was endorsed unanimously by the local Labour Party and elected with a 2,000 majority in 1924.

This kind of official and often unofficial cooperation, (for example in Motherwell) between the Communist left and the Labour left was not uncommon at a time when the Labour Party itself was searching for a firm role and a programme that could be endorsed by the electorate.

It only came to an end when decisions of the Party Conference between 1922 and 1925 banned Communists from individual membership of the Party and selection as Parliamentary candidates.

This culminated in 1927 with the NEC disaffiliating 23 constituency Labour parties which had been taken over by the Communist Party.

Henry Pelling[319] describes the Labour Party before 1914 as 'a pressure group under pressure,'[320] and also says that it was 'largely deficient in Parliamentary and administrative talent,'[321] and we know that in relation to the Labour movement outside Parliament the PLP was very weak.

The socialists in the PLP were 'restive and embittered,' in Pelling's

---

318. Shapurji Saklatvala, MP for Battersea North 1924-29
319. *A Short History of the Labour Party*, Macmillan 1961
320. Op. cit., page 18
321. Op. cit., page 19

phrase, and the extra Parliamentary socialists even more restive and bitter. The point is that certainly before 1914, and for a period after 1918, the PLP was not in control and that the movement as a whole was searching for a role and for the right balance between Parliamentary activity and other methods of pushing the cause. And in the period before the war, they were yoked in practice to support for the Liberal Government which in 1910 lost its overall majority and relied on Labour and the Irish Party to pass legislation.

But in that critical period after 1918, 'Parliamentary politics had little importance for the Party as a whole.'[322] In 1919, a composite resolution was overwhelmingly carried at Party Conference instructing the NEC to consult the Parliamentary Committee of the TUC 'with the view to effective action being taken' to enforce their claims 'by the unreserved use of their political and industrial power.'[323]

It was not only resolutions which flagged this mood: Beatrice Webb was at this time arguing that the Parliamentary Labour Party had lost its way with the result that the faith of politically active members was becoming 'dim or confused' and that the rank and file 'become every day more restive.'[324]

The PLP in Charge – for a While

The decisive point in the growth of Parliamentary hegemony came between 1922 and 1926, with the growth in the number of Labour MPs and the defeat of the General Strike.

In addition, the TUC abolished its Parliamentary Committee in 1921, strengthened the Congress secretariat, and established the General Council as the leading voice of industrial workers.

This period is therefore the tilt point at which the PLP became relatively dominant on political matters and the TUC on industrial matters.

After the experience of 1926, it became clear that concerted industrial action on a widespread scale was little short of revolution.

This history shows that before 1922 the PLP was largely ineffective as an organising body and it was only after 1926 that the PLP became dominant.

---

322. Pelling, page 49
323. Labour Party Annual Conference Report 1919 page 156
324. *Beatrice Webb's Diaries 1912-24*, ed. M Cole, Longman 1952, page 23

The great economic crisis of 1929-31 and the formation of the National Government by MacDonald, followed by catastrophic electoral defeat for Labour as an independent Party, had in effect the consequence that the TUC General Council took over the running of the PLP after the split.

Arthur Henderson was elected the new leader in a joint vote of the PLP and the General Council and led Labour into the General Election of 1931. Later, Citrine as General Secretary of the TUC demanded that the Council 'should be regarded as having an integral right to initiate and participate in any political matter which it deems to be of direct concern to its constituents.'[325]

If the Labour Party was founded to represent working people in Parliament, it also began to adopt some elements of liberalism such as support for free trade, internationalism, and religious nonconformity. Partly because of this, it also attracted some Liberal party figures as that party disintegrated. This strengthened the PLP, and the Parliamentary Party began to attract more power to itself over time, and rely on control through liaison between the trade unions which had the largest block votes at Conference and the key figures in the PLP.

But in the 1920s it was touch and go whether the Labour Party would become a Parliamentary-dominated Party at all or would adopt some other form of organisation and policy. Some argued for syndicalism, some for guild socialism, some for a combination of trade union action and Parliamentary action to change the law.

It was not clear where the dice would land for some time, but they did, and by the end of the 1930s it was clear that they had landed on the side of the PLP.

By 1945, the PLP had attracted prestige because of its successful membership of the Coalition, and the general performance of the Labour Cabinet up until 1951 cemented the power, prestige and authority of the Parliamentary Party and the leadership.

But back in the 1930s, a revolt by the constituency Parties had created a nucleus of potential opposition within the NEC.

---

325. Report of a meeting in a TUC file, quoted by VL Allen *Trade Unions and the Government*, Longmans 1961

Revolts and Resolution

The key feature of the disputes between the leadership and a left grouping between the 1950s and the 1970s was that the revolt contained both Parliamentarians and trade union leaders, and at some points – certainly in the 1960s – the trade union element in these revolts were dominant.

Later, the Benn resurgence of the left was focused on the CLPs with significant trade union backing and a slice of the PLP; later the Corbyn left, based itself on the opportunity provided by the new Party rules and the organising power of the internet. This depended heavily on the membership and the new people that could be attracted to vote as registered supporters, with minimal PLP support and only modest trade union backing with the exception of Unite.

So, there were significant differences between the Corbyn putsch against the status quo and those movements for change which had occurred before.

Corbynism depended heavily on forces external to the PLP but there was a new praetorian guard in the form of Len McCluskey, with some smaller unions providing money and premises to Momentum.

All the revolts against Parliamentary domination since 1945 depended on a combination of forces, with Bevanism, Bennism and Corbynism all requiring substantial slices of extra Parliamentary membership power to come close to winning, or to win arguments.

All the revolts were based on leaders with charismatic power who could mobilise followers and overcome bureaucracy but only Corbynism triumphed – not because he was intrinsically better than Benn or Bevan but because circumstances had changed the terrain over which battles were fought.

The 2014 change in rules had enabled rapid and substantial expansion of the membership, and because the internet had delivered a means of organising which was favourable to mobilising the kinds of followers who wanted to revolt.

So, what were the historic barriers to a successful revolt against the Labour establishment based in the PLP?

In the mid-1960s, politics students were told that the central feature of British political parties in terms of the internal distribution of power within them was that:

If the Party accepts the conventions of Cabinet and Parliamentary Government, then the prospect of office is of far greater importance in determining the distribution of power within the Party than are any of the Party's internal constitutional arrangements.[326]

This central thesis was still true, argued Crossman, in the case of a Party pretending to be democratic, by his argument that these democratic pretensions were severely modified and curtailed by the practical independence of the PLP, and the control of Party Conference by the trade unions wielding the most substantial block votes.

Crossman and McKenzie were the pillars on which academic analysis of power in political parties was based at that time and they did not discount the work of Michels, which seemed to have been vindicated by events subsequent to the publication of his book.[327]

Michels argued that there was an 'iron law of oligarchy' which stemmed from the nature of organisation itself. Sub-classes and groups formed themselves, developing eventually into cliques that obtained and sequestered power to themselves. The leadership's domination of a Party was not, said Michels, the function of a low level of social and economic development or

inadequate education or capitalist control of the opinion forming media ... but rather was characteristic of any complex social system.[328]

This iron law of oligarchy implied that pressure for leadership control came from the top and was incapable of being overturned. There was an echo of this 'inevitability' in the arguments of McKenzie and the emphasis he placed on Parliamentary norms as governing the character of the power distribution within a party.

So, in 1965, whether you believed McKenzie or Michels, the result was the same: a seemingly permanent domination of a so-called democratic party by a Parliamentary elite, subject, of course, to challenge but in the end nearly always winning and beating back the opposing forces.

Even the great attack on Labourism and the domination of the PLP by Ralph Miliband[329] descended in the very last paragraphs of the book into what he clearly thought was a despairing choice between a party inevitably declining towards a politics which was a

decreasingly meaningful activity, void of substance, heedless of principle, and rich in election auctioneering, the responsibility is not only that of the

326. RT McKenzie, *British Political Parties*, 1955, reprinted and updated 1963, Mercury, preface
327. Robert Michels, *Political Parties*, reprinted by Crowell-Collier 1962
328. Op. cit. Introduction by SM Lipset, page 15
329. Ralph Miliband, *Parliamentary Socialism*, George Allen and Unwin 1961, reprinted by Merlin Press 1964.

hidden or overt persuaders: it is also ... that of Labour's leaders.

Therefore, argued the academic Miliband, a consensus Parliamentary-dominated Labour Party would almost certainly lose.

But he also described the alternative – a socialist Labour Party – as having 'to take the longer view' and it would have to ignore the inevitable defeats that would occur and regard them

not as the occasion for retreat but as a spur to greater efforts in its task of political conversion.

He goes on to say that a socialist Labour Party:

would be subject to attacks infinitely more fierce than it had to endure (previously) but ... it would elicit and enlist the kind of devotion and support which a consolidating Labour Party now finds it increasingly difficult to engender.[330]

So, according to Miliband, it was heads you lose if a consolidating Party continued, and tails you lose if a socialist Party emerged.

It was a counsel of despair as he could not see the circumstances under which such a party could be formed from the ashes of the old, and which could then win elections. In practice, he accepted the consensus view that permanent Parliamentary Party domination was inescapable unless circumstances changed radically. Forty years later, they did.

A Transformed Membership – the Working Class Largely Gone

However, it is easy to identify in the Labour Party some of the trends which Michels said would occur in political parties: he said that a left Party would suffer from what he called embourgeoisement. Petty bourgeois elements would adhere to the Party as new administrative elements were created by the very organisational structures which the Party needed to survive and because new bourgeois elements were created by capitalist society.

He also argued that 'an entry into the Party hierarchy becomes an aim of proletarian ambition.'[331]

What can we make of these arguments in the light of 21st century Labour politics?

It is true that the kinds of people who now join the Labour Party in

330. Quotes from Miliband, op. cit., page 349.
331. Michels, op. cit., page 258

the 21st century are very different from those who joined before and just after 1918 when the new constitution made it possible for individuals to do so.

Even in the 1950s, when the first serious studies of local Labour Parties were undertaken, the dominant groups in local Parties were working class, with a sprinkling of lower middle class people disproportionately represented in the local 'officer class' undertaking the necessary administrative work.

The first studies at constituency level in Glossop, Greenwich, Stretford, Gorton, Banbury and Newcastle-under-Lyme in the 1950s suggested that:

the social structure of the membership of each of the two main parties seems to correspond with the social structure of its electorate.[332]

More specifically in this context:

[that] the Labour membership should be overwhelmingly composed of manual workers and the Conservative membership should be almost equally divided between manual and non-manual workers. Labour members are generally distributed in this way, Conservative members are not. The local leadership of both parties (taken in the widest sense and including NCOs as well as top leaders) is more middle class than the membership.

Blondel goes on:

Manual workers are overwhelmingly strong among Labour members and electors but they only formed one third of the leaders in Glossop, half the leaders in Greenwich, rather more in Newcastle-under-Lyme.[333]

Despite this caveat, the contrast between the 1950s and 2020 could not be more profound: in 2020 it is unusual to find manual workers at Labour ward meetings and constituency meetings, except those from the public sector; and the local leadership is now overwhelmingly middle class in most constituencies.

The Labour membership has been transformed in a process starting from the mid 1960s, and it is now on some counts the most middle class party in Britain. Its voters too have become significantly more middle class and in the 2019 General Election Labour did not win a plurality of votes in the social groups which define the working class, for the first time since the 1920s. So, the Labour Party membership is still aligned with its voting support but only because its voter base in the working class has been extensively culled.

---

332. J Blondel, *Voters Parties and Leaders*, Penguin 1963
333. Op. cit., page 101

The extent of the changes in voting behaviour are not fully understood in Labour circles. The tables in Figures 5 and 6 show the position over time with Labour's middle class vote stable and its working class vote collapsing.

What is going on here is remarkable: at the great Blair triumph of 1997, about a third of the middle class was voting Labour. At the great Corbyn defeat of 2019, almost the same proportion of the middle class were voting Labour.

The position in the working class is radically different. In 1997 well over half the working class voted Labour; by 2019 just over a third were doing so. Labour has lost about a third of its working class vote over the last 23 years.

The conclusion that we are driven to is that Labour has maintained its appeal to middle class voters as a group under leaders of very different stripes, but that the working class has peeled away substantially over the same period. Many of them are now voting Conservative. And critically, almost all this fall in working class votes happened before the Brexit referendum of 2016.

Sub Culture Development

This process of 'middleclassification' in political organisations is not new. As early as 1968 Frank Parkin[334] described groups of people who were alienated from dominant values and who

experience a sense of powerlessness, an inability to influence events which affect their lives are felt liable to grow disenchanted with domestic politics and to become susceptible to the appeals of mass movements with a direct political approach.

Parkin quotes the work of Arendt, Kornhauser, Hoffer, Shils and Lederer in support of this argument and illustrates the point through his analysis of CND. He continues:

CND is not to be understood wholly as an expression of protest against the Bomb … much of the movement's attraction derived from the fact that it also served as a rallying point for groups and individuals opposed to certain features of British society which were independent of the issue of the Bomb but which the latter served dramatically to symbolise … the Pacifists, the New Left, the Communists and Anarchists, the Quakers, the Labour left

334. F Parkin *Middle Class Radicalism*, Manchester University Press, 1968

and so on were generally less committed to unilateralism as such than to an array of quite distinct aims which were thought to be furthered by support for the Campaign.[335]

The development of a strong grassroots and victory for Corbyn in 2015 can be seen as a development and extension of this longstanding process of sub-culture development.

Between 1968 and 2015 very large changes occurred in the structure of the social classes, through the creation both of more middle class jobs but also a gig economy which provided only basic wages and much insecurity to those it employed.

It was not the gig workers that flooded in to the Labour Party in 2015 and 2016 but large numbers of middle aged, middle class sometime radicals, some of whom resented the way in which capitalism had developed in Britain, with its emphasis on significant rewards for the very rich and stagnating incomes and security at best for everyone else. And it is clear that many of them believed that the Parliamentary Labour Party had lost its way in dealing with these problems.

Some were also radicalised by the moral imperatives they thought flowed from the wars in the Middle East and especially the invasion of Iraq, which lent a high moral tone to the middle class radicalism which emerged to sweep Corbyn into power.

In explaining the social structure of such radical movements Parkin showed that:

middle class occupations embrace a spectrum of values wide enough to provide niches compatible with almost any set of attitudes and beliefs. Considerations of this kind have little relevance for industrial workers since the types of jobs open to them are comparatively undifferentiated in the values they embody.[336]

This meant that increasingly, as the growth of middle class employment continued, more individuals were faced with making a strategic choice about which job was most congruent with their moral and political views. This has meant that the public sector in particular has recruited large number of quite radical individuals, sensitised to unfairness of varying kinds.

This explains the availability of large numbers of (overwhelmingly) public sector workers to join the Labour Party at a critical moment and the difficulty in persuading 'moderate' people to join.

---

335. Op. cit., page 5
336. Parkin, Op. cit., page 191

However, we must not be overawed by the influx of 2015: individual Labour membership had been moderately stable at just under a million from the early 1950s to the late 1970s, when it collapsed. Despite a campaign by Smith and the early Blair, it maintained a low level until 2015, when the Corbyn resurgence occurred – but the re-growth of membership did not take it back to the levels seen from 1951 to 1978.

It may be the case that if Corbyn had been more competent, less disorganised, less hindered by baggage, and more appealing in personality to voters generally, that the experiment in left radicalism would not have folded as dramatically as it did in 2020.

What we can say with confidence is that membership of the Labour Party has soared, but not back to where it was in the immediate post-war period. It has become far more middle class, and less working class, in comparison to the baseline of the 1950s, and the rule changes made during the Miliband leadership enabled a mass influx of returning or new members and supporters which directly created the victory for Corbyn.

This rule change made it possible, but it was only made certain by the power of internet politics. And it is, as far as can be ascertained, the only occasion in British political history when very large groups of individuals were motivated to join a political party with the specific objective of changing the direction of the leadership, and then winning the day.

This incident in 2015 goes much further than the implications of the General Incentives Model used by some political scientists to explain why individuals join political parties.[337] In this case, and only in this case, were very large numbers motivated to join a party to stop it being what it was and to change its direction through the election of an 'alternative' leader.

The Benn revolt in the late 1970s and early 1980s did not produce such swingeing increases in Party membership. The General Incentives Model really goes no further than saying that people join parties in order to gain traction for the policies and ideology that they espouse. But the 2015 case is in a class of its own. We know, because they were asked in several polling iterations by reputable companies, that the new members and registered supporters joined to support Corbyn because he was different.

It is true that the motivations of this large group are well known, and they overwhelmingly believed that their intervention would make a difference. They had a sense of political efficacy.

---

337. See T Bale P Webb and M Polletti, *Footsoldiers, Political Party Membership in the 21st Century*, Routledge 2020, page 15

Is the Revolt Repeatable?

The interesting question for the Labour Party is whether such events are repeatable. If access to membership remains open as it is now, and people are encouraged to join as registered supporters, then there is no reason to think that a second surge in membership would not be possible.

However, a further condition would be required: that there is someone who a large group of radical members would want to join for, and vote for.

Even if there was, there would need to be a properly funded network supporting that candidate through internet and social media mechanisms if they were to come close to winning.

All of these conditions would have to be fulfilled if a left radical candidate were to succeed – but it is not impossible to think that those conditions might in principle be fulfilled.

Is it likely?

Probably not in the foreseeable future, because the impact of the 2019 General Election has been profound. It has thrown a bucket of ice water over the membership and has shown in the clearest possible way that the broader electorate does not care for very radical politics with a political face like Corbyn's attached to it.

The second important lesson to be clear about is that the insurgency of 2015 is unique in Labour Party history and upended Parliamentary control of the Party in a decisive way.

In its early years, Labour denounced the Conservatives and the Liberals as undemocratic organisations that did not listen to their membership, definitely so in the case of the Conservatives and sometimes so in the case of the Liberals. This was, however, a straw man and did not reflect reality.

As the franchise was expanded in the 19th century, in waves, it did indeed become necessary for the two major Parliamentary forces to develop their own grassroots organisations which could organise elections and support candidates in the new environment with a much bigger electorate and the secret ballot.

Commentators such as Ostrogorski[338] believed that a caucus system would develop in these external organisations which would undermine Parliamentary democracy, but this danger was recognised by the leaders of the parties and in practice it did not occur.

---

338. *Democracy and the Organisation of Political Parties*, M Ostrogorski, London 1902

McKenzie goes further and says:

The Parliamentary leaders of the two older parties were so successful in shackling and controlling their mass organisations that the emergent Labour Party managed to convince itself that this was crowning proof of the undemocratic nature of the two older parties.[339]

This view that the Labour Party was better and should be better in giving its members a serious voice in determining events crystallised in the aftermath of the 1931 débacle when the Labour Prime Minister MacDonald defected and formed a National Government with a few colleagues.

In the powerful reaction to this there was much discussion about the accountability of a Labour Cabinet and Prime Minister to the rest of the Labour movement. This culminated in an extensive report submitted by the NEC to the Party Conference in 1933[340] which suggested procedures which would control how consideration of taking office and the selection of a Labour Prime Minister should be structured.

There were also suggestions about the appointment of the Cabinet. The key point was that three members of the PLP should be elected to advise the Party Leader, together with the General Secretary of the Party, in respect of taking office.

Further controls on freedom of political movement were suggested about the circumstances under which a dissolution of Parliament should be agreed (which was to happen only with the approval of the whole Cabinet), and on limiting the powers of the Chancellor of the Exchequer to make untrammelled financial decisions. The NEC report proposing all these controls was adopted by Conference.

Power decisions 1945: Ushering in the Dominance of the PLP

The historically fraught relationships between the PLP and the Party generally came to a head in 1945 with the election of the first majority Labour Government.

At that point Professor Harold Laski, a significant Labour intellectual and Chairman of the NEC, had said that Attlee should attend the 1945 Potsdam Conference determining the future of the defeated Germany

339. McKenzie op. cit. page 10
340. *1933 Labour Party Annual Conference Report,* pages 204-9

'as an observer only' and also wanted the NEC to be consulted about the membership of the incoming Labour Cabinet. This had been prefigured by the NEC report and Conference decisions in 1933. It is clear that in his remarks he was only seeking to ensure the adoption of those procedures.

Attlee agreed that the NEC had a right to be consulted but vigorously denied that it had 'power to challenge the actions and conduct of a Labour Prime Minister.'[341]

In his later autobiography[342] Attlee describes the abandonment of the 1933 Conference decisions and his behaviour in 1945 in this way:

The passage of time and further experience has led to these proposals being tacitly dropped.[343]

Laski had not overstated the case for demanding NEC control because the long shadow of 1931 still fell across Labour politics in 1945, and he was not alone in thinking that a Labour Government needed guide rails to prevent its leading members 'going rogue.'

However, the ease with which Attlee dismissed these demands when confronted with a request from the King to kiss hands and form a Government was remarkable: he just threw off the constraints, faced down Laski, and ignored the 1933 Conference decision.

He could do so because of the prestige that he and his colleagues had built during the war as part of the Coalition which had defeated the Nazis and also, critically, because he had been endorsed by the people in the unexpected victory of 1945.

So, the dominance of the PLP was cemented *de facto* if not *de jure* by Attlee, and this lasted for 30 years until the rupture with Keynesianism engineered by Callaghan and Healey.

But it is clear that PLP dominance of the Party was in fact not at all normal. It was not normal before 1945, it was not in the 1976-83 period, and it was fatally undermined by the Miliband reforms in 2014.

We can see that powerful leaders such as Attlee and Blair, and to some extent Kinnock, can make the weather and prevent serious revolts affecting the structure of the Party from occurring. However, it is ironic that the leader who is probably the most revered by the left in the history of the Party, should have been the one who cemented that PLP dominance for two generations.

---

341. *1946 Labour Party Conference Report,* page 5
342. C R Attlee *As it Happened* Heinemann, 1954
343. Attlee, op. cit., page 148

We can say therefore that the relative dominance of the PLP changed too. It went from extensive control in the 1940s and 1950s, to a seriously challenged position in the 1976-83 period, back to extensive Prime Ministerial control under Blair and Brown. The great sea change occurred in 2014 with the rule revisions which undermined the position of the PLP.

As McKenzie states:

Under his leadership (Attlee's) the Labour Party, almost without realising it, came to accept a principle of party leadership fundamentally similar in its essentials to that which operates in the Conservative Party.[344]

That was clearly not the case under Corbyn. Rule changes, lack of PLP legitimacy, changes in the class structure enabling larger numbers of middle class Party entrants, and the development of internet politics, upended the internal power structure of the Labour Party and made many question its continuing viability as a governing party.

Return to Normalcy?

The election of Sir Keir Starmer in 2020 is perhaps an indication that relative dominance by the PLP has returned following the serious shock of the 2019 election.

Internal power is now concentrated in the hands of a supportive majority on the NEC and the appointment of a pro-Starmer General Secretary. The new leadership has the benefit of a semi-traumatised left which is predictably splitting after defeat, and a rump left wing group in the PLP which is isolated and lacks credibility following the total failure of their experiment.

However, it is not yet clear that the *sine qua non* of an effective Labour Parliamentary leadership (the creation of a supportive group of trade union leaders) has been completed.

The group of trade union leaders supporting Attlee and his colleagues in the 1950s is not yet entirely visible in 2020 and may not emerge, thus calling into question the viability and permanence of the reversion to PLP control of the Party.

It is still possible that circumstances will be created which will allow a reinvigorated grassroots to claim power again – but not before the PLP has lost credibility again because of political errors, as seen by the rank and file. Such a time is perhaps years away.

344. McKenzie op. cit., page 334

However, it is impossible to put the democracy genie back in the old PLP bottle. It can't be done and it is impossible to revert to an MPs-only franchise for leadership elections, with Conference decisions made by trade unions supporting that leadership. The Party must create structures and systems which allow the rank and file members to co-exist in a sensible way with the PLP leadership.

Class Structure and Party Identification

There are other changes to the underpinning of the British political system which have occurred and which affect the operation of Parties and the likelihood of them winning elections. Most important of these are the sweeping changes to the class structure which have taken place, upending the dominance of the working class, and the increasing fluidity of party identification.

As described earlier, the changes to class composition are staggeringly large and call into question the ability of a Labour Party rooted historically in the working class to win elections.

However, the Blair victories do lend credibility to the argument that a coalition can be created to affect some degree of progressive change. More important, however, is the issue of fading party identification – for all the main UK parties – which creates a political landscape very different from that of the 1960s.

There is data on this, which the splendid David Cowling has ransacked from the files (see Figure 7).[345]

This precipitate decline in the strength of party identification has provoked a significant increase in the churning of votes.[346]

Whilst the two-party share of the national vote in 2017 might have seemed like a return to normal service in which the two main parties gathered the overwhelming proportion of votes, Cowling observes that in the context of the party identification numbers above:

The contrast (between low party identification and a high two-party share of the vote) perhaps helps explain why the large votes for the two main parties

---

345. David Cowling, former head of Political Research for the BBC
346. If you are not very much attached to a political party, you are more likely to switch from one party to another, sometimes multiple times in a short time period.

in 2017 reflected all the strength and robustness of sea mist on a summer's day barely two years later (in 2019).

The three elections of 2010, 2015 and 2017 also provided important data on the degree of switching between parties between three closely packed elections in the timeline. British Election Study (BES) data published on 8th October 2019 shows that:

The General Elections of 2015 and 2017 saw the most vote switching since the BES began in 1964.

- 13% of voters switched between the 1964 and 1966 elections

- 43% of voters switched between the 2010 and 2015 elections

- 33% of voters switched between the 2015 and 2017 elections.

Across the three elections 2010/15/17, only 51% voted for the same party in each election.

Voters Switching Between the Conservative and Labour Parties

2017 saw the highest switching between Labour and Conservative voters in BES data – 11% of 2015 Lab or Con voters went from one party to the other.

- 1 in 8 Conservative voters from 2015 switched to Labour in 2017

- 1 in 11 Labour voters in 2015 switched to Conservative in 2017

Small Parties Don't Hold on to Voters

In 2017, small parties lost many of their 2015 voters:

- 47% of 2015 Lib Dem voters defected in 2017

- 78% of 2015 UKIP voters defected in 2017

- 88% of 2015 Green voters defected in 2017

In 2015, some smaller parties lost a huge proportion of their previous voters: 76% of 2010 Lib Dem voters defected in 2015.[347]

So, we have declining party identification, huge voter volatility from one election to the next, and complex views held by the electorate on left-right issues. This has always been true, far more so than some observers think. But the position now is extraordinary.

Left Wing Right Wing All in One Person

A YouGov poll in 2019 asked respondents to identify left wing policies and right wing ones. In the light of these definitions by voters themselves, they found that only 50% of respondents knew what (in their view) was a left wing policy and what was a right wing policy. YouGov gave them a list of issues which might be one or the other.

Of 100 political views put to voters by YouGov, not one was thought to be a particularly left wing or right wing view by more than 53% of people. Left and right wing views were not distinct at all and some ('global population growth is a problem' and 'converting to green and renewable energy is a priority') were supported by substantial majorities of both self-identified left and right wing voters.

There were some clearly differentiated views, as on the EU, nuclear weapons, and multiculturalism. But the polling company identified a number of views that were held by left and right wing voters that they 'should not have held', if the idea of a coherent left perspective or right perspective were correct.

YouGov commented:

For instance, a majority of left wing Britons (59%) believe that school discipline should be stricter, making it the most commonly held right wing view among the left. Likewise, 55% of left wingers believe criminal justice in Britain to be too soft, a plurality of 47% want to see tighter restrictions on immigration, and sizeable minorities of 39% support capital punishment and 36% support Britain having a nuclear arsenal.

This is perhaps best illustrated by one fact: 61% of voters in the YouGov survey who thought there should be a wealth tax also thought there should be capital punishment (see Figure 8, showing the views that most differentiate left and right wing voters).

---

347. Source: British Election Study Press Release, 8th October 2019

What is the context and importance of this?

In the late 1960s, Butler and Stokes produced interesting material arguing that issues in political debate needed to 'touch values that make it a widespread popular feeling.'[348] But, for an issue to have an impact on the standing of the two major parties, opinion on the issue must be skewed rather than equally balanced, and that the public must see the parties differently in relation to that issue.

They said in conclusion:

The sharpest impact on party strength will be made by issues which simultaneously meet all three conditions, that is to say on issues which attitudes are widely formed, on which opinion is far from evenly divided, and on which parties are strongly differentiated in the public's mind.[349]

In the 2020s, such sharply differentiated issues are few and far between, especially with the move against austerity by Prime Minister Johnson (at least in 2020).

But on the other hand, the issue of Brexit was not only highly divisive but also strongly differentiated between the parties. In the planning for a future election with underlying data like this, where low party identification is prevalent and voter churning between parties is extensive, it is important to recognise that these contours are not just a problem but are also an opportunity. It gives chances to a party significantly behind in terms of seats (as Labour is now) in a way that would not have been true in the 1950s and 1960s under conditions of greater electoral stability and where political issues were highly differentiated over policies such as nationalisation.

The Disappearing Working Class – in Labour's Leadership Cadre

Another major change in politics since the 1960s, overturning previously held stereotypes, is the transformation in the composition of the Parliamentary Labour Party.

Other parties have seen similar kinds of changes congruent with their ideology and recruitment points of entry, but the changes in Labour have been the most extreme.

---

348. Butler and Stokes, op. cit., page 341
349. Ibid., page 342

At the 1964 General Election, 103 of the elected Labour MPs were in these manual worker groups: railway clerks (10), miners (31), skilled workers (41) or semi or unskilled workers (21).[350]

It is difficult to classify MPs, especially longstanding ones, by previous occupation, but this was the position in 1964: 37% were manual workers in 1951 and 32% in 1964. The proportion of Labour MPs with a professional occupational background rose to 41% in 1964, on its long upward trajectory.

By 1997, there were only 12 miners, 40 skilled workers and two semi-skilled workers: the share of manual workers in the PLP had reduced to 13%.

Educational background was also analysed in 1964: 99 Labour MPs had elementary education only and 134 had been to a university. By 1997 only two had just elementary school education and 275 had been to a university, doubling the share who had been in higher education in 1964.[351]

The elimination of most working class occupations in the PLP continued apace so that by the General Election of 2017, there were only four identifiable manual workers in the Parliamentary Party, a tiny 2% of the whole. And there were 129 who had been employed in what the Nuffield study calls Instrumental Occupations (i.e. councillors, political and social researchers, Party officials, journalists, trade union officials and lobbyists).[352]

The domination of the PLP by those in working class occupations, so prominently the case before and after the first world war, has now been replaced by a Parliamentary Party dominated by professionals, some trade union officials, and staffers previously employed by MPs and MEPs.

From a Party of Outsiders to a Party of Insiders

This staggering change has transformed the explicit Party of outsiders, hammering loudly on the locked doors of Parliament in a famous early Labour Party image, and founded explicitly to launch working men into

---

350. See DE Butler and A King, *The British General Election of 1964,* page 235
351. D Butler and D Kavanagh, *The British General Election of 1997*, Macmillan 1997, pages 203-5
352. P Cowley and D Kavanagh, *The British General Election of 2017*, Macmillan 2018, page 401

Parliament, into a deeply changed Party of insiders. They know how the system works, can manipulate it and enjoy advantage from it.

The cultural implications of this are hugely important and have been almost entirely ignored. Labour has replaced representation in Parliament based on class, by representation based on attributes. Being a woman or a member of an ethnic minority is now regarded as being far more important as an attribute than having working class occupational roots.

Of course, it is true that these groups are not mutually exclusive – there are many women and BAME people who have manual worker jobs, and it is also highly desirable that the Party seeks to redress its longstanding imbalance in Parliamentary representation from both of these important groups. But very little has been done to attract recruit and retain working class candidates per se.

That's what the data says about Parliamentary candidates and MPs in the last 70 years: a continuing decline in working class representation, accelerating slowly at first and then rushing towards oblivion.

It shows that any pretence at encouraging, finding and ensuring the election of working class candidates has been clattered into the dustbin of history.

It also demonstrates how the Labour Party and its leaders have consistently ignored the importance of political culture amongst a big chunk of the electorate it was trying to appeal to in the Labour voting coalition, and how it relates in the future to the voting blocs which they want to engage with.

A further issue that the political parties have failed to deal with is the need to obtain and keep competent Parliamentary candidates, get them elected and keep them as MPs.

In the 1970s and previous decades there were several trade union and labour movement colleges which provided courses of various kinds on political education and they also supported life skills training which helped individuals get better jobs and ensured that they had access to administrative power.

Some of these have now closed (Fircroft), some courses have atrophied to a shadow of themselves (the political courses at Ruskin), and the TUC postal courses run from Tillicoultry, Scotland have been replaced with a more modern online approach. They have classroom teaching in normal times – but the focus is entirely on trade union skills, health and safety, and employment law and do not touch on politics at all.

Some of the major unions, like Unison and Unite (and there are others) provide a few short courses but they are again a shadow of their former selves.

Unite in particular has a schedule of political courses, some at Ruskin, and some deliberately attempting to train active members in skills such as chairing meetings and becoming a candidate for office. But because there are so few of them it follows that few members can attend and develop their skills.

The Labour Party has two support schemes for people wanting to be candidates but none of these specifically target working class individuals; they target women and BAME people. Of course, some of these may have manual worker jobs but many will not. In short, the gateway for talented and intelligent working class activists into the Labour Party has closed and many say that it is not just the PLP which is finding it hard to recruit bright working class youth.

The trade unions are also finding it hard to recruit competent full time organisers too. This is partly because many 18-year-olds are flying off to university given that almost 50% of that age cohort go into higher education – but it is also the result of the shrivelling of routes into labour movement education.

But there is a further serious problem.

The pipeline has dried up but it is also true that local Labour Parties in many parts of the country are full of middle class people and higher education graduates. It is also the case that the selectorate want to choose people like themselves.

Localism is often cited as a reason for choosing Freda rather than Fred but the process in train is actually one of weeding out those who do not fit the selectorate's conception of what an MP or a councillor should look and sound like.

Many candidates who do slide through the sieve have earned their spurs in university politics societies rather than anywhere else, and, of course, there is little money to train or support those with lower incomes or advanceable skills to win selection and move up.

This really has to change if Labour, in particular, is to get better candidates who will reflect the culture of the communities that used to return Labour MPs.

Support and Training

There is therefore a problem about recruiting people who may be good candidates. There is also a serious issue about the level of support and training given to MPs who hurdle the obstacle course to be an MP: in 1979 there was precisely nothing. I did not even receive a letter telling me where to go or when to attend, either from the House authorities or the Labour Party; you had to infer what to do from the national media.

In order to assess what needs to be done to support potential MPs it is worth looking at the skillsets required of elected Members.

In the United States there has been some reflection on these required attributes, both in respect of elected Members and of the staff they employ, and whether Congress meets these criteria. Responses from a survey of senior staff undertaken by the Congressional Management Foundation (CMF)[353] showed low levels of satisfaction with the institutional support systems underpinning elected Members' roles.

The percentages of senior staff who said they were 'very satisfied' with their chamber's performance was as follows:

- The chamber's human resource support and infrastructure is adequate to support staffers' official duties (e.g. training, professional development, benefits, etc.): 5%

- Members have adequate time and resources to understand, consider, and deliberate policy and legislation: 6%

- The technological infrastructure is adequate to support Members' official duties: 6%

- The chamber has adequate capacity and support (staff, research, capability, infrastructure, etc.) to perform its role in democracy: 11%

- Members and staff have a strong understanding of the chamber's role in democracy: 20%

As one US house legislative director told the CMF:

---

353. *State of the Congress: Staff Perspectives on Institutional Capacity in the House and the Senate*

Offices don't have nearly enough money for a good legislative staff. My boss wants issue experts on most issues, and unfortunately, with our budget that is just impossible. He is a fresh member and was definitely shocked by the youth and lack of resources for staff upon entering Congress.

Perhaps the most serious and disturbing finding was that only 20% of senior staff felt very satisfied that 'Members and staff have a strong understanding of the chamber's role in democracy.'

There are, of course, significant differences of role between the UK House of Commons and the US legislature.

Elections to the US House are every two years rather than four or five in the UK. And the bicameral nature of the US legislature is not as strongly replicated in Britain – the House of Lords has limited powers, unlike the US Senate.

In addition, the separation of powers does not exist in the same way in the UK and the Executive is much more powerful in Britain than across the pond, at least in most Parliaments – except when the Government of the day has no effective majority.

The Effectiveness Deficit

Despite large amounts of evidence of need, the Labour Party in particular has been slow to remedy the effectiveness deficit of its elected MPs.

Although there is more 'induction' after election in 2019 than in 1979, there is little attempt to find and nurture competent people who could be effective representatives. Parties are focused much more on weeding out politically unacceptable individuals and on placing special advisers in safe seats.

The Labour Party has also been insistent about recruiting women and to a lesser extent black and minority ethnic candidates, and has not necessarily tested whether these individuals are competent.

Various kinds of screening processes have been used at pre-selection stage but they are not – in the Labour Party at least – rigorous. In 2001, going through the process before being placed on the panel, I was struck by the limited ability and poor levels of information of some of the potential candidates that I met.

In 2017, many candidates were selected without real invigilation by very small panels – in effect one person – looking through CVs, not checking backgrounds or social media records, and certainly not interviewing any of them.

Notoriously, some candidates were selected and then elected who were wildly incompetent and unsuitable to be anything more advanced than a school governor in a bad year.

Peterborough is one example but there are many others – including the MP who was due to meet a local NHS Chief Executive in charge of a critical reconfiguration of services. Before the meeting was due to start, another attendee was phoned by the MP's Chief of Staff saying that the MP could not get out of bed and would be late.

Then there was another call saying they would be very late and that the MP was not yet in the car standing outside the house. When the MP finally arrived, disgracefully and discourteously late, a good briefing paper pre-circulated and clearly never read was turned over and notes were started on the back. The MP's first words to the Chief Executive were, 'I don't know anything about the NHS, do tell me.'

This was not untrue. This MP's practice was never to read briefing or reports on anything at all.

You would not select candidates for a top job in a leading company or public sector organisation in the way that it is done in politics.

Potential candidates need to be selected after extensive training, with mentors who will actively support and extend their vision, train them how to be good administrators and staff employers, support them on how to invigilate those in authority, and teach them the basics of legislative work.

These are critical tasks if the quality of politics is to be enhanced. And Labour needs to do it, especially for its working class people of whatever gender and ethnicity they happen to be.

Experience of Running Absolutely Nothing

This failure is compounded by the kinds of people in Labour politics who want to get into Parliament, who get selected and who end up sitting on the green benches.

Very few Labour candidates and MPs have ever run anything as a senior manager or business leader. Some have experienced high level roles as councillors in local government but have not actually run the services they are controlling and some have been teachers or lawyers.

This absence of high level 'running stuff' experience is one of the reasons why Labour ministers are often ineffective when in government at controlling civil servants and working with them in choosing options and implementing policy.

This is not just my view: the evidence collected by Anthony King and Ivor Crewe[354] indicates that Parliament as an institution is entirely peripheral to the implementation of policies.

They say that interviewees:

[W]hen asked directly about Parliament's role in the commission of any particular blunder, responded more often than not by shrugging and saying that Parliament had been 'lax' or even 'useless'... None of the people we spoke to, although many of them were MPs or ex-MPs, spontaneously attributed any significant influence to either the House of Commons or the House of Lords.[355]

This was true whether the blunder involved primary legislation or the implementation of a policy using existing powers, such as entry to the European Exchange Rate Mechanism.

King and Crewe conclude that Parliament failed to exert effective scrutiny, let alone control, over such massive blunders as joining the ERM, the way that payments were made to farmers under the CAP, the development of the poll tax, the mis-selling of personal pensions arising from the Social Security Act 1986, the Child Support Act 1992 and the workings of the Child Support Agency, Individual Learning Accounts arising from the Learning and Skills Act 2000, and the private finance programme for the London Tube.

They make the point that blunders are not party political. They occur under both Conservative and Labour governments with almost equal frequency. The latest iteration of this string of failure is the outcome of the court case on the Government's implementation of the pension reforms following the Hutton Review started in 2010.

Eventually the Government changed the recommendations of the review in such a way that it discriminated against younger members of pension schemes, and this was challenged by the Fire Brigades Union and the judges.

The Government lost the case comprehensively and was refused leave to appeal.

The Treasury then had to find the resources to correct the error at a cost of £17bn, in the middle of having to spend an extra £350bn to keep the economy afloat during the coronavirus pandemic.

---

354. *The Blunders of Our Governments*, Oneworld Publications, 2013
355. King and Crewe, op. cit., pages 361-2

Fundamentally, in this case, the Government failed to comply with its own equalities laws and specifically the Equality Act 2010. It seems no one thought that was important.

As Paul Johnson, the Director of the Institute for Fiscal Studies, wrote in the Times:[356]

[T]his episode demonstrates yet again the importance of competence in politics, something sadly missing for a long time and at great cost to us all.

King and Crewe concluded that Parliament as a body was bedevilled by having far too few people of quality, and I conclude that political parties have completely failed to ensure that supply of competent and capable people. Being an MP is not an easy job, especially in the 21st century: the hours, travelling, constant abuse, threats, and lack of public esteem are all real, and significant disincentives to recruiting sensible people. It follows that determined and serious efforts need to be made to overcome these hurdles in order to recruit and retain people of real quality.

There have always in modern times, in my view, been a core group of 20 or 30 people on each side of the House 'keeping the show on the road.' And that's all.

However, King and Crewe argue that government backbenchers are still influential on some issues and that Bagehot's phrase describing Conservative backbenchers as 'the finest brute votes in Europe' is no longer true.

But it is still the case that a government with a majority can ram through almost any piece of legislation or an administrative policy without great fear of being defeated, provided that it has a mandate for the policy.

Votes in the chamber and in public bill committees are structured almost entirely on partisan lines with the only real exception in modern times being the various bills setting out the Withdrawal Agreement following the referendum on EU membership of 2016, when significant sections of the Conservative Parliamentary Party were influenced more by the referendum mandate than by the requirements of the Government whips.

Ministers are also prone to the same disease of incompetence as are civil servants: the King and Crewe analysis leads to the conclusion that many huge errors were caused by lack of brightness, experience and understanding of complexity on the part of quite senior ministers in both parties.

Attempts have only been made to deal with this problem obliquely. It

---

356. 20th July 2020

is like 'pouring on quality' at the end of a manufacturing process through inspections and codes, when what is needed is something very different. That is, a cohort of trained people who can work together and who know the limits of administrative power and the sinkholes which can suck in a well-intended policy until it is destroyed.

This failing is also present amongst some senior civil servants, who find it difficult to design systems that can stand the worst effects of humans when following the administrative rules which they have created.

The attempts to improve things by micro-reform have failed. As far as legislation is concerned, the Wright Committee proposals to improve the functioning of the Commons have proved to be little more than window dressing.

The election by MPs as a whole of most select committee chairs since 2010 rather than them being appointed by the whips, simply removes a small layer of patronage, and the introduction of the Backbench Business Committee has allowed a little more Parliamentary time to be given to the concerns of MPs, but it has not changed the balance of forces within Parliament determining policy.

It is clear that six decades of Parliamentary reform, starting in the mid 1960s, have not caused a reduction in the numbers of administrative blunders, the executive is still dominant, and the system still relies on complex policy implementation through computer software support to very junior civil servants who on the basis of that system determine entitlements, liabilities, and access to services.

It is these complex systems and the human problems they produce that have become both the bane of MPs lives at surgeries and also the cause of much distress to users of these services. No amount of Parliamentary reform or changes to the balance between the executive and legislature can mitigate these problems. But perhaps better quality MPs, with more experience of leadership and management roles, could.

Parliamentary Reform Fails

That is not to say that the tone of Parliament has stayed the same over the last 60 years. It has not, and I would pray in aid a conversation with a House of Commons secretary and her boss, a cabinet minister who I was trying to persuade to address the new Kent University Labour Club in the 1960s. The Secretary came on the line and snootily said, 'You are about to receive a telephonic communication from the Right Honourable xxxxx Member of Parliament for yyyyy who will speak to you now.'

If tone has changed, 60 years of reform has not changed the place in useful ways. It is true that salaries now are better, facilities are much better for elected Members, the Short money supports opposition Parties in a way that did not exist before 1974, departmental Select Committees have been established on a wide scale under the St John-Stevas reforms of 1979, and greater invigilation of financial policy has been made possible by the creation of the Office for Budgetary Responsibility and the existence of important independent units such as the Institute for Fiscal Studies.

Also, more MPs work full time rather than part time, the pretence that ministers are responsible for every small administrative act of their civil servants has been quietly and sensibly dropped; more widespread use of technical and expert advice has been made in Government; secrecy is rather less used than before and consultation on the development of policy and practice has been extended enormously (some would argue far more extensively than is good for us).

The great list of needed reforms to Parliament and the Machinery of Government published in the early 1960s has only been blocked in respect of the renewal of the House of Lords and the extension of sitting time by reducing the length of recess.[357] In accordance with the mood of the time Crick then argued that:

Britain today suffers under the burden of three native curses: that of amateurism, that of inner circle secrecy and that of snobbery. All three serve to debase both the quality of political life and the energy of economic activity.[358]

His list of reforms was designed to address all three 'curses.' Amateurism, however, is still present at the highest levels of politics and government and, the Labour Party has been silent on the issue.

Looking back, great store was placed by Parliamentary reformers in the 1960s on these structural changes and in advocating more resources, better facilities for Members, and structures that made deeper invigilation of Government possible.

Much of what was advocated has been implemented but the striking thing absent from consideration is that the role of political parties in ensuring the selection and election of able Members is completely

---

357. See Bernard Crick, *The Reform of Parliament*, Weidenfeld and Nicolson, 1968 edition, pages 244-252.

358. Crick op. cit., page 252

omitted. It is almost as if the role of parties was thought to be illegitimate, a necessary but unfortunate part of constitutional life.

Concern about the quality of Members has been expressed only erratically: a survey of MPs by Rudolf Klein for the *Observer*[359] asked MPs themselves whether they thought that 'in your period in the House of Commons, has the quality of Members gone down, remained the same, or gone up?'

At that point, 37% though that quality had gone up, 30% thought it had remained the same, and 15% said it had gone down. Labour MPs were more critical, with 23% of them saying that quality had gone down.

But for the most part since the early 1960s, political parties have been silent on the issue of recruiting high quality Members, with only occasional quotes from unnamed sources suggesting that 'there are no stars in the new Parliamentary intake.'[360] This was attributed to the impact of the One Member One Vote selection process maximising the selection chances of local councillors. In addition, newspapers repeat the phrase that 'the Cabinet is not terribly competent,' a refrain expressed frequently in every Parliament, whichever party is in power.

These paraphrases of common views are repeated *sotto voce* on telephone calls with members of the PLP and it is a widely held opinion amongst senior Members now that the quality of MPs has gone down in their own Party. There is also concern at the deficit in effectiveness on procedural matters and making trouble. The real ability of backbenchers such as Bob Cryer, Dennis Skinner, Willie Hamilton, and Jeff Rooker to get under the skin of Ministers, delay proceedings, and undermine carefully prepared plans, is largely missing today and consequently the Government gets away with more. Labour needs troublemakers as well as high-flying academics.

Despite the prevailing view in the 1960s, based on McKenzie's work, that political parties were there to sustain alternative teams of Parliamentary leaders, almost no work has been done on how parties could in fact sustain and improve recruitment to elected Member roles.

McKenzie argued that:

The selection and sustaining of the teams is mainly the job of the party outside Parliament; the organisation of the teams (and the allocation of roles, including the key role of party leader and potential Prime Minister) is the

---

359. *Observer* newspaper, 17th March 1963
360. Quoted in D Butler and D Kavanagh, *The British General Election of 1997*, page 189 as the view from Labour head office.

function of the party within Parliament.[361]

The unspoken assumption then and now was that political parties would somehow ensure the availability of adequate numbers of competent people to fill the ranks of their Parliamentary parties; but there has been remarkably little discussion of how this might be done, or evidence that it is.

PLP: A Tool of Pressure Groups?

What has actually happened in the Labour Party is that emphasis has been placed on making the Parliamentary Party more accountable and more reflective of society as a whole rather than being, largely, the preserve of white middle-aged men.

This is a laudable aim, but it can be argued that Labour in 2020, much more so than the Conservatives, has become the tool of powerful pressure groups concerned to ensure that their voice is heard, rather than in ensuring effective Government. In the 21st century these pressure groups are overwhelmingly NOT those of manual workers but are instead those advocating greater roles for women and ethnic minority groups, those advocating specific cultural claims, and that of the organised ultra-left.

If we go back to previous arguments for democracy in the Party, the relative failures of the 1964-70 and especially the 1974-79 Labour Governments raised the issue of control by provoking claims designed to ensure that the Party when in Government did not abandon its manifesto commitments – exactly the same concern that was expressed and acted on after the débacle of 1931.

This concern about limiting the power of leaders is why the issues of election of the leader, control over the manifesto, and mandatory reselection of MPs emerged at all in the 1970s, and they emerged gradually as evidence piled on evidence that Ministers were out of control. The reforms were all of a piece – designed to stop the leadership running away from manifesto commitments and agreed policies as hard as it could once in power.

This is very clear from the published findings of a national panel I chaired in 1980 to devise ways in which democracy could be advanced in the Labour Party. Its members included Hilary Benn as Secretary,

---

361. *Political Quarterly* vol 24 1958, edition 1, reprinted in *Crisis in British Government*, WJ Stankiewicz, Collier Macmillan 1967, page 314

Vladimir Derer, Michael Meacher, Frances Morrell and Barrie Sheerman, and we published a little book on our findings.

In the Introduction, which I wrote, I quoted Crossman's famous piece on the methods through which top level control was maintained over the Party and said that if we examined the political record of the last ten years

... *it is clear that the activists and the Party Conference have been correct on a number of important issues, and the Parliamentary leadership wrong. Vietnam, cuts in public expenditure and the 5% pay policy are examples.*[362]

What is interesting, however, is not that this book reflects the concerns of the time, which it did, but that it ignored the glaring problem before us all: the quality of MPs.

It talked a lot about reform of the PLP, reselection and selection of MPs, and changes to the role of Conference. But in all the talk of process improvements it failed to utter a word about how the Party obtained individuals who could take on civil servants, ensure that policies were crafted and adapted and implemented, how oversight of the administrative consequences of decisions could be ensured, and finding the systems which could deal with these complex issues and the mindset of the bureaucracy in government.

Despite the allegedly left wing character of the process changes advocated, we paradoxically accepted the longstanding Fabian tradition of the neutrality of the civil service and its supposed benign influence.

Tony Benn did not fully agree with this Webbian tradition and described in detail the frustrations and barriers he had encountered as a minister. But he did not put forward a convincing recipe for change.

He advocated more select committees (implemented) a Freedom of Information Act (disastrously implemented), and argued for vague elements of 'more prime ministerial accountability' and the 'abolition of patronage.'[363]

These seemed to me to be weak arguments at the time and even more so now. Weakening the central structures of government is a recipe for less control and less coherence, rather than more. The missing element again was having politicians with an agenda who were capable of implementing it.

---

362. *Democracy and Accountability in the Labour Party*, Spokesman Books, ed J Burnell, 1980, page 11
363. See *Arguments for Democracy*, ed. Chris Mullin, Jonathan Cape, 1981, pages 65-66

The Minimalist Blair Revolution Inside the Party

Recent political history has not helped either.

The great positive about the Blair regime in particular was that it acknowledged the changes that had occurred in the British social structure and accepted that an alliance had to be created between Labour's traditional working class base and rafts of the newly enlarged middle class in order to obtain a Parliamentary majority.

This was in a sense nothing more than re-emphasising the view of Gaitskell that:

The success of the middle class alliance depended on the acceptance by the working class element of middle class leadership and middle class ideas.[364]

Even though this was early Gaitskell and he was discussing the failure of the Chartist Movement, it formed the core of modern establishment thinking on how Labour could proceed and win votes.

Blairism accepted this entirely, and the differently contoured nature of the electorate, but did little to address the changes required inside the Party – recruiting and retaining more working class members and ensuring the recruitment of able people who could reinvigorate the PLP.

The 'Blair Revolution' was, in fact, nothing like a revolution at all and consisted of a thin layer of top people committed to change, with little underpinning amongst the membership, and this was one of the reasons that its successors were swept away by Corbyn in 2015.

It is thus clear that both the internal distribution of power within political parties and their relationship with the electorate has fundamentally changed since the early 1960s. In particular, the Labour Party has experienced multiple reorientations of power within itself and the character of its 'winning strategy' has been forced to change in these dozen ways:

The Upending of Internal Power

The classic definition of power within parties has changed and, in fact, has been upended. It is no longer the case that a Parliamentary elite, supported in the case of the Labour Party by a cohort of trade union leaders, is bound to be dominant and in most cases have its positions supported by Conference. Now, because of the reduced prestige of the

364. H Gaitskell, *Chartism*, Longmans 1929

PLP, the growth of social media and the internet, it is possible to conceive of circumstances that would mean another significant attack from an activist left that would stand a good chance of success. Looking back to the era of stable Parliamentary dominance under Attlee, it is easy to see that this period was unusual rather than normal. If the PLP's prestige wanes again because of political failures the conditions for a second successful left putsch could be created. They think it's all over, but it isn't yet.

The Problems of Sharing Power

The democratisation of power relations inside the Labour Party has fundamentally changed the relationships between the PLP, the unions and the individual members. This cannot be unwound in the sense that reversion to votes only for the PLP in leadership elections is impossible and undesirable, and indeed it could not be contemplated without creating an enormous crisis. It probably means that it is now very difficult for top people in the Party to reverse course fundamentally and implement different policies from those on which they were elected. To this extent therefore, democratisation has made the prospect of another 1976-79 reversal of policy much more difficult, as it was indeed intended to do.

Leaders will in future have to work harder to keep all three parts of the Labour internal electorate on side. The changed power distribution in the form of OMOV[365] has also had serious effects on the recruitment of candidates for office and has accelerated the decline in working class representation.

The kinds of people who now get selected for Parliamentary seats are councillors, special advisers, prominent locals, and a few trade union officials. There are exceptions: Jim Murphy[366] organised the tapping-up of some military people which resulted in the recruitment of notable new MPs. And the trade unions have discussed the means by which more working class candidates can be selected. But little has changed.

---

365. One Member One Vote
366. MP for Eastwood 1997-2015

Working Class Candidates Gone

The character of the Parliamentary Party has fundamentally morphed. Out are the cohorts of trade union sponsored MPs, largely of manual worker origins; in are the women and significant numbers of ethnic minority MPs. The PLP looks, sounds and is more representative of some significant and important parts of the wider electorate. However, there has been a disastrous elimination of working class candidates with little attempt made to renew the Party's links with its own traditional supporters, leading embarrassingly to the loss of a majority amongst working class voters for the first time in 2019. Instead, in are the inhabitants of student politics societies and those who have already become part of the professional political class. They are different from most people, as was admirably described in *Why We Get the Wrong Politicians*[367] describing a survey commissioned by Gloria de Piero.[368] This showed that many voters were thoroughly alienated from politics but that many might also be interested in pursuing election to the Commons if mechanisms of advancement were clear to them. The barriers, however, are profound: the Labour Party now sounds and feels alien to many working class voters.

The Most Middle Class Party in Britain

The membership of the Party has been transformed from an essentially working class one to one which is very largely middle class, and a special kind of middle class at that. By and large excluded are the gig workers, the factory workers, and the business people. Included are the public sector professionals and a few others. From the Party of the people, Labour has transformed itself into the Party of staff from the public sector.

In 1900 the Labour Representation Committee was formed by frustrated trade unionists and a few intellectuals who thought that working men would not be advanced by the Liberal Party, which was too self-consciously middle class or aristocratic to give ground to such working men candidates. From that place, Labour has become in large part a haven for the educated middle class, acting at distance for the interests of a patronised set of working class voters. So, the great cause of 1900 has

---

367. I Hardman, Atlantic Books 2019, pages xxxi to xxxii
368. MP for Ashfield 2010-19

been eliminated and the Labour position in 2020 is exactly the same as in the Liberal Party in 1900: a seeming unwillingness to allow working class candidates to go forward. The ultimate product of this position was the advocacy of a wildly pro-European policy which would have been anathema to both Gaitskell and the early stage Harold Wilson, and which – to many voters north of Watford – made the Labour Party sound like a teacher telling them what to do.

Brexit in 2016 was, however, the end product of the long gestating malaise and not the proximate cause of Labour's defeat in 2019. Working class voters didn't like the patronising tone, the *de haut en bas*, 'Oh, how dreadful!' posting of England flags on Facebook by Shadow Cabinet members. They wanted more control over their lives because the political class had deserted them, and voted Tory in revolt. The apotheosis of the decline of working class politics came in 2019.

This is not just my view. Oliver Heath argues that,

'The results of (my) analysis show that the decline of working class MPs in the Labour ranks has had a substantial impact on the relative popularity of the Party among working class voters, even controlling for a host of other factors commonly associated with class voting. Working class people are significantly more likely than middle class people to vote Labour when the Party contains a substantial number of working class MPs, and variation over time in the number of working class Labour MPs in office closely tracks the strength of class voting.

'For example, all other things being equal, the difference between a person from the middle class and the working class voting for Labour is about 42 percentage points if there is a high level of social difference between the parties, but only 25 percentage points if there is a much lower level of social difference between the parties. Over time the two parties have become ideologically more similar, but also socially more similar, and it is this social similarity that appears to have the strongest impact on class voting.' [369]

In further detailed work, Heath describes the precise ways in which working class voters were alienated by wealthy or middle class candidates:

'The results from the British context suggest that the social background of political representatives influences the ways in which voters participate in the political process, and that the decline in proportion of elected representatives from working-class backgrounds is strongly associated with the rise of

---

369. University of London Royal Holloway College, LSE blog February 12th 2015

working-class abstention.[370]

Has the Labour Party reacted in any way to this evidence? It seems not.

The Working Class Say Goodbye

The Party's voter base has been transformed too. In the 1960s, the vast majority of the Party's voters were working class, and now most of them are middle class. In geographic terms the destruction of the old alliance between manual workers and a small part of the middle class has meant a Labour retreat to the cities and a few isolated enclaves. The constituencies in the legacy industrial areas have been shredded, with Durham now returning four Tories and the string of Labour-supporting seats along the eastern edge of the Pennines, following the pattern of the deep coalfields, has been reduced to a tiny urban rump between Leicester and Sheffield. Labour is now much more dependent on city-based middle class voters and ethnic minorities and far less on working class voters, however defined. As the middle class has grown in size and the working class shrunk, the geographic reach of progressive politics has shrunk too. Labour has said goodbye to the working class and the working class has said goodbye to Labour.

No Voter Loyalty

The electorate as a whole is more fungible. It is less committed to a particular party than ever, with tiny numbers now identifying strongly with Labour – and the Conservatives. This is a transformation of the landscape with serious implications for any party that fails to appeal to voters – that party can no longer rely on automatic loyalty because that party is what it is.

Labour National Agent Reg Underhill once told me, 'We can get 11 million votes without trying.' Not any more. The great selling point of Corbynism to the Party membership was that instead of appealing to the traditional kinds of swing voters, it would expand the electorate by motivating, organising and mobilising huge swathes of potential voters who were inherently sympathetic to Labour but who had been disillusioned

---

370. *Policy Alienation, Social Alienation, and Working Class Abstention in Britain 1964-2010*, Cambridge University Press, 2016

by what was described as years of centrist leadership.

At the height of success in the 2017 election, when Labour 'only' lost by 64 seats, the Corbynistas claimed that a 'youthquake' had occurred with many more 18-24s coming out to vote with the proportion of them voting Labour increasing too. This was later proved to be nonsense. The Corbyn project, mobilised through Bernie Sanders type community organisers, at vast expense, proved to be an almost complete, and totally predictable, failure. The solidaristic working class communities, with strong trade unions and deep family and work structures reinforcing each other, have almost completely gone and have been replaced with a vast army of floating, de-oriented voters with little connection to Labour as an institution.

Right and Left – Can't Tell the Difference

And the level of awareness is low: voters now have a conception of what is progressive and what is not which defies all ideological conceptions. Many voters favour both left and right wing positions on different issues at the same time and do not associate a party with a coherent ideological position. It is often the case that radical activists of all stripes fail to understand how disengaged normal people are from politics.

Voters' level of factual information is low, their awareness of political leaders is low, they are often unaware of issues until they become extremely prominent, and are in essence a sleeping tiger. They are uninterested in what passes for action in politics, until their awareness is spurred by significant events which are visible to them and are important.

As an example of the low level of political information in the minds of voters, the annual Hansard Society survey of electors found in 2013 that only 22% of those surveyed could accurately name their local MP, down from 38% in 2011.

Just 23% were satisfied with the way MPs were doing their job, and 57% did not know that Britons elected Members to the European Parliament. One in three believed that members of the House of Lords were elected.

Higher levels of awareness on these issues were achieved when the name of the local MP was prompted to the respondent along with five fake names, but even then, awareness was under 70%.[371]

The attempts by Labour radicals to turn its public image into a Corbyn-style suite of leftist positions, based on a posited willing engagement by millions of voters who would be radicalised by such positions, was doomed to failure when confronted with a disengaged, confused and somewhat uninterested electorate.

But instead they did succeed in mobilising and radicalising significant numbers to overturn the balance of power inside the Labour Party.

The Elephant in the Room

There is the inability of the Party to deal with its own internal problems in selecting and keeping top quality Parliamentary candidates, or working class ones, and in dealing with the incompetence of some parts of local government. This clouds voters' perceptions of the Party as a whole.

The long time ago issues of incompetence in Haringey, the GLC, Derbyshire and Lambeth, all in my own field of vision, have been accompanied in many other places by out-and-out corruption. Think also of Glasgow and Newcastle in the 1960s and the inability to deal with the slew of rapes, grooming and attacks on white working class girls by Asian men in Rotherham, Rochdale and elsewhere, ignored by local politicians because it was politically inconvenient. The problems in places like Haringey continue as a long running tableau of horror, and there is now suspicion that organised crime has penetrated parts of local government.

Labour has in most cases turned a blind eye to the inconvenient truth of the character of some of its one-party States until it was impossible not to notice, and has failed to root out those who are using public office to feather their own nests. It has to be much more serious about getting rid of the rotten apples and the out-and-out bozos who couldn't run a whelk stall.

It must also, as a matter of the utmost seriousness, take steps to produce Parliamentary candidates who can count, get out of bed in the morning, read their briefing documents and know what to do with them, and demonstrate that they can govern.

---

371. See P Cowley, Guest Contributor to the *British Election Study*, 4th September 2014

The local government horror stories also show clearly that in some places Labour simply does not know how to deal with money.

Defining and Defending the Boundaries

The Party has to define its own boundaries and defend them – but to do it in such a way that it respects natural justice and does not revert to the longstanding tradition that it will expel or discipline members the leadership of the day does not like because they have differing political views.

The Party has traditionally used administrative means to do this, with greater or lesser degrees of efficiency, supported by a limited number of principles which are accepted by almost everyone – such as expulsion if you campaign for another political party.

Even then, on a principle that was supposed to be universal, it has hedged – overtly in the case of Michael Cocks who was photographed in a car covered in SDP stickers campaigning for them and using a microphone to do so. He was instead rewarded for his disloyalty by receiving a peerage. But in other cases, like that of Ken Coates, it exercised the right of an organisation to defend itself against defectors planning mayhem.

However, since the 1940s, it has mainly used expulsions and discipline against the left of the day. In the 1940s against the Soviet Union fellow travellers, in the 1960s against the infiltrating sectarian Trotskyist groups like the WRP and in the 1980s against Militant and others.

The real issue here is not the legitimacy of discipline – it has every right to defend those boundaries – but that sometimes the leadership overreaches badly and takes action against people who aren't in grouplets but who merely don't conform to general opinion in the Party.

The new leadership under Starmer has to develop methods of discipline which conform to natural justice and legal rules, but to make clear what it will tolerate and what it will not. It is worth pointing out that in general the Corbyn regime was as bad at discipline as its more right wing predecessors. It too enjoyed the idea of being in power and of drumming out people it didn't like, or protecting its own, a policy described in detail by Pogrund and Maguire.[372]

---

372. *Left Out*, G Pogrund and P Maguire, Bodley Head 2020, see page 53 for examples of political interference in disciplinary matters by Corbyn-appointed officers

Communities Largely Gone

The influence which the trade unions have exercised over their members has significantly declined, partly because of the fall in overall trade union membership and partly because the composition of the trade unions has changed forever. There are now far fewer trade unionists employed in manufacturing and extractive industries and far more in public sector jobs than was the case in the 1950s and 1960s.

This matters because being a member of a trade union seems to influence voting behaviour, both for working class and middle class trade union members, and for family members of trade unionists. The disappearance of this socialising effect is significant.

Individuals and communities are socialised and create a constructed reality of their lives and relationships with others: voting behaviour studies up to the 1980s showed that some very solid working class communities, and some occupational groups, had a higher propensity to vote Labour in aggregate than did others in other occupations or geographic locations that were not as solidaristic.

Living and working in a working class community and family, with friends and family doing the same, and with significant numbers of workmates experiencing the same pressures and life chances, created an institutional order which was legitimated and reinforced through experience.

These communities, trades, and neighbourhoods supported each other and the presence of a trade union underpinning these bonds, values and behaviours meant that parts of the working class were experiencing multiple reinforcements of their identity. Together they created a social construction of reality which was in many senses 'their world.'

The best practical description of this effect is embedded in *Coal is Our Life*[373] which described Yorkshire mining communities in the 1950s, an environment that nationally has now almost completely disappeared.

Norman Dennis, the son of a tram driver and the recipient of a first in Economics from the LSE, described the very different lives of men and of women in Ashton (in the real world, Featherstone) in the deep Yorkshire coalfield, and the interaction between the planes of work, family and leisure which dominated these communities.

These planes of experience have now dissolved and have been replaced with more fragmented communities where there are multiple cross-pressures on behaviour of all kinds, including voting behaviour.

373. N Dennis, F Henriques and C Slaughter, Eyre and Spottiswoode, 1956

The decline of the trade unions and of solid working class communities has thus steepened the decline in support for Labour. The consequences of heterogeneity in communities has been discussed over many decades in political literature, perhaps best expressed in tabular form in *Political Man*[374] in describing who votes and who doesn't.

Lipset says that three factors create stronger pressures to vote: under-privilege and alienation, strength of class political organisation, and the extent of social contacts. Voting studies across many western democracies all trended in the same direction.

All three factors were strongly present in the working class communities of Britain after 1945 and have now dissipated rapidly. There is even early talk of the decline of this influence in specific constituency reporting of the 1964 General Election, where slum clearance had wiped out Labour's community roots in Swansea West, leading to a narrow Conservative victory at the previous election of 1959.

But the strongest empirical evidence of working class disengagement from Labour is early, at the 1970 General Election; the Nuffield election study[375] showed that if non-voters were treated as a Party, the number of constituencies where non-voters had a higher 'vote share' than the winning candidates rose from only 8 in 1959 to 89 in 1970. The authors state that, 'it was in the large cities and mining areas that non-voting has spread most spectacularly since 1955 ... the movement since 1966 was higher in all urban areas.'[376] This is the beginning of the great ungluing of voters from Labour in working class seats. Those who think this problem is recent and can be pinned on particular individual leaders are misinformed.

Has Labour addressed this properly at national level? Not to my knowledge.

From the Top Judgements and Misjudgements

Recent events have given pause to those convinced by Michels' work that the bureaucracy of a political party deradicalises it and distorts its vision. There is now concrete proof that bureaucratic actions, imposed

---

374. SM Lipset, Heinemann 1960, see page 185 in 1963 edition
375. *The British General Election of 1970*, D Butler and M Pinto-Duschinsky, Macmillan 1971, page 393.
376. Op. cit., page 393

by a top leadership, can fundamentally change the operation of that organisation by producing radical and sometimes unexpected effects.

Two examples will suffice.

The changes to the rules of the National Union of Public Employees in the 1970s, entirely sponsored from above and mobilised through the mechanism of a report by Professor Bob Fryer,[377] were intended to rectify the exclusion of women from power in a union that was in membership terms dominated by women.

It was successful and introduced significant tranches of women activists into powerful positions over time and is regarded as a positive and forward looking policy that rebalanced influence between men and women in the union in a way that would not have happened otherwise. This was radical change sponsored from above by a bureaucracy.

The second example is that of the Miliband reforms of Party voting proposed at the leader's request in the Collins Report of 2014. In the introduction, former General Secretary Collins said that:

the central objective is to transform Labour so that it becomes a genuinely mass membership party reaching out to all parts of the nation

The 2014 report does not contain the warnings that Collins gave Miliband about the potential consequences of opening up the membership, with voting rights, through a registered supporters scheme and OMOV. What was intended was the broadening of Labour support into communities. An attempt to curtail the power of the unions in the leadership process, through eliminating the painstakingly created 1980s Electoral College, resulted in an unexpected transformation of power relations in the Labour Party which was disastrous.

What actually happened was that imposed structural change led to a stellar opportunity for highly motivated (largely) public sector radicals to join, and by doing so to impose a candidate who would not have won without those rule changes. The Miliband leadership thought that structural changes in rules would enable it to reconnect with working class communities: instead, it enabled the greatest takeover of a political party in British history. The bureaucracy had found a policy it thought it liked, and rued the day in 2015.

---

377. Research fellow, lecturer and senior lecturer at Warwick University; Principal of the Northern College for 15 years; Sheffield Hallam University's first professor of lifelong learning; Assistant Vice Chancellor at Southampton University; Chief Executive of the NHS University and national 'Tsar' for Widening Participation in Learning in the NHS

Leaderships and bureaucracies can thus impose change with either benign or disastrous consequences. What is clear is that you cannot mend the Labour Party's connection with working class communities by giving votes in internal elections to a narrow section of the middle class.

Leaden-Footed Responses

We have seen the Party's inability to change tack quickly and respond to new and legitimate demands.

The failure to respond to the question of low pay and to delink it from incomes policies, from 1969 all through to the Thatcher victory a decade later, was the most fundamental rejection of demands from working class people as a whole in my lifetime.

Cabinet ministers found it appalling that they were being asked to support the lowest paid, perhaps the least well-educated and most deprived sections of the working class – and openly said so.

The essence of the period is captured best in Barbara Castle's diaries[378] when, as a minister and especially as Minister for Employment and Productivity 1968-70 she spent inordinate amounts of time – as did other senior ministers – in trying to deal with the economic challenge posed by the trade unions (at least those sections of them which were already entrenched with strong negotiating positions based on the level of membership penetration and coherent negotiating machinery).

What was going on in this period of almost continuous pay restraint, or at least attempts at pay restraint, was action to prevent economic crises under fixed exchange rates and serious outfall political effects for the Government.

It is remarkable looking back at this period to see how the exchange rate, and the ability to borrow on the markets in circumstances where currency traders could determine the policy of the Government, was the ultimate determining factor.

It was true, of course, that during this period, the important Equal Pay Act (1970) was carried through but the Government otherwise lost its way on low pay. They simply did not rate the ability of those workers to cause sufficient trouble and they felt they could hose down the situation pretty easily.

---

378. *The Castle Diaries* 1964-70, Weidenfeld and Nicolson, 1984

Over time this became more difficult to do, especially after the great inflationary spikes of 1974 and 1978-9.

The contrast with today is revealing. In a world of floating exchange rates and liberalised financial policy, very few care deeply about the exchange rate and its immediate effects in the same way that they did in the 1960s.

The rejection of action on low pay, and the adoption of a form of monetarism, opened the door for Thatcher in 1979 and the undermining of the social settlement imposed and legislated for by Attlee in 1945. It is also remarkable that 'new' demands – and I hesitate to use that word in this context – for women's rights were sidelined and mocked by the very same people who would not act on low pay.

Wilson's *de haut en bas* responses to the women MPs who wanted a review of women's rights on the 50th anniversary of the franchise extension in 1918 is remarkable to read in the pages of Hansard.

There is a connection between these two examples of failure: the connection is an uneasiness in dealing with the new, a difficulty with being imaginative, a nervousness in dealing with less privileged people, which is surprising for a party that pretends to be the champion of those with the fewest rights and least power.

This is not new.

One of the best known analyses of the failure of the 1929-31 Labour Government said this:

[I]t is a misconception to believe that the second Labour Government failed because its dependence on Liberal support prevented it from carrying out the bold measures on which it had set its heart. It failed because no amount of Liberal pressure would induce it to adopt bold measures … it revealed neither the capacity nor the will to surmount it (the economic recession). The economic dogmatism of Snowden, the pusillanimity of MacDonald and JH Thomas, and the unhappy combination of doctrinal radicalism and innate caution amongst its followers rendered it incapable of dealing with the crisis.[379]

The truth is that Labour, from early on, was a conventional, quite scared Party at the top, determined not to be too controversial on issues that might frighten the horses.

Labour has enjoyed the fruits of multiple failures of nerve and understanding going back 60 years. It has been at its best when working with the grain of public opinion, developed in a wide population during the

---

379. T Wilson *The Downfall of the Liberal Party*, Collins 1966, page 387

1930s depression, who wanted hope, and a new beginning in a post war settlement that would not ignore working people again. The conditions of 1945 were uniquely favourable to Labour, as were those of the early 1990s with a combination of economic failure and perceptions of 'sleaze' in the Conservative Party.

These kinds of conditions are unusual and infrequent, but during the coronavirus crisis, which has swept away millions of jobs and killed scores of thousands of citizens – some of them abandoned to their fate by the Johnson Government – Labour faces serious choices and opportunities for crafting a new settlement.

How will it respond to a combination of job losses and astronomically high public borrowing? How will it give extra funding to bolster the NHS and schools and deal with the scandalous neglect of social care when there is little money to do so?

There are more gigantic challenges facing the principal party of opposition and no obvious means of addressing them. Will it fudge and hedge and go conformist yet again and hope it will all be all right on the night? Previous history is not encouraging on prospects for the future.

CHAPTER 9

THE FAILURE OF PARTIES AS INSTITUTIONS

The failures of leadership experienced by the Labour Party in the late 1970s under Callaghan and in the 2015-20 period under Corbyn have roots in the same failure of understanding.

In the 1970s, Callaghan and Healey seriously underestimated the reaction in the Party to the adoption of monetarism as the basis of their policy. In the Corbyn era there was a similar failure to understand that society had changed so considerably that it was impossible to run policies and strategy on the basis of what might have worked 40 years before.

Both leaderships, very different in approach, style, and ideology, made the same class of mistake: failure to recognise that the world was changing underneath their feet.

There was one difference, however, which made it possible for the 'let's do nothing' forces to prevail in the early 1980s.

In that period, external pressure group politics had not developed sufficiently for them to be hegemonic. With the arrival of the internet and social media it was possible in 2015 for external pressure groups to overwhelm a Parliamentary leadership in an election for the Party leader in a way that was not possible earlier.

However different they are, these periods are linked by one ideological strand which is not fully appreciated – the demand to make leaderships accountable to Party members.

Therefore, have Parliamentary leaderships had their day in both the major parties? The power of extra-Parliamentary forces is now potentially so great that moderate constitutional leaderships have found it difficult to resist.

Since Cameron at the latest, the Parliamentary Tory leadership have felt it necessary to throw red meat to the Tory backbenches and to appease the extra-Parliamentary constituency associations, especially on Europe, in a way that would have been thought extraordinary by earlier leaders in the One Nation mould.

The position in Labour is different in that rule changes and technology have enabled the chances of extra-Parliamentary revolt. But there is also the growth of wider social organisations that have a degree of influence over the Parliamentary leaderships.

1960s pluralist theory proposed that in a western style democracy there would be a number of mediating groups between the State and the Citizen – a balance of forces which, in the end, produced social consensus and helped define social policy.

This limited role of pressure groups has now broken down completely and has been replaced by an internet/social media driven powerhouse which is overwhelming representative politics and is even seeking to undermine decisions made by the people in referenda.

The 1960s typology of pressure groups delineated them as:

- First, those protecting sectional interest, for example, the National Farmers Union, which are still much as they were, albeit using a wider range of techniques and channels

- Second, those set up to influence or control attitudes, for example, those to the EU, or to sections of society.

It is this second kind of group which has advanced in power and size because of the democratisation of media and opportunities for influence. Everyone's a journalist, everyone's a paparazzi.

Insofar as these kinds of groups can reach into the professions and Parliament, they can be more powerful than political parties and the media.[380]

In 2020, the campaigns by Black Lives Matter and others demonstrate the power of organised pressure groups to change policy and attitudes quickly in a way that was almost unheard of in the 1960s. At that time, large external pressure groups such as the campaign against the Vietnam War, CND, and the Anti-apartheid movement – powerful and important though they were at the time – did not shift politics instantly as some campaigns do now.

---

380. ee FG Castles *Pressure Group Theory and Political Culture*, Routledge and Kegan Paul, 1967

Worse still, these modern pressure groups set an agenda, ask for political parties to support it, and then denounce them and their leadership if they don't. They can exert extreme antagonistic pressure to conform. They are setting the agenda, drawing lines in the sand, and daring anyone to cross them on pain of excommunication. In the new century it is not about changing items of policy such as the hill farm subsidy or even creating a minimum wage. It is about defining a moral position and urging conformity to it.

The issue here is not whether these modern campaigns are correct or not, the point is that they have taken over many of the functions of political parties to a significant degree, with Parliamentary leaderships being susceptible and vulnerable to fast change, criticism and denunciation. Consequently their power to make independent decisions is diminished and their legitimacy curtailed.

Marcus Rashford, the Manchester United striker, can change school meals policy in two days with one BBC interview and a surge in social media attention. He attacked the Government's position and got £120m extra in spending almost overnight.

This did not and could not happen in the 1950s and 1960s or any time previously and we can contrast this modern extraordinary fluidity with the campaign to obtain bare representation for the constituency Parties on the Labour NEC in the 1930s. Only because that campaign persuaded a few top people in the PLP that it had a degree of credibility was it supported.

And even mass 1930s campaigns such as that of the Peace Ballot, with wide and deep support, achieved nothing because its long-term influence was ineffective in stopping rearmament – essentially because the Baldwin leadership of the Conservative Party out-argued and defeated it.

Parliamentary leaderships still ruled. The traditional modes of pressure group campaigning in the 1930s, subject to the overpowering influence of Parliamentary parties, have been quite overtaken by the role of celebrity. Immediacy is everything with large numbers of individuals able to mobilise thousands at the drop of a hat to influence political leaderships – who then find it difficult to resist.

It is a kind of continuous trial by ordeal with the Emperor asking the assembled throng of Coliseum Romans to decide on thumbs up or thumbs down, with a final endorsement by the token ruler ratifying the rule of the mob. Sometimes the ruler is in charge of the mob, as Trump was, but more often they are diminished in stature by the campaigns driven by instantly mobilised public opinion.

Tony Benn used to argue that democracy would be modernised by creating a button at the side of the bed from which citizens could express their opinions on matters of the day and vote in electronic referenda.

The button is now on the smartphone, and the users are setting the questions, not the Government. It is impossible to know what will come up next, and this instability gives further reason to doubt whether the seeming reversion to the norm of Parliamentary dominance in the Labour Party is anything of the kind.

From Social Class to the Internet

The levelling forces driven by the internet and social media have thus undermined the means of communication previously dominated by the Parliamentary elites. The forces corrosive to elite democracy prefigured by many commentators in the 1960s is now a reality, and the long rule of the Parliamentary parties may now be over.

This process has dissolved political legitimacy and the triumph of the extra Parliamentary forces make leaderships look weak and useless. Populism and extremism in identity politics have corroded party structures, undermined the distribution of power within parties, and affected the ability of that party to win elections, certainly in the case of the Labour Party.

What my experiences illustrate is that we have seen a shift from a politics based largely on class to one based on segmented pressure groups. This in turn has changed the distribution of power within parties and Parliamentary parties, which are bullied and cajoled by powerful internet driven and sometimes unrepresentative pressure groups completely unlike anything we have seen before.

A new reality has emerged in which the internet and social media create the terms of exchange and force those who wish to participate in politics to endorse the language and the agenda of the 'movements.'

The emergence of these powerful, morphing, pressure groups has undermined political consent. Instead of a mandate being given by the electorate at general elections, with politicians trying to follow it, politics has changed to one in which mandates can be varied or overthrown by powerful forces based on a sectional view of issues. These can, in principle, override electoral mandates or change their content. Even the courts are influenced by waves of dissent mobilised through powerful pressure groups funded by rich individuals.

Is this a problem?

It calls into question not just mandate theory, but also the aggregative nature of political parties. It is making it much more difficult to govern and create a political leadership that can drive policy through, if these powerful external forces limit, confine, change, and sometimes distort, the options available to the Prime Minister, Cabinet and the Shadow Cabinet.

It is a particular problem for the Labour Party, as we know that it has been slow to change policies and leaders who fail, and is reliant extensively on its creation myth: that it was more democratic than other parties and that it represented the interests of the overwhelming mass of the people and that therefore they would see its intrinsic merit.

The problem for Labour is that the world has changed. It has casually abandoned representation by working class people, the working class has left Labour by abandoning it in the voting booth or by not voting at all, and a new pressure group politics is dominating discourse. Strangely, it is not clear that it has noticed the reasons for these fundamental changes.

Parties and Government

Political parties, especially those that wish to change society in significant ways, have a relationship with government in a way that is not always understood clearly by those in charge of them.

We have seen how the 1960s attempts at Parliamentary reform had been successful in the sense that most of the items that Crick and others argued for have been implemented. But little changed at the level of Parliament as an institution, or in respect of the efficiency and competence with which ministers and MPs run departments and the centre of government.

That is because the Labour Party, the principal reforming party in Britain since the 1920s, has paid too little attention to the need to ensure that it can actually make things happen, ensure that the civil service implements the actions required, ensure that there are sufficiently large numbers of high-quality MPs and potential ministers available, and that they are trained to undertake the tasks in hand.

Perfunctory efforts have been made in opposition – for example as reported by Harriet Harman before the 1997 election victory – but these have been skin deep and were not always effective at getting buy-in from those concerned, as Harman herself confesses.

The Labour Party's own organisation at national level is a disaster area.

Within the Party and from the perspective of late 2020, there is no national strategic plan, no people plan, no learning and development strategy, and the NEC debates on any subject are based almost entirely on factional argument.

Although the Business Board, in effect a sub-committee of the NEC, has done good work precisely because it was left alone to deal with the internal financial crisis after the 2005 General Election, all other aspects of decision making are politicised, contested, and sharply divisive.

The organisations representing head office staff (the GMB and Unite) act as if they are Constituency Labour Parties, sending resolutions to the General Secretary about the way in which frontbench PLP spokespersons have made statements, and they complain about sackings in the shadow team in the Commons.

There are vast numbers of staff copied in to emails and huge meetings where no one wants to make decisions or be responsible for them. Everything is designed to slide away responsibility from an individual so that others can be blamed and to attack those who want change.

This follows appalling practice in some Labour local authorities, but it is a sign that no one is allowed to be in charge or is in charge, and this malaise has to be stopped.

General Secretaries have no key performance indicators about their own tasks, nor is there are any performance review of the issues that have been decided on, whether political or administrative.

This is a large organisation, incapable of governing itself and being distracted by nonsense every day.

If Labour wants to be taken seriously ever again, this morass has to be reformed quickly. And, of course, there is no training of the people in Parliament who are tasked with being an alternative Government. Hollow attacks on Conservative 'incompetence' will not wash in these circumstances.

It is reform or die.

The Party has done very little about the recruitment of intelligent, high-flying, capable people to its candidates lists, save for (as an unsatisfactory proxy) recruiting them from the ranks of special advisers and Parliamentary assistants. In fact, the introduction of OMOV has maximised the chances of local councillors in Parliamentary selections, and minimised the chances of able national figures. This is not a strategy for successful government.

Second, the Party does not have clear ideas about how to reform the centre of government – the Prime Minister's personal office, the Cabinet Office and the roles of the Cabinet Secretary and the departmental Permanent Secretaries – to ensure that decisions made will be implemented as quickly as is practical and with finesse.

In the service delivery departments, we have seen scandalous incompetence in structuring services and systems which can be implemented easily by junior civil servants (as is always a risk) and there are numerous examples, as King and Crewe put it, of the blunders of our governments under administrations of both parties.

Great improvements were made to financial planning and performance review under the Blair Government, with the creation of rolling funding programmes for departments, programme agreements at high level for each department, and with the creation of the Prime Minister's Delivery Unit.

But some of those reforms have been nullified or dismantled and there is a need to look at the whole structure of central government again to ensure greater degrees of compliance where necessary. But despite the electoral success, there is serious evidence about the inability of the Blair Government at the time to get to grips with the civil service machine: Cabinet Secretary Richard Wilson quoted Blair as saying:[381]

he felt that he was sitting in a Rolls Royce and he can't find the key.

Alastair Campbell also divulged that he himself believed that:

being in government would be just like opposition, except that things would happen.[382]

These notes of concern and surprise were in contrast to Blair's initial positioning that he

was fully committed to a command and control model of government, at variance with the modus operandi of even Lloyd George and Churchill when guiding the country through two world wars.[383]

The Blair relationship with Wilson became more difficult over time and when his replacement was being appointed Wilson said to Blair:

Your problem is that neither you nor anybody in No. 10 has managed anything on a large scale. Blair replied: 'I have managed the Labour Party.' Wilson responded: 'You have never managed them you have led them …

---

381. Quoted by him in an interview on 29th September 2016
382. Wilson interview, source as above
383. A Seldon, *The Cabinet Office 1916-2016*, Biteback 2016, page 244

there is a huge difference giving orders to Party officials and managing a public service.[384]

The Cult of Amateurism

This is the central Labour problem in its relationship with modern government.

It is about time that the Labour Party as an institution considered these issues carefully to ensure that the pipeline supply of good people is radically improved and that it sets itself internal goals which will maximise the chances of this happening.

It is often said that politics has been professionalised, but we can argue that it is not professional enough. One could almost say that the cult of amateurism is alive and well in the 2020s, and that some of the worst features of the grouse moor mentality and the challenges set out in the Fulton Report on the civil service in 1968 still stalk the land.

This is not a plea for more middle class people in charge: intelligence and aptitude is not structured on the basis of social class and it is often the case that working class youngsters, disadvantaged by their background and family circumstances, face a glass ceiling as adamantine in its structure as those which operate still for women and for ethnic minorities.

It is not enough to ask of candidates for office whether they are politically correct or agree with the thrust of the Party's position at any one time. Questions must also be asked of their seriousness, ability, understanding of systems of control and review, and their determination to get things done.

On the matter of effectiveness in power, I have found that ministers entering government after a first election victory often have little specific guidance from a manifesto, let alone minimalist pledge cards. And the tendency in modern times to have less detail in manifestos does not help.

This has always been so, as Richard Crossman found when appointed as Housing Minister in 1964. He discovered that there was hardly any Labour housing policy at all.

There is sometimes an underwhelming steer from a new Labour Prime Minister on what priorities should be pressed forward, as was the case for Frank Dobson in 1997.

---

384. Exchange quoted in Seldon op. cit., page 253

There are also junior ministers who are immensely frustrated at the lack of coherence in government, and its obsessions with 'flavour of the month' policies that unravel when touched. As an example, there was plenty of 'new money for capital' for local projects under the Blair government, but with no continuing revenue funding bolted onto projects, with the consequence that once built, they could not survive.[385]

The list could go on.

Then there is the issue of lack of control from the centre. Whitehall is essentially a series of fiefdoms, carefully and jealously guarded by both departmental ministers and Permanent Secretaries, with only a moderate ability for the Prime Minister of the day to get their way.

The Cabinet Secretary has limited managerial rights over Permanent Secretaries, principally through their annual performance review. The Prime Minister can, therefore, pull levers all day long but may not have traction on an issue if the department in question does not believe that the policy is a priority, or that it presents itself in the way that the Prime Minister thinks it does.

Better Political Parties Mean Better Government

So, the missing piece in the jigsaw of better government in Britain is the role of political parties. If parties do not present effective potential ministers, if they fail to control the bureaucracy effectively when in power, and if they fail to recognise the complexity of modern administration and design policy in ignorance, they will fail spectacularly in their mission. And that is to implement what the voters have sent them there to do. They also need to have very clear ideas on priorities and policies before they win an election, whether they publish these or not.

For the Labour Party, as the party of serious reform in the British political system, these challenges are profound. It has to provide a team of suitably qualified leaders – at least a hundred out of a PLP of 330 plus when in government – who are capable, dynamic, educated, representative, and strategic.

They need a detailed platform to work from and they need central direction from the Prime Minister of the day. They need systems in place to ensure that departments deliver what is required, and they need

---

385. Set out so clearly and with multiple examples in Chris Mullin's diaries, e.g. *A View from the Foothills*, Profile Books 2010.

the civil service to work as a team rather than in competing managerial silos. The result of that is minimal formalistic supervision by the Cabinet Secretary, or high level financial and managerial agreements which are easy to finesse for a quiet life.

In order to do all these things, Labour must reform itself.

Its staff numbers vary, dependent on the point in the electoral cycle but after a national election are between 200 and 300. Its income is around £46m a year.

This is a significant undertaking and it needs a strategic plan which will encompass a number of elements. It needs to develop new links with working class communities alongside a plan to recruit and retain working class candidates of all kinds.

Further, a plan to recruit and retain high-quality candidates at all levels, a scheme not inconsistent with other priorities. In addition, a system of performance review should be developed internally to ensure that objectives are met.

And lastly, an understanding that pitching your wares to the electorate in the circumstances that exist in 2020 is not just about tweaking a few policies and arguing for them better. It is about building trust and competence and demonstrating that you are capable of running the country.

All political parties are closed organisations with limited memberships and a market for acquiring votes that is different from that encountered by commercial organisations.

The CEO of Sainsbury's knows what is selling in store or online on an hourly or daily basis and can adjust the company's commercial policy accordingly. They can expand or contract or change the offer very quickly as the market dictates.

The market for political parties is quite different and is governed, in Britain at least, by the overriding need to win a general election, usually at four-year intervals – an eternity in commercial life or in the life of a major public service like the NHS adapting to fast-moving change in medical treatment and practice.

For political parties in opposition, in between general elections, there are local polls of various kinds, but the ideology of Party members is the controlling feature enabling or limiting the ability to change quickly in response to events.

Closed organisations can also have a limited view on their own performance. They will know if they are losing or gaining members, losing or winning council seats, and they will know what the opinion polls are saying about voter dislikes and perceptions of them.

Parties may or may not have strategic plans – and regrettably in this department the Labour Party seems to be about as far away as it is possible to get from a rational Weberian bureaucracy.

It discusses objectives at an annual away-day each year, and there are reports to the various sub-committees of the NEC which flow from those objectives. But normal practice is that the findings of an NEC sub-committee are not discussed or amended by the full National Executive. So, there is quite literally no strategic oversight of its plans because measuring is poor, and they have decided that discussion of sub-committee decisions is simply not done.

At times, Labour gives the impression of being an unregulated morass, when it should be planning, controlling and delivering a strategic plan. Labour talks incessantly about the need for planning and the incompetence of ministers when they act foolishly, but it does little to change its own *modus operandi*.

In addition, the Corbyn regime in its twilight acted as if it was planting long fuse bombs in out-of-the-way corners to greet the new people who were their hated replacements.

Labour will not be able to govern Britain if it can't govern itself.

Poor Ministers Cause Problems

The internal organisation, power structures and culture of parties affect the way government works, and these interlocking roles are recognised in the modern world, most recently by the Institute for Government.

Its CEO Bronwen Maddox published a paper in July 2020 entitled *Reform of the Centre of Government* in which she says:

Ministers are right in much of their diagnosis of the weaknesses of the British government 'machine' ... More seriously, they do not acknowledge enough the part of ministers themselves in causing the problems. Their efforts at change will be more successful if they do.[386]

There is a lesson for Labour there.

Political parties of all stripes need to up their game to deliver the competent ministers and shadow ministers that are required for McKenzie's idea of democracy to be achieved: political parties must

386. IoG Paper, July 2020

in reality deliver teams of leaders between whom the electorate can choose, in the knowledge that they are capable and competent, albeit with different offers and policies.

The Conservative Party has always had it much easier in principle in this department. They have the pick of the output of some of the finest schools in the country and of the top universities; of key players in industry, commerce and finance; of self-made people who are entrepreneurial; and they can recruit advisers at the drop of a hat who have been used to running things.

That does not make them automatically wonderful, of course, and the top layers of the Tory Party are beset by endless and continuing sexual misdemeanours and sometime financial scandals – but they have an accessible talent pool which is congruent with a party that, generally speaking, wishes to maintain a comfortable *status quo* for the monied.

The Labour Party does not enjoy these luxuries and has a different kind of talent pool. It must learn to grow its own, to become a real organisation which is developing key people, and which has a plan to reconnect with the communities and classes it has lost. Labour's talent pool has also changed fundamentally because of the long-term impact of the Robbins report; swathes of bright working class students have gone off to university and (by and large) have not returned to live in the areas where they grew up.

This means that local trade unions, constituency Labour parties, and voluntary organisations outside London but especially outside the major cities, are denuded of talented leadership over time. This effect is profound: there is a fundamental difference between the number of voluntary organisations that exist in working class areas outside London and those that exist in the capital.

When, as Chief Executive of Derbyshire, I asked for a list of all the voluntary organisations in the County, as a start in testing the County's voluntary sector strategy (there wasn't one), I was presented with a list on two pages of A4 paper. As a resident in North East Derbyshire, this was apparent too: it was almost a desert.

As a generalisation, the third sector was absent from the lives of local people apart from the ubiquitous Miners Welfares, which often treated women as second class citizens. This process of weeding out talent as they move away to university means that the rather better educated workers that Labour always depended on to do the administrative work in the local Party structures and provide leadership are far harder to find now than they were 50 years ago, and this is a particular problem outside the big cities with universities. When there are no pits, there are no NUM lodges. When the big factories go, the trade union branches melt away too.

The culture of the Party at national and local level also needs to change. It is often snooty and unwelcoming; one of the first lessons I learnt in Canterbury was that working class Party members felt discriminated against: Alf Walker, a local miner at Chislet Colliery, said that he was never allowed to stand in the ward where he lived because he might win. He felt he was the 'utility candidate', sent to fight hopeless areas but never allowed to have a chance at getting elected in the most pro-Labour ward in the City.

In the PLP individualism is rampant. Some MPs regard others on the same side as competitors rather than colleagues bound in a single project, with a premium being placed on removing potential competitors for future office.

Leadership groups often ignore those who they don't like, walk past them in the corridor without a word or gesture, rather than trying to engage with them. In terms of building a team and a positive culture this is impossible.

Leaders at all levels have to learn the names of everyone, try to engage them in discussion, be respectful to the needs of newer representatives, and try and build a team with a common purpose. Establishing a set of common objectives is top of the list, followed (dare I say) by a tailored appraisal system for MPs inside the PLP. It should be designed to maximise input and questions from individuals with the objective of learning what is bugging and disturbing Members. Train newcomers, give them real support to manage their staff, provide a positive research and strategic political function, and don't leave it all to individual enterprise.

The contrast with the professions is marked: in the NHS it is widely accepted that single-handed GP practices are more liable to error and poor practice than practices with multiple partners and a range of services. Hospital doctors work with their peers in a collective effort, training is readily available, and the concept of continuous professional development is wholly accepted. The other professions run similar systems. But at times it feels that the only way that elected MPs learn about each other is if they serve on a Public Bill Standing Committee together, when any barriers that may exist dissolve as they are engaged in that very common purpose that is so sadly lacking in other domains in the PLP. 'Training' is almost a foreign concept although there are a few placement opportunities available through which MPs can learn about industry and commerce.

The question Labour has to ask itself is why strong groups of leaders – for example the wartime generation tested in important positions then, and the new wave of Scottish first-raters who arrived in the 1970s and 80s – did not ensure a continuing stream of bright and competent candidates coming up behind them. I suspect that the answer is that there is no structure to ensure that this happens and a culture which magnifies the importance of individualism.

The Party leadership also have to address the drinking culture, which is corroding trust and respect and which fuels unacceptable behaviour by men against young staffers. Excessive drinkers need support to change their behaviour, and it is not acceptable to argue that the Whips will deal with it – they just don't. Binge drinking is an issue in all parts of the so-called Labour Movement, with trade union officials being some of the worst offenders. At the ACTT in the 1980s, the union was spending several hundred pounds a week on Alan Sapper's private drinks cart in his office and a senior national officer of the union was seen crawling in the gutter to the office in Soho Square, in the middle of the afternoon, after a lengthy lunch.

It really has to stop being like that in the 21st century. There are still Labour MP 'regulars' in the Strangers Bar who never miss a session, and others who hold themselves upright on lampposts (because otherwise they would fall over) outside the St Stephens entrance. It is not social drinking, it is alcohol abuse in a work situation, and it would not be tolerated anywhere else. One of the consequences is that it kills people early.

At the heart of this is the need to change the tendency to prima donna behaviour. This is exhibited in all aspects of the job of being an MP, with many regarding themselves as different and superior to others. It flows from the absence of collective support and from the way in which their salaries and expenses are determined and their taxes and pensions are set. They are on their own, they are invincible, and this all led inexorably to the expenses scandal in which absurd claims for duck houses, moat cleaning and the renting of pornographic films was somehow regarded as expensable to the taxpayer.

This reached public consciousness big time, but the rot set in decades ago. Many on the left of the PLP saw Bevan as a loner, seeking help only when it suited him, and others thought that of Benn too. Benn said he was hopeless at maintaining contact with the PLP, misjudged the impact of what he was saying and doing on Ministerial colleagues, and in 'man management', as he put it. These failings are common tendencies of political leadership cadres.

Labour must stop being an amateur party, recklessly behaving like the very different Tories of the early 1960s. The Douglas-Home Tories, after three consecutive election victories, thought they were untouchable too and that the Establishment would protect them. Labour is different because the Establishment will never protect them, and it is more vulnerable to erratic behaviour, boozing and groping than others because of its traditions. Its culture is a problem, and it must be changed.

Hubris in Labour has indeed brought nemesis closer. The Party has an institutional crisis of considerable proportions about its structures, rules, and behaviours, and has a lack of professional focus on the skillsets that will enable it to move forward.

Labour has a Problem with its Culture

One of the reasons for this close call with nemesis is that many in the Party define themselves as being against what their opponents stand for: against the Tories, against public expenditure cuts, against all bad things, against whatever aspect of culture you don't like.

It is impossible to win general elections if the voters as a whole do not have a sense of what you are for, and how you will govern. Contrast the position now with what voters knew about Attlee and his team in 1945. They knew then that Labour ministers had played a significant role in the defeat of Hitler, had worked hard to create and sustain the sinews of war, and had plans to make the peace one which would benefit working people.

This was a clear message. But these days, it is sometimes difficult to ascertain what some Labour politicians believe, beyond defining themselves as against aspects of language, and being angry about everything. Some MPs also restrict themselves to saying what they believe the leader at the time wants.

In other words, Labour has a culture problem.

It is also about the behaviour of Party members; about the types of candidates selected;[387] about the way in which the PLP conducts itself; and about its approach to the problems of modern government.

In the 21st century, decisions about expensive services such as the NHS are being made via the analysis of complex large scale datasets to drive decisions and by the application of science. Labour needs to position itself to use data effectively to drive policy in opposition and to effect change in government. Data does not replace values – it enhances our ability to put values into practice. Decision-making is now so complex that no one person can be omnipotent in decision making: the law of asymmetric expertise now rules, where those in charge of the data or the methodology of collecting it are bound to have more information than the average MP or a moderately competent special adviser. In these circumstances, what the PLP needs is sufficient numbers of people who know what questions to ask, who are bright enough to follow the argument, who know when they might be wrong, and who understand the limitations of knowledge itself.

As Professor Anthony King wrote recently:

From the poll tax onwards, governments have blundered again and again when ministers bright ideas have been tested against reality and found wanting. Ministers often behave as though announcing a new policy or putting legislation on the statute book were an end in itself. But policy is useless, or worse, unless effective. Sadly, Britain's political class is conspicuously more adept at speechmaking than hands on management.[388]

King argues that governments have abjectly failed to achieve their own objectives and have wasted vast amounts of public money. Past failures such as the Tanganyika ground nut scheme of the 1940s when Labour Ministers raced ahead with a disastrous programme that cost £1 billion, after serious warnings that it was bound to fail, and the DeLorean fiasco of the late 1970s, when incompetent Labour Ministers[389] ladled millions

---

387. See Note on Candidate Selection, appendix B
388. *Financial Times*, July 6th 2014
389. Roy Mason, Secretary of State for Northern Ireland, and Don Concannon, his junior Minister, failed to check whether DeLorean's claims of having 30,000 sales for the car agreed by US distributors and dealers was true. The Irish Government, which had also been considering funding DeLorean, had checked and found that the claims were without foundation and refused to sanction support for the car company. Mason and Concannon failed to check and landed the British taxpayer with millions in unrecoverable debts as the company quickly burnt through the cash they had been given by Whitehall. DeLorean, it later transpired, siphoned off the bulk of the British

of pounds of taxpayers money to a corrupt businessman without checking his claims on the car firm's order book, are further confirmation that Labour people are just as liable to error as Conservatives.

The moral of King's story – and he is right – is that we must not just concentrate on policy formation but also on detailed implementation by committed people who will not be moved onto another task in a few months.

Our task is to craft policy to win, to craft detailed, credible policy for delivery and to follow it through with a competent and knowledgeable implementation team.

This is the kind of culture that Labour needs to develop, and it needs to do so fast, and sweep away the obstacles to change. I regret to say that my personal experience with Labour MPs and ministers is that we are light years away from getting close to a culture like this.

Talk about complexity to many MPs, talk about data, talk about strategic objectives, and their eyes glaze over and feet shuffle. And Harold Wilson's famous dictum that 'this Party is a moral crusade or it is nothing'[390] is no longer nearly enough to describe a strategy for governing. It is important to have values and to apply them in the context of modern society, but it is important too to understand the terrain that you are working on. If you don't, your public representatives become merely reactive to other Parties' initiatives.

It is also true that Labour has alienated itself from working class communities and that those communities have noticed, in large numbers, that the Party they thought was on their side is no longer in their corner.

This is reversible but only if Labour understands that it is no longer 1945, 1964, or 1997.

The brief flurry of interest in forgotten communities and in Northern England's Murdered Towns (as the *Financial Times* put it in September 2019) was transient. It needs to build a new hegemonic alliance, excluding no one, rebuilding its working class base whilst understanding the need to change.

Mass unemployment and further austerity may be on the horizon again and Britain needs an opposition that can be a competent government.

---

taxpayer money for personal use and was also put on trial in California for distributing hard drugs after a sting operation by the FBI.
390. Speech at the Labour Party Conference 1962, quoted in the *Times* 2nd October 1962

And far worse is to come. In a speech at the TUC in June 2018 Bank of England Chief Economist Andy Haldane suggested this:

What we can I think say with some confidence … is that given that the scale of job loss displacement, it is likely to be at least as large as that of the first three industrial revolutions … Technology appears to be resulting in faster, wider and deeper degrees of hollowing-out than in the past. Why? Because 20th-century machines have substituted not just for manual human tasks, but cognitive ones too. The set of human skills machines could reproduce, at lower cost, has both widened and deepened.

With machines becoming ever smarter, Haldane said, a wider array of jobs were at risk from automation than in the past. Low-paid jobs were most at risk, but the hollowing out would increasingly affect mid-skill jobs as well.

Haldane said the Bank had used methodology pioneered in the US to model the impact of smarter machines on the UK labour market and its more than 30m employees.

This methodology classified jobs into three categories – those with a high (greater than 66%), medium (33-66%) and low (less than 33%) probability of automation and made an adjustment for the proportion of employment those jobs represented. Haldane continued:

For the UK, roughly a third of jobs by employment fall into each category, with those occupations most at risk including administrative, clerical and production tasks.

Taking the probabilities of automation, and multiplying them by the numbers employed, gives a broad brush estimate of the number of jobs poten-tially automatable. For the UK, that would suggest up to 15 million jobs could be at risk of automation.

If the option of skilling up is no longer available, this increases the risk of large scale un- or under-employment. The wage premium for those occupying skilled positions could explode, further widening wage differentials.

This potential future brings into sharp focus the question of what the Labour Party is for. Traditionally, it has concentrated on social and economic issues which seek to ameliorate the lot of the most put-upon strata in society: sometimes it has argued for economic change by modernising the way in which the British economy works. However, not only has the lot of the poor and the poorest been made worse by the coronavirus pandemic, it is also the case that the ability of the British economy to produce productivity gains and thereby produce wealth has decreased too.

UK average annual gross fixed investment was the lowest in the G7 countries between 2010 and 2018 and it was the second lowest in research and development investment too.[391] In this environment, the ability of the UK economy to produce taxable wealth to fund better social programmes is fatally undermined. So, in this context the traditional Croslandite policy of taxing profits and incomes for the benefit of all looks stretched as a concept and one must wonder whether Labour has any future at all unless it embraces policies to deal with the R&D and productivity problem and to enhance the performance of the British economy.

Labour is also challenged by the changes in the economy and society accelerating towards us in the next ten years. Ageing populations worldwide, combined with falls in the birth rate, further advances in life expectancy, the widespread use of artificial intelligence, and the continued growth of the digital economy, will make the Labour Party's origins in the era of coal, steam and cotton look increasingly anachronistic.

The political challenges flowing from these events will make both Marx and Attlee irrelevant in the new world, at least on a literal meaning. What is required is an adoption of new ideas and a new relationship with the electorate. In Labour, this process has hardly begun and evidence of understanding of the problem of fast pace change is thin on the ground.

Labour In 2050

In the last 50 years, Labour has lost huge chunks of its core working class support. It has allowed its Parliamentary wing to be completely dominated by the middle class and political operatives. It has not reformed itself except by endorsing the need for more women and ethnic minority MPs. It has foolishly allowed untested expansion of its own electorate to happen, creating the required conditions for putsches against the leadership, which have underlined the fragility of the power structure inside the Party.

It is simply not true that Labour has always been dominated by the PLP, and there may be further massive revolts to come.

It has historically failed to engage with new issues and has given the impression that it sneers at elements of society that should be and were its core constituency. It has failed to control incompetent and sometimes

391. Source: World Bank

corrupt local groups and has allowed itself to be infiltrated many times over by ultra-extremists. Labour needs to get a grip.

This matters because there needs to be an electable, competent party of government other than the one that happens to be in Downing Street. By the year 2050, Labour will have had to reinvent itself as a political Party. Its core message can still be to address the needs of the excluded, but it will have to find new ways of running the economy, finding resources for itself as an organisation, recruiting a well informed and effective political class of its own, and finding new ways to communicate with an atomised electorate.

The idea that the old ways will be capable of ensuring electoral victory is quite ridiculous, but some in Labour are still persuaded that they are. Political parties will have to adjust to a swiftly changing world but in the absence of change in the electoral system, it is probable that the two major parties will continue to dominate: Duverger's law will still be operational.

However, Labour has one trend working in its favour that will undermine politics as usual: the reduction in the birth rate in most advanced countries.

This means that in the near term future there may be fewer people available to join the workforce, who may as a consequence have a higher level of bargaining power: the price of labour will rise. However, it also means fewer people to tax, and higher inflation based on rising costs, which can only be contained by the rapid expansion of artificial intelligence, robotics and technology, all challenges for a party that built its policy on spending more and sometimes taxing more. The alternative would be to import more foreign-born workers, a policy that will be challenging given the history leading up to Brexit. The next 50 years for Labour may be even more traumatic than the last 20, if it survives as an organisation.

Labour's failure to accept the reality of constant change is not the fault of one individual or groups of individuals. To argue that is foolish and counterproductive. However, the task of this generation of leaders is to deal with the structural and strategic problems of the Party and to understand how it has climbed voluntarily into the quicksand that may engulf it.

Is the Labour Party finished as a serious party of government? The great irony of the Party's trajectory is that it has come full circle: a Party that began because the Liberal Party establishment would not allow working class candidates to be selected in their safe seats, has transformed itself from being a party that promoted working class candidates to a party that has hardly any left amongst its ranks.

It has not learnt from the mistakes of the 1970s and has certainly not learnt from the evidence of the Blair victories, when a brilliant communicator who engaged with a very broad swathe of the electorate and won three times was sidelined and treated as if nothing his team did was ever positive.

Labour has sounded as if it is more concerned with ideological purity than winning and some of its MPs have been obsessed with culture wars that can never be won and which alienate huge swathes of the electorate.

There is now a choice: accept its marginalisation and become a party only of the woke and the inner cities, or be a broad-based progressive party appealing to large parts of our society, including the relatively comfortably off respectable working class voters in the North and the Midlands that it has so expertly alienated. Big decisions have to be made, explicitly and clearly, as to the Party's degree of adaptation to reality.

Will there ever be another Labour Government? It is hard to be positive. There are simply not enough places like Canterbury, changed fundamentally in the last 50 years, to compensate for the loss of the working class and lower middle class vote that was the bedrock of Labour support.

APPENDIX A

A NOTE ON STATISTICS

Goodbye to the Working Class relies on a range of statistical sources to identify trends in the economy and society which might influence trends in politics.

Choosing which data to use has to be informed by the proposition being tested. The Labour Party created its own theory of representation: it was formed to advance the cause of 'working men' in Parliament, principally by ensuring that working class candidates were selected and won seats in the House of Commons. Only the existence of working class candidates and MPs could ensure that policies to support working class interests would be implemented, it was argued. It was a clear objective, as was the quite explicit need for reliance on working class votes to achieve that aim. Therefore, the size of the working class in the electorate, the number of manual workers in particular, and the size of particular occupational groups such as miners and cotton workers, were important from the beginning in measuring the audience for the Party's message.

It is therefore important to identify facts which can illuminate and measure the class theory of electoral representation, in order to establish the chances of a Labour Party actually achieving its goals of representing working people.

Labour's founding myth assumed that, through a process of education and propaganda, working class voters would increasingly identify with the Party and vote for it over time, and that progress would be assured. However, this assumption of continuing progress was maintained even when Labour's electoral performance was rocky: the explanation of the 1931 election débacle by Herbert Tracey is a good example of this, and is almost Marxist in its belief that eventually the workers would see the errors of their ways and vote Labour in their own interests.

Tony Benn's strange formulation of 'ten million votes for socialism' after the terrible defeat of 1983 is in the same vein. This was not just whistling in the wind to keep the spirits up, it amounted to a theory of history in which gradual progress would always be made. Perhaps we can see in it an extension of the Whig version of history in which a form of continual progress was the governing principle of history, extending Victorian democracy in fundamental ways to the benefit of working men and their families.

In its own terms therefore, Labour assumed that a significant working class would continue as an available reservoir of votes. So, measuring the size of the working class, the numbers of manual workers within it, and the size of the group of non-manual workers and the size of the middle class, could potentially give the observer an indication of whether such continuous progress was possible.

It is therefore reasonable to use social class and occupational group as indicators because the Labour Party has itself, since its foundation, assumed that these groups, who might be said to share a common way of life with common problems, would be available to them as a potential voting bloc. It may also be helpful to show the number of those employed in key occupational groups with significant weight, such as miners, engineering workers and transport workers – all of which were critical to the functioning of society in the 1920s and before, who had considerable bargaining power, and who were considered at the time to be the core of the 'Labour Movement.'

But this cannot be the whole story. 'Objective' social class measurements based on occupation or a manual/non-manual dichotomy, only give a certain flavour. Individuals have their own 'subjective' views about their own social class position and where they are in society. It is now, in 2021, consistently the case that more people say they are working class than are working class as defined by objective occupational criteria, although the number subjectively describing themselves as working class is dropping sharply.

New evidence published in the journal *Sociology* (published 19th January 2021) suggests that middle class people with working class grandparents create a narrative life story by massaging their past, which makes their own individual success more socially acceptable. In this narrative, this generation has risen by hard work from poverty-stricken roots to a sunlit pinnacle of achievement, made more splendid by where their forebears were from. If this theory is validated by larger surveys, it is still likely that there are many different constructions of reality created by individuals to explain and justify the social and political positions they take.

The modern constructs of social groups (for example through Mosaic) attempt to sub-divide the great classes in to more manageable and more numerous freezer-size chunks, but they still do not capture entirely the reality of subjective class positioning by individuals. The point is that the advent of a much larger middle class does not entirely eliminate the possibility of a progressive Government being elected; it depends partly on who people think they are, which may influence how they behave in the voting booth.

Identifying useful data and trends flowing from them is easier said than done, even in countries with a long history of publishing detailed official data sets. The problem is that data definitions morph and change constantly, especially in response to economic change. There is no reason to collect data about the numbers of knocker-uppers or Vesta match-makers when both of those occupations, amongst many others, have disappeared because of social and technological change.

Even if you are an academic who knows where to look, things can get difficult, especially the further you go back in time. But there are two useful books which everyone interested in the development of our society and politics should have on their shelves: the first is *British Social Trends since 1900, A Guide to the Changing Social Structure of Britain* (ed A. H. Halsey, Macmillan, updated edition 1988), which brilliantly examines how Britain has changed over time; and the more recent *The Official History of Britain, Our Story in Numbers* as told by the Office for National Statistics (ed B. Starling and D. Bradbury, Harper Collins 2020). Despite being irritating in not labelling its charts effectively, it is the most up to date description of our land and its people. The Government used to publish an excellent annual publication, *Social Trends*, which performed this function but was an early victim of the Thatcherite public expenditure axe. It is time it was revived.

Evidence on voting behaviour arrived more recently than official statistics on the economy and society. The first public opinion polls were started in the late 1930s in Britain by Gallup, under the guise of the British Institute of Public Opinion. Some of the early data has been lost or is incarcerated on paper that has disappeared (articles were published in the now defunct *News Chronicle* newspaper which I used to read when my father brought it home from the hot metal production office where he worked.)

Some of these early articles have vanished, but things improved in the early 1960s with the advent of the British Election Study which provides longitudinal data on elections and voting behaviour to the present day. In addition, there are the invaluable Nuffield *Guides to the General Election*, published since 1945, largely under the guiding hand of David Butler, which are the best landing place for anyone who wishes to understand British elections more fully. That's where you should point yourself if you want to know more about the development of voting behaviour in Britain.

Hard-core data addicts will also want to analyse the post-general election voting behaviour data published by many of the nationally known polling companies, and widely available on the internet, and read the excellent publications from the House of Commons Library. These useful volumes (the latest being *UK Election Statistics 1918-2019: A century of Elections*, CBP 7529, July 2019) show the results of each general election in detail, the backgrounds of candidates etc., and are invaluable to historians of our democracy.

APPENDIX B

A NOTE ON THE SELECTION OF CANDIDATES

One of the reasons that Labour fails to recruit well organised, intelligent and focused people as candidates in sufficient numbers is that its candidate selection process is a shambles. Political scientists have called this the 'secret garden' of the British constitution – the process whereby parties select and therefore advance the careers of those who will eventually become MPs and potentially Ministers in Government.

In Labour's case it has almost always been local people who decided who the candidate should be rather than the Party centre (with the exception of vetoes on individuals, the selections for some by-elections, and late retirements by sitting MPs, in which the NEC plays a more prominent part).

Very little has been written about this process, but as someone who has been involved in Parliamentary selections in different capacities between 1970 and 2001, there are a number of propositions which can be put forward about the topography of this secret garden.

First, selections are never open in the sense of an Athenian democracy mechanism for selecting the very best candidate that is available. This almost never happens. There are prejudices – for example, the perceived need to have a 'local' candidate who knows the area, and there is a strong feeling against people who are 'outsiders', on the basis that the selectorate can be aware of local candidates' faults and can calibrate a decision on whether those faults are impediments to office in a way that is impossible with those outsiders.

Second, in some constituencies there was domination of the delegations by one or two powerful trade unions such as the NUM, which frequently had a clear majority of delegates in mining areas (in the days when decisions were made by delegates rather than postal ballots of the whole membership). This domination by local trade unions did mean that there was a guaranteed route for at least some working class candidates to be selected, but this route has now been closed by rule changes and the decline of working class trade union branches.

Third, there were enthusiasms about particular kinds of people. In the early 1960s it was regarded as a bit trendy to have a candidate who was a university lecturer, and several of them slipped through, and in the early 1980s there was a moment when it was *de rigeur* to select a woman or a BAME candidate in London and elsewhere, and no others could stand a chance of success – but this was righting a complete imbalance in the PLP which at the time had no BAME MPs and hardly any women.

Fourth, enormous efforts were made by ruling elites in constituencies to minimise the chances of anyone who wasn't under their control. In Liverpool Walton, for example, the constituency Executive invited 20 candidates to attend a short-listing meeting, and gave each of them one minute to speak, giving no notice and announcing this 'rule' as the candidates arrived at the meeting.

Naturally, no one could say anything useful and the local favourite son sailed through. In South Wales, there was the well-known 'Valleys shortlist' ruse, in which the preferred candidate would be shortlisted alongside four or five utter no-hopers, in order to ensure that the favourite would be selected in a landslide.

Fifth, rule changes and the creation of one vote for each Party member made it possible for hard work to be repaid, as lengthy timetables meant that some candidates who were prepared to put in the work could doorstep hundreds of Party members who had votes, introduce themselves and persuade those members to vote for them.

But the most important attribute of Parliamentary selections is undoubtedly factionalism. This is most powerful in marginal seats or where a Labour MP is retiring and there is every hope that the new Labour candidate will be elected to Parliament. In safe Conservative or Liberal constituencies factionalism has often been less powerfully present because of the lesser chances of electoral success.

Factionalism has had many different faces. Sometimes it is the espousal of strongly favoured policies, such as unilateral nuclear disarmament, support for the Alternative Economic Strategy, or (as a proxy) support for radical leaders such as Benn or Corbyn. Other leitmotifs indicating a candidate's general position have been an individual's attitude to democracy in the Party, support for Palestine, opposition to Gulf War 2, and so on. This is not to say that these policy items are of overwhelming importance to delegates or voters in themselves, but they give the selectorate a clear view of a candidate's politics.

What is almost never on the table is whether an individual can actually do the job and has the brainpower to undertake what is a complex and demanding role. The closest approach to this are vague questions such as, 'Will you live in the constituency?' (A question that is easy to answer in London, but more difficult in Inverness); and 'Will you have an office in the constituency?' On occasion these have been used against women candidates in particular to suggest that they are placing too much weight on their family's needs if they fail to answer 'correctly.'

What is almost always lacking, however, is a thoughtful examination of the policy issues, because individual Party members may not have sufficient information to make judgements about responses from candidates. Almost all potential Labour candidates will today, at selection hustings meetings, go on at length about the dreadful state of the NHS, with little chance that anyone will pick up any errors in their argument.

Sadly, the quality of the list of candidates, taken as a whole, is inadequate. For most of the last 100 years of Labour history, candidates have not been effectively tested by the NEC. In many cases you simply filled in a form, sent it in to Transport House, they had a quick look over it, and that was that. Entry to the 'B' list of Parliamentary candidates was always like that; and entry to the 'A' list – that constructed from people nominated by trade unions – was even more perfunctory.

The line was that if the union had nominated them, they must be OK. The theory was that constituencies could look at the list and have a free choice as to whom to invite, but this was always done by a small committee, usually the Executive who tended to choose people who were relatively local or who were well known in a local authority like the County or Borough Council.

In the Blair years, complex processes were constructed to ensure that potential candidates had to jump through some quality control hoops, but the field was weak and the bar to access the approved list was not high.

In some cases, there was outright intervention by senior NEC officers to exclude people because they were disliked or regarded as politically unacceptable. Today, however, rule changes have meant that aspirants can nominate themselves without any reference to their local Party at all, without reference to any set of objective criteria at all, and can construct their own submission rather than answer set questions. It is also the case that NEC panels of one person have invigilated these submissions, with no interviews or vetting of social media accounts, and in practice they determined who was selected for a constituency and in some cases elected to the Commons. There was a selection committee of one.

The opportunities for administrative meddling are also substantial at constituency level. Under the old system before OMOV, those sending out initial invitations to candidates would have their own prejudices and concerns; the local Executive might choose to stop candidates with substantial numbers of nominations from getting on the shortlist; delegations to the selection conference could be admitted or not; affiliations from organisations can be ramped up before a selection; and the opportunity for manoeuvring at a delegate-based selection conference was high.

So, the structure of the election system is critical and under the new OMOV arrangements it is no less important. But the key issue now is the time available for the assiduous to knock on doors and win votes, and to have the financial resources available to camp out in a constituency for weeks on end. Only relatively local people and those with financial resources at their back can do this if it is a normal selection and not one close to an election with a truncated timetable. The rules basis of selection is therefore critical.

What is not known reliably is why individuals vote for particular candidates in a selection process. Little work has been done on this in recent times, but it is clear that broad political position is key; whether the candidate is known widely in a constituency, or has proven links with it, is another. There have been notable occasions when it is believed that rhetoric on the day has carried the day. I am extremely suspicious of this and do not believe that a 'performance' carries much weight with those present unless there are other factors at work.

Who gets selected depends fundamentally on the nature of the selectorate. Some Party members may not be terribly well informed, some have eccentric views and prioritise fringe issues over others, and many have a view of the world that assumes it is the 1940s.

It is now clear that the Party membership is wholly unrepresentative of voters as a whole, and is heavily skewed to the public sector middle class. As Churchill said, the best argument against democracy is a five-minute conversation with the average voter, and that cynical view is unfortunately confirmed when dealing with some Labour Party members. They are better informed than the average voter sometimes, but have radically different and more extreme views as a group. They see their task in selections of candidates as being that of selecting 'people like themselves', who have the same social characteristics and political views as themselves and their friends.

There is no prospect whatever of moving away from democracy in selections of candidates, nor is it desirable to do so. The key issue is to ensure that there is a pipeline of capable, competent and able candidates of a range of backgrounds available to select – and that provision and winnowing can only be done by national-level institutions. That is what a serious political party needs to ensure happens.

If Labour wants to ensure the selection of good, competent people and working class candidates then it needs to revisit its selection process and ensure much greater invigilation and screening of those putting themselves forward. At present in 2021, anyone can put themselves forward without restraint provided they have been a member of the Party for a very short period. In some general elections, especially those called suddenly, there is almost no invigilation of who these people are at all, and in 2017 this produced some disastrous results. As the quality of political candidates feeds through to the quality of governance in the British state, this is not a minor problem, and great efforts must be made to construct a fair screening process which will encourage the bright and well-organised and competent, and those from groups like the working class which are grossly underrepresented in Parliament, and discourage the dubious and useless.

INDEX

General Election (1931) 18, 34, 349
General Election (1945) 259
General Election (1950) 20, 42, 45, 80, 187
General Election (1959) 48–50, 81
General Election (1964) 365, 387
General Election (1970) 20, 84, 387
General Election (1974) 82, 99, 108, 146
General Election (1979) 156, 184, 188
General Election (1983) 195, 199–201
General Election (1987) 289, 308
General Election (1992) 93, 251
General Election (1997) 261, 266, 292–293, 309, 396
General Election (2005) 298, 397
General Election (2010) 180, 272
General Election (2015) 315, 339, 362
General Election (2017) 74, 362, 365, 383
General Election (2019) 126, 275, 336–338, 353, 357
General Galtieri of Argentina 184
General Incentives Model 356
General Problems of Low Pay 97
General Strike (1926) 119
George, John 236
George, Lloyd 398
Germany 35, 38, 49, 86, 137, 358
    East 188
Gifford, Tony 206
Gilby, Terry 294–296
Gilets Jaunes (France) 30
Glasgow (UK) 37, 45
Glass, Jack 37
GLC (Greater London Council)
199–221, 233, 237–238, 241, 244, 309
globalisation 47, 103, 260, 269, 318, 326
GMWU (General and Municipal Workers Union) 79, 120–123
Godsiff, Roger 336
Goering, Hermann 64
Gold Standard 18, 272–273
Golding, John 117, 184
Goldthorpe, John 47
    et al. 341–342
Goodman, Elinor 101
Gorbachev, Mikhail 229
Gormley, Joe 112, 205
Gowing, Margaret 77
Grant, Bernie 128–129
Grant, John 115
Great Britain 17–19, 23, 24–27, 30–31, 35, 37, 44–48, 51, 65, 68, 82–85, 95, 99–100, 103, 108, 111, 183, 252, 255–257, 260, 321, 329, 338, 342–343, 346, 355, 396, 400–402, 408
Green Party 362
Greenspan, Alan 268
Grenada 303
Guardian 77, 199
Guides to the General Election 416
Gulf War (1991) 291

H
Hague Convention 166
Haines, Joe 146
Haldane, Andy 409
Hamilton, Willie 134, 165, 174, 375
Hansard 186
Hardy, Peter 92

99, 123
Weber, Max 30
Welfare, Damien 202
West 231, 267–271
West Midlands (UK) 48, 222
       Dudley 159
Western Europe 17, 49
Western World 5
Wheatley Act (1923) 64
Whit Week Walks 37
white collar jobs 21
White, James 156
White Paper (1976) 87
White Paper (1977) 112
White Paper (1978) 112–113
Whitehead, Phillip 309
Whitemore, Fred 5, 36, 60–61, 65,
      72–73
Whitty, Larry 215, 288
Why We Get the Wrong Politicians
      (Hardman) 380
Williamson, Catherine 64
Williamson, Chris 300
Williamson, Tom 135
Wilson, Harold 20, 28, 35, 50–51,
      83–86, 91, 100, 136–138,
      144–146, 164, 198, 273,
      286, 307, 326, 381, 390,
      398, 408
Wilsonism 95
Windscale Fire (1957) 179
Winnick, David 61
Winter, Colin 289
Withdrawal Agreement 372
Women's Action Committee
      (WAC) 160–161
women's rights 22, 39, 134,
      156–161, 191, 198
Women's Rights Committee 150
women's right's legislation 164–165
Wood Green (London) 148

working class community 386–389,
     408
working class party 17, 24
working men 21
world trade 49
Worswick, David 137

Y
Yalta 230–231, 234
YouGov 363
Young, George 166

Z
Zilliacus, Konni 187